SEPM REPRINT SERIES NUMBER 12

Beach and Nearshore

Sediments and Processes

Selected Papers Reprinted from

JOURNAL OF SEDIMENTARY PETROLOGY
SEPM SPECIAL PUBLICATION NO. 24
SEPM EASTERN SECTION FIELD GUIDE
SEDIMENTOLOGY

Compiled by

RICHARD A. DAVIS, JR.

Tulsa, Oklahoma

January 1987

ISBN 0-918985-66-8

© 1987 by
Society of Economic Paleontologists and Mineralogists
P.O. Box 4756
Tulsa, OK   74159-0756

Printed in the United States of America

PREFACE

This volume of reprinted research articles on beach sedimentation is somewhat of a milestone in the series in that in addition to regular Society publications, it includes papers from a publication of one of the Society's sections (Eastern) and from the publication of another organization (IAS). This expansion of sources is designed to provide the reader with a complete spectrum of research on beach sedimentation. The need for such a reprint volume is the result of a combination of Special Publication No. 24, *Beach and Near-shore Sedimentation*, going out of print and the desire to have a single volume that includes older, often cited papers with the more recent papers.

The process-response approach to sedimentology has resulted in both expanded effort and increased sophistication in studies of the beach and related environments. These studies remain field intensive and combine good observations with electronic data gathering devices. Primary efforts among those involved in beach research are directed toward a combination of two objectives: 1) obtain a thorough understanding of modern process-response systems or morphodynamics (Wright, et al., 1979) in order to make predictions that will permit better management and utilization of the coast, and 2) develop tools and models which can be applied to the ancient stratigraphic record and thereby help to interpret properly the details of ancient environments. The papers included in this volume provide a variety of approaches to both of these objectives, although all are concerned with the modern beach environment.

In order to understand completely process-response systems, it is important to consider the processes themselves and the controlling factors in generating these processes. The first paper in the volume does that by considering basic meteorological phenomena and how they control coastal processes. Fox and Davis devoted several years to such studies in a broad spectrum of coastal settings (e.g. Fox and Davis, 1973, 1978; Davis and Fox, 1975). They describe the basic and predictable interrelationships between weather and coastal processes with the resulting changes in morphology.

Miles Hayes' study on the impact of hurricanes on the Texas coast (Hayes, 1965) has been a hallmark paper and one that demonstrates the old axiom of being in the right place at the right time. In this volume he and Boothroyd provide what is probably the first detailed account of the effects of a storm on the beach environment and the subsequent recovery. The guidebook from which this paper is taken has become a classic of the "gray literature." In order to show that coastal morphodynamics are similar in drastically different environments, Davis and others compared the Massachusetts example from the previous paper with Lake Michigan. This demonstrated that only scale and rates are different between the two areas. Hine's paper also documents the repair of the beach after erosion due to storm conditions. He concentrates on the development of the berm in the recovery profile and how this takes place at the end of an active recurved spit.

The interaction of waves and currents with the nearshore bottom is well shown in the related papers by Clifton and others, and by Davidson-Arnott and Greenwood. In one case the setting is a non-barred high-energy coast where the sequence of bedforms closely mimics that described by the fluvial researchers (Simons et al., 1965). Symmetrical ripples formed by orbital motion give way to asymmetric bedforms and eventually to plane beds as the shore is approached. Davidson-Arnott and Greenwood go a step further in looking at a barred coast by considering the stratification and structures across profiles of the nearshore. They found distinct patterns across each bar-and-trough pair that relate to the findings of Clifton and colleagues and that are repeated as each bar is traversed.

Textural parameters have been used to characterize and distinguish between depositional environments for decades. Two of the most often cited examples are those by Mason and Folk and by Fox and others. The former is the oldest paper included in the volume. It provides not only a look at distinguishing among coastal environments using textural properties but it also represents the first coastal application of the nearly standard formulas presented initially by Folk and Ward (1957). Fox and his colleagues consider more traditional moment measures but show the systematic variation of these statistical parameters across the beach and nearshore zone.

Although research efforts have been focused on sandy beach environments, it is appropriate to include gravel and muddy beaches in a volume of this type. Bluck's paper on gravel beaches from Wales remains one of the most detailed studies of its kind. Of particular interest is the distribution of clast shapes over the beach and the broad spectrum of fabrics that develop on gravel beaches. The opposite end of the spectrum is provided by Wells and Coleman in their companion papers on the muddy coast of Surinam. Some might argue that this is not really a beach environment. It is, however, an open exposed coast so that the niche is that of a beach but the physical energy level is quite low. Nevertheless, the papers provide very interesting data and they broaden the spectrum presented.

Beaches are wave-dominated and as such, the environment presents some problems for benthic organisms and also for their study. The two papers included here demonstrate a common general approach to animal-sediment relationships but they come from distinctly different environments, thereby providing a good spectrum of conditions. Hill and Hunter studied the north end of Padre Island, Texas, a distinctly wave-dominated area with low tidal range and only a modest nutrient supply. In contrast, the Sapelo Island, Georgia area studied by Howard and Dorjes is one of very low wave energy, high tidal range and tremendous nutrient supply. The faunas and their interrelationships provide good data for zonation of sedimentary features in these contrasting areas.

From this brief introduction, it should be apparent that the 13 papers included herein provide a broad and fairly comprehensive treatment of the sedimentology of beach and nearshore environments. Included are process-response morphology, sediments, sedimentary structures and animal-sediment relationships. Data contained in these papers provide a good basis for understanding beach dynamics for application to coastal management or engineering, or for interpretation of apparent beach/nearshore sequences in the rock record.

Richard A. Davis, Jr.
Department of Geology
University of South Florida
Tampa, Florida 33620

REFERENCES

DAVIS, R. A. and FOX, W. T., 1975, Process-response mechanisms in beach and nearshore sedimentation, I. Mustang Island, Texas: Jour. Sed. Petrology, v. 45, p. 852–865.

FOLK, R. L. and WARD, W. C., 1957, Brazos River Bar: a study in the significance of grain size parameters: Jour. Sed. Petrology, v. 27, p. 3–26.

FOX, W. T. and DAVIS, R. A., 1973, Simulation model for storm cycles and beach erosion on Lake Michigan: Geol. Soc. Amer. Bull., v. 84, p. 1769–1790.

FOX, W. T. and DAVIS, R. A., 1978, Seasonal variation in beach erosion and sedimentation on the Oregon Coast: Geol. Soc. Amer. Bull., v. 89, p. 1541–1549.

HAYES, M. O., 1965, Hurricanes as Geological Agents: Case Studies of Hurricanes Carla, 1961 and Cindy, 1963: Univ. Texas, Bur. Econ. Geol., Rept. Inv. 61, 56 p.

SIMONS, D. B., RICHARDSON, E. V., and NORDIN, JR., C. F., 1965, Sedimentary structures generated by flow in alluvial channels. in Middleton, G. V. ed., Primary Sedimentary Structures and Their Hydrodynamic Interpretation: SEPM Spec. Publ. 12, Tulsa, OK, p. 34–52.

WRIGHT, L. D., CHAPPELL, J., THOM, B. G., BRADSHAW, M. P. and COWELL, P., 1979, Morphodynamics of reflective dissipative beach and inshore systems, southeastern Australia: Mar. Geol., v. 32, p. 105–140.

CONTENTS

Reprinted from BEACH AND NEARSHORE SEDIMENTATION, SEPM Special Publication No. 24,
PP. 1–23, FIGS. 1–17, October 1976

WEATHER PATTERNS AND COASTAL PROCESSES

WILLIAM T. FOX and RICHARD A. DAVIS, JR.
Williams College, Williamstown, Massachusetts 01267, and
University of South Florida, Tampa, 33620

ABSTRACT

Waves and longshore currents, which are responsible for deposition and erosion on sand beaches, are closely tied to storm patterns. Three coastal areas, the eastern shore of Lake Michigan, Mustang Island, Texas and the central Oregon coast, were studied to develop coastal process-response models. Time-series analysis of weather, waves and current data was coupled with frequent beach surveys to construct the models.

Thirty-day studies were completed at Holland and Stevensville, Michigan, during the summers of 1969 and 1970. Longshore current was correlated with the first derivative of barometric pressure, and breaker height was correlated with the second derivative. During storms, longshore currents were shunted offshore by beach protuberances and cut through nearshore bars. After the storms, the bars reformed and migrated toward the beach.

At Mustang Island, Texas, beach studies were undertaken during the fall and winter of 1971–1972. Weather patterns were dominated by intense, offshore-moving cold fronts or northers marked by a rapid rise in pressure, drop in temperature and sudden reversal in wind direction. Broad beaches are relatively straight with a low seaward slope and two or three nearshore bars. Saddles in the bars are not related to protuberances on the beach.

Waves and currents on the Oregon coast are controlled by the East Pacific High in the summer and the North Pacific storm track in the winter. In summer of 1973, strong north winds set up southward flowing longshore currents and frequent upwelling. The summer beaches are characterized by broad intertidal sand bars separated by longshore troughs and rip channels. During winter storms of 1973–74, sand was removed from the beach and stored offshore on subtidal bars.

The three areas differ in their response to coastal processes because of their position relative to storm tracks, orientation of the shoreline, tidal range and nearshore topography.

INTRODUCTION

Weather patterns and storm tracks play a major role in the development and destruction of coastal features. Large coastal land forms such as continental shelves, submarine canyons, deltas and barrier islands are influenced by global tectonics and eustatic changes in sea level. Smaller features including beaches, nearshore bars and rip channels are created and removed by the local waves, swells and longshore currents which are generated by surface winds and storms. Therefore, the existing coastal configuration of an area is a combination of large erosional or depositional features influenced by tectonic controls or sea level changes upon which smaller features are superimposed as a function of the local wave regime.

Several coastal areas in the United States, including the east and west coasts of Lake Michigan, Mustang Island, Texas on the Gulf of Mexico, and the central Oregon coast, were studied to develop a model for predicting the relationships between weather patterns and coastal processes. The east coast of Lake Michigan was studied from 1969 through 1974. It provided a simple model for the rapid response of beaches, and adjoining nearshore bars provide ideal conditions for developing and testing a coastal process-response model. The model developed for the eastern shore of Lake Michigan was also tested on

the western shore of the lake where the weather systems move offshore.

Two time-series studies were conducted during the fall of 1971 and the winter of 1972 at Mustang Island on the central Texas coast. The fall and winter weather pattern for the Texas coast is dominated by cold fronts or northers which move seaward across the coast. A broad gently sloping beach with two or three nearshore bars characterizes the Texas coast. Tides of 1.0 to 1.5 meters spread out the effects of waves and currents over the broad, flat beaches. Reversals of wind direction and longshore currents recorded on Lake Michigan were also evident on the Texas coast. Although the cold fronts moved offshore, the general model developed for Lake Michigan accounted for the succession of waves, longshore currents and beach erosion observed on the Texas coast.

The Oregon coast has frequent winter storms which produce huge waves and also has a large tidal range which provides a marked contrast with Lake Michigan and the Texas coast. Weather and wave conditions were studied for one year, from June, 1973 through May, 1974. During the summer, the Oregon coast was dominated by the East Pacific High, which resulted in strong north winds and upwelling, with waves from 1 to 2 meters high. A few small low pressure systems which

1

moved through the area in the summer caused short reversals in wind direction and currents along the coast. During the fall and winter, a series of large storms moved across the Oregon coast with heavy rains and high winds. Sand, which built up as a series of intertidal bars in the summer, was removed by waves and longshore currents during the winter storms. The waves during the winter storms were more than 8 meters high and caused considerable erosion along the coast. In the spring, the sand returned to the beach in the form of large broad sand bars.

The relationships between weather patterns and coastal processes were studied by time-series analysis of waves and currents in conjuction with maps of the beach and nearshore area. The time-series studies of coastal processes ranged from 15 days to one year. The beaches studied ranged from 244 to 488 meters in length and ranged in width from a few meters on Lake Michigan to several hundred meters on the Oregon coast. Although the sizes of the areas and the energy conditions encountered on the coasts varied considerably, definite similarities emerged for the relationship between weather patterns and coastal processes.

COASTAL PROCESSES

Scale of coastal processes.—Coastal features are constructed and destroyed by processes which operate at different scales in time and space. Large coastal features such as mountain ranges, deltas and continental shelves are strongly influenced by crustal plate movements and develop over millions of years. Intermediate scale features including estuaries, spits and barrier islands are more closely related to changes in sea level caused by tectonic processes or glaciation and may be formed in hundreds or thousands of years. Small scale features including beaches, nearshore bars and ridge and runnel topography are controlled by waves, longshore currents and tidal currents. The waves and currents which control beach and nearshore topography are strongly influenced by local weather patterns and major storm tracks. Small scale features are often formed in a few days or destroyed by a single storm. In unravelling the geomorphologic and sedimentologic history of a coast, it is necessary to consider the processes operating at each of the different scales with the smaller features superimposed on the larger features.

Plate tectonics and coastal processes.—The major geomorphic configuration of a coastal area is closely related to the movement of crustal plates away from spreading centers, toward subduction zones or along transform faults. Inman and Nordstrom (1971) have classified coasts into three groups; trailing edge coasts which face a spreading

center, collision coasts which abut a subduction zone or transform fault, and marginal coasts which adjoin an island arc. As seafloor spreading progresses and continents move away from a spreading center, a full cycle of shoreline development occurs. Near the spreading center or ridge, the trailing edge coasts are bouyed up by the thermally elevated spreading centers and form steep, tectonically active coasts. As the spreading continues and the continental margin moves away from the spreading center, the coastline subsides and the gradient of the continental shelf decreases. At the same time, sediment eroded from the interior of the continent is dumped along the continental margin forming a broad flat continental shelf. Barrier islands frequently develop on the trailing edge coastlines where the slope is very low. At collision coasts, on the other hand, rugged mountains form where one plate is subducted beneath another, or fault blocks form where transform faults delineate the continental margin.

Sea level changes.—Eustatic and tectonic changes in sea level have an influence on the formation of coastal features such as barrier islands, cliffs, wave-cut terraces and submerged shorelines. Eustatic changes in sea level can be directly related to tectonic forces which cause the vertical movement of a portion of the coast. Changes in sea level can also be created by the horizontal movement of crustal plates. With increased spreading rates, the volume of elevated material in the mid-oceanic ridges is increased (Sclater and others, 1971) and the continental margins are flooded by a widespread marine transgression. When the spreading rate decreases, the elevation of the ridges drops and the marginal seas withdraw resulting in a margin regression. Because the volume of the ridges adjusts slowly to changes in spreading rates, the transgressions and regressions endure for hundreds of thousands or millions of years. With slow transgressions or regressions, the coastal processes are able to adjust to the changes in sea level and the products of sedimentation are spread over a wide area of the sea floor.

Valentin (1952) recognized the nonequilibrium conditions along coastlines related to changes in sea level and glaciation. When sea level is dropping or the coast building out by accretion, there is a gain of land or an advancing coast. Under weak tidal action, lagoon-barrier and dune-ridge coasts form, while under strong tidal action, tidal flat and barrier-islands coasts develop. With a rapid rise in sea level on a coast which has been excavated by glaciers or rivers, a fjord or embayed coastline forms. If the submergence takes place over a broad coastal plain, there is development of barrier islands and spits, typical of an emergent coastline. Shepard (1963) shows a rapid rise in sea level between 20,000 and 5,000 years ago, with a fairly slow rise in sea level for the past 5,000 years.

Waves and currents.—Weather patterns which influence wave and current conditions are responsible for small scale coastal features. Davies (1964) developed a world wide dynamic classification of coastal environments based on the distribution of wave types. He distinguished four major types of wave climate; first, the storm wave environment, second, the west coast swell environment, third, the east coast swell environment and fourth, the low energy environment. The coastal features formed within each environment are related to the waves impinging on the coast. The storm wave environment is generally restricted to the higher latitudes where storm tracks are concentrated and a belt of strong and variable winds generates storm waves (Fig. 1). In the northern hemisphere, the storm belt shifts from 46°N in the winter to 62°N in the summer with the occurrence of larger storms more frequent in the winter. On the North American continent, the zone of storm wave activity extends northward from California on the west coast and from New York and New England on the East coast. Because the storms approach from the west in the mid-latitudes, the wave activity on the west coast is generally much greater than on the east coast. In Europe, the storm wave zone extends from northern France to northern Norway and in Asia, from Japan northward. In the southern hemisphere, the storm belt varies from 54°S in the winter to 56°S in the summer. Because only the tip of South America extends into the storm belt, storm wave coasts are much more restricted in the southern hemisphere.

In addition to waves, longshore currents are important in the formation of small scale coastal features. Where storm paths move directly across a coast, the reversal of wind direction during the passage of a storm will result in a change in angle of wave approach and a shift in longshore current direction. If the storm track is roughly parallel to the coast, the winds may shift from onshore to offshore, but the dominant direction of longshore transport remains the same. A constant angle of wave approach or longshore current direction causes the enhancement of longshore coastal features such as spits, bars and rhythmic topography. Where storms are less frequent and long period swells dominate the wave climate, the waves are refracted so that they approach the coast at a smaller angle and generate slow longshore currents. Although long period swells do not generate strong longshore currents, they

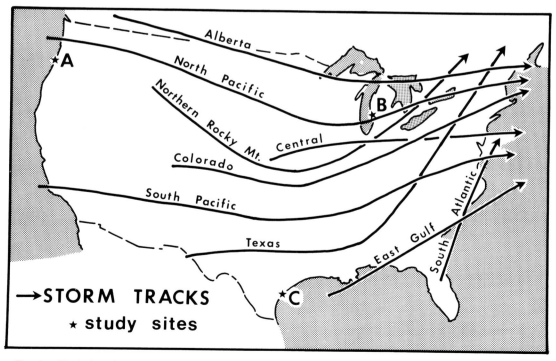

Fig. 1.—Typical paths of cyclones appearing in various regions of the United States and location of study sites at *A*, central Oregon coast; *B*, eastern shore of Lake Michigan; and *C*, Mustang Island, Texas.

often set up standing waves or edge waves which may form cusps or rhymthic topography along the coast.

Lake Michigan study area.—The relationship between weather patterns and coastal processes has been studied at several locations on Lake Michigan by the authors (Fig. 2). In July, 1968, a two-week pilot study was completed at Stevensville, Michigan, to test field procedures and make preliminary environmental observations. A 30-day field study was conducted at Stevensville, Michigan, during July and August, 1969, with weather and wave observations taken at 2 hour intervals (Fox and Davis, 1970a, 1970b). Daily topographic profiles were surveyed across the beach and nearshore bars to measure erosion and deposition under varying wave conditions. In July, 1970, a similar 30-day study was conducted at Holland, Michigan, about 95 kilometers north of Stevensville (Fox and Davis, 1971a; Davis and Fox 1971, 1972b). During the summer of 1972, a field study was completed at Sheboygan, Wisconsin, on the western shore of Lake Michigan (Fox and Davis, 1973a). A pair of simultaneous field studies were conducted at Zion, Illinois, and South Haven, Michigan, during July, 1974 to determine the effects of a single storm on the eastern and western

shores of the lake (Davis and Fox, 1974).

Lake Michigan lies across and to the south of the major North Pacific and Alberta storm tracks (Fig. 1). Summer storms which originate in the Pacific northwest proceed from west to east across the northern United States and southern Canada and generally pass over or somewhat to the north of Lake Michigan. During a typical summer, a storm moves through the area every 7 to 10 days. The general storm pattern during the summer is quite regular with a predictable shift in wind direction and angle of wave approach as the storms move across the Great Lakes region.

Stevensville, Michigan.—The typical wind, wave, and current pattern generated by a storm on the eastern shore of Lake Michigan can be shown by studying the effects of a fairly large storm which passed north of Stevensville, Michigan, in July, 1969 (Fox and Davis, 1970b). On July 26, 1969, a large circular low pressure system moved across the northern United States and the center of the low passed over Lake Michigan (Fig. 3). The surface winds circulated around the low in a counterclockwise direction and produced large waves on the lake. As the low pressure system moved across to the north of the study area, waves approached the shore out of the southwest. After the passage of the low, the wind shifted around to the northwest and large waves built up from that direction. The waves moved across Lake Michigan and resulted in extensive erosion and coastal damage along the southeastern shore of the lake. In many places the beaches were eroded back to the base of the dunes; at some places the dunes were cut back from 6 to 10 meters.

When the low pressure system passed over the lake, a 30 day time-series study was in progress at Stevensville, Michigan. Observations on 17 variables were collected at 2 hour intervals to obtain a detailed plot of weather and coastal processes during the passage of the storm. Weather related variables include barometric pressure, wind speed and direction, air temperature and cloud cover. Wave measurements were made offshore on a staff 180 meters from the beach in a depth of 5.5 meters, in the surf zone at a depth of one meter, and in the plunge zone at a depth of 0.4 meters. Wave measurements include offshore wave height and period; breaker height, period, angle, distance and type in the surf zone; and breaker height and depth in the plunge zone. The direction and speed of the longshore current was measured in the trough between the sand bar and the shore. Daily beach profiles were used to determine rates of erosion and deposition before, during, and following the storm.

Weather and wave measurements taken at 2-

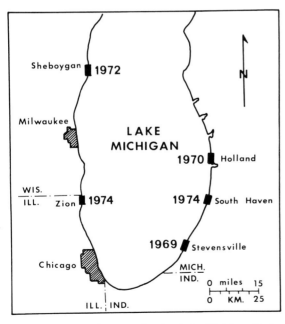

Fig. 2.—Location map showing Lake Michigan Study site for Stevensville, Michigan (1969), Holland, Michigan (1970), Sheboygan, Wisconsin (1972), Zion, Illinois (1974) and South Haven, Michigan (1974).

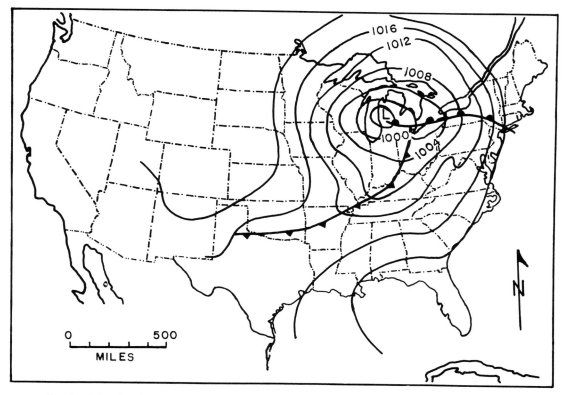

FIG. 3.—Map showing position of intense low pressure area over Lake Michigan on July 28, 1969.

hour intervals provide a time series with 360 observations which can be smoothed using Fourier analysis. The period, phase and amplitude of the first 15 Fourier components were computed for each of the variables. In order to study the effects of the passage of the storm, the cumulative curves for the first 15 harmonics for barometric pressure, longshore wind, longshore current and breaker height were plotted for a 15-day period from 8 a.m. on July 21 through 6 a.m. on August 4, 1969 (Fig. 4). The curve for barometric pressure shows a sharp drop when the low passed through the area reaching a minimum of 1000.4 millibars (29.54 inches) on July 27. Following the storm, the barometric pressure rose to 1017.3 millibars (30.04 inches) on July 30 and 1020.0 millibars (30.12 inches) on August 3. There is a sharp rise in breaker height with the drop in barometric pressure, reaching 1.8 meters on July 28. The peak in the breaker height curve is displaced somewhat to the right (later) relative to the low point in barometric pressure.

As the storm passed over Stevensville, a cold front moved in on July 28 with a shift in wind direction from the southwest to the northwest and an increase in wind velocity from 9.5 to 12 m/sec. The southwest winds preceding the storm produced waves 0.5 meters high from the southwest forming an angle of 21 degrees with the nearshore bar and generating a northward flowing longshore current with a speed of 120 cm/sec. Following the passage of the cold front, the wind shifted to the northwest and the wave height increased to 1.8 meters. The northwest waves formed an angle of 23 degrees as they crossed the bar and generated a longshore current of 210 cm/sec to the south. The highest winds, waves and longshore current occurred after the low pressure system had passed and the wind had shifted over to the northwest. Strong northwest winds following the passage of the cold front accounted for the high waves and strong longshore current to the south.

On the eastern shore of Lake Michigan where the shoreline is almost perpendicular to the storm path, breaker height and longshore current velocity can be roughly predicted directly from the curve for barometric pressure (Fox and Davis, 1971b, 1973a). The curve for longshore current closely resembles the curve for a constant multiplied by the first derivative for barometric pressure. Since the cosine is the derivative of a sine, and the

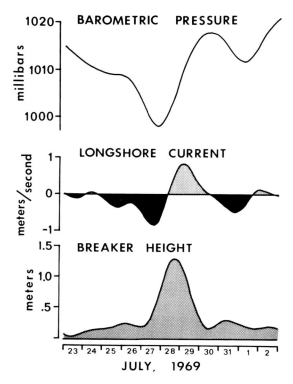

FIG. 4.—Smoothed curves for barometric pressure, longshore current and breaker height at Stevensville, Michigan, July, 1969.

vals from 8 a.m. on June 29 through 6 a.m. on July 29, 1970. During the 30-day study, the barometric pressure varied from a low of 1002.7 millibars (29.61 inches) to a high of 1023.4 millibars (30.22 inches) with a mean of 1011.8 millibars (29.88 inches). Four distinct storms, indicated by low points in the barometric pressure curve, occurred on July 4, 9, 15 and 19 (Fig. 5).

The longshore component of the wind reversed from south to north as each low pressure system passed over the study area. Because the storm paths typically are located to the north of the study area and the surface winds circulate in a counterclockwise direction around the center of the low, the winds which preceed each storm are from the southwest.

For the first storm which moved through on July 4th, the northern component of the longshore wind following the reversal was much stronger than the southern component. The reversal in wind direction for July 4 was accompanied by a rapid rise in barometric pressure. For the second storm

Fourier curves are formed from a summation of a series of sine curves, it is possible to take the derivative of barometric pressure and generate a curve for longshore current. The curve for breaker height resembles the second derivative of barometric pressure. If a time lag of 3 to 6 hours is incorporated in the equations for predicting longshore current and breaker height, it is possible to reproduce the curves for longshore current and breaker height with a fair degree of accuracy.

Holland, Michigan.—During July, 1970, a series of summer storms passed over Lake Michigan at approximately one week intervals. In that month a 30-day time series study was in progress at Holland, Michigan (Fox and Davis, 1971a). Holland is located on the eastern shore of Lake Michigan about 95 kilometers north of Stevensville and 150 kilometers northeast of Chicago (Fig. 2). The beach at the Holland study site trends in a north-south direction and is bounded on its landward side by a low cliff cut into grass-covered sand dunes.

Observations were made on weather and wave conditions at Holland, Michigan for 2-hour inter-

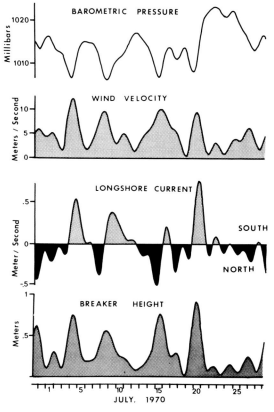

FIG. 5.—Smoothed curves for barometric pressure, wind velocity, longshore current and breaker height at Holland, Michigan, July, 1970.

on July 8, the north and south components of the longshore wind are approximately equal, and the depression in the barometric pressure for July 8 is nearly symmetrical. The curve for the third storm which occurred on July 15 shows a stronger southern wind component followed by a weak north wind (Fig. 5). The barometric pressure curve for July 15 shows a long gradual drop in pressure followed by a rapid rise in pressure. The fourth storm which moved through on July 19 had a short drop in pressure followed by a large increase as a strong cold front and high pressure system moved into the area. The high pressure system was accompanied by strong northwest winds on July 19 and 20. The different patterns displayed by the curves for barometric pressure and longshore winds are determined by the locations, sizes and paths of the individual storms and cold fronts. When a small intense storm moves directly across the study area, the barometric pressure curve is steep and the curve for longshore wind is symmetrical. When a broad, less intense storm system moves diagonally across the shore, an asymmetrical curve is produced for the longshore wind and current.

The peaks and valleys in the curve for longshore current velocity closely match the highs and lows for longshore wind (Fig. 5). The longshore current measured in the trough between the nearshore bar and the shore is roughly parallel to the shore. On the curve for longshore current velocity, the positive longshore current flows to the south and corresponds to the north and northwest wind, whereas the negative longshore current is flowing to the north and related to the southwest winds. Longshore current velocity is a function of breaker angle, wave period, breaker height and bottom topography. Because breaker angle is controlled by wind direction and wave refraction in the nearshore zone, one would expect a close correspondence between the longshore component of the wind and longshore current velocity. There is a close alignment between the smoothed curves for longshore wind and longshore current with minor differences in the amplitude of the peaks. The longshore wind reached a maximum of 15 meters/second on July 4, while the maximum longshore current of 115 centimeters/second was recorded on July 20 (Fig. 5). Although the longshore component of the wind was lower on July 20 than on July 4, the onshore component, which influences breaker height, was greater.

The curve for breaker height has four peaks which occur shortly after the troughs in the barometric pressure curve (Fig. 5). The highest breakers were recorded on July 4 and 20, with lower breakers associated with the storms on July 9 and 15. Lake Michigan waves are generated by local winds with a maximum fetch of about

150 kilometers. Therefore, there is a very rapid response of the waves to increase in wind speed and changes in wind direction. As the low pressure center approaches, the wind picks up out of the southwest generating waves from the same direction. As the waves break on the coast, a northward flowing longshore current is produced. After the storm passes, there is a rapid shift in wind direction which is followed a few hours later by a change in angle of wave approach and a reversal in longshore current direction. On Lake Michigan, the time lag in this shift is usually 3 to 6 hours after the change in wind direction.

Conceptual model for Lake Michigan.—A conceptual model was formulated to study the relationship between storm cycles and beach erosion on Lake Michigan (Davis and Fox, 1972b; Fox and Davis, 1973b). The model is based on field studies conducted at Stevensville and Holland, Michigan, during the summers of 1969 and 1970. Generalized curves are plotted for barometric pressure, wind speed, longshore current and breaker height (Fig. 6). In the model, two low

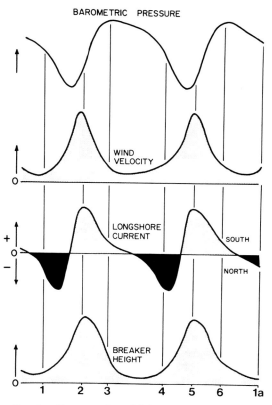

FIG. 6.—Conceptual model for barometric pressure, wind velocity, longshore current and breaker height for 2 storm cycles on Lake Michigan. Numbered vertical lines refer to stages in the model shown in Figure 7.

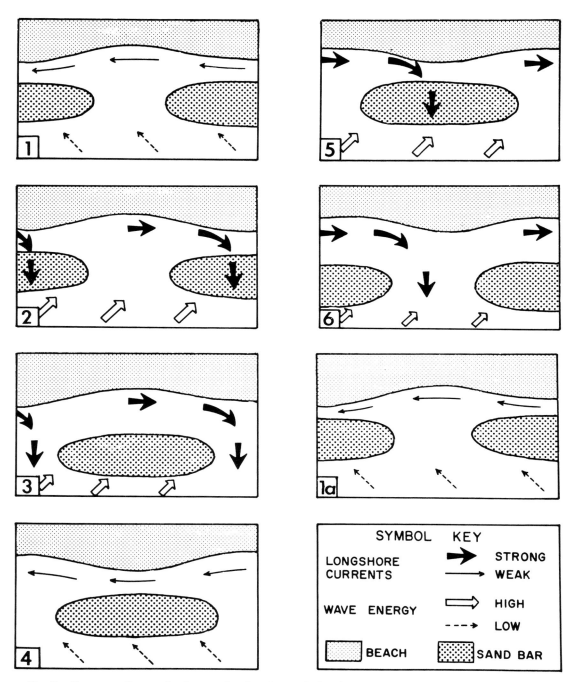

Fig. 7.—Sequence of generalized maps showing changes in beach and bar topography in response to changes in magnitude and direction of the waves and currents on Lake Michigan.

pressure systems pass through the area forming two storm cycles which are separated by a post-storm recovery period.

Six stages in the model (Fig. 6) are numbered to correspond to maps of the beach and nearshore area (Fig. 7). The first storm cycle is marked by a sharp drop followed by a rise in barometric pressure between stages 1 and 3. The interval between 3 and 4 represents the post-storm recovery. The second storm cycle occurs between stages 4 and 6 with a post-storm recovery between stages 6 and 1a. In the model, stage 1 represents falling barometric pressure, low wind speed, weak longshore current to the north and low breaker height as a storm approaches. Between stages 1 and 2, the low passes over and the longshore wind and current reverse direction. During stage 2 the cold front or high pressure ridge moves in. As the barometric pressure rises, wind speed, breaker height and longshore current reach a maximum. At stage 3, barometric pressure is at its highest while wind speed, longshore current and breaker height die down. In the post-storm recovery between stages 3 and 4, the wind slowly shifts over to the southwest, generating low waves and weak currents to the north.

Seven generalized maps show changes in beach and bar topography as the storms pass over the coastline (Fig. 7). The initial shoreline has a rhythmic pattern with two nearshore bars separated by a saddle or rip channel (Evans, 1940). As the low waves approach from the southwest, a weak longshore current flows to the north. At stage 2, high waves build up out of the northwest with strong southward flowing longshore currents between the bars and the shore. The longshore currents are shunted offshore by the protuberance on the beach and cut a channel across the nearshore bar. At stage 3, a new bar is formed in the old saddle and currents cut across the position of the earlier bar. During the post-storm recovery, between stages 3 and 4, small waves move across the bar which advances toward the beach (Olson, 1958). At the same time, a protuberance builds out behind the bar and sets the stage for the next storm cycle. In stages 5 and 6, the storm cycle is repeated again and the bar returns to its original position (Fig. 7).

In the conceptual model, the bar oscillates back and forth during storms exchanging positions with the rip channels or saddles between bars. The post-storm recovery with the shoreward migration of the bars and the growth of the protuberances behind the bars, plays an important role in the model. During the post-storm recovery, erosion takes place on the beach at the head of the rip channels. The sand is transported along the beach by the weak longshore currents forming a protuberance behind the bar. During the next storm cycle, the longshore current is directed offshore by the protuberance and cuts across the nearshore bar forming a rip current. A new bar is formed between the pairs of rip currents near the center of the nearshore circulation cell (Fig. 7). If two storm cycles are closely spaced in time, the protuberance will not have an opportunity to form and the bars will not shift position. On the other hand, if the time interval between storm cycles is long enough, the bar will migrate onto the shore and become welded to the beach (Davis and others, 1972). In a tidal environment, the bar migration would correspond to the ridge and runnel formation described by Hayes and others (1969).

MUSTANG ISLAND, TEXAS

Texas study area.—Two time-series studies were conducted on the Texas coast during October and November, 1971, and January and February, 1972 (Davis and Fox, 1972a). The study area is located on Mustang Island near the middle of the extensive Texas barrier island system (Fig. 8). The barrier islands are approximately 2 to 3 kilometers wide with the major shoreward portion covered by vegetated barrier flats and wind tidal flats. A narrow foredune complex and a gently sloping beach extend along the seaward margin of the islands. The dunes are generally 5 to 8 meters high, but may reach 15 meters locally. In front of the foredunes, the backbeach slopes toward the sea slightly and often is covered with small wind-shadow dunes.

During the fall and winter of 1971-72 when the studies were being made, a prominent berm was not present but there was a noticeable slope difference between the foreshore and backshore. The berm which is normally present on the beach was destroyed by tropical storm Fern in September, 1971, and was not reconstructed because of the relatively high wave conditions during the fall and early winter of 1971-72 (Davis, 1972). The foreshore zone is typically covered by low antidunes generated by swash runoff on the low angle foreshore. During most of the study, three bars were present in the nearshore zone spaced at about 80, 170, and 260 meters from the mean high tide line. Rip currents frequently cut across low saddles in the bars. Although the bars shifted slightly with varying wave conditions, they did not migrate onto the beach and remained relatively stable in position.

The beach study site was located about 5.6 kilometers southeast of the jetty at Aransas Pass. The study site extends approximately 460 meters (1500 feet) southeast of Access Road #1.

Field observations.—The fall time-series study was conducted for 30 days from 8 a.m. on October 18, 1971, through 8 p.m. on November 16. The

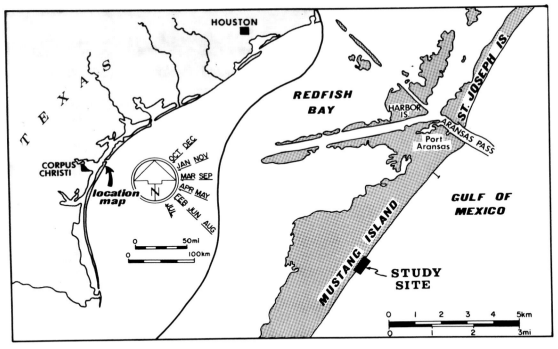

FIG. 8.—Location map showing study site at Mustang Island, Texas.

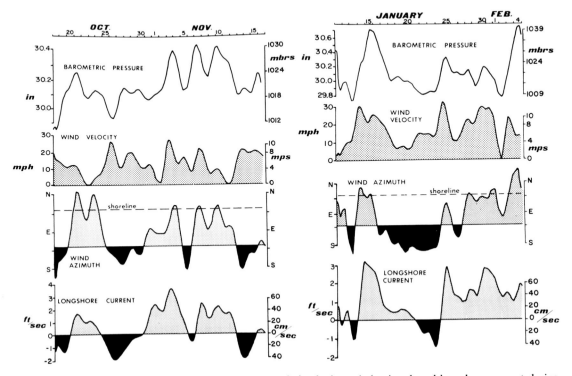

FIG. 9.—Smoothed curves for barometric pressure, wind velocity, wind azimuth and longshore current during fall 1971 and winter 1972 at Mustang Island, Texas.

winter study which lasted from 8 a.m. on January 11, 1972, through 8 p.m. on February 4, was terminated after 25 days because of cold weather and high winds. Wave period, offshore wave height, breaker height, distance, angle and type, and longshore current velocity were measured in the surf at the beach study site or from wave staffs mounted on the Horace Caldwell Pier about 3 kilometers northeast of the beach study site. The wave and current data were taken at 8 a.m., 2 p.m. and 8 p.m. each day. Barometric pressure, tides, wind speed and direction, and water temperature were recorded continuously at the University of Texas Marine Science Institute at Port Aransas, Texas. Readings were extracted at 2-hour intervals for the time-series study in order that they could be compared directly with the wave and current data.

During each of the field studies on the Texas coast, several cold fronts passed over the study area. During the fall of 1971, the range in barometric pressure was 1010.5 to 1031.8 millibars with a mean of 1019.0, while in the winter of 1972, the range was 1007.8 to 1039.6 millibars with a mean of 1019.3 (Fig. 9). The greater range in barometric pressure reflects the more intense cold fronts which passed through the area during the winter.

Wind data were recorded on a two channel recorder, with the directional vane and anemometer mounted approximately 15 meters above sea level at the Marine Science Institute pier. A rapid increase in wind velocity and sudden shift in wind direction are associated with the passage of cold fronts. During the fall, the range in wind velocity was from 0 to 16 m/sec with a mean of 7.5, while in the winter, the range was 0 to 14 m/sec with a mean of 8.2. In both the fall and winter, the wind velocity increased from zero to the maximum in less than one hour when a norther passed over the coast. In the fall, high wind velocities occurred on October 26 and November 3 and 7. On October 26, a storm moved onshore from the Gulf of Mexico and hence was not a typical norther and did not display a rapid rise in barometric pressure and reversal in wind direction (Fig. 9). The events on November 3 and 7 are typical of northers with a sudden increase in wind speed and reversal in wind direction as the front passed through the study area.

Three distinct northers passed over the Texas coast during January and early February of 1972 (Fig 9). During the first norther on January 13, the wind increased from 4 to 14 m/sec and reversed direction from south to north. For the second norther on January 25, the wind increased from 7 to 17 m/sec with a similar reversal in wind direction. In the third norther of the winter on February 3, the wind increased from 2.3 to

15 m/sec, but shifted more to the northwest instead of northeast. The cold front extended in a northwest-southeast direction, so that the south to north reversal in longshore wind was not as prominent and the offshore component of the wind was larger. The strong offshore wind subdued the incoming waves resulting in a decrease in breaker height, wave period and the longshore current velocity. The tides were also almost 0.3 meters lower than predicted because water was forced out of the estuary by the offshore wind.

In the fall study, wave height reached a maximum of 1.2 meters on October 26, and in winter, the wave height reached about 1.3 meters on January 17. The mean breaker height in the winter was the same as in the fall, both were about 0.65 meters. The maximum breaker heights occurred shortly after the maximum wind velocity with a slight time lag. Because the strongest winds were blowing along the shore or slightly offshore, a long fetch was not available to build up large waves.

Longshore current velocity was measured just shoreward of the inner bar using a whiffle ball attached to a 15 meter (50 foot) nylon line. The morning and evening measurements (8 a.m. and 8 p.m.) were made at the Caldwell fishing pier, and the mid-afternoon readings (2 p.m.) were taken at the beach study site. During the fall, the longshore current velocity ranged from −90 cm/sec to the northeast to 120 cm/sec to the southwest (Fig. 9). During the winter, the velocity varied between −50 and 110 cm/sec. The mean current velocities for the fall and winter of 1971–72 were 12 and 24 cm/sec respectively. The lows in the barometric pressure curves are aligned with negative longshore currents and high barometric pressure corresponds to positive longshore currents (Fig. 9). The curve for longshore current during the winter shows a greater asymmetry with positive currents from the northeast being both dominant and prevailing.

The cold front or norther which moves across the Texas coast in an offshore direction creates a pattern of coastal processes which is quite similar to that observed on Lake Michigan. In both areas, the center of the low pressure cell moves from west to east, but passes several hundred kilometers north of the study sites. On Lake Michigan, the counterclockwise circulation around the center of the low pressure cell in conjuction with weak cold fronts produces a shift from southwest to northwest winds as the storm passes. Along the Texas coast, intense cold fronts extending as a southwest line from the low pressure center, exert a strong influence on the coastal processes. In Texas, the shift from southwest to northeast winds is much more abrupt as the cold front passes. Therefore, the curves for barometric pressure, wind velocity and longshore current are more asymmetrical on the Texas coast where strong cold fronts dominate the fall and winter weather pattern and coastal processes.

Conceptual model for Texas coast.—A conceptual model showing the environmental variables on the Texas coast (Fig. 10) was plotted to contrast with the conceptual model developed for Lake Michigan (Figs. 6, and 7). As a cold front or norther approaches the Texas coast from the northwest, barometric pressure drops steadily and the wind velocity is moderate at 8 to 10 m/sec. The waves are generally low, ranging between 0.5 to 0.8 meters, and longshore currents are slow, between 35 to 50 cm/sec to the southwest. Immediately after the passage of the cold front, there

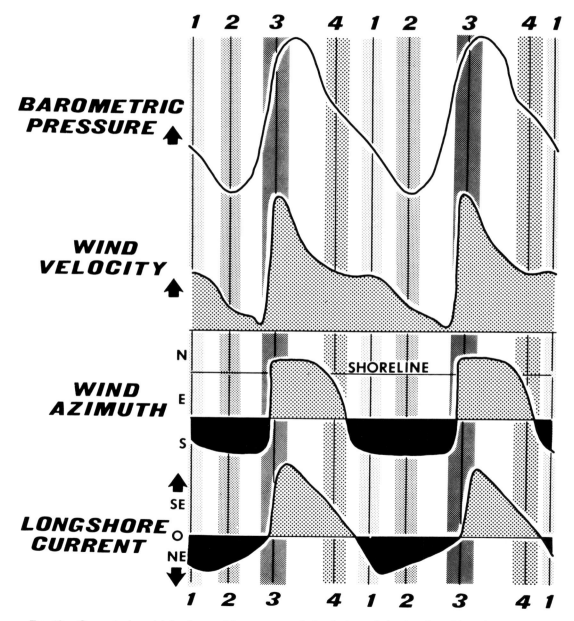

FIG. 10.—Conceptual model for barometric pressure, wind velocity, wind azimuth and longshore current on the Texas coast.

is an abrupt rise in barometric pressure and a sudden drop in air temperature. Wind direction changes to the northeast and the wind velocity increases to about 15 m/sec. The waves approach the shore at an angle open to the southwest and generate longshore currents of 60 cm/sec to the southwest. After the front passes seaward of the coast, the barometric pressure falls, wind shifts toward the southeast and slackens, and the longshore current decreases.

Because the strongest components of the wind are blowing along the shore or slightly offshore, the wave height on the Texas coast does not build up as rapidly as on Lake Michigan. The curves depicted on the model for the Texas coast (Fig. 10) are more asymmetrical than those for Lake Michigan because of the rapid change in wind direction with the passage of cold fronts. The wind speed curve on the Texas model shows an extended hump behind the initial rise as the front passes. The abrupt changes in wind speed, wind direction and longshore current occur somewhat later with respect to barometric pressure on the Texas coast as compared with Lake Michigan (Figs. 6, 10). In general configuration, the models for Lake Michigan and Texas are quite similar, with differences in symmetry for longshore wind and current and a significant difference in wave height with offshore versus onshore wind.

OREGON COAST

Oregon study site.—During 1973 and 1974, a summer study of 45 days and a full year study were conducted on the Oregon coast in the vicinity of Newport, Oregon. In the summer of 1973, a 45-day study extended from July 1 through August 14, when wave conditions were low and longshore currents were relatively slow (Fox and Davis, 1974). Wave and current conditions were measured three times each day in the surf zone. Hourly readings for barometric pressure, wind speed and direction, air temperature, humidity and tide level were taken from the continuously recording instruments at the U. S. Weather Station located in the Oregon State University Marine Science Center at Newport, Oregon. Significant wave height and period were interpreted four times each day from microseismograph records which were correlated directly with pressure sensor observations (Longuet-Higgins, 1950). For the full year study, the continuously recording weather instruments and microseismograph were used exclusively to record the weather and wave data (Creech, 1973). Direct surf observations of waves and currents were not attempted in the winter because of the inherent danger and possible loss of men and equipment in the heavy surf.

During the summer months, three beach areas were surveyed on a rotating basis with one area

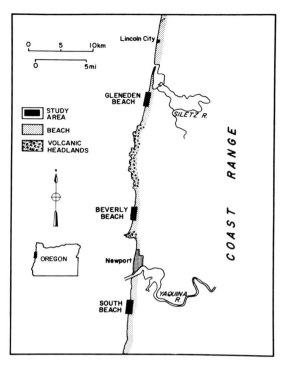

FIG. 11.—Location map of 1973–74 study sites at Gleneden Beach, Beverly Beach and South Beach, Oregon.

mapped each day. The primary study site at South Beach, Oregon, was located about 3 kilometers south of the jetty at the mouth of Yaquina Bay in Newport, Oregon (Fig. 11). The study area extended 488 meters along the coast and about 300 meters seaward from the base of the cliff. Additional beaches were also monitored at the south end of Beverly Beach State Park about 12 kilometers north of Newport, and at Gleneden Beach about 35 kilometers north of Newport (Snavely and MacLeod, 1971). The study site at South Beach was mapped once every two weeks at spring low tide for the full year study. The Oregon coast has a mixed, diurnal-semidiurnal tide with a spring tide range of 4.0 meters and a neap tide range of 2.0 meters (Cox, 1973).

During the summer months, the weather pattern on the Oregon coast is dominated by the East Pacific High (Frye, Pond and Elliot, 1972). The high, which is frequently situated a few hundred kilometers off the Oregon or Washington coast, influences the flow of wind and weather patterns along the coast (Fig. 12). In the fall, the high is displaced to the south and the North Pacific storm track moves across the Oregon coast (Cramer, 1973).

The smoothed curve for barometric pressure

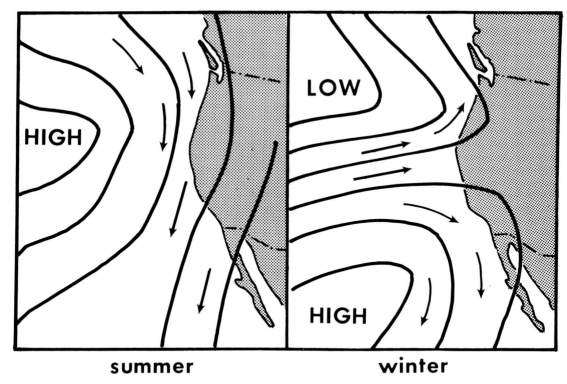

summer   winter

FIG. 12.—Schematic diagram of the seasonal shift of the East Pacific High and associated wind patterns.

has several low points which correspond to weak fronts which moved in from the Pacific Ocean or up from California (Fig. 13). The major frontal systems which had an effect on the coastal area moved across on July 7, 14, 16 and 28 and August 6 and 10, 1973 (Fox and Davis, 1974). The barometric pressure ranged from a low of 1013.2 millibars on July 16 to a high of 1026.2 millibars on July 11. Under the influence of the East Pacific High, north to northwest winds dominate the summer wind pattern and wind-induced coastal upwelling is frequent and long lasting (Smith, 1972). During the upwelling which started on July 17, the water temperature in the surf zone dropped from 14.4°C to 6.6°C (58°F to 44.4°F) in two days.

During July and August, the East Pacific High generally produced strong north to northwest surface winds, roughly parallel to the coast. The surface wind pattern is shown by the longshore component of the wind (Fig. 13). During the study, the longshore wind blew out of the north for 35 days reaching a maximum of about 15 m/sec on July 12, and out of the south for 10 days reaching a peak of 5 m/sec on July 8. On July 1, a high pressure system dominated the weather with winds about 12.5 m/sec out of the north. On July 2 through 8, a weak front stalled offshore

with southwest winds reaching 6 m/sec. From July 9 through 16, north winds swept along the coast reaching 15 m/sec on July 12. A low pressure system moved up the coast from California on July 16 and displaced the East Pacific High seaward until July 21, producing southwest winds of 3 to 4 m/sec. The longest continuous period of north winds and upwelling occurred for 18 days between July 22 and August 8, 1973. A weak low started to move up from California on July 28 and decreased the north component of the longshore wind, but did not push the subtropical high offshore. Low pressure systems moved in from the Pacific on August 9 and 13, producing weak southwest winds on the 9th and stronger winds, up to 5 m/sec, on August 12th and 13th.

The longshore winds on the Oregon coast have a definite diurnal component which was smoothed out on the plotted curves (Fig. 13) but shows up in the observed data (Fox and Davis, 1974). The longshore wind reaches a peak in the afternoon and drops off considerably at night. The sea breeze pattern is deflected along the coast by the large difference in air and water temperature. The onshore component of the wind shows a fairly regular pattern with an onshore peak of about 5 m/sec in the mid-afternoon, and an

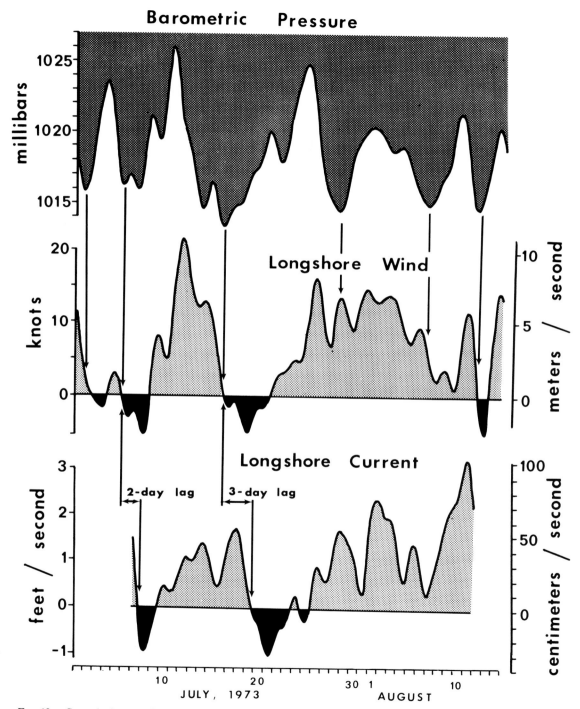

FIG. 13.—Smoothed curves for barometric pressure, longshore wind and longshore current at Newport, Oregon.

offshore breeze of about 2 m/sec at night. Normally, one would expect a sea and land breeze to show a 12-hour pattern with the onshore breeze picking up in the afternoon and an offshore breeze during the late evening. However, along the northwest Pacific coast of the United States, the diurnal wind field is superimposed on the subtropical high and the result is a strong 24-hour, instead of 12-hour, periodicity in the wind speed (Frye, Pond and Elliot, 1972). The cold surface water which reaches a low of about 6°C during upwelling, tends to inhibit the development of a land breeze at night.

The nearshore current speed and direction was measured at least twice each day at the South Beach study site (Fox and Davis, 1974). When the South Beach site was being surveyed in the mid-afternoon, longshore current was also measured at 2 p.m. However, when surveys were being made at Beverly Beach or Gleneden Beach, the afternoon current measurements were not taken. Because rip currents were present in the intertidal zone at different times in the tidal cycle, the azimuth as well as speed of the nearshore current was recorded. Therefore, current speed and azimuth measurements were taken in the center of the rip channel, as well as 30 meters north and 30 meters south of the channel. The average longshore component of the nearshore current was recorded as the longshore current velocity. The offshore component, which represents the rip current, was strongest on July 25 when it reached 25 cm/sec. The longshore component of the current was generally much stronger than the offshore component and reached a maximum of 90 cm/sec on August 11.

There is a close relationship between barometric pressure, longshore wind and longshore current on the Oregon coast (Fig. 13). For the first half of the study, the lows in barometric pressure corresponded quite closely to reversals in wind direction from north to south. The lows in pressure on July 2, 5 and 17 were coincident with changes in wind direction from north to south. A similar pattern of reversals in longshore current direction was observed, but the current showed a 2 to 3 day lag in the reversal. Because the longshore currents are closely related to rip currents on the Oregon coast, the lag time in reversal of current direction may be related to the shifting of nearshore bars and rip channels.

Ocean wave periods and heights were derived from microseismograph records at the Marine Science Center, which were verified twice each day by visual observations (Creech, 1973). During the 45-day study, the significant breaker height varied from a minimum of 0.76 meters on July 2 to a maximum of 2.60 meters on July 16 (Fig. 14). The plot of breaker height shows a general increase for the first 16 days, then low waves for the remainder of the study with small peaks of about 1.2 meters on July 26 and 1.6 meters on August 8. The low points on the barometric pressure curve correspond with the peaks on the breaker height curve similar to the general model developed for Lake Michigan. During the latter half of the study, from about July 24 through August 5, strong winds were blowing along the coast with speeds up to 15 m/sec, but they did not produce high waves. Because the high waves correspond to the lows in the barometric pressure curve and not the local wind conditions, it can be assumed that the waves were produced by the winds offshore as the low approached the coast. At the coast, the winds are predominantly along the shore and do not correspond closely with local wave conditions.

Topographic changes.—The primary study site at South Beach, Oregon was located about 3 kilometers south of the jetty at the mouth of the Yaquina River in Newport, Oregon (Fig. 11). The study area extends for 488 meters along the coast and about 350 meters seaward from the base of the cliff. The beach covers a wave-cut terrace in the Nye Mudstone which is overlain unconformably by Pleistocene marine terrace deposits which crop out in the upper half of the cliff (Lund, 1972). The layer of sand on the beach is up to two meters thick during the summer with portions of the wave-cut terrace exposed during the winter.

Two lines of bars were present in the intertidal zone on July 4, an inner set (bars A and E) about 140 meters from the cliff and an outer set (bars B, D and C) about 230 meters from the cliff (Fig. 15a). Between July 4 and 10, bars A and B advanced toward the shore at about 5 m/day, and to the south at about 16 m/day (Fig. 15h). Bar C advanced toward the beach at 4 m/day and bars E and F welded onto the beach. Some rip channel excavation took place in front of the bars as they advanced toward the beach.

Between July 10 and 18, significant changes took place on the beach and in the intertidal zone (Fig. 15c). Bars A and C merged and advanced across the beach and to the south. On July 16, strong longshore currents due to high waves from the north excavated a trough more than a meter deep and 15 meters wide in front of bar C. Large megaripples in the trough provided evidence of strong longshore currents at high tide. A new bar, G, developed about 80 meters seaward from bar A and started to migrate toward the beach.

Between July 18 and 25, low wave conditions persisted on the Oregon coast and the intertidal sand bars advanced shoreward across the beach (Fig. 15d). Bar G moved toward the shore at 14 m/day and built up in elevation. A rip channel developed between the south end of bar G and

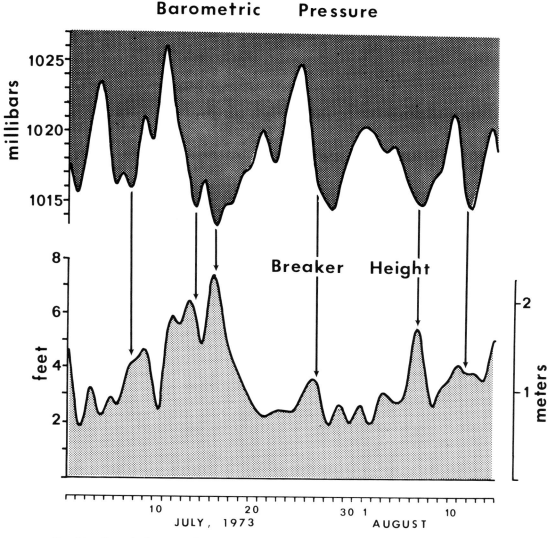

FIG. 14.—Smoothed curves of barometric pressure and breaker height at Newport, Oregon.

bar C. At the same time, bar C advanced toward the shore at about 2 m/day and closed the southern exit from the longshore trough. Therefore, the water carried over bar C by the waves was no longer able to drain out to the south and increased the discharge out the rip channel between bars G and C (Fig. 15d). From July 25 through August 4, the south end of bar G continued to enlarge southward forcing the rip channel between bars G and C to the south. As the current emerged from the rip channel, the northwest waves directed the current southward along the shore. The seaward face of bar C was eroded by wave action and longshore currents from the

rip channel. A portion of the sand from the seaward side of bar C was transported across the bar and deposited on the longshore trough as the bar advanced up the beach.

Between August 4 and August 12, bar G continued to build out to the south until it extended beyond bar C. It then proceeded to advance shoreward and merge with bar C forming a continuous bar the full length of the study area. At the same time, two new bars, H and I, formed seaward of bars G and C and started their advance across the beach. At the end of the study, one long continuous bar extended along the entire beach with a longshore trough which drained to

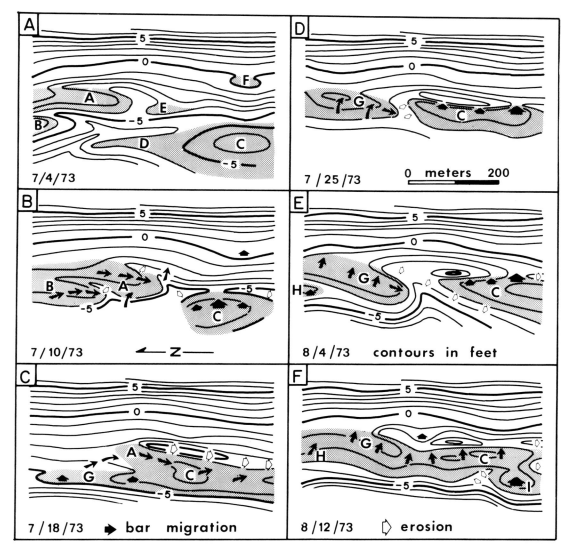

Fig. 15.—Sequence of maps showing bar migration and beach erosion during July and August, 1973, at South Beach, Oregon.

the south. Two smaller bars were forming seaward of the long bar and were moving across the beach.

In summary, the major mode of sand transport across the Oregon beaches in the summer is in the form of large intertidal sand bars. The bars form at a depth of 1 to 2 meters and advance toward the cliff at 1 to 5 m/day. During the summer, the wind is generally out of the north to northwest at 5 to 15 m/sec with waves 1 to 3 meters high. The northwest winds and waves generate longshore currents to the south resulting in a southward migration of the bars. The rate of bar movement to the south varies from 10 to 15 m/day. During storms or high waves longshore troughs and rip channels are excavated by the longshore currents. During times of low wave activity, the bars advance toward the cliff and bury the longshore trough.

Seasonal trends on the Oregon coast.—Very definite seasonal trends are present in the weather and wave conditions on the Oregon Coast. In order to separate the seasonal trends from the shore period fluctuations due to individual storms, the first 18 Fourier harmonics were computed from the data, and the cummulative curves were plotted for barometric pressure, longshore wind,

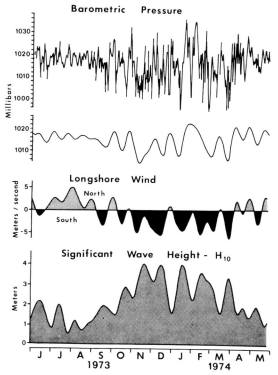

FIG. 16.—Observed curve for barometric pressure and smoothed curves for barometric pressure, longshore wind and wave height from June, 1973, through May, 1974, at Newport, Oregon.

and significant wave height (Fig. 16). The first 18 Fourier components filter out any fluctuations with a period of less than 20 days.

The smoothed curve for barometric pressure shows minor broad oscillations from June through October, 1973, with the first major low in mid-November. The remaining low points on the smoothed curve for barometric pressure occur in mid-December, mid-January, late March.

The curve for significant wave height reaches a low point in late August and builds up to several broad peaks in the late fall and winter. Offshore waves of more than 7 meters in height were recorded during storms in November and February. The peaks in the wave height curve for mid-November, mid-December, mid-January, late February and late March correspond to the low points on the pressure curve. Each broad peak on the wave height curve consists of several distinct storms, but the groups of storms are separated by 8 to 10 days of relative calm with low wave activity. The longest break in the weather occurred in early January when it was clear for 10 days and the wave heights dropped

below one meter. The range in oscillation of barometric pressure varied from a minimum of 8 millibars during the summer to a maximum of 43 millibars in the midwinter storms. The wave height reached maximum of 2 meters during late July and early August compared with about 7 meters in November and February.

No attempt was made to measure longshore current velocity during the winter months, but the longshore component of the wind was recorded (Fig. 16). Because there is a close correlation between longshore current velocity and the longshore component of the wind during the summer (Fig. 13), it is assumed that the longshore current and longshore wind would also be correlative during the winter. This assumption may not be justified because the larger waves in the winter would be refracted and approach the shore more closely parallel to the beach. However, based on the deep excavation of longshore troughs, and the general build up of sand on the south side of jetties during the winter, it is assumed that the northward flowing longshore currents play an important role in coastal erosion and sediment transport during the winter months. The smoothed curve for longshore wind shows the dominant north wind under the influence of the East Pacific High during the summer months (Figs. 12, 16). The dominant wind direction shifts to the southwest in September and remains from the south until the following April. The peaks in the longshore wind from the south also line up with the peaks for the smoothed curve for breaker height. Although they are masked in the smoothed curve, reversals in wind direction occur within each individual storm, but the south component of the wind generally is stronger than that from the north. The onshore component of the wind also increases during the winter from a minimum of about 2 to 3 m/sec during the summer to maximum of almost 15 m/sec in the winter. The strong onshore winds significantly build up the winter waves. Offshore winds of up to 10 m/sec reduce the wave height in early January.

During the summer, intertidal sand bars were formed on the lower foreshore and advanced across the beach under low wave conditions. In September and October, the intertidal bars were removed from the beach and the beach surface was concave upward. In November, more than 0.6 meters of sand was stripped from the entire surface beach. During the winter storms, portions of the beach were eroded down to bedrock. In the calm intervals between major storm periods, large bars formed and started to migrate across the beach. Deep rip channels and longshore troughs were cut on the shoreward margin of the bars as they advanced across the beach. Therefore, the sand on the backbeach was removed when the longshore trough was excavated, and more sand was deposited as the bar advanced across the trough. Because a deep trough is frequently excavated on the shoreward side of the sand bar and filled in as the bar progresses up the beach, a new layer of sand is accumulated by each successive set of bars. Therefore, the new sand is not simply laid down as a carpet of sand over the existing sand on the beach, but the pre-existing sand is eroded on the shoreward edge of the trough and the bar fills in the trough as the bar and trough migrate together across the beach.

DISCUSSION

Three coastal areas, the eastern shore of Lake Michigan, Mustang Island, Texas, and the central Oregon Coast were selected for detailed analysis of the relationship between weather patterns and coastal processes. The shoreline on the eastern coast of Lake Michigan extended perpendicular to the storm paths and the storms moved onshore

to the north of the study area. With a tidal range of less than 10 centimeters and fetch of about 150 kilometers, the waves respond quickly to changes in weather conditions, and swells and tidal currents do not influence beach erosion. A simple storm cycle model was developed for Lake Michigan relating breaker height and longshore current velocity to barometric pressure. The general shapes for the barometric pressure, longshore current and breaker height curves for Lake Michigan are given in Figure 17. The curve for barometric pressure is symmetrical with the rate of pressure drop about equal to the rate of pressure rise. The curve for longshore current is again symmetrical with a somewhat faster longshore current to the south than to the north. The maximum longshore current of the three areas was 210 cm/sec at Stevensville, Michigan, in July 1969. Wave heights reached a maximum of 1.8 meters during summer storms, but were generally less than 1.0 meter on Lake Michigan.

On the Texas coast, Mustang Island is oriented in a northeast-southwest direction with the Gulf

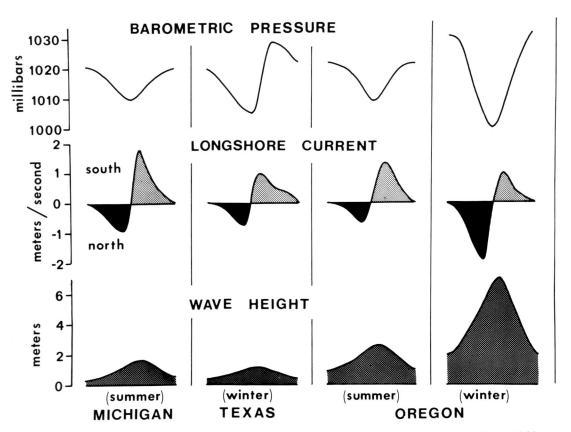

Fig. 17.—Generalized curves for barometric pressure, longshore current and breaker height at Holland, Michigan; Mustang Island, Texas; and Newport, Oregon.

of Mexico to the east. In the fall and winter, low pressure systems move to the north of Mustang Island with intense cold fronts trailing off to the southwest. As a low pressure center moves to the east, a cold front sweeps across the coast accompanied by a sharp rise in barometric pressure and rapid reversal in longshore current direction. Because winds blow along shore or offshore, the fetch is short and breaker height does not increase very much. Maximum breaker height during the fall and winter studies at Mustang Island was about 1.2 meters, whereas the breaker height reached 1.8 meters on Lake Michigan during the July 1969 storm. Although the fetch is less on Lake Michigan, onshore winds generally produced larger waves and faster longshore currents on Lake Michigan than on the Texas coast (Fig. 17). The warm gulf air contrasted sharply with the polar air masses in the late fall and winter producing intense cold fronts or northers which crossed the Texas coast. Cold fronts connected with the low pressure systems that passed over Lake Michigan during the summer were not as intense because of the smaller difference in temperature. The asymmetry of curves for barometric pressure and longshore current, and the smaller breaker heights are plotted at the same scale as the curves for Lake Michigan (Fig. 17).

The summer weather pattern on the Oregon coast is dominated by the East Pacific High. The high pressure system is situated a few hundred kilometers off the Oregon coast. North winds circulating around the high blow along the coast from April through September. Weak low pressure systems move over the coast during the summer, causing a reversal in wind direction and longshore current (Fig. 17). The south component of the longshore wind reaches only 5 m/sec, while the north component is frequently over 15 m/sec. Breakers on the Oregon coast reached heights of 2.5 meters and longshore currents approached 100 cm/sec. Usually the high waves were refracted so that the wave crests were almost paralled to the coast, and longshore currents were more strongly influenced by the topography of the intertidal sand bars. The tide range on the Oregon coast is up to 4 meters in spring tides which contrasts with the 1 meter spring tides on the Texas coast and 10 centimeter tide on Lake Michigan.

During the winter, the East Pacific High moves to the south and the major Pacific storm track shifts over the Oregon coast. During 1973–74, storms passed with regular frequency during the fall and winter months boosting the rainfall on the Oregon coast to 92 inches. Wave height during the winter storms reached 8 meters with wave periods of 8 to 14 seconds. Most of the storm activity was concentrated between the months

of November and March with breaks of 8 to 10 days between sets of 3 to 5 storms. The onshore wind generally dominated over the offshore wind with speeds reaching 15 m/sec. During the storms, the south component of the longshore winds reached 20 m/sec, while the north component was only 10 m/sec. Although it was not possible to measure the longshore currents during the winter, there was a positive correlation between longshore wind and longshore current during the summer. It can be assumed that the strong south winds during the winter were also responsible for strong longshore currents to the north.

Regular patterns of topographic change were recorded in each of the three study areas. On Lake Michigan, the beach and nearshore bars responded quickly to waves and longshore currents within each storm cycle. In the intervals between storms, protuberances built out along the shore, and the bars migrated toward the beach. During storms, the waves approached the shore at a large angle and generated strong longshore currents. The currents were shunted offshore by the protuberances and eroded a channel through the sand bars. Thus, the position of the bars shifted with each storm cycle under the influence of waves and longshore currents.

Along the Texas coast, the beach is broad with 2 to 3 well developed longshore bars. Although low amplitude cusps were present on the foreshore during most of the study, the rhythmic shoreline pattern found on Lake Michigan was not as pronounced on the Texas coast. With the straight shoreline, longshore currents were confined to the nearshore trough and rip currents were not regularly spaced. However, the shoreward migration of bars during low energy conditions, and seaward expansion of the trough during high energy were observed on both the Michigan and Texas coasts. Saddles are present on the Texas sand bars, but they are not related to protuberances along the beach.

On the Oregon coast, the 4 meter tidal range exposed an intertidal beach almost 300 meters wide. Sand bars migrated across the intertidal beach with large rip channels developed between the bars. The rip channels are affected by rising and falling tides which flood and drain the beach. During the summer, the bars advanced across the beach at 1 to 5 m/day, and new bars formed at the seaward margin of the intertidal zone. During the winter, high waves and strong currents stripped a large portion of the sand off the beach. During occasional quiet conditions in midwinter, however, large bars would form and move across the beach. Most of the sand which was removed from the beach by large winter storms apparently was stored below mean low tide on large sand bars. An equivalent volume of sand was returned to the intertidal beaches during the spring and summer.

CONCLUSIONS

The following conclusions can be drawn concerning weather patterns and coastal processes on Lake Michigan, Mustang Island, Texas and the central Oregon Coast.

1. On the eastern shore of Lake Michigan, longshore current velocity is a function of the first derivative of barometric pressure, and breaker height is a function of the second derivative.

2. On Lake Michigan, rip channels between bars occur offshore from protuberances on the beach. During storms, longshore currents are shunted offshore by protuberances and form rip channels between the bars.

3. On the Texas coast, fall and winter weather patterns are dominated by intense cold fronts or northers marked by a rapid rise in pressure, drop in temperature and sudden shift in wind from northeast to southwest.

4. Beaches along the Texas coast are relatively straight with 2 to 3 offshore bars. Rip channels forming saddles between the bars are not related to protuberances along the coast.

5. During the summer, the weather pattern on the Oregon coast is dominated by north winds circulating around the East Pacific High. Waves are 1 to 3 meters high with strong longshore currents to the south.

6. During the winter on the Oregon coast, the East Pacific High shifts to the south and the Pacific storm track passes over the Oregon coast. Wave heights reach 6 to 8 meters during the storms and southwest winds predominate forming strong northward flowing longshore currents.

7. The 4-meter tides on the Oregon coast play an important role in spreading the influence of waves and currents over a 300 meter wide intertidal beach.

8. Broad intertidal sand bars migrate across the Oregon beaches during the summer at a rate of 1 to 5 m/day. During the winter storms, between November and March, sand is removed from the beach and stored in subtidal sand bars. In the spring the bars migrate onto the beach returning the sand lost by the winter storms. Large sand bars also form on the beach in the winter during the quiet intervals between major storms.

9. Beach erosion and bar migration observed in the three study areas are closely related to waves and longshore currents during storms. The areas differ in their response to wave and currents because of their position relative to storm tracks, orientation of the shoreline, tidal range, and nearshore topography.

ACKNOWLEDGEMENTS

This research was carried out under the sponsorship of the Geography Branch of the Office of Naval Research under Research Contract N00014-69-C-0151 Task No. NR 388-092. Several student assistants including: E. Cartnick, C. Collinson III, J. Cunningham, H. Flint, C. Foster, T. Getz, R. Kerhin, D. Lehman, R. LoPiccolo, D. McTigue. P. Murphy, W. Murphy, K. Murray, D. Rosen and E. Thorp helped with various aspects of the field work, laboratory analysis and computer programming for the project. Computer facilities at Williams College, Western Michigan University and Oregon State University were used for plotting the curves. Wind and weather data were made available from the Marine Science Institute at the University of Texas and from Oregon State University.

REFERENCES

Cox, W. S., 1973. Oregon estuaries: Oregon State Land Board, Salem, Oregon, 48 p.
Cramer, O. P., 1973, Mesosystem weather in the Pacific Northwest, a summer case study: Monthly Weather Rev., v. 101, p. 13-23.
Creech, C., 1973. Wave climatology of the central Oregon coast: Oregon State Univ., Marine Sci. Center Tech. Rep. NOAA Sea Grant Project 04-3-158-4, 19p.
Davies, J. L., 1964, A morphogenetic approach to world shorelines: Zeitschr. Geomorphologie, v. 8, Sonderheft, p. 127-142.
Davies, R. A., Jr., 1972, Beach changes on the central Texas coast associated with Hurricane Fern, September 1971: Contr. Marine Sci., v. 16, p. 89-98.
—— and Fox, W. T., 1971, Beach and nearshore dynamics in eastern Lake Michigan: Williams College, Tech. Rep. 4, ONR Contract 388-092, 145 p.
—— and ——, 1972a, Coastal dynamics along Mustang Island, Texas: Williams College, Tech. Rep. 9, ONR Contract 388-092, 68 p.
—— and ——, 1972b, Coastal processes and nearshore bars: Jour. Sed. Petrology, v. 42, p. 401-412.
—— and ——, 1974, Simultaneous process-responses study on the east and west coasts of Lake Michigan: Williams College, Tech. Rep. 13, ONR Contract 388-092, 61 p.
——, ——, Hayes, M. O., and Boothroyd, J. C., 1972, Comparison of ridge and runnel systems in marine and non-marine environments. Jour. Sed. Petrology, v. 42, p. 413-421.
Evans, O. F., 1940, Low and ball of the eastern shore of Lake Michigan: Jour. Sed. Petrology, v. 48, p. 476-511.

Fox, W. T., and Davis, R. A., Jr., 1970a, Fourier analysis of weather and wave data from Lake Michigan: Williams College, Tech. Rep. 1, ONR Contract 388-092, 47 p.

—— and ——, 1970b, Profile of a storm-wind, waves and erosion on the southeastern shore of Lake Michigan: Internat. Assoc. Great Lakes Res., Proc. 13th Conf. on Great Lakes Research, p. 233-241.

—— and ——, 1971a, Fourier analysis of weather and wave data from Holland, Michigan, July 1970: Williams College, Tech. Rep. 3, ONR Contract 388-092, 79 p.

—— and ——, 1971b, Computer simulation model of coastal processes on eastern Lake Michigan: Williams College, Tech. Rep. 5, ONR Contract 388-092, 114p.

—— and ——, 1973a, Coastal processes and beach dynamics at Sheboygan, Wisconsin, July 1972: Williams College, Tech. Rep. 10, ONR Contract 388-092, 94 p.

—— and ——, 1973b, Simulation model for storm cycles and beach erosion on Lake Michigan: Geol. Soc. America Bull., v. 84, p. 1769-1790.

—— and ——, 1974, Beach processes on the Oregon coast: Williams College, Tech. Rep. 12, ONR Contract 388-092, 86 p.

Frye, E. E., Pond, S., and Elliott, W. P., 1973, Note on the kinetic energy spectrum of coastal winds: Monthly Weather Rev., v. 100, p. 671-673.

Hayes, M. O., et al., 1969, Coastal environments, northeastern Massachusetts and New Hampshire: Univ. Massachusetts Coastal Res. Group, Contr. 1, 462 p.

Inman, D. L., and Nordstrom, C. E., 1971, On the tectonic and morphologic classification of coasts: Jour. Geology, v. 79, p. 1-21.

Lund, E. H., 1972, Coastal landforms between Yachats and Newport, Oregon: The Ore Bin, v. 34, p. 73-91.

Longuet-Higgins, M. S., 1950, A theory of the origin of microseisms: Royal Soc. London Philos. Trans., Ser. A, v. 243, p. 1-35.

Olson, J. S., 1958, Lake Michigan dune development; 3. Lake level beach and dune oscillations: Jour. Geology, v. 66, p. 473-483.

Sclater, J. G., Anderson, R. N., and Bell, L. M., 1971, Elevation of ridges and evolution of the central eastern Pacific: Jour. Geophys. Res., v. 76, p. 7888-7915.

Shepard, F. P., 1963, Thirty-five thousand years of sea level: In R. L. Miller (ed.), Essays in marine geology in honor of K. O. Emery: Univ. Southern California Press, p. 1-10.

Smith, R. L., 1972, A description of current, wind, and sea level variations during coastal upwellings off the Oregon coast, July-August, 1972: Jour. Geophys. Res., v. 79, p. 435-443.

Snavely, P. D., Jr., and Macleod, N. S., 1971, Visitors guide to the geology of the coastal area near Veverly Beach State Park, Oregon: The Ore Bin, v. 33, p. 85-105.

Valentin, H., 1952, Die Küsten der Erd: Petermanns Geog. Mitt. Ergänzunashelf, 246 p.

STORMS AS MODIFYING AGENTS IN THE COASTAL ENVIRONMENT

Miles O. Hayes and Jon C. Boothroyd
Coastal Research Group
Department of Geology
University of Massachusetts

ABSTRACT

Northeasterly storms play a dominant role in the generation of cycles of erosion and deposition on the beaches of New Hampshire and northeastern Massachusetts. Measurement of bimonthly, and often closer-spaced, beach profiles at 8 stations from September 1965 to April 1969 revealed the following stages of low-tide beach morphology relative to storm occurrences:

1) Early poststorm (up to 3 or 4 days after storm) – Profile is flat to concave, and beach surface is generally smooth and uniformly medium-grained. Severest storms leave erosional dune scarps.

2) Early accretion (usually 2 days to 6 weeks after storm) – Small berms, beach cusps, and ridge-and-runnel systems are quick to form.

3) Late accretion, or maturity (6 weeks or more after storm) – Landward-migrating ridges weld onto the backbeach to form broad, convex berms. On some beaches, welding does not occur and gigantic ridges (up to 4 feet in height) lie between the backbeach and the low-tide terrace.

No stage is unique to any particular season and the cycle is frequently interrupted by recurring storms.

During the period of observation, over 20 moderate-to-severe northeasters affected the study area. The role of these storms as geological agents was controlled by (1) size and intensity of storm; (2) speed of storm movement; (3) tidal phase (i.e., spring or neap tide); (4) path of storm with respect to beach; and (5) time interval between storms.

INTRODUCTION

The importance of coastal storms in shoreline processes is now widely recognized (Blumenstock et al., 1961; Stoddart, 1962; Hayes, 1965). Observations of the effects of over 20 northeasterly storms during the past four years indicate that these storms are the dominant factor controlling cycles of erosion and deposition of the sand beaches of northern New England. The "northeaster," which develops as a low-pressure center over the southwestern or southeastern United States and swings in a northeasterly course along the Atlantic coast, is the most important storm affecting the northern New England coast. Tracks of some of the major storms that occurred during the interval between 7 August 1966 and 29 May 1967 are shown in Figure 1. Because of the counterclockwise rotation of winds around these low-pressure centers, strong northeasterly winds blow against the northern

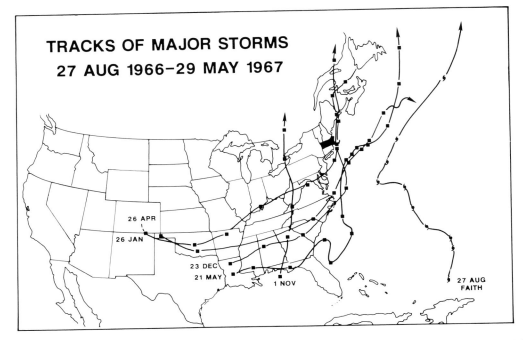

FIGURE 1. Tracks of major storm centers for the period of 27 August 1966 to 29 May 1967. The most effective storms occurring during this interval were the storms labeled 25 January and 21 May. The track of Hurricane FAITH is the easternmost track.

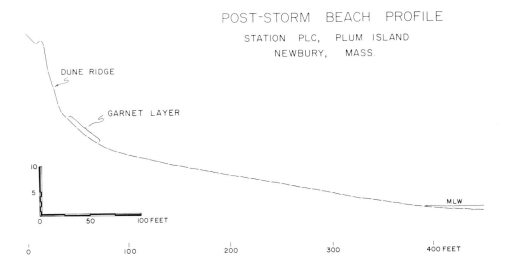

FIGURE 2. A typical poststorm beach profile on Plum Island (Profile PLC). This profile was cut by the major northeaster of 25-26 May 1967. Profile measured on 27 May.

New England coast as the storm center swings over the continental shelf east of southern New England. During the span of our observations, September 1965 to April 1969, no major hurricanes have passed through the area. Figure 1 shows the track of Hurricane FAITH in late August 1967. This hurricane generated large, long-period waves which had only a minor erosional effect on the northern New England coast.

THE BEACH PROFILE

The measurement of over 600 beach profiles at 8 permanent beach profiling localities in northeastern Massachusetts and New Hampshire reveals a consistent recurrence of 3 basic beach profiles: (a) early poststorm (up to 3 or 4 days after storm); (b) early accretion (usually 2 days to 6 weeks after storm); and (c) late accretion, or maturity (6 weeks or more after storm).

The early poststorm profile is flat to concave-upward, and the beach surface is generally smooth and uniformly medium-grained. The most severe storms leave erosional dune scarps. An example of such a profile is shown in Figure 2, which was taken on the day following the major northeasterly storm of 25-26 May 1967. Two views of the beach profile cut by that storm are shown in Figure 3.

Typically, the constructional beach profile (Fig. 4) consists of a ridge-and-runnel system, sometimes accompanied by a small, incipient berm. The ridge grows in size through the constructional period and will eventually weld to the backbeach if the interval between storms is long enough. This cycle of beach accretion is further illustrated in the descriptions for Stops 4 and 19 (this guidebook).

After welding of the ridge, the beach continues to accrete on the beach face, forming a broad depositional berm that is convex-upward. This is the mature profile. The profile for 10 September 1967 in Figure 5 is a typical example of such a profile. During the development of the mature profile, beach cusps are very common along the beach face. Our observations indicate that at least 90 percent of the cusps we have observed were formed during the constructional phase of beach development and are, hence, depositional features.

Therefore, the cycle of erosion and deposition of the sand beaches of Massachusetts and New Hampshire is a cycle related directly to storm activity. Although storms are most common during the months of December to March, no single erosional or accretional stage is unique to any particular season. The cycle is frequently interrupted by recurring storms.

There is no distinct "summer beach" or "winter beach." The profiles on Figure 5 show that summer beach profiles can be either of the extreme end members of the erosional-accretional cycle on northern New England beaches. Figure 6 illustrates the rapid rate with which sediment can accumulate on the beach during the winter. In a period of only 18 days, the high-tide mark advanced seaward a distance of over 100 feet, and a large, welded neap berm accumulated in the middle of the beach profile. This sediment accumulation was eroded away by the large northeaster of 27-28 January 1967.

FIGURE 3a.   View looking north from Profile PLC on 27 May 1967. Compare
photograph with the beach profile at that position (Fig. 2).
Note logs protruding from the wave-cut scarp. The amount of
retreat of the dune scarp at this position during the storm was
between 5 and 10 feet.

FIGURE 3b.   Same date and orientation as Figure 3a, from the foredune
ridge. Note broad, flat profile. Dark zone at the base of the
dune scarp is a garnet-rich, heavy mineral deposit.

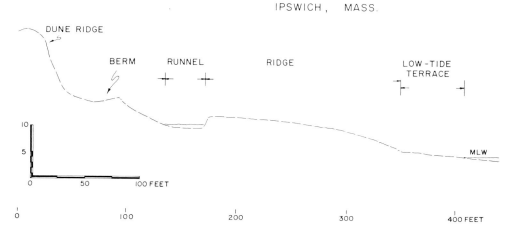

FIGURE 4. Typical constructional beach profile for the coast of northeastern Massachusetts and New Hampshire. This profile was measured at profiling station CBA at the northern end of Crane Beach on 22 August 1967.

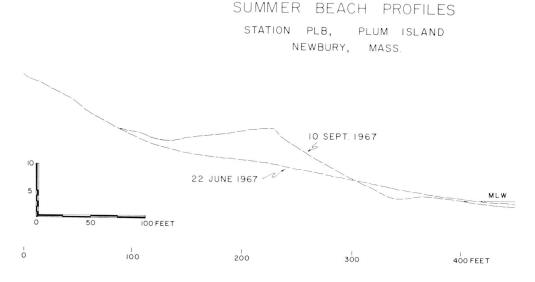

FIGURE 5. Summer profiles at station PLB on Plum Island. These profiles represent the two extreme end members of the erosional-accretional cycle, poststorm (22 June 1967) and late accretion (10 September 1967).

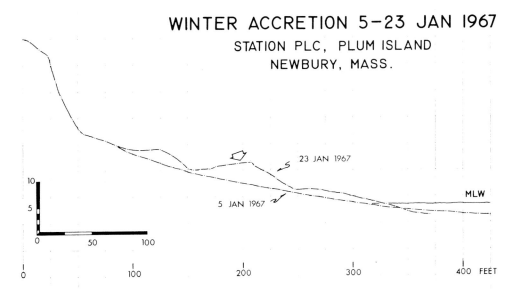

FIGURE 6.   Profiles depicting winter accretion at station PLC, Plum Island,
             for the period 5-23 January 1967. During this 18-day period,
             the high-tide mark advanced seaward over 100 feet, and a large
             neap berm (arrow) developed.

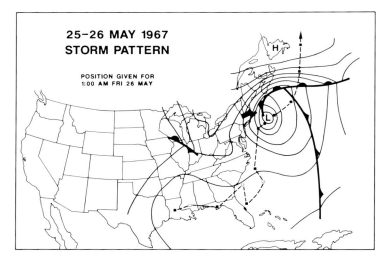

FIGURE 7.   Location of a large northeasterly storm at 1:00 AM on Friday,
             26 May 1967. The track of this storm is shown by the dashed
             line. The distance between blocks along the track represents
             the distance the storm center traveled within a 12-hour
             interval. This is one of the largest storms to affect the study
             area during the last four years. Note the slow progress of the
             storm once it reached a position directly offshore from the
             southeastern coast of Massachusetts. It was practically
             stationary for a period of two full days.

IMPORTANT STORM CHARACTERISTICS

During the period of our observations, the role of northeasterly storms as geological agents appears to be controlled by five factors--size and intensity of storm, speed of storm movement, tidal phase, path of storm with respect to beach, and time interval between storms.

Size and Intensity of Storm

The most obviously important characteristic of a storm with respect to geological processes is its size and intensity. Northeasterly storms occasionally attain hurricane proportions on the New England coast. Northeasterly wind velocities of 50-60 mph are very common. These storms sometimes generate storm surges, but the surges seldom exceed three feet. An example of a very large and intense northeasterly storm is shown in Figure 7.

Speed of Storm Movement

Regardless of the size of the storm, if it moves through an area so fast that winds cannot build up from a given direction for several hours, then it will be of only minor importance. Inasmuch as most erosion on the beach takes place during high tide, the waves have only approximately 4 to 6 hours per day to effectively cut back the beach profile. Generally, at least two high tides are necessary in order for beach erosion to be very severe. Usually, during the first high tide, the beach profile is simply smoothed out, with not much loss of sediment. It is during the following high tides that the beach begins to cut down and back (Fig. 8).

A fast-moving storm can easily pass completely through the New England area within a 24-hour period. The two storms that have been most effective during our period of observation, the storms of 25-26 May 1967 and 24-27 February 1969, have both been very slow-moving storms. Note the almost stationary position of the 25-26 May 1967 storm off Nantucket for a period of two full days (Fig. 7).

Tidal Phase

Whether the storm occurs during the spring or neap tide is another important consideration. Even if a storm surge of 3 feet accompanies a neap tide, the high-water mark will only reach its normal level (MHT) during the storm. If, however, the storm occurs during a spring tide and a minor surge is added to the high-water mark, then the dunes and the backbeach are exposed to intense wave erosion (Fig. 9). Most of the very effective northeasters we have observed occurred during spring tides.

Path of Storm with Respect to Beach

When a storm is centered offshore from Nantucket, northeasterly winds blow directly across the Gulf of Maine with a very long fetch. Hence, large waves can be formed. If a storm passes to the west of the northern New

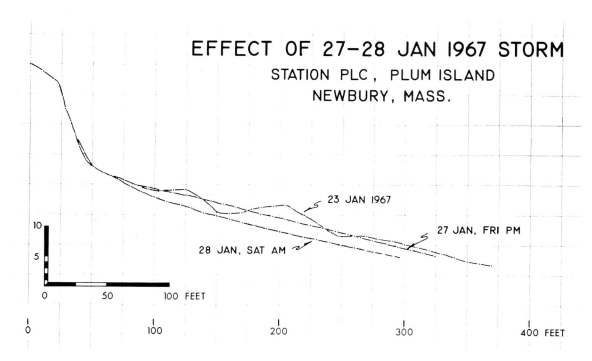

EFFECT OF 27–28 JAN 1967 STORM

STATION PLC, PLUM ISLAND
NEWBURY, MASS.

23 JAN 1967

27 JAN, FRI PM

28 JAN, SAT AM

10

5

0   50   100 FEET

0   100   200   300   400 FEET

FIGURE 8.   Profiles illustrating the erosional effect of the 27–28 January
1967 storm at profiling station PLC on Plum Island. Most of the
month of January had been very mild, as indicated by the large
accumulation of sediment shown on the 23 January profile.
Compare these profiles with those in Figure 6. Strong winds
from the northeast first started blowing on the morning of 28
January. Our first profile, at low tide in the late afternoon of
28 January, showed that the waves had simply rearranged the
sand on the beach into an extremely flat, featureless profile.
The profile measured at low tide the next morning showed that
the whole beach profile had been eroded downward a vertical
distance averaging around 3 feet. This fast-moving storm left
the area on Saturday, 28 January, and erosion of the profile
ceased.

FIGURE 9. Storm waves.
a. [Top] The erosion zone on northern Plum Island.
b. [Bottom] Dune erosion near profile PLB.

England coast, or far offshore, then winds will approach the shore from a different angle, usually at smaller velocities, and the resultant waves will be relatively small. Therefore, the path followed by storms that are the most effective is in a northeasterly direction across the continental shelf off southeastern New England (Fig. 1), just east of the island of Nantucket.

Time Interval Between Storms

One of the most effective deterrents against dune erosion or loss of shore property is a large mass of sand on the beach profile itself. Much of the erosive energy of the storm waves may be used up in removing this sand.

An example of the protective effect of a broad berm is illustrated in Figure 10. A relatively severe storm of 3 November 1966, cut away approximately two-thirds of the berm at profiling station PLB. The profile was left with a high beach scarp; however, there was no erosion below the normal storm profile or into the dunes. Figure 11 has three photographs illustrating the destruction of the berm by this storm. If, on the other hand, storms follow each other very closely without an interim period for sand to return to the beach, erosion will be much greater than normal.

CONCLUSIONS

1) The cycle of erosion and deposition on the sand beaches of New Hampshire and northeastern Massachusetts is closely related to the periodic northeasterly storms that pass through New England. The cycle consists of three stages: (1) an early poststorm profile that is flat to concave-upward; (2) an early accretionary profile which normally consists of a ridge-and-runnel system, with the ridge migrating toward the backbeach area; (3) a late accretionary or mature profile that occurs after the ridge has welded to the backbeach and a broad berm has developed. On some beaches, welding does not occur and gigantic ridges (up to 4 feet in height) lie between the backbeach and the low-tide terrace (Figs. 12 and 13).

2) The concept of "winter" and "summer" beach profiles does not hold true in this area. Although there is a general tendency for storms to be most frequent during the winter months, and for accretion to be slightly more prevalent during the late summer months, any of the three basic profiles can occur during any particular season.

3) The role of northeasterly storms as geologic agents is apparently controlled by size and intensity of the storm, speed of storm movement, tidal phase (i.e., spring or neap tide), path of storm with respect to beach, and time interval between storms.

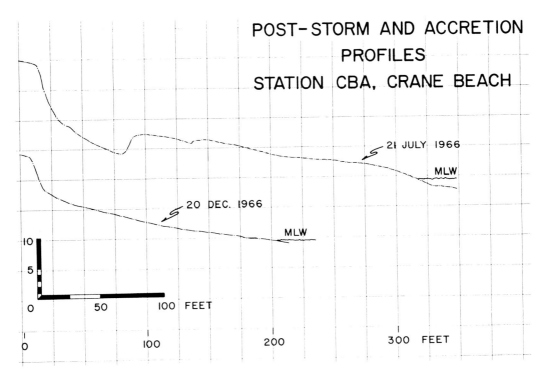

FIGURE 12. Accretional and poststorm profiles at station CBA on Crane Beach. The 20 December 1966 profile was measured the day following a mild, fast-moving northeaster. The 21 July 1966 profile was measured after a long period of mild weather. Ridges developed on this profile migrate very slowly and, hence, very seldom weld to the backbeach.

FIGURE 11. Observations during the northeaster of 3 November 1966.
a and b. Wave attack at high tide on the beach at the northern end of Plum Island.
c. Destruction of the berm (at high tide) on central Plum
Island.

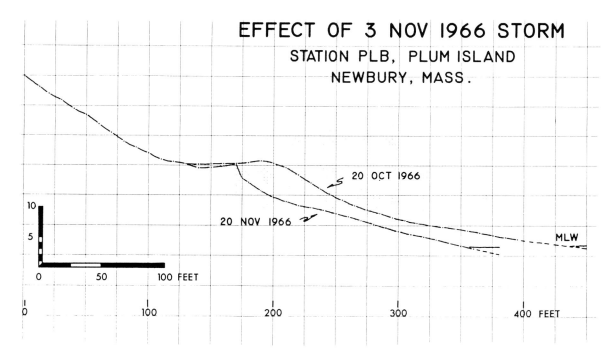

EFFECT OF 3 NOV 1966 STORM
STATION PLB, PLUM ISLAND
NEWBURY, MASS.

20 OCT 1966

20 NOV 1966

MLW

10

5

0   50   100 FEET

0   100   200   300   400 FEET

FIGURE 10.   Profiles illustrating the erosional effect of the 3 November 1966
storm at station PLB on Plum Island.   The main effect was the
removal of approximately two-thirds of the large mature berm
that had been deposited during the late summer and early fall
months and the carving of a steep beach scarp.

FIGURE 13. Views from profiles CBA at the time of measurement of the profiles shown in Figure 11. Both views look southeast and were taken from the dune crest at approximately the same position.
a. 21 July 1966.
b. 20 December 1966.

REFERENCES CITED

Blumenstock, D. I., F. R. Fosberg, and C. G. Johnson, 1961, The resurvey of typhoon effects on Jaluit Atoll in the Marshall Islands: Nature, Vol. 189, pp. 618-20.

Hayes, M. O., 1965, Sedimentation in a semiarid wave-dominated coast (south Texas) with an emphasis on hurricane effects: Ph.D. thesis, Univ. Texas, 350 pp. (unpublished).

Stoddart, D. R., 1962, Catastrophic storm effects of the British Honduras reefs and cays: Nature, Vol. 196, p. 515.

JOURNAL OF SEDIMENTARY PETROLOGY, VOL. NO. 2, P. 413-421
FIGS. 1-11, JUNE, 1972

COMPARISON OF RIDGE AND RUNNEL SYSTEMS IN TIDAL AND NON-TIDAL ENVIRONMENTS[1]

RICHARD A. DAVIS, JR
Department of Geology, Western Michigan University, Kalamazoo, Michigan 49001

WILLIAM T. FOX
Department of Geology, Williams College, Williamstown, Massachusetts 01267

MILES O. HAYES AND JON C. BOOTHROYD
Coastal Research Center, University of Massachusetts, Amherst, Massachusetts 01003

ABSTRACT

Beach and inner nearshore areas of Lake Michigan are basically the same as northern Massachusetts except for scale of the morphologic features and tidal range; in Lake Michigan spring tides reach 0.25 feet whereas in Massachusetts they reach 13 feet. Ridge and runnel topography is developed in the inner nearshore zone at both locations is the result of storm activity. These ridges migrate shoreward during low energy conditions and eventually weld onto the beach. Overall morphology, surface features and internal structures are quite similar in both areas. The only appreciable differences between the two areas are the scale and rate of migration. Apparently tides have no appreciable affect on the sediment sequence that accumulates as ridges weld to the beach although tides are significant in determining the rate at which the shoreward migration of the ridges takes place.

INTRODUCTION

During the past few years the authors have been conducting research on various aspects of beach and nearshore sedimentation on the New England coast and Lake Michigan. Davis (1970a; 1970b) has been surveying coastal areas along most of eastern Lake Michigan with emphasis on the southern portion, Fox and Davis have studied two small areas along the southeastern coast of Lake Michigan in great detail (Davis and Fox, 1970; 1971; Fox and Davis, 1970a; 1970b; 1971), and Hayes and Boothroyd have studied the new England coast from Cape Cod to Maine (Hayes, et al., 1969). Over the course of these investigations each of the authors has had the opportunity to visit the study areas of the others. We were uniformly impressed by the striking similarity in the processes operating in the two areas and in the resulting topographic features. This is particularly true for the ridge and runnel systems (King and Williams, 1949), both in terms of their configuration and their dynamic nature.

The areas of study exhibit some contrast as well as many similarities. Eastern Lake Michigan is bounded by Pleistocene glacial deposits as is most of the upper New England coast. Both areas contain beach and nearshore zones dominated by sand. Plum Island and Crane Beach on

Castle Neck, which are barrier islands along the northern Massachusetts coast, and dune areas of Berrien and Ottawa counties, along the southeastern shore of Lake Michigan (fig. 1), both display ridge and runnel features during many times of the year. Coastal morphology is quite similar in both areas except that dunes along Lake Michigan are generally much larger than those of Massachusetts. Both areas have rather continuous offshore sand bars at distances of a few to several hundred feet from shore. Bars off Massachusetts are somewhat less stable in position and have more relief between trough and bar than comparable Lake Michigan features.

Waves in both areas usually have small wave heights and short periods. Average breaker height on Lake Michigan during summer is 0.80 feet and average period is 3.2 seconds (Fox and Davis, 1970a; 1971). Along the northern New England coast the average breaker height is 1.40 feet and wave period averages 7.0 seconds (Galvin and Hayes, 1969). The northern Massachusetts coast is somewhat protected by Cape Ann except from intense northeast storms. Lake Michigan has a short fetch although storms from the north and northwest may generate relatively large waves.

By far the most impressive contrast between the two areas is the tidal range. In Lake Michigan spring tides reach 0.25 feet whereas the northern Massachusetts coast has a mean range of almost 9 feet and a maximum spring range of 13 feet. It

[1] Manuscript received August 23, 1971; revised December 9, 1971.

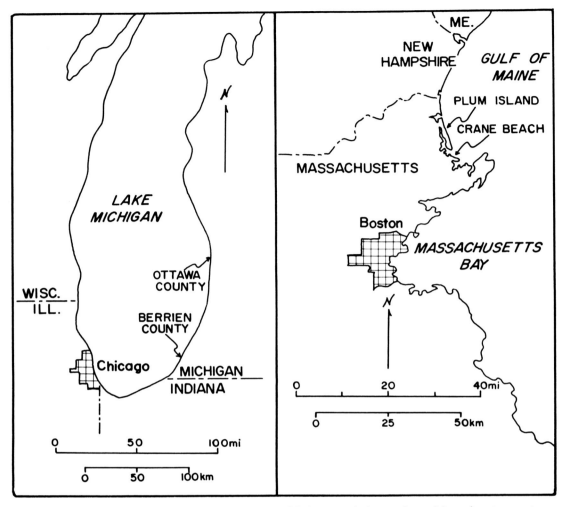

Fig. 1.—Location maps of areas studied in Lake Michigan and the northeast Massachusetts coast.

would seem that such tidal differences would cause appreciable contrasts in sedimentation in the beach and inner nearshore area. This report will demonstrate that both study areas are characterized by similar processes and topographic features leading to the conclusion that perhaps tidal fluctuations are not of major importance in controlling the nature of sediments which accumulate on the beach as the result of ridge and runnel sedimentation.

PREVIOUS WORK

Little published material is available on the morphology and processes associated with the ridge and runnel system. The first detailed description was by King and Williams (1949) who actually recognized two different types of near-beach sand bars. They chose to restrict the application of ridge and runnel to coasts with considerable tidal range and used the term "barred beaches" for non-tidal areas (King and Williams, 1949, p. 70). Morphology and genesis are apparently quite similar in both situations which has led the present writers to use ridge and runnel to apply in both tidal and non-tidal environments.

King and Williams (1949) noted that the formation of shallow bars in either tidal or non-tidal areas seems to be restricted to places where fetch is limited. The experiences of the authors indicates that these bars are restricted to areas not commonly exposed to long period swell. Comparable ridge and runnel development has been

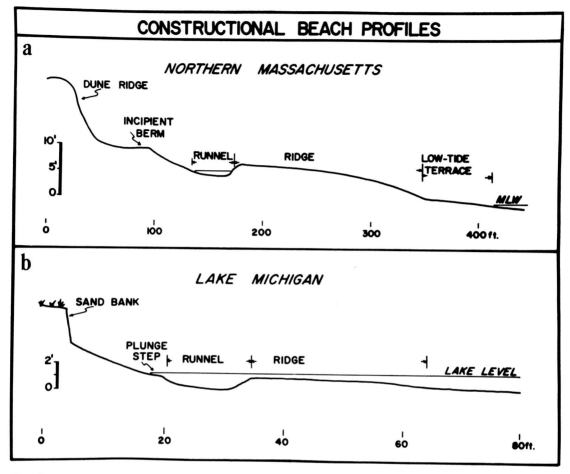

FIG. 2.—Generalized ridge and runnel profile for a) northern Massachusetts and b) Lake Michigan. Note that although the profile configuration is quite similar there is considerable difference in the scale.

described from the North Sea coast of Germany (Reineck, 1964) and along Padre Island in the Gulf of Mexico (Hayes, 1967).

Miller and Zeigler (1964), Sonu (1969) and Niedoroda and Tanner (1970) are among several investigators who have studied somewhat similar sand bars that are oblique to, and connect with, the shore. Some of the dynamics of these features are comparable to those of ridge and runnel processes.

BEACH AND INNER NEARSHORE TOPOGRAPHY

Under normal conditions the beach and nearshore profiles of non-tidal and tide dominated areas are alike in their general morphology. Constructional beaches have a rather broad and nearly horizontal berm with a fairly steep foreshore slope or beach face, whereas erosional beaches are flat to slightly concave upward with an overall slope toward the water. Due to the lack of tides in Lake Michigan, the plunge step is more prominent than along the Massachusetts coast.

The ridge and runnel topography in both locations (fig. 2) is formed as a post-storm feature. Generalized profiles show a well developed berm and gently sloping nearshore area prior to wave attack. After the storm subsides the beach profile generally shows significant erosion and the offshore ridge is developed (fig. 3). A quantitative study of the volume of eroded beach material and subsequent deposition of the ridge during a storm in July, 1969 showed that the ridge accounted for approximately twenty-five percent of the total beach loss in southeastern Lake Michigan (Fox and Davis, 1970a). The remainder of

Fig. 3.—Oblique aerial views of ridge and runnel systems in a) Massachusetts and b) Michigan. Outlet channels persist in Massachusetts whereas they have been closed by longshore drift in Lake Michigan. The satellite ridge seen in the Massachusetts area is also present in Lake Michigan but is submerged.

the eroded sediment was carried both alongshore and further offshore from the ridge.

MORPHOLOGY AND MIGRATION OF RIDGES

The formation of ridges in both Massachusetts and Lake Michigan (fig. 3) is associated with storm activity. Along the northern New England coast ridges usually occur a few days after strong northeasterly storms which are commonly called "nor'easters." Erosion of the beach and adjacent dune areas serves as a source of sediment for these ridges. The amount and rate of erosion is closely related to the tidal phase and the rate of movement of the storm through the area, as well as to storm intensity. In order for significant erosion to take place the storm must move through slowly during spring tide. Similar conditions during neap tide, even if accompanied by a 3 foot storm surge, would only reach mean high tide level (Hayes and Boothroyd, 1969).

In comparison, most of the severe erosion to beach and dune areas of southeastern Lake

Michigan is caused by storms from the north-northwest. These are commonly generated by winds on the trailing side of a low pressure system as it moves across the lake. Such storms utilize the maximum fetch of the lake and are particularly destructive when they move slowly. Storm surges in excess of one foot have been monitored (Fox and Davis, 1970a). Slowly increasing lake levels during the past five years and the absence of tidal fluctuation have the same effect as storms during spring tide in Massachusetts.

Ridges are present the day following storm subsidence. In both areas they are nearly symmetrical in profile with the landward slope slightly steeper than the basinward side (fig. 4). Ridge crests in Lake Michigan are generally about 50 feet from the strand line. The sand body is 40 to 50 feet wide and initially rises a foot, or slightly less, above the level of the runnel. Along the Massachusetts coast the same features are about one-half an order of magnitude larger (fig. 2).

Within a few tidal cycles after formation, the ridge begins to migrate shoreward and its shape is modified. The profile becomes sharply asym-

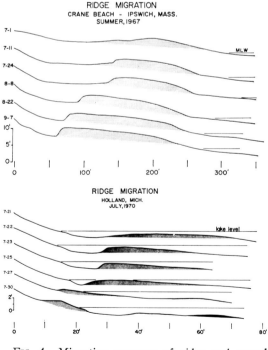

Fig. 4.—Migration sequence of ridge and runnel profiles in a) Massachusetts and b) Lake Michigan. In addition to scale differences there is also a difference in rate of migration. Note the satellite ridges in the Lake Michigan profile.

metrical with the leading or landward edge quite steep, at the angle of repose of the migrating sand (fig. 4). The slip face is inclined at near 30 degrees in both areas. At the same time the basinward slope is slightly convex upward and very gently inclined basinward ($<5°$). The ridge retains this overall profile until it becomes welded to the beach. Note that although the scale is different between the two study areas, the geometry is quite comparable.

The profile change described above is caused by wave activity and wave generated currents moving across the ridge. On the Massachusetts coast the rising tide gradually covers the ridge. Initially the upper surface is under upper flow regime conditions (fig. 5a) as the thin water layer of the swash flows over the ridge. This results in plane bed deposition with flow separation occurring at the leading edge of the ridge. Sand migrates across the gently sloping surface and avalanches down the steep, prograding edge of the ridge. As the water level continues to rise, lower flow regime ripples (fig. 6) are formed by wave generated currents passing over the ridge crest and progradation continues but at a much slower

Fig. 6.—Lower flow regime conditions on the ridge causes formation of ripples. These occur during high tide in Massachusetts and until the bar emerges during migration in Lake Michigan.

rate. The ridge retains the above character for most of its existence.

The absence of tides in Lake Michigan causes some temporary differences in surface features between this area and the Massachusetts coast as the ridge migrates shoreward. The ridge is initially under lake level with several inches to a foot of water over the crest. Small waves generate ripples over the entire upper surface of the ridge (fig. 6). As migration takes place the ridge may be elevated more than a foot above the runnel. This progradation and steepening of the ridge decreases the depth of water above the ridge. Eventually upper flow regime conditions are reached as wave generated shallow sheet flow moves over the ridge (fig. 5b). About 3 to 5 days are required for this change.

Once the ridge welds onto the back beach (fig. 7) the overall profile changes. The seaward face of the ridge steepens as a beach face of near 10° develops in both tidal and nontidal environments. Beach face development (with accompanying accretion) in Massachusetts is especially marked during neap tides. The crest of the welded ridge is smoothed into a broad, uniform berm by waves that overtop the welded ridge crest during spring tides. The resultant profile in both areas is a convex-upward, accretionary berm with a gently dipping landward surface and a relatively steep foreshore slope. This entire welding process usually takes 5-6 weeks in the tidal area (Hayes and Boothroyd, 1969) whereas in Lake Michigan the same configuration may be achieved in a week or ten days.

Thus far all discussion has centered around the ridge, where most of the changes in morphology take place. The runnel remains nearly flat and horizontal during ridge migration. Its surface is

Fig. 5.—Upper flow regime conditions with plane beds as swash creates currents over the ridge in a) Massachusetts and b) Lake Michigan.

Fig. 7.—Welded ridges in a) Massachusetts and b) Lake Michigan.

covered with asymmetrical ripples which are parallel to the strand line. Water spilling over the ridge due to wave action becomes trapped in the runnel and moves parallel to shore and eventually enters rip channels where it travels seaward in the form of rip currents. The current moving parallel to shore generates small current ripples in the runnel which are superimposed on, and at right angles to, the wave generated ripples (fig. 8). The term ladder backed ripples has been applied to this combination of bed forms (Hayes, et al, 1969).

Rip channels last only for a few days in Lake Michigan. As soon as the ridge crest approaches lake level there is sufficient longshore current caused by wave swash to fill in the rip areas. In Massachusetts however, these outlet channels may persist throughout migration of the ridge because of the large amount of water being flushed from the runnels during tidal fluctuations.

In summary, the morphology of the ridge and runnel systems in Lake Michigan and Massachusetts are quite similar. Changes in ridge profile occur during similar stages in the migration at both places. Surface features on the ridge are the same but they occur at different times because of

the differing relationship to water level in both areas. Runnel features are also alike.

Sizes of the ridges are not comparable and the rates of migration differ markedly. The size difference may be a function of the amount of erosion, the slope of the nearshore zone, the size of waves, or the tidal range. Migration rate in the tidal environment is slower because the forces causing it, namely waves, only cover the ridge during high tide and because the ridges are much larger in the tidal environment. These differences are not of consequence however, in the type of sedimentary sequence that forms as a result of ridge migration and welding.

INTERNAL STRUCTURES

The large tidal range along the northern Massachusetts coast provides excellent opportunity for examining internal structures in the ridge and runnel system. During low tide the entire system is exposed and trenches can be dug to determine the internal structures of both ridge and runnel. Due to the absence of tides this is not possible on Lake Michigan until welding takes place.

Fig. 8.—Ladder-backed ripples in the runnel in a) Massachusetts and b) Lake Michigan. These features form as currents flowing parallel to shore cause development of ripples over those previously formed by wave generated motion.

RIDGE CROSS-SECTION

CRANE BEACH - IPSWICH, MASS.
21 JULY 1966

◄ 200' TO DUNES

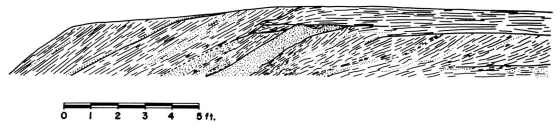

0   1   2   3   4   5 ft.

FIG. 9.—Internal structure of ridge during migration in Massachusetts.

During most of the migration of the ridge, plane beds are present across the entire upper surface. These may be horizontal or they may dip slightly seaward ($<5°$) reflecting the surface configuration. The slip face is characterized by stratification which dips near 30° in a shoreward direction (fig. 9). Although there is difficulty in examining the internal features of a submerged ridge in the non-tidal environment there appears to be close parallel with the tidal environment. Similar processes and morphology in both areas strongly imply that submerged Lake Michigan ridges have the same internal structures as those in Massachusetts.

As the ridge migrates and builds up to a berm configuration these steeply dipping beds are covered by increasing thickness of plane beds. When swash action occurs on the welded beach face these plane beds are truncated and the sediment is reworked into seaward dipping beds at angles of 10 to 15 degrees in both areas (fig. 10).

By digging below the projected ridge surface the ripples of the runnel environment can be observed. This surface is easily recognized and is preserved due to burial by the migrating ridge.

PALEOENVIRONMENTAL IMPLICATIONS

One of the primary benefits derived from study of modern environments is application of process-response features to the rock record. In the case of the ridge and runnel structures such application is warranted and of value. The regular stratification of sedimentary structures may be preserved in vertical sequence as suggested by Hayes, Anan and Bozeman (1969). The transgressive sequence of beach deposits they describe from the Massachusetts coast is also applicable for non-tidal Lake Michigan.

In this sequence the basal beds are low angle and dip offshore, generally with heavy mineral concentrations. They represent storm beach conditions (fig. 11). Immediately above are similarly oriented beds dipping at somewhat higher angles. These beds represent the incipient berm which is often present in the tide dominated environment of Massachusetts but is uncommon in Lake Michigan. Ripple cross bedding representing the runnel overlies this unit with asymmetrical land oriented ripples. High angle, land ori-

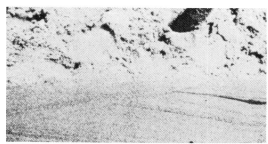

FIG. 10.—Internal structure of welded ridge showing foreshore stratification inclined at 10–12° in a) Massachusetts and b) Lake Michigan.

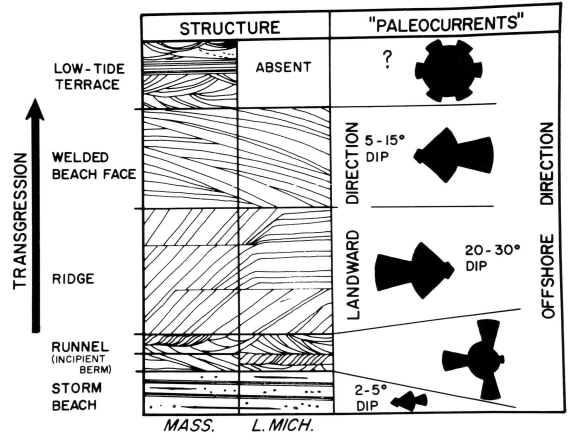

Fig. 11.—Sequence of structures in transgressive sequence of ridge migration in tidal and non-tidal environments. Although the scale and rate of migration may be different, the sequence that accumulates is essentially indistinguishable between the two contrasting environments.

ented ripples of the migrating ridge overlie this unit (fig. 11). The sequence is capped by seaward dipping beach face deposits. In the tide-dominated environment interbedded festoon beds and planar beds of the low tide terrace are present. The latter unit represents the only real difference between the tidal and nontidal sequence (fig. 11).

The above discussion strongly implies that interpretation of tidalites and intertidalites (Klein, 1970) in the rock record must be approached with caution when dealing with beach and associated inner nearshore zones. Although similar warnings have been issued in the past (Klein, 1971), the present report is the first demonstration that comparable sedimentary processes and their resulting depositional sequences do indeed occur in both tidal and non-tidal environments. Appreciable differences have not been found in the sequences of modern sediments in areas without tides and comparable areas with tidal ranges of more than 10 feet. We assume that the same is true for the intermediate tidal ranges.

ACKNOWLEDGMENTS

The bulk of the data that led to the findings reported above were collected during research while under contract with the Office of Naval Research, Geography Branch. Fox and Davis were supported by contract 388-092 and Hayes and Boothroyd were supported by contract 388-084. Some of the beach studies in Massachusetts were also supported by Coastal Engineering Research Center, U.S. Army Corps of Engineers contract DACW72-67-C-0004 to Hayes. These agencies are gratefully acknowledged for this financial support.

The authors also extend appreciation to numerous students who have assisted in collecting field data. The manuscript was typed by Cynthia Howard.

REFERENCES

DAVIS, R. A., 1970a, (abs.), Beach dynamics in southeastern Lake Michigan: Geol. Soc. America, Abs. with Programs, v. 2, p. 384–385.

DAVIS, R. A., (ed.), 1970b, Coastal sedimentation in southeastern Lake Michigan: Western Mich. Univ., Studies in Geology, No. 1, 50 p.

DAVIS, R. A., AND FOX, W. T., 1970 (abs.), Sediments, Processes and topography in the nearshore environment: Geol. Soc. Amer. Abs.with Programs, v. 2, n. 7, p. 534.

DAVIS, R. A., AND FOX, W. T., 1971, Beach and nearshore dynamics in eastern Lake Michigan: ONR Tech. Rept. No. 4, Contract 388–092, 145 p.

FOX, W. T., AND DAVIS, R. A., 1970a, Fourier analysis of weather and wave data from Lake Michigan: Tech. Report. ONR Contract 388–092, 47 p.

———, 1970b, Profile of a storm-wind, waves and erosion on the southeastern shore of Lake Michigan: Proceedings, 13th Conf. on Great Lakes Research, part 1, p. 233–241.

———, 1971, Fourier analysis of weather and wave data from Holland, Michigan, July, 1970: ONR Tech. Rept. No. 3, contract 388–092, 79 p.

GALVIN, C. J., AND HAYES, M. O., 1969, Winter beach profiles and wave climate along the New England coast: unpublished manuscript.

HAYES, M. O., 1967, Hurricanes as geological agents: case studies of hurricanes Carla, 1961, and Cindy, 1963: Univ. Texas Univ. Bur. Econ. Geology Rept. Inv. 61, 56 p.

———, ANAN, F. S., AND BOZEMAN, R. N., 1969, Sediment dispersal trends in the littoral zone: a problem in paleogeographic reconstruction *in* Eastern Section S.E.P.M. Guidebook, May 9–11, 1969, p. 290–315.

———, AND BOOTHROYD, J. C., 1969, Storms as modifying agents in the coastal environment *in* Eastern Section S.E.P.M. Guidebook, May 9–11, 1969, p. 245–265.

HAYES, M. O., *et al*, 1969, Coastal environments, northeastern Massachusetts and New Hampshire: Contrib. No. 1, Coastal Research Group, Univ. Mass., Eastern Section S.E.P.M. Guidebook, May 9–11, 1969, 462 p.

KING, C. A. M., AND WILLIAMS, W. W., 1949, The formation and movement of sand bars by wave action: Geog. Jour., v. 113, p. 70–85.

KLEIN, G. D., 1970, (abs.), Paleotidal sedimentation: Geol. Soc. America Abs. with Programs, v. 2, p. 598.

———, 1971, A sedimentary model for determining paleotidal range: Geol. Soc. America Bull., v. 82, p. 2585–2592.

MILLER, R. L., AND ZEIGLER, J. M., 1964, A study of sediment distribution in the zone of shoaling waves over complicated bottom topography: *in* Papers in Marine Geology, Shepard Commemorative Volume, Macmillan Co., New York, N.Y., p. 133–153.

NIEDORODA, A. W., AND TANNER, W. F., 1970, Preliminary study of transverse bars: Marine Geology, v. 9, p. 41–62.

REINECK, H. E., 1964, Layered sediments of tidal flats, beaches, and shelf bottoms of the North Sea in Lauff, G. H. (ed.), Estuaries, Am. Assoc. Adv. Sci., Pub. 83, p. 191–206.

SONU, C. J., 1969, Collective movement of sediments in littoral environment: Proc. 11th Conf. on Coastal Engineering, p. 373–400.

JOURNAL OF SEDIMENTARY PETROLOGY, VOL. 41, No. 3, P. 651–670
FIGS. 1–27, SEPTEMBER, 1971

DEPOSITIONAL STRUCTURES AND PROCESSES IN THE NON-BARRED HIGH-ENERGY NEARSHORE[1,2]

H. EDWARD CLIFTON, RALPH E. HUNTER AND R. LAWRENCE PHILLIPS
U.S. Geological Survey, Menlo Park, Calif.

ABSTRACT

The marginal marine environment consists of an offshore where the wave form is approximately sinusoidal and a nearshore where the wave form is either solitary or that of a bore. Within the nearshore, shoaling waves become progressively higher and steeper until they break. After breaking, the waves progress as bores through a surf zone; these bores ultimately terminate within a swash zone on the beach itself.

In a high-energy coastal environment where long-period swell enters a nearshore uncomplicated by off-shore bars, sedimentary structures develop on the seafloor in facies that trend parallel to the zones of different wave activity. In the offshore, small sand ripples are the most common depositional structure, but in the nearshore larger bed forms predominate. Seaward from the line of breakers, in the zone of wave build-up, are landward-oriented lunate megaripples. Near the outer portion of the surf zone the bed form is planar (outer planar facies), but, in the inner portion of the zone, a area of large-scale bed roughness (inner rough facies) commonly is present. Within the swash zone, the bed form is again planar (inner planar facies). The boundaries of the facies shift in response to changes in waves or tide, and certain of the zones are sometimes missing. The relative position of the zones, however, is invariable.

The major features of the bed forms can be interpreted in terms of flow regime. The stronger of the two opposing transient currents caused by passing waves produces structures analogous to those produced by continuous, unidirectional currents. Landward wave surge is dominant in the outer three structural facies, whereas seaward surge predominates in the innermost (inner planar) facies. Wave surge over the intermediate inner rough facies is more complex, and the direction of strongest surge may be variable.

In the outer three facies, the landward sequence from small asymmetric ripples to lunate megaripples to plane bed suggests an increase in flow regime from the lower part of the lower regime to the upper regime; this shoreward increase in flow regime is associated with a shoreward increase in orbital velocity at the bottom. The inner planar facies is produced by flow in the upper regime. The inner rough facies, situated between two zones of flow in the upper regime, is apparently a product of flow in the upper part of the lower regime.

Within each of the structural facies a distinctive set of internal structures is produced. Internal structure of the asymmetric ripple facies consists of shoreward-inclined ripple cross-lamination and gently inclined cross-stratification. The lunate megaripples produce medium-scale landward-dipping foresets. Within the outer planar facies bedding is nearly horizontal. Structures in the inner rough facies produce medium-scale foresets that mostly dip directly or obliquely seaward, although landward-dipping foresets also occur. Within the inner planar facies bedding is gently inclined seaward. Migration of the facies in response to changes in waves or tide produces distinctive assemblages of structures where the facies overlap. These assemblages provide criteria for paleoenvironmental interpretation, particularly where interrelated assemblages occur in a meaningful spatial distribution.

INTRODUCTION

Few systematic observations of wave-generated depositional structures have been made in and near the high-energy (breaker heights greater than 1 meter) surf zone. Conditions there are extremely unfavorable for scientific research; visibility is generally restricted to a few feet, and the violence of the waves makes systematic study of bottom features very difficult. Nonetheless this environment contains a unique set of oceanic forces that profoundly affect the sediment, and ignorance of this area hinders understanding of nearshore processes and interpretation of ancient environments. This paper describes depositional structures in the topographically simple high-energy nearshore along the southern coast of Oregon (fig. 1) and discusses their origin. The observations provide criteria for recognition of this depositional environment in the stratigraphic record.

Swell approaching the shore from the deep ocean can be described either by the Airy equations for sinusoidal waves or by the somewhat more accurate Stokes equations for waves of trochoidal form (Inman, 1963, p. 55–56). At some relatively shallow depth a short distance seaward from the breaker zone, the wave undergoes a transformation from a basically sinusoidal or trochoidal form to a basically solitary form (fig. 2). For long period waves such as those typically present during this study (fig. 3B), this transformation occurs where the ratio of the wave height to water depth reaches about

[1] Manuscript received March 15, 1971.
[2] Publication authorized by the Director, U.S. Geological Survey.

0.2 (Inman and Nasu, 1956, p. 41). Under the general wave conditions observed during this study (fig. 3), the water depth of the transformation generally is between 3 and 5 meters.

In this study we apply the term "nearshore" to the area lying between the location of the transformation to solitary waves and the shoreline. This definition basically corresponds to that of Shepard (1963, p. 169), who defines the

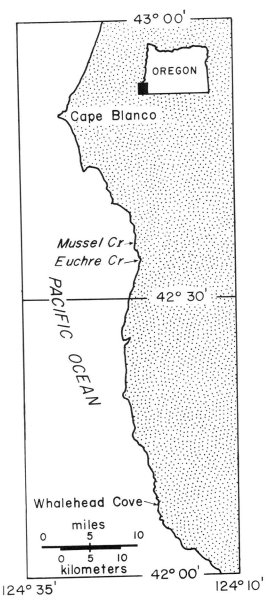

FIG. 1.—Locations of nearshore observations, southern Oregon.

nearshore as "A relatively narrow zone extending seaward of the shoreline and somewhat beyond the breaker zone. The zone of wave-induced nearshore currents." The area seaward of the nearshore we herein term "offshore."

The nearshore can be subdivided. After beginning its transformation to a solitary wave, the swell travels shoreward, increasing in height and becoming progressively more steep and asymmetric until it breaks at a point where the water depth is about 1.3 times the breaker height (Munk, 1949, p. 390). For typical summer coastal conditions in Oregon (fig. 3) this depth varies between 1.5 to 2.5 meters. From the point of breaking, the wave progresses as a bore through a surf zone. Near the beach in some areas a zone exists that is transitional between the surf zone and the swash zone of the beach (Schiffman, 1965, p. 259).

Studies described here were largely centered at Whalehead Cove on the southern coast of Oregon (figs. 1 and 4). This location provided the advantages of access, relatively clear water, sufficient protection to permit nearly daily observations with SCUBA, and enough heavy minerals in the sediment to define small scale stratification features. Additional observations were made on the open coast just south of Whalehead Cove, near the mouths of Euchre Creek and Mussel Creek in southern Oregon (fig. 1) and off La Selva beach in Monterey Bay in central California. At each of these locations, the direction of wave approach in the nearshore is approximately normal to the shoreline, either because the beach is oriented approximately normal to the dominant swell direction, or, as at Whalehead Cove, because of refraction and diffraction in the offshore (fig. 4).

During most days of diving operations, the highest tenth breaker heights ranged between 1.5 and 2 meters and the wave period generally was between 8 and 12 seconds (fig. 3). The largest breaker measured while divers were in the water was approximately 3 meters high. At each of the locations, the beach to offshore bottom profile was topographically simple, i.e. sloping seaward continuously (fig. 4) without the complication of offshore bars, at least within the area of observation.

Because observations were made during summer non-storm conditions, generalizations drawn therefrom are distinctly limited. Presumably, however, the data should be generally applicable to any situation having wave conditions similar to those that obtained during our studies, regardless of season. Probably the major factor introduced by the high seas generated by winter storms is a great intensification of rip

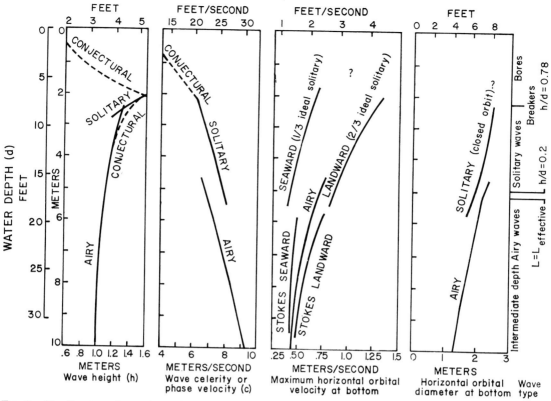

Fig. 2.—Shoaling transformations of waves having a period of 10 seconds and a deep-water height of 1 meter.

currents (Bascom, 1964, p. 179; Cook, 1969, p. 39–40), which had negligible effects on depositional structures during the summer.

METHODS

Nearly all observations were made underwater using SCUBA. Profiles across the nearshore established the position of the different depositional structures. A nylon line from a fixed shore station indicated horizontal distances along the profile. Periodic recalibration of the line overcame the problems of progressive line stretch during use. At each measurement the same degree of tension, verified by spring scale, was placed on the line; experiments indicated that even gross differences in tension produced errors of less than 5 percent. Although longshore currents occasionally tended to cause a bowing of the line during measurement, the actual errors as found by repeated measurements to a fixed station about 800 feet offshore from the shore station were less than plus or minus 3.5 percent.

Water depths were obtained with a stadia rod. The surface reference used in depth measurement was the average wave trough, which in the nearshore where the waves are basically solitary should approximate the still-water level at any one time. Checks on the depth measurement using a shore-based level indicated that the errors in depth measurement did not significantly alter the observations.

Wave data were mostly obtained from shore-based observations. Wave period was calculated from the number of waves that were observed to pass a fixed point during a four-minute interval. Breaker heights were measured by aligning the observer's eye, the breaker crest, and the horizon, and then measuring the vertical distance between eye level and the median lower limit of swash, which is at approximately the same level as the average wave trough.

Direction of the wave approach was also measured but was relatively constant at Whalehead Cove during the period of observation. Other wave data, such as deep-water wave height, wave celerity (phase velocity) and wave length at any depth, and orbital velocities and

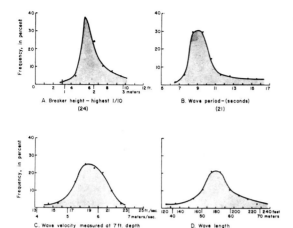

FIG. 3.—Wave parameters observed at Whalehead Cove, Oregon, during 18 days.

diameters can be calculated from these data (Munk, 1949; Inman, 1963). Observed wave velocities in the nearshore, as measured by the time required for a wave to pass between points a known distance apart, agreed to within plus or minus 10 percent with those predicted by solitary wave theory.

The internal structure of the sediment was ascertained using Senckenberg boxes (fig. 5) (Bouma, 1964, p. 349–354; Bouma, 1969, p. 309). Like most marine sediment coring devices, the boxes were too small (20.1 cm high, 15.4 cm wide, and 7.7 cm deep) to fully define the bedding structure. Emplacement of the boxes 2–3 cm apart in an aligned series (fig. 5a), however, permits reconstruction of a section of internal structures 1 m or more in length and 20 cm high, an area comparable to that seen in many outcrops. The series of boxes could be aligned either normal to or parallel to the shoreline, or if a 3-dimensional view was desirable, in a "T" or "L" configuration.

The Senckenberg boxes are in general difficult to use for subaqueous sand sampling (Bouma, 1969, p. 310), and sampling within the turbulent surf zone presented special problems. Through a combination of perseverence, improvisation, and considerable effort, the problems were eventually circumvented. The boxes were bound tightly with tape, numbered sequentially, and marked with orientation data prior to the sampling. A metal rod about 1 cm in diameter twisted to form a spiral about 75 cm long and 10 cm in diameter made an effective hand anchor when screwed into the sand. Such an anchor proved necessary not only to maintain position against the surge of the waves but also to sup-

ply leverage for the almost neutrally buoyant diver to emplace the boxes. The boxes could generally be pushed all the way into the sand with a gentle rocking motion. Because of the rapid wave scour around each box, all the boxes had to be at least partly emplaced very quickly. Once embedded, the boxes were removed individually by digging the sand away from one side, slipping a metal plate beneath the box and pulling the box and the plate upward. A strong elastic band was then placed around the box and the bottom plate (fig. 5b) and the secured box placed in a rigid plastic container and carried to the beach. If the box were not protected by the container, the strong currents generated by the waves would readily erode much of the sample along the seam between the box and the bottom plate. Small holes in the bottom of the containers permitted a gradual draining of the water and prevented sample loss due to flushing.

The boxes were opened in the laboratory, and the central 20 mm of sand within the box was placed in a metal tray inscribed with the orientation data and dried (fig. 5c-f). Maintenance of the orientation data of the sample at every step of the processing proved to be vital. Use of

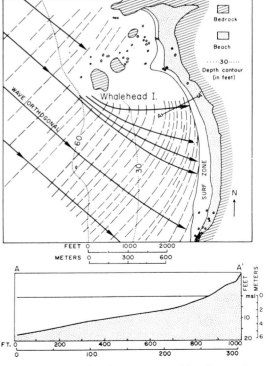

FIG. 4.—Wave refraction pattern and beach-nearshore bottom profile, Whalehead Cove, Oregon.

only the central portion of the box reduced the structural distortion which occurred at the sides of the box. After the sample had dried, sufficient (about 120 cc) epoxy resin was poured over the sand surface of the tray to partially penetrate the sample (fig. 5g). Partial penetration provived sufficient surface relief on the cemented block to define much of the internal structure (fig. 5h). Additional details of internal structure appeared in X-ray radiographs of the cemented block. The final structural interpretation, in which stratification was correlated across the individual boxes and artificial bedding disturbances were disregarded, was based on both surface relief features and radiographs (fig. 6).

DEPOSITIONAL STRUCTURES

The nearshore contains a rather limited set of depositional structures that consistently occur in a set of well-defined facies (fig. 7). The structural facies, which in part coincide with the different zones of wave activity, occur in bands parallel to the shoreline, except where the pattern of the waves is complicated by offshore rocks. Although certain of the structural facies were not always present, depending on wave conditions, the relative positions of the different facies remained constant.

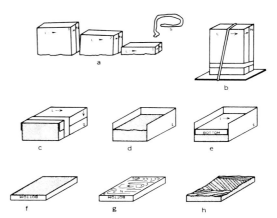

FIG. 5.—Taking and processing of sand box cores to identify internal structure.

Inner planar facies

The shoreward-most structural facies, the inner planar facies, is characterized by a planar surface. This facies occupies the swash zone and commonly extends below still-water level into the zone transitional between surf and swash (Schiffman, 1965). The internal structure produced within this facies is the normal parallel swash lamination that is visible on many beaches (fig. 8) and has been described

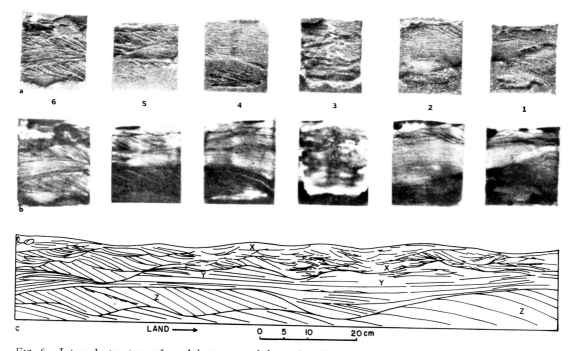

FIG. 6.—Internal structure of sand just seaward from the offshore-nearshore boundary on an average day.

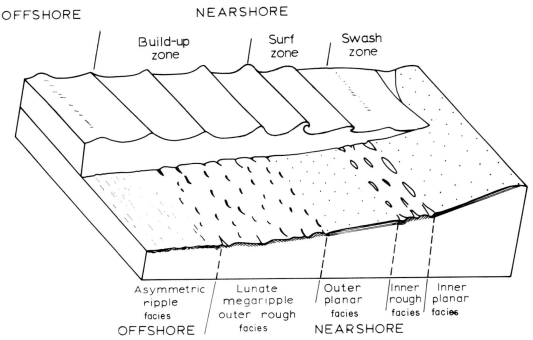

FIG. 7.—Zonation of wave activity and facies of sedimentary structures within and adjacent to the high-energy nearshore.

by Thompson (1937) and discussed genetically by Clifton (1969).

Inner rough facies

The inner planar facies commonly is bounded seaward by an area of bed irregularity, here designated the inner rough facies. On steep beaches, the rough facies occurs immediately seaward from the topographic step at the inner base of the beach. On gently sloping beaches, such as the one at Whalehead Cove, where no abrupt topographic change occurs between the beach and nearshore profile (fig. 4), the inner rough facies generally lies within the transition between surf and swash or within the inner portion of the surf zone. The bed configuration of the inner rough facies off a steep beach differs distinctly from that off a gently sloping beach.

Off steep beaches (Euchre and Mussel Creeks, fig. 1), the inner rough facies consists of a series of 3 to 10 large (15–20 cm high, 30–60 cm wavelength), steep-sided, symmetrical ripples composed of coarse sand or fine gravel. The crests of these ripples continue for long distances more or less parallel to the beach.

The first ripple seaward from the topographic step onto the beach generally contains the coarsest sediment, commonly fine gravel. The grain size of sediment composing the ripples typically

decreases in a seaward direction to coarse sand, and the ripple height likewise diminishes seaward. The bedding within these ripples is complex and may dip either landward or seaward.

Off gently sloping beaches the inner rough facies consists largely of sets of troughs or depressions, 1–2 m across and 10–50 cm deep, elongate parallel to the shoreline and separated by broad, flat "ridges." The seaward-facing side of the troughs is generally steep (fig. 9) and contains the coarsest sand. These structures over a period of time migrated in a seaward di-

FIG. 8.—Swash zone (inner planar facies) lamination exposed by Hubbard Creek, Oregon.

rection, and the internal structure of the inner rough facies accordingly tends to consist predominantly of medium-scale (units 4 to 100 cm thick), seaward-dipping trough crossbedding (fig. 10). Longshore currents, which commonly reach their maximum velocities over the general area occupied by the inner rough facies, modify the shape of the depressions and the direction of their migration. Under the influence of longshore currents, the steepest side shifts toward the up-current end of the depressions and cross-stratification shows a pronounced longshore component (B, fig. 10). Under very strong currents the internal structure within the inner rough facies may be directed essentially longshore, as postulated for Pleistocene "coquina" off South Carolina beaches (DuBar and Johnson, 1964).

Occasionally, the inner rough facies at the beach in Whalehead Cove contains both seaward-facing depressions and straight-crested, nearly symmetrical ripples. The symmetrical ripples, which occur seaward from the depressions, migrated in a shoreward direction. Rarely, shoreward-facing lunate megaripples about 10 cm high and a meter in span were present in the seaward portion of the inner rough facies. Both the shoreward-migrating symmetrical ripples and the shoreward-facing megaripples would likely produce landward-dipping foresets, possibly similar to those shown in profiles A and D, figure 10.

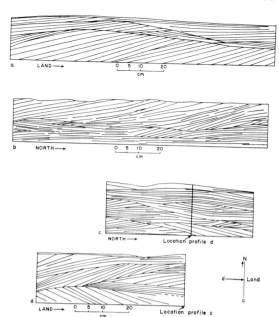

Fig. 10.—Internal structure of the inner rough facies on a relatively gently inclined beach nearshore profile.

The inner rough facies ranges in width from 3 to 10 meters and is generally the narrowest of the structural facies. Off gently sloping beaches it commonly is totally absent, particularly at high tide. The sand in the inner rough facies generally is relatively coarse and quite loosely packed.

Outer planar facies

Seaward from the inner rough facies, under the outer portion of the surf zone and the inner portion of the zone of wave build-up, is the outer planar facies, which generally is between 10 and 30 m wide. Except for broad gentle undulations a few centimeters high and about 2 m in wave length that commonly occur near its outer margin, the surface of the outer planar facies is flat and devoid of large-scale bed features. The sand here is generally somewhat finer than that in the bordering structural facies and is more densely packed; emplacement of Senckenberg boxes in this facies requires more effort than elsewhere.

Sand transport on the outer planar facies is dominantly by sheet flow over a planar surface. Under certain wave conditions, however, small sand ripples may cover the surface of the outer planar facies (fig. 11). These ripples are very regular and have a very long crestal length compared to their wave length (about 10 cm)

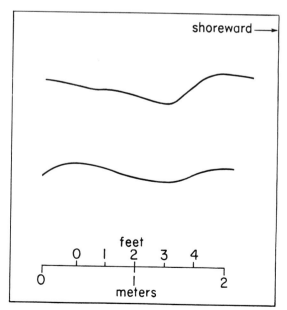

Fig. 9.—Profiles normal to shoreline across bedforms of the inner rough facies.

Fig. 11.—Photograph of bed of outer planar facies.

and amplitude (less than 1 cm). In profile the ripples are flat-bottomed or solitary (Inman, 1957, p. 6). The ripple crests are relatively straight and are normal to the direction of wave approach. As a wave crest passes, the underlying ripple commonly is obliterated and sand is transported by sheet flow over a smooth planar bottom. When the landward surge wanes, however, the ripples reappear on the bottom, at which time they have steep sides facing landward. This asymmetry is reversed during the seaward surge under the wave trough. In most

characteristics, such as solitary form, long crestal lengths, and reversing asymmetry, these ripples resemble those observed by Inman (1957, p. 35) in water depths generally less than 6 meters. The internal structure produced by the sheet flow of the outer planar facies consists of horizontal or nearly horizontal lamination.

Lunate megaripple (outer rough) facies

Seaward from the outer planar facies, approximately beneath the outer portion of the zone of wave build-up, is an area generally 30–120 m wide of large-scale bed features. The dominant bed form in this zone is a very distinctive landward facing lunate megaripple (fig. 12) that shows considerable variation in size and spacing. Using the descriptive terminology of Allen (1968, p. 60–63), most megaripples have heights between 30 and 100 cm, spans between 1 and 4 m, chords between .5 and 5 m, and semi-chords between 30 and 80 cm (fig. 12). Each of the megaripples has a landward-facing slipface generally between 10 and 30 cm high (fig. 13). The structures are comparable in size to those termed "dunes" by Simons *et al.* (1965, p. 38) and by Harms and Fahnestock (1965, p. 91) or "largescale ripples" by Allen (1968, p. 36).

In profile, some of the megaripples have their summit point (Allen, 1968, p. 61) at the top of the slipface, but in the most common form, the summit lies well to the rear of the slipface, and a nearly horizontal crestal platform occurs between the summit and the slipface (fig. 12). Where this occurs, the inclination to the trough of the trailing ripple commonly exceeds 20 degrees. This inclination, however, consistently is less than that of the slipface which generally equals the angle of repose, about 33 degrees.

As shown in figure 10, the megaripples range from isolated lunate forms, sometimes arranged crudely en echelon, to laterally connected, or cat-

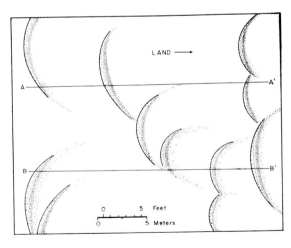

LAND ⟶

A ———— A'

B ———— B'

```
0        5   Feet
0        5   Meters
```

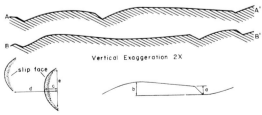

A ——— A'
B ——— B'

Vertical Exaggeration 2X

slip face

Fig. 12.—Plan view and profiles across a portion of the lunate megaripple facies.

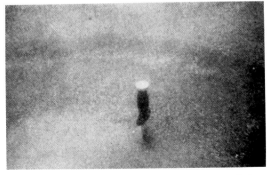

Fig. 13.—Photograph of lunate megaripple slipface.

TABLE 1.—*Distribution and character of small sand ripples in the nearshore as a function of wave conditions*

	Lunate megaripple facies (outer part)	Lunate megaripple facies (inner part)	Outer planar facies
High-energy conditions	Solitary ripples on megaripple crests	No ripples on megaripple crests	No ripples
Low-energy conditions	Trochoidal ripples on megaripple crests	Solitary ripples on megaripple crests	Solitary ripples

enary forms (Allen, 1968, p. 62–63). All of the megaripples observed near the inshore boundary of the facies were fully developed and had active slipfaces. In the outer part of the facies, the megaripples commonly increase in span. Rarely, the ripples with the longest spans (5 m or more) seem to take the form of a nearly straight-crested ripple without a well-defined slipface. At the nearshore-offshore boundary, the character of the megaripples depends on whether the boundary is migrating seaward or shoreward. If the shift is seaward, the newly formed megaripples tend to be small (height less than 10 cm, span less than a meter) but with active slipfaces. If the shift is shoreward, the megaripples are large but, except under the largest individual waves, have an inactive slipface crossed by smaller sand ripples. Commonly small, straight, flat-troughed (solitary) sand ripples similar to those from the outer planar facies coexist with the megaripples; the distribution of the smaller ripples apparently depends on the prevailing wave conditions (table 1). Small ripples also commonly occur in the megaripple troughs, oriented approximately normal to the megaripple crest.

The lunate megaripples migrate landward, commonly at a rate of about 30 cm per hour. The resulting internal structure is medium scale cross-stratification with foresets dipping steeply to landward (fig. 14a). The internal

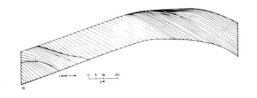

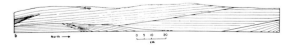

FIG. 14.—Internal structure produced by lunate megaripples.

structure viewed in a section parallel to shore (fig. 14b) is low angle cross-stratification without a consistent direction of inclination. Most of the cross-bedding produced by lunate megaripples therefore seems to be of a trough geometry, although the rare, relatively long, straight-crested megaripples may produce more tabular units. Within the zone of wave build-up, longshore currents are generally more feeble than those within the surf zone, and seem to have little effect on the orientation of the foresets. Under the influence of the strongest longshore currents observed, the megaripples were slightly asymmetric in plan view; the limb of the trough extending in the direction of the longshore current is somewhat longer than the other limb. The megaripple orientation follows the direction of wave propagation, and where the waves obliquely approach the shore, the cross-bedding produced by the megaripples will be similarly oblique to the shoreline. Due to the refraction of the waves at Whalehead Cove (fig. 4), for example, the seaward-most megaripples commonly were oriented obliquely to the shoreline; in contrast, the megaripples closer to shore faced nearly directly landward.

The grain size of sand in the lunate megaripple facies differs according to its position on a megaripple. Sand on the seaward-sloping surface and on the crestal platform is uniformly fine. Coarse sand and fine gravel is concentrated within the megaripple trough, especially on the lower part of the slipface (fig. 13). Strong eddies generated by the landward surge carry this coarse material up a slipface. As the surge wanes and the eddy dissipates, the coarse sand avalanches back down the face, producing a distinct size grading up the slipface, which is preserved in the foresets as the megaripple migrates. The foresets thus tend to be composed of relatively coarser sand, especially near the base.

Asymmetric ripple (inner offshore) facies

Seaward from the megaripple facies the bottom is profusely rippled, but under most wave conditions it lacks large-scale bed irregularity. Sand ripples adjacent to the offshore-nearshore boundary are generally short-crested (less than 30 cm long) and wavy, 2–5 cm high, and have a chord length ("wave length") of 10–20 cm. The ripple crests lie approximately normal to the direction of wave surge, and in profile, the ripples are asymmetric either landward or seaward depending on the direction and strength of the latest surge across them. If the seaward surge is sufficiently weak, the ripples will show a persistent asymmetry with steeper faces to landward. Seaward, in progressively deeper water, the ripple crests lengthen and become straighter as the ripple height diminishes.

Sets of interference ripples are also commonly present in the inner offshore. Such ripples consist of two sets that are nearly normal to one another. One set (generally but not everywhere in the study area oriented approximately northwest-southeast) is dominant and has long, straight, uninterrupted crests. Ripple crests in the other set occur in the troughs of the dominant ripples. The ripples in each set are straight crested and range up to 15 cm in height and 50 cm in wave length; in profile, they are nearly symmetrical. The angle between the ripples is bisected by the direction of wave surge. Each surge generates movement on ripples of both orientations; the interference pattern is not produced by waves approaching from two different directions. The interference pattern may initiate lunate megaripples if the offshore-nearshore boundary migrates seaward. Small megaripples commonly develop at the intersection of the larger cross-ripples.

The internal structure produced in the asymmetric ripple facies consists of small-scale (units less than 4 cm thick), shoreward-inclined ripple cross-lamination (*cf.* Newton, 1968) in some places suggestive of climbing ripples. The cross-laminated sand interfingers with gently dipping medium-scale scour and fill units (fig. 6). Careful scrutiny of the radiographs shows that many of the gently dipping laminations have faint internal foresets. This observation suggests that the laminations are produced by ripple trains migrating across bottom irregularities induced by abnormally large waves (Newton, 1968, p. 287; Clifton and Boggs, 1970, p. 896).

The offshore-nearshore boundary marks changes other than those in the depositional structures. Water near the bottom in the offshore commonly is more charged with fine suspended particulate matter than that in the nearshore. Faunal differences also occur. Off the Oregon coast, the small gastropod *Olivella biplicata* is much more abundant in the offshore than in the adjacent lunate megaripple facies. Off La Selva beach in Monterey Bay, California, the inner offshore is densely carpeted by living specimens of the sand dollar *Dendraster excentricus,* whereas the adjacent lunate megaripple facies contains only scattered empty or broken tests.

ORIGIN OF THE STRUCTURES

Hydrodynamic conditions

In topographically simple nearshore areas forming the subject of this paper, by far the strongest currents are landward and seaward surges associated with the passage of wave crests and troughs. Longshore and rip currents are much weaker and tidal currents negligible. The waves during most of the period of study formed a fairly regular swell, so that the hydrodynamic conditions can be described with some confidence by classical wave theory.

As a wave travels into shoaling water, the orbital velocity at the bottom increases (fig. 15). Given the wave period and deep-water wave height, Airy wave theory may be used to predict the increase in maximum horizontal orbital velocity at the bottom as the water shoals (Inman, 1963, p. 57–62). If the wave has a period of 10 seconds and a deep-water height of 1 meter, which are approximately average summer conditions off the Oregon Coast (fig. 3), the maximum horizontal orbital velocity will be 0.18 meters per second when the water depth is 30 meters. This velocity is great enough to move fine sand and to form ripples (Harms, 1969). Airy wave theory predicts the magnitude of the velocity increase with decreasing water depth but does not predict an asymmetry of orbital motion that becomes greater as the water shoals. In the absence of currents other than the orbital motion due to waves, the maximum landward velocity becomes greater than the maximum seaward velocity. This asymmetry, as predicted by Stokes wave theory (Dean and Eagleson, 1966, p. 107), is shown in figure 2.

As a wave travels into the nearshore, it begins to approximate in character the solitary wave (Inman, 1963, p. 62; Munk, 1949). If the waves were ideal solitary waves, the water motion would be entirely in the direction of wave travel. In reality, however, the waves are moving toward a beach which halts shoreward water transport and necessitates a seaward return flow. If the return flow is not channelized in rip currents, the water motion must be oscillatory even if the waves are essentially solitary.

Measurements of orbital velocity slightly seaward of the surf zone under wave conditions similar to those in Oregon have shown that the

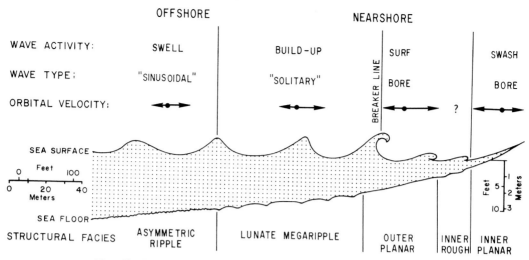

Fig. 15.—Relationship of depositional structures to wave type and activity.

maximum landward velocity is about two-thirds of that predicted by solitary wave theory and that the maximum seaward velocity averages about one-half the landward velocity (Inman and Nasu, 1956; Inman, 1963, p. 65). The same kind of asymmetry was felt qualitatively while diving in the areas studied.

As water depth decreases and the wave begins to build in height, the orbital velocity, as predicted by solitary wave theory, continues to increase until the wave breaks (fig. 2). Shoreward of the breaker line, wave theory is inadequate to predict water motion, and extensive measurements have been made on only a few beaches (Nagata, 1964; Schiffman, 1965). In the areas we have studied, the orbital velocities at the bottom seem qualitatively to increase into at least the outer half of the surf zone, and the landward surge remains stronger than the seaward surge.

In and immediately seaward of the swash zone, however, the seaward water movement or wave backwash commonly seems to be more significant in the transport of sediment along the bottom than the landward water movement or wave uprush. In the transition between surf and swash, the backwash seems to be especially dominant at the bottom because the broken wave or bore commonly overrides the seaward flow (Schiffman, 1965). The pattern of orbital velocities within the swash zone may differ among beaches; in contrast an opposite asymmetry was observed on the lower foreshore by Nagata (1964). Moreover, although landward surges may be strong for a brief moment as the wave

passes, high velocities during backwash are of longer duration and a much greater quantity of sediment is transported along the bottom.

Probable Existence of Wave-produced Flow Regimes

Perhaps the most striking aspect of the depositional structures in and adjacent to the high-energy nearshore is their resemblance to structures produced in alluvial channels. Each of the structural facies has a bed configuration similar to the configuration in part of a flow regime as described by Allen (1963) and by Simons *et al.* (1965). The asymmetric ripple facies, for example, is similar in bed configuration to the lower part of the lower flow regime, the inner and outer rough facies are similar to the upper part of the lower flow regime, and the inner and outer planar facies are similar to the lower part of the upper flow regime.

This resemblance is found in spite of the fact that flow conditions in the high-energy nearshore are very different from those in alluvial channels. The dominant currents in the areas studied are oscillatory wave-induced surges, whereas currents in alluvial channels are unidirectional and, to a first approximation, steady and uniform. Moreover, the period of oscillatory movement due to waves is considerably smaller than the time required for the full development of depositional structures. Despite the obvious differences in flow conditions, the similarity in sedimentary structures suggests that flow conditions in the high-energy nearshore zone are similar in their effects on bed configuration to flow conditions in alluvial channels.

For the flow conditions to be similar in their effect, a necessary characteristic of the oscillatory flow is that the surges in opposite directions be unequal. The greater the asymmetry of the oscillatory flow, the greater must be the tendency of the flow to act as a undirectional current in the direction of the stronger surge. The condition of unequal shoreward and seaward wave surge is certainly met in most parts of the high-energy nearshore and in the shoreward part of the offshore. This asymmetry is predicted by wave theory, has been measured on some beaches, and is easily sensed qualitatively while diving.

Variation in the period of oscillatory flow may affect the tendency of the flow to act as a undirectional current in the direction of the stronger surge. Certainly this is true if the period approaches the time required for the full development of depositional structures. In such long-period oscillatory flows, the flow in each direction must tend to act as a unidirectional current and to produce structures independent from those produced by the preceding opposed flow. As the period becomes smaller, it is conceivable that another limit is reached, below which the rate of oscillation is so rapid that all similarity to unidirectional flow is lost. However, the presence of persistent asymmetric structures in the high-energy nearshore indicates that the period of the waves must be in the proper range for the asymmetric oscillatory flow to act similarly to a unidirectional current.

Relations between Facies in Terms of Flow Regimes

The relations between facies, each of which formed in one specific part of a flow regime, can be examined in terms of varying hydrodynamic conditions and consequently varying flow regime. The hydrodynamic parameters on which flow regime is dependent have not been definitely established (Simons, Richardson, and Nordin, 1965; Allen, 1968, p. 133–138; Harms, 1969), but certainly flow velocity is a paramount factor.

A first obvious distinction to be made is that the asymmetry of structures in the two outer facies, *i.e.* the asymmetric ripple and lunate megaripple facies, is opposite in orientation to that in the inner rough facies, at least as the latter is typically developed on gently sloping beaches. Structures in the two outer facies reflect the dominance of landward currents, a dominance that can be observed and is predicted by wave theory. The structures in the inner rough facies

on gently sloping beaches, on the other hand, imply the dominance of seaward currents, a dominance that is supported by limited observational evidence (Schiffman, 1965). On steep beaches, the structures in the inner rough facies are nearly symmetrical, and the degree and polarity of flow asymmetry are not known.

The inner planar facies resembles the inner rough facies of gently sloping beaches in having seaward currents that are dominant. Evidence for the dominance of such currents is strong despite the absence of asymmetric structures. The dominance of wave backwash in producing lamination in the inner planar facies has been documented by Clifton (1969). The outer planar facies likewise has no asymmetric structures, but qualitative observations of flow velocity suggest that it resembles the facies seaward of it in having shoreward wave surges stronger than those to seaward.

The facies in the nearshore and inner offshore can thus be grouped into two series: an outer series of three facies in which landward currents have the dominant effect on the bottom, and an inner series of one or two facies in which seaward currents are dominant. On steep beaches, the inner rough facies is apparently transitional between the two series. Even on gently sloping beaches, we have no quantitative evidence that the line along which landward and seaward flow velocities are equal coincides exactly with the boundary between the outer planar and inner rough facies.

A shoreward traverse across the outer three facies suggests a gradual increase in flow regime from the lower part of the lower flow regime to the lower part of the upper flow regime. The existence of this progression is supported by changes across individual facies. In the asymmetric ripple facies, the change from relatively long-crested forms in the outer part to short-crested forms in the inner part is suggestive of the change from low-energy to high-energy current ripples described by Simons *et al.* (1965, p. 38) and by Harms (1969). In the outer part of the lunate megaripple facies, the common superposition of ripples on megaripples is similar to the bed configuration described by Simons *et al.* (1965) in the transition between ripple and dune configurations.

An upper flow regime interpretation of the outer planar facies is supported by several features in addition to the lack of bed form roughness and the shoreward position of the facies in a progression of shoreward-increasing flow regimes. Among these features, which are characteristic of the upper flow regime (Simons, Richardson, and Nordin, 1965), are intense sediment movement and firm packing of sand.

An interpretation of the outer three facies as representing a shoreward increase in flow regime is in agreement with the shoreward increase of orbital velocity at the bottom (fig. 2). In marine waters, this velocity increase is associated with decreasing water depth, in contrast to the well-described increasing velocity and flow regime associated with increasing water depth in a stretch of alluvial channel whose slope varies little with discharge (Dawdy, 1961; Nordin, 1964).

The progression of bed forms in a traverse across the inner two facies may also be explainable in part by variation in flow regime. That the inner planar facies is a product of flow in the upper regime is attested by the common occurrence of primary current lineation (Allen, 1963), standing waves and antidunes, which have been called swash-zone ripple marks by Tanner (1968) or regressive sand waves by Panin and Panin (1967), and rhomboid markings (Woodford, 1935; Tanner, 1968). All these features are produced by wave backwash.

The step at the base of the swash zone on low-energy beaches and on steep high-energy beaches probably marks the transition between upper and lower flow regimes (Tanner, 1968). The inner edge of the inner rough facies on gently sloping high-energy beaches is evidently equivalent to the simple step found on other beaches. The inner rough facies thus appears to occur in an area of flow in the lower regime situated between two areas of flow in the upper regime. It is not surprising, therefore, to find in the inner rough facies structures similar in scale to those formed in the upper part of the lower flow regime. On gently sloping beaches, the asymmetry of these structures reflects the continuing dominance of seaward surge for some distance seaward at the swash zone. On steep beaches, where the seaward surge rapidly spreads out as it moves past the step at the base of the swash zone, seaward surge is evidently not dominant in shaping the structures.

The unique character of the inner rough facies on steep beaches may in part be due to the coarse grain size of the sediment. Moreover, limited observational data suggests that long-crested large ripples are present across much of the nearshore where the sediment is fine gravel. The possibility that bed configuration in the nearshore is a function of sediment grain size as well as of hydrodynamic conditions is in accord with the findings of Simon *et al.* (1965).

Complicating Factors

Although the major features and interrela-

tions of the structural facies seem to be adequately explained in terms of flow regime, several features are not entirely similar to features produced by unidirectional flows. Considering the differences between transient, bidirectional wave-induced flow and continuous, unidirectional flow, this is not surprising.

Ripples in the offshore facies differ in several ways from those produced by unidirectional flow. The wave-formed ripples are commonly irregular in plan view but never approach a truly linguoid form. Also, their average asymmetry is not as great as that of ripples in alluvial channels. These differences are probably due to the modifying action of seaward surges, which prevent the stronger landward surges from forming current ripples of fully mature form.

Nearshore lunate megaripples differ in several aspects from those produced by unidirectional flow. Although megaripples produced by unidirectional flow may have summit points located upcurrent from their slipface brinks (Allen, 1968, p. 61), the summit points are apparently never as far back as they are in the nearshore lunate megaripples. Moreover, the stoss sides of nearshore lunate megaripples are commonly much steeper than those of megaripples formed by unidirectional flow. Probably the unique features of the nearshore lunate megaripples are modifications caused in some way by seaward surges.

The sea floor in the outer planar facies differs from a plane bed produced by unidirectional flow in the upper regime by commonly being marked by ripples. These ripples resemble the incipient ripples described by Carstens and Neilson (1967) and by Tanner (1963). They also resemble the ripples (illustrated by Guy, Simons, and Richardson, 1966, p. 115) that form during the shutdown of a flume and that are probably of incipient nature. The fact that the ripples are eliminated during the peak of every strong landward wave surge indicates that their form is indeed a result of their incipient nature. Their presence in the outer planar facies is thus a result of the highly unsteady nature of the flow. Although these ripples occur in a high-energy area, in many ways they closely resemble ripples formed under low energy conditions.

The greatest structural complexity occurs in the inner rough facies. The variability of bed forms in this facies suggests that no single interpretation is completely valid. One flow characteristic that may be important in producing bed form roughness in this facies is strong turbulence due to bores first reaching the bottom and due to the interference of incoming and outgoing surges. However, only a flow-regime interpretation seems capable of explaining the persistent asymmetry of structures found in the inner rough facies of gently sloping beaches.

Because of the complex oscillatory nature of wave-induced flow, a wave surge having a certain maximum horizontal velocity at a given water depth may not produce the same bed configuration as would a unidirectional current having the same velocity at the same depth. Therefore, changes in wave character may be as important as changes in maximum surge velocity in causing changes in flow regime. For example, an increase in asymmetry of orbital motion may be more important than a simple increase in orbital velocity in producing the change from asymmetric ripples to lunate megaripples. Similarly, the change from lunate megaripples to a planar bottom could conceivably be due more to a change in orbital asymmetry or to an increase in turbulence than to a simple increase in orbital velocity.

FACIES MIGRATION

Observations made under different conditions of waves and tides show that the structural facies readily shift both landward and seaward. Certain of the facies may also change considerably in width and may disappear altogether. Their position relative to one another, however, is invariable.

The inner rough facies seems to be the most variable in location and presence. Commonly the facies is not at all developed, particularly where the beach-nearshore system bottom profile is relatively flat. In such a situation, widely spaced (1–3 m), straight sand ripples about 1 cm high, oriented slightly oblique to the shoreline, commonly occur at the position generally occupied by the inner rough facies; otherwise, the outer and inner planar facies merge and are indistinguishable. The inner rough facies at the lowest tide observed occurred adjacent to the lunate megaripple facies and the outer planar facies was absent. Where in contact with the lunate megaripples, the inner rough facies structures can be recognized by seaward slipfaces and geometric form.

The outer boundary of the lunate megaripple facies also is sensitive to changes in water depth (tidal state) or wave conditions. In one five-hour period on the Oregon coast during which wave conditions remained nearly constant, the boundary shifted shoreward more than 80 m as the tide rose 2 m (fig. 16). The boundary location also seems in part dependent on wave height (fig. 17) and on other wave parameters such as period, wave length, and, possibly, on the regularity of the wave patterns; on days of

even, regular swell the boundary seemed to be further offshore than on days when the sea surface was irregular or disturbed by a strong wind chop. The complexity of the sea surface precludes, at least at present, precise definition of interrelationships between the boundary location and the different wave parameters, and the location of the boundary cannot yet be accurately predicted.

The landward boundary of the lunate megaripple facies is far less variable than its seaward boundary. Even during marked tidal rise or fall, the boundary shifted no more than ten or twenty meters (fig. 16). The relative stability of the position of this boundary possibly may be explained in terms of flow regime. The bed forms of the upper and lower flow regimes tend to maintain themselves despite changes in flow conditions towards the other regime (Simon, Richardson, and Nordin, 1965, p. 37). Thus, in the surf zone, the boundary between lunate megaripples and the outer planar facies may hold its position despite changes in water depth or wave conditions. Changes in the structural zonation as the tide rises from its lowest levels support this hypothesis. As described previously,

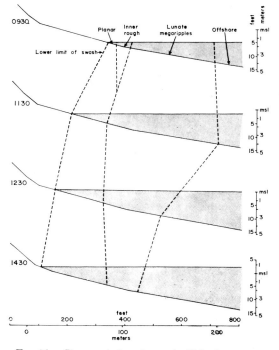

FIG. 16.—Changes in location and width of structural facies on a day (July 31, 1969) during which the tide rose more than 2 m.

the inner rough facies commonly occurs near the lunate megaripple facies at the lowest tidal levels. As the tide rises, the irregular bed forms of the inner rough facies are quickly converted to lunate megaripples, whereas the planar facies separating the inner rough facies from the megaripples persists for some time before it develops megaripples.

The lunate megaripple facies may, under small short-period waves, become so modified as to be nearly unrecognizable. Under the smallest waves encountered (highest 10 percent of breakers equaled 0.8 m, average wave period of 6 seconds, and average wave length of 33 m), the facies generally occupied by lunate megaripples contained a combination of straight symmetric sand ripples 10 to 15 cm high and irregular megaripples which mostly lacked a lunate form. During the period of observation, however, the wave height increased and typical lunate megaripples began to form.

STRUCTURAL ASSEMBLAGES

Because the structural facies readily migrate seaward or landward as wave or tidal conditions change, the internal structures sampled at any one place in the nearshore are likely to reflect deposition in several different facies. Recognition of the assemblage of structures produced by facies overlap in different portions of the high-energy nearshore constitutes a useful tool for identifying these environments in the stratigraphic record.

Many of the series of box cores contained evidence of deposition in two or more structural facies. Figure 18 shows the internal structures in a set of cores taken in the lower part of the swash or inner planar facies. The parallel, nearly horizontal lamination produced under wave backwash (Clifton, 1969) is truncated by wedges of seaward inclined cross-stratification produced at the landward edge of the inner rough facies. Box cores from the outer portion of the outer planar facies commonly contain parallel lamination produced in that facies over-

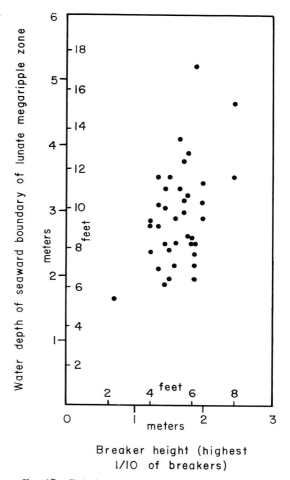

Breaker height (highest 1/10 of breakers)

Fig. 17.—Relation between observed breaker heights (highest 10 percent) and measured water depth at the seaward boundary of the lunate megaripple facies.

lying medium-scale landward-dipping foresets produced previously by lunate megaripples (fig. 19a). Cores from the central portion of the outer planar facies commonly show (fig. 19b) a

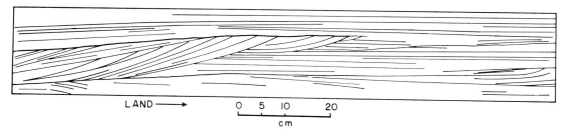

Fig. 18.—Internal structures from the seaweed edge of the inner planar facies (swash zone).

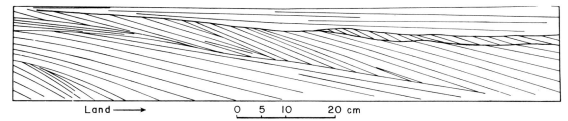

a. Outer portion outer planar facies

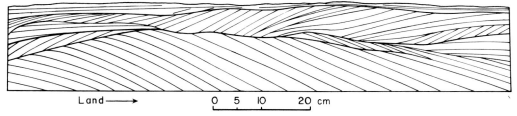

b. Central portion outer planar facies

FIG. 19.—Internal structures from the outer planar facies.

combination of parallel, essentially horizontal lamination, seaward-inclined foresets formed within the inner rough facies and landward-inclined foresets produced by lunate megaripples. Cores from the inner part of the offshore include ripple cross-lamination, gently inclined scour and fill structure, and medium-scale landward-dipping foresets produced by lunate megaripples (fig. 6). The medium-scale cross-bedded units commonly consist of coarser sand than do others in the section.

EQUIVALENT STRUCTURES IN THE
STRATIGRAPHIC RECORD

The preservation potential of high-energy nearshore deposits may be relatively low, but in a subsiding basin into which sedimentation was rapid, nearshore deposits such as beach deposits are incorporated in the sedimentary record. Such deposits may also include a complex array of depositional features not covered in this paper, such as rip channel deposits, offshore bars, and tide-swept river-mouth deposits, and these might greatly complicate the simple nearshore-beach system described herein. Nonetheless, a number of different deposits of shallow marine origin contain structural assemblages similar to those of the topographically simple contemporary high-energy nearshore environment.

One of the most distinctive assemblages encountered is the combination of ripple cross-lamination, gently inclined scour-and-fill struc-

ture, and medium-scale landward-dipping cross-bedding produced near the nearshore-offshore boundary (fig. 6). Similar assemblages occur in late Pleistocene marine terrace deposits along the coast of southern Oregon (fig. 20) and in the marginal marine Branch Canyon Sandstone (Hill *et al.*, 1958) in the southeastern Caliente Range of southern California (fig. 21). In both of these examples, the sand composing the crossbedded unit is coarser than that composing the ripple lamination and gently dipping scour-and-fill structure. The crossbeds in the Pleistocene marine terrace sands dip eastward, undoubtedly the landward direction when the sand

FIG. 20.—Assemblage of sedimentary structures in outcrop of marine terrace deposits of late Pleistocene age near Cape Blanco, Oregon.

FIG. 21.—Assemblage of sedimentary structures in outcrop of the middle and upper Miocene Branch Canyon Sandstone in the southeastern Caliente Range, California.

FIG. 23.—Assemblage of structures in marine terrace deposits of late Pleistocene age about 5 meters west (seaward) from the portion of the exposure shown in figure 23.

was deposited. The crossbeds in the examples from the Branch Canyon Sandstone dip eastward towards the shoreline inferred for that time (Clifton, 1967, p. B37).

The interface between the inner planar and the inner rough facies (fig. 18) also is quite distinctive. At two localities in the late Pleistocene marine terrace deposits in southern Oregon, very gently seaward-dipping, parallel lamination characteristic of the lower swash zone could be traced laterally seaward into a cross-bedded sequence in which foresets were dominantly inclined seaward (figs. 22 and 23). The cross-stratified sequence shown in figure 23 also shows a considerable amount of soft-sediment deformation, which was not observed in box cores taken from contemporary beaches.

Although the recognition of individual structures and structural assemblages may be useful in environmental interpretation, most of these features may be nearly duplicated in other dissimilar depositional environments. For example,

the assemblage of structures found by Imbrie and Buchanan (1965, fig. 9) in intertidal deposits are quite similar to those encountered near the nearshore-offshore boundary (fig. 6). Therefore, the interrelation of associated structural assemblages may provide the best documentation of paleoenvironments using sedimentary structures. Fitting the different assemblages into a meaningful pattern, either laterally or vertically (assuming the Walther Law of Facies, Visher, 1965, p. 41), provides a powerful tool for the interpretation of the depositional environment of ancient sedimentary deposits. An excellent example occurs in a marine terrace deposit of Quaternary age near the mouth of the Pajaro River in central California (California Dept. of Water Resources, 1970, pl. 1).

A roadcut in the south bank of the Pajaro River about 1 kilometer northeast from its mouth (SE corner, sec. 25, T. 12 S., R. 1 E., Monterey Co., Calif.) provides an excellent exposure of well-bedded Quaternary sand and

FIG. 22.—Assemblage of sedimentary structures in outcrop of marine terrace deposits of late Pleistocene age in cut on road to Cape Blanco, Oregon.

FIG. 24.—Quaternary marine terrace deposits exposed in south bank of Pajaro River 800 meters from river mouth.

FIG. 25.—Isolated lens of cross-bedded sand and gravel truncating flat lamination in lower part of evenly bedded pebbly sand shown in figure 25.

gravel. The lowermost 2 meters of this exposure consists of cross-stratified gravel in which crossbedding dips 15°–20° to the west and southwest (fig. 24). Overlying this gravel is approximately 3 meters of evenly laminated pebbly sand in which the laminations dip uniformly about 5° toward the southwest. In its lower portion, this evenly laminated sediment is pebbly and contains a few thin dark laminations composed of heavy minerals. The pebbles occur in discrete beds and in many beds show a south-west-inclined imbrication. The pebble beds are locally interrupted by small (15 cm thick), isolated lenses of gravel in which crossbedding dips to the southwest (fig. 25). The evenly laminated sandy gravel changes in character up-sec-

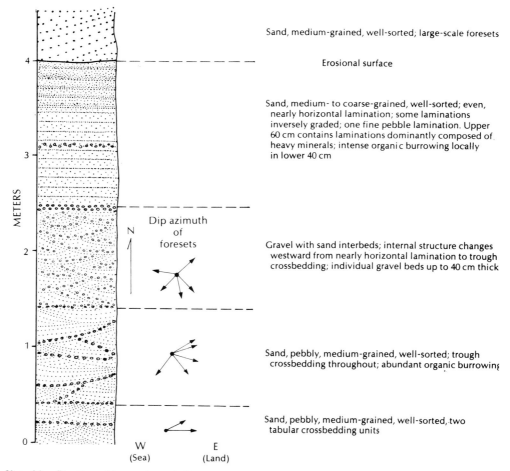

Sand, medium-grained, well-sorted; large-scale foresets

Erosional surface

Sand, medium- to coarse-grained, well-sorted; even, nearly horizontal lamination; some laminations inversely graded; one fine pebble lamination. Upper 60 cm contains laminations dominantly composed of heavy minerals; intense organic burrowing locally in lower 40 cm

Dip azimuth of foresets

Gravel with sand interbeds; internal structure changes westward from nearly horizontal lamination to trough crossbedding; individual gravel beds up to 40 cm thick

Sand, pebbly, medium-grained, well-sorted; trough crossbedding throughout; abundant organic burrowing

Sand, pebbly, medium-grained, well-sorted, two tabular crossbedding units

METERS

W (Sea)   E (Land)

FIG. 26.—Stratigraphic section of Quaternary marine terrace deposits exposed on south bank of Pajaro River about 100 meters upstream from exposure shown in figure 25.

FIG. 27.—Lower part of section described in figure 26.

tion vertically and also laterally up-dip, parallel to the lamination. Pebbles become less abundant and the heavy mineral content increases. Near the top of the sequence concentrations of heavy minerals form dark laminations up to 2 cm thick. Many laminations in the upper part of the sequence are inversely graded in grain size. A second roadcut, approximately 100 meters upstream, exposes a more complete section through the deposit (fig. 26).

These exposures contain many features similar to those found in the contemporary high-energy beach and nearshore, assuming that the trend of the Quaternary shoreline at the time of deposition approximated that of the present-day coast. The landward (eastward)-dipping crossbeds in the lowest part of the section (figs. 26 and 27) resemble those produced by lunate megaripples in the zone of wave build-up. The combination of both landward and seaward-dipping crossbeds in the immediately overlying pebbly sand (fig. 26) occurs in contemporary surf zone deposits. The gravel which overlies this pebbly sand contains crossbeds that dip dominantly seaward; sedimentary structures in this gravel resemble those formed in some inner rough facies of contemporary high-energy nearshores. The evenly laminated pebbly sand above the gravel compares well with that produced in the swash zone. Seaward-inclined pebble imbrication is common on beaches (Cailleux, 1945, p. 391), and individual sand laminae exhibit the inverse size grading characteristic of swash lamination (Clifton, 1969). Isolated lenses containing seaward-dipping crossbeds in the lower part of the laminated sequence resemble those found on the lowermost part of some present beaches. Concentrations of heavy minerals such as those

present in the upper part of the sequence characteristically develop in the uppermost part of the swash zone on Oregon beaches.

Depositional structures in the Pajaro River exposures thus suggest the following environmental sequence (in ascending order): zone of wave build-up, surf zone, lower swash zone changing seaward into inner surf zone, and upper swash zone. This sequence implies a simple beach progradation, a seaward overlapping of adjacent depositional facies. Environmental associations can also be related in meaningful patterns within the Branch Canyon Sandstone and in other ancient marginal marine deposits.

CONCLUSIONS

The identification of sedimentary structures and their distribution in contemporary depositional environments can promote insight into depositional processes in complex environmental systems and provide criteria for recognizing these systems in the stratigraphic record. The high-energy nearshore depositional system contains well-defined, interrelated facies of depositional structures that are interpretable in terms of sequential changes in shoaling waves. Knowledge of the spatial relationship of these facies enhances interpretation of the geometric distribution of depositional structures in the stratigraphic record.

The topographically simple high-energy nearshore depositional system is but one of many existing in the marginal marine environment. Similar studies in the other depositional systems should provide an abundance of information regarding contemporary depositional processes and greatly increase our understanding of ancient shallow marine deposits.

ACKNOWLEDGMENTS

The following individuals, C. H. Carter, R. A. Cook, C. B. Johnson, A. G. McHendrie, and S. F. Stringham, shared the rigors of working in the high-energy nearshore of southern Oregon. K. E. Clifton assisted in the profiling operations. We also thank R. J. Janda for showing us exposures in Pleistocene marine terrace deposits in southern Oregon that provided comparisons with the contemporary environment. Drs. E. D. McKee, C. F. Nordin, H. E. Jobsen, G. S. Visher and J. C. Ingle critically read the manuscript and their comments are gratefully acknowledged.

REFERENCES

ALLEN, J. R. L., 1963, Internal sedimentation structures of well-washed sands and sandstone in relation to flow conditions: Nature, v. 200, p. 326–327.
———, 1968, Current ripples: their relation to patterns of water and sediment motion: North-Holland Publishing Co., Amsterdam, 433 p.

BASCOM, W. A., 1964, Waves and beaches—The dynamics of the ocean surface: Anchor Books, Doubleday and Co. Inc., New York, 267 p.

BOUMA, A. H., 1964, Sampling and treatment of unconsolidated sediments for study of internal structures: Jour. Sed. Petrology, v. 34, p. 349–354.

———, 1969, Methods for the study of sedimentary structures: John Wiley and Sons, New York, 458 p.

CAILLEUX, 1945, California State Department of Water Resources, 1970, Sea-water intrusion into the lower Salinas Valley: Progress report 1968–1969, 28 p.

CARSTENS, M. R., AND NEILSON, F. M., 1967, Evolution of a duned bed under oscillatory flow: Jour. Geophys. Research, v. 72, p. 3053–3059.

CLIFTON, H. E., 1967, Paleogeographic significance of two middle Miocene basalt flows, southeastern Caliente Range, California, in Geological Survey research 1967, U.S. Geol. Survey Prof. Paper. 575–B, p. B32–B39.

———, 1969, Beach lamination—nature and origin: Marine Geology, v. 7, p. 553–559.

———, AND BOGGS, SAM, JR., in press, Concave-up pelecypod (*Psphidia*) shells in shallow marine sand, Elk River Beds, southwestern Oregon.

COOK, D. O., 1969, Sand Transport by shoaling waves: Geol. Soc. America, Abstr. Pt. 7, p. 39–40.

DAWDY, D. R., 1961, Depth-discharge relations of alluvial streams-discontinuous rating curves: U.S. Geol. Survey Water-Supply Paper 1498-C, p. C1–C16.

DEAN, R. G., AND EAGLESON, P. S., 1966, Finite amplitude waves; p. 93–132, in Ippen, A. T., ed., Estuary and coastline hydrodynamics: McGraw-Hill Book Co., New York, 744 p.

DU BAR, J. R., AND JOHNSON, H. S., JR., 1964, Pleistocene "coquina" at 20th Avenue South, Myrtle Beach, South Carolina, and other similar deposits: Southeastern Geology, v. 5, p. 79–100.

GUY, H. P., SIMONS, D. B., AND RICHARDSON, E. V., 1966, Summary of alluvial channel data from flume experiments, 1956–61: U.S. Geol. Survey, Prof. Paper 462–I, 96 p.

HARMS, J. C., 1969, Hydraulic significance of some sand ripples: Geol. Soc. America Bull., v. 80, p. 363–396.

———, AND FAHNESTOCK, R. K., 1965, Stratification, bed forms, and flow phenomena (with an example from the Rio Grande); p. 84–115 in Middleton, G. V., ed., Primary Sedimentary Structures and their Hydrodynamic Interpretation—A symposium: Soc. Econ. Paleontologists and Mineralogists Spec. Pub. no. 12, 265 p.

HILL, M. L., CARLSON, S. A., AND DIBBLEE, T. W., 1958, Stratigraphy of Cuyama Valley-Caliente Range area, California: Am. Assoc. Petroleum Geologists Bull., v. 42, p. 2973–3000.

IMBRIE, JOHN, AND BUCHANAN, HUGH, 1965, Sedimentary structures in modern carbonate sands of the Bahamas; p. 149–172 in G. V. Middleton, ed., Primary Sedimentary Structures and their Hydrodynamic Interpretation—A symposium: Soc. Econ. Paleontologists and Mineralogists Spec. Pub. no. 12, 265 p.

INMAN, D. L., 1957, Wave-generated ripples in nearshore sands: U.S. Army Corps Engineers Beach Erosion Board Tech. Mem. 100, 42 p.

———, 1963, Ocean waves and associated currents, p. 49–81 in Shepard, F. P., Submarine Geology, 2nd ed.; Harper and Row, Publishers, New York, 557 p.

———, AND NASU, N., 1956, Orbital velocity associated with wave action near the breaker zone: U.S. Army Corps Engineers Coastal Eng. Research Center Tech. Memo. 79, 43 p.

MUNK, W. H., 1949, The solitary wave theory and its application to surf problems: New York Acad. Sci. Annals, v. 51, p. 376–424.

NAGATA, YUTAKA, 1964, Deformation of temporal pattern of orbital wave velocity and sediment transport in shoaling water, in breaker zone, and on foreshore: Oceanog. Soc. Japan Jour., v. 20, no. 2, p. 7–20.

NEWTON, R. S., 1968, Internal structure of wave-formed ripple marks in the nearshore zone: Sedimentology, v. 11, no. 3/4, p. 275–292.

NORDIN, C. F., JR., 1964, Aspects of flow resistance and sediment transport, Rio Grande near Bernalillo, New Mexico: U.S. Geol. Survey Water-Supply Paper 1498-H, p. H1–H41.

PANIN, N., AND PANIN, ST., 1967, Regressive sand waves in the Black Sea shore: Marine Geology, v. 5, p. 221–226.

SCHIFFMAN, ARNOLD, 1965, Energy measurements in the swash-surf zone: Limnology and Oceanography, v. 10, p. 255–260.

SIMONS, D. B., RICHARDSON, E. V., AND NORDIN, C. F., JR., 1965, Sedimentary structures generated by flow in alluvial channels; p. 34–52 in Middleton, G. V., ed., Primary Sedimentary Structures and their Hydrodynamic Interpretation—A symposium: Soc. Econ. Paleontologists and Mineralogists Spec. Pub. no. 12, 265 p.

SHEPARD, F. P., 1963, Submarine Geology, 2d ed.: Harper and Row, Publishers, New York, 557 p.

TANNER, W. F., 1963, Origin and maintenance of ripple marks: Sedimentology, v. 2, p. 307–311.

———, 1968, High-Froude phenomena in sedimentology [abs.]: Geol. Soc. America and associated societies, Ann. Mtgs., New Orleans, La., 1967, Program, p. 220.

THOMPSON, W. O., 1937, Original structures of beaches, bars, and dunes: Geol. Soc. America Bull., v. 48, p. 723–752.

VISHER, G. S., 1965, Use of vertical profile in environmental reconstruction: Am. Assoc. Petroleum Geologists Bull., v. 49, p. 41–61.

WOODFORD, A. O., 1935, Rhomboid ripple mark: Am. Jour. Sci., 5th ser., v. 29, p. 518–525.

Reprinted from BEACH AND NEARSHORE SEDIMENTATION, SEPM Special Publication No. 24,
PP. 149–168, FIGS. 1–11, October 1976

FACIES RELATIONSHIPS ON A BARRED COAST, KOUCHIBOUGUAC BAY, NEW BRUNSWICK, CANADA

ROBIN G. D. DAVIDSON-ARNOTT AND BRIAN GREENWOOD
Scarborough College, University of Toronto, Canada

ABSTRACT

Bedforms and sedimentary structures formed by wave oscillatory and wave-generated unidirectional currents in modern nearshore environments provide a useful analogue for the interpretation of ancient sediments. This paper presents: (1) a basic facies model for a modern, barred nearshore environment, and (2) an examination of the application of the flow regime concept to flow and bedform generation in the nearshore area. Work was carried out in Kouchibouguac Bay, New Brunswick, Canada in an area characterized by two marine bar systems: (1) an inner system of bars up to 1 m in height and breached at intervals by rip channels and (2) a single continuous, crescentic outer bar system up to 2.5 m high, located 200 to 300 m offshore. Fetch restrictions limit waves to a maximum of 2.5 m high and 7 to 8 second period during northeasterly storm winds. Bedforms were observed using SCUBA, but only in the inner system during high energy conditions. Sedimentary structures were studied in resin peels made from 90 box cores taken from the nearshore zone.

Four subfacies associated with each bar and trough, and extending parallel to the shoreline were identified: (1) a seaward slope facies characterized by sets of small-scale oscillation ripple cross-lamination and units of seaward dipping plane bed. Considerable bioturbation may be present particularly in the outer system; (2) a bar crest facies characterized by units of sub-horizontal plane bedding and medium-scale cross-bedded units produced by migration of lunate megaripples. Cross-bedding dip may be both landward and seaward; (3) a landward slope facies characterized in the outer system by oscillation ripple cross-lamination and units of low-angle, landward-dipping plane bed, and in the inner system by high-angle landward dipping, medium-scale cross-bedding up to 1 m in thickness produced on an avalanche slope by bar migration; (4) a trough facies characterized by poorly preserved oscillation and current ripple cross-lamination, dipping roughly parallel to shore. A distinct organic component produces a dark coloration. A fifth subfacies, the rip channel facies, is found only in the inner system associated with distinct rip channels. It is characterized by units of medium-scale cross-bedding dipping seaward and produced by megaripple migration under the influence of rip currents.

Comparison of the sequence with that of Clifton and others (1971) and consideration of flow conditions in the nearshore area suggests the existence of three distinct flow regime sequences: (1) a symmetric oscillatory flow regime controlled by near-symmetric oscillatory currents with a bedform sequence, no movement-ripples-plane bed; (2) an asymmetric oscillatory flow regime controlled by highly asymmetric oscillatory and translational flow with a bedform sequence, no movement—ripples—lunate megaripples—plane bed; (3) a unidirectional flow regime controlled by unidirectional longshore and rip currents with a bedform sequence, no movement—ripples—megaripples—plane bed.

INTRODUCTION

The transport of sediment, whether in water, air or some other fluid, is usually accompanied by some deformation of the sediment-water interface. It has long been recognized that these deformations or bedforms exhibit regular variations in shape in response to differences in flow conditions and flow velocities. If the sedimentary structures produced by these bedforms are subsequently preserved, they can be used to characterize the depositional environment. Bedforms and structures have been studied from a wide range of depositional environments, including rivers, dunes, turbidity currents and coastal areas. There is a considerable body of literature dealing with field, laboratory and theoretical studies, particularly concerning bedforms generated by unidirectional currents flowing over cohesionless material. There are, however, comparatively few studies of bedforms produced under oscillatory flow conditions, particularly those associated with breaking waves in the nearshore area.

Most studies of bedforms and structures produced by wave action have been carried out either seaward of the area where rapid wave transformation begins, or on the beach face. Early work in the lower shoreface was carried out by Evans (1941) and a detailed study was made by Inman (1957). Other notable works include those of Tanner (1959, 1963, 1971), Davis (1965), Risk (1967), Newton (1968) and Cook (1969). The structures found in the swash zone and beach face have been described in even greater detail, probably because of their accessibility at low tide. Among the earliest work was that of Thompson (1937) and subsequent studies have included those of Emery and Stevenson (1950), McKee (1957), Andrews and van der Lingen (1969), Hayes (1969) and Clifton (1969). Studies of berm and intertidal bars (ridge and runnel) include those of Thompson (1937), Davis and others (1972) and Reineck (1963).

Studies of bedforms and structures in the inner nearshore area, however, have been very limited, the notable exceptions being those of Clifton and others (1971) on the high energy Oregon coast, Hunter and others (1972) on the Gulf coast and Reineck and Singh (1971, 1973) on the Mediterranean coast. Risk (1967) studied bedforms associated with bar and trough topography in Lake Huron but the observations were made only under low energy conditions and did not include examination of structures. A search of the literature fails to reveal any other significant field studies of bedforms and structures associated with waves breaking either on plane or barred coasts.

The nearshore, shoreface marine environment is complex, being dominated by the processes of waves, tides and secondary currents associated with breaking waves. The primary objective of this study is to provide information on the types of bedforms and resulting sedimentary structures present within the barred nearshore system in Kouchibouguac Bay, New Brunswick, Canada, and on the size characteristics of the sediments themselves. Because direct observations on the manner by which sediment is transported during high energy conditions is difficult, the study of sedimentary structures can provide: (1) useful information on bed conditions in the different zones; (2) relationships to changing energy levels and (3) the direction of sediment transport. By taking cores from all zones within the bar systems, together with direct observations of bedforms, it was anticipated that a general model could be formulated relating bedforms and sedimentary structures to wave and current processes and topographic features within the systems. Such a model complements studies on the form and movement of the bars and provides additional information on the nature of the wave and current processes which control their formation and movement. Finally, the model should be useful in the study of bedforms in other shallow water areas and in the study of ancient sediments.

Two major aims of this paper are: (1) to establish the basic facies characteristics of a modern nearshore barred environment as an analogue for future paleo-environmental reconstruction and (2) to examine the concept of flow regime and bedform generation under oscillatory flow conditions.

LOCATION AND DESCRIPTION OF STUDY AREA

The study was carried out in Kouchibouguac Bay, which is located at the western end of the Northumberland Strait on the New Brunswick coast of Canada (Fig. 1). A series of barrier islands and barrier spits 29 km long extends in a gentle arc from Pt. Sapin in the north to Richibucto Cape in the south. The barrier islands are separated by three permanent inlets located opposite the tidal estuaries of rivers draining into the bay. The general characteristics of the barrier island system have been described by Davidson-Arnott (1971) and Bryant and McCann (1973).

Detailed work was carried out on one of the barrier islands, North Richibucto Beach, primarily in the two study areas shown in Figure 1 and in a third area located midway between them. North Richibucto Beach is characterized by the presence of two distinct bar systems in the nearshore area: (1) an outer system consisting of a single bar, crescentic in form, which is continuous for most of the length of the barrier island; and (2) an inner system of one, two or, occasionally, three discontinuous bars which are frequently crescentic in form (see Fig. 2) although straight and transverse forms also occur. An example of the morphology of the bar systems is shown in Figure 3.

The outer bar along North Richibucto Beach ranges in height from 1.5 m to 2.5 m and its crest is located 200 m to 300 m offshore in 2.5 m to 3.5 m of water. It is separated from the inner system by a distinct deep trough. The inner bars range in height from 0.5 m to 1.25 m and extend up to 150 m offshore. The shoal areas of the innermost bars may be exposed for short periods at spring low tides but otherwise the bars are submerged. Both bar systems are permanent features of the nearshore bathymetry. The bars maintain their form and position over periods of several months with only gradual changes and are not destroyed during storms. The morphology of the bars and their response to wave and current processes have been described in detail by Greenwood and Davidson-Arnott (1975).

The average beach slope off North Richibucto Beach is 0.5% from 0 to 10 m and 0.1% from 10 to 20 m. The beach and nearshore area is composed of sand-sized sediments (to a depth of 10 m) but some relict Pleistocene gravels and bedrock are found in deeper water (Kranck, 1967). Size characteristics of sediments associated with the inner and outer systems are given in Table 1.

During the summer months the predominant winds blow offshore from the southwest (Fig. 1). Important wave generation occurs under the influence of winds blowing from the northeast (the direction of maximum fetch) during the passage of storms which occur on the average two to three times a month. Mean wave height during the storms ranges from 1.0 to 2.0 m with periods of 4 to 8 seconds. Because of the effects of refraction by a large shoal area extending in a northwesterly direction from Prince Edward Island, and by further refraction at the entrance to the Strait, waves generated in the Gulf of St. Lawrence with periods greater than 8 seconds

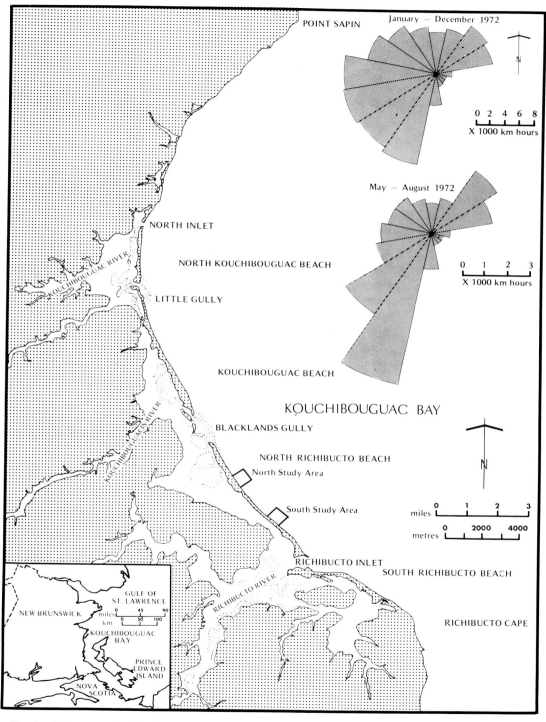

POINT SAPIN

January — December 1972

N

0 2 4 6 8
X 1000 km hours

NORTH INLET

NORTH KOUCHIBOUGUAC BEACH

May — August 1972

LITTLE GULLY

0 1 2 3
X 1000 km hours

KOUCHIBOUGUAC BEACH

KOUCHIBOUGUAC BAY

BLACKLANDS GULLY

N

NORTH RICHIBUCTO BEACH

North Study Area

South Study Area

miles 0 1 2 3

metres 0 2000 4000

RICHIBUCTO INLET

SOUTH RICHIBUCTO BEACH

RICHIBUCTO CAPE

GULF OF ST. LAWRENCE

NEW BRUNSWICK

miles 0 45 90

km 0 50 100

KOUCHIBOUGUAC BAY

PRINCE EDWARD ISLAND

NOVA SCOTIA

Fig. 1.—Index map showing location of study area. The wind diagrams summarize the product of average wind speed and duration for each direction.

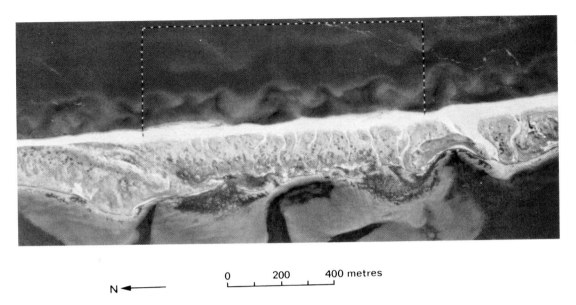

0   200   400 metres

N ◄────

FIG. 2.—Aerial photograph, taken July 18, 1973, illustrating inner and outer bar systems. The area outlined is illustrated in detail in Figure 3.

LINES BP   CZ
SURVEYED JUNE 3, 1973

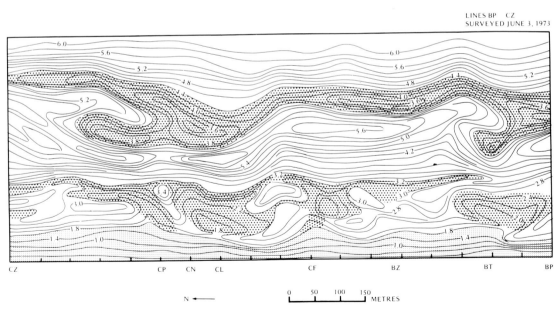

CZ   CP   CN   CL   CF   BZ   BT   BP

N ◄────   0   50   100   150
                 |____|____|____| METRES

FIG. 3.—Map of the North Study Area illustrating inner and outer bar systems. Survey carried out by echo sounding along lines 60 m apart, and by levelling in the inner system along lines 30 m apart. Depths are in meters below a fixed datum on the beach (0.5 m above high high water) and the contour interval is 20 cm. Light stipple denotes beach above low low water; heavy stipple outlines bar form.

TABLE 1.—MEAN AND RANGE OF SIZE-FREQUENCY STATISTICS OF SEDIMENTS FROM THE INNER AND OUTER BAR SYSTEMS

Location	Number of Samples	$m\phi$			$s\phi$		
		min.	av.	max.	min.	av.	max.
Inner bar-trough system	103	1.61 (0.33 mm)	2.25 (0.21 mm)	2.57 (0.17 mm)	0.24	0.39	0.69
Outer bar-trough system	62	0.83 (0.56 mm)	2.12 (0.23 mm)	2.83 (0.14 mm)	0.36	0.53	1.10

Note: $m\phi$ = phi mean; $s\phi$ = phi standard deviation: computed using the method of moments.

do not affect the Bay (McCann and Bryant, 1972). Waves from the easterly and southeasterly directions are of limited importance because of the low frequency of winds from this direction and the limited fetch length (maximum 35 km). Significant wave heights and periods for waves recorded over a two month interval during the 1973 field season are given in Table 2.

During storms the short, steep waves break as spilling breakers on the outer bar, reform in the trough and repeat the process in the inner system. Rip cell circulation patterns are well-defined in the inner system, where longshore currents flow in the troughs, and rip currents flow seaward not only in distinct channels but also across the center of crescentic bars. Measured current velocities in the trough frequently range from 20 to 40 cm/sec and rip current velocities may exceed 75 cm/sec. Current velocities in the outer system are less well documented but seem to be considerably lower than in the inner system. Maximum tidal range is 1.25 m and tidal currents seaward of the outer system rarely exceed 15 cm/sec.

FIELD METHODS

Observations and measurements of bedforms were carried out by diving, with and without SCUBA. However, during storms these were limited to the inner system because the difficulties

TABLE 2.—FREQUENCY DISTRIBUTION OF SIGNIFICANT WAVE HEIGHT AND PERIOD FOR A 2 MONTH INTERVAL, SUMMER 1973

Height (cm)	Period (seconds)					
	1–1.9	2–2.9	3–3.9	4–4.9	5–5.9	6–6.9
20–39	36	168	79	32	6	2
40–59	0	27	37	38	8	6
60–79	0	5	21	23	13	3
80–99	0	0	4	5	18	8
100–119	0	0	0	2	5	8
120–139	0	0	0	0	2	1
140–159	0	0	0	0	2	1
160–179	0	0	0	0	4	1
180–199	0	0	0	0	1	0

of operating a small boat under such conditions and poor underwater visibility made diving impossible.

Sedimentary structures were studied in resin peels made from cores taken with a box corer (modified after Klovan, 1964) with all coring being carried out under low-wave conditions. The corer is 45 cm high, 30 cm wide and 20 cm deep. Cores were obtained in shallow water by wading and in deep water by a SCUBA diver working from a small boat. In order to preserve the surface bedforms, an open metal frame 5 cm high was placed over the selected area and dyed sand spread over the surface (Newton, 1968).

Peels were obtained using the method of Burger and others (1969). After removing the peels, individual units within the core were sampled for size analysis. Approximately 90 cores were obtained from the area extending from the beach face to the seaward side of the outer bar. These form the basis for identification of the facies discussed in this paper.

FACIES MODEL FOR BARRED SHORELINES

Although the entire nearshore zone from the point at which waves first begin to shoal to the point of final wave collapse may constitute one environment associated with the zone of wave transformation, it is evident that distinct subenvironments can be identified associated with the varying bar topography. Each of these subenvironments has distinct bedforms and sequence of sedimentary structures; five subfacies can be documented on the basis of sediment characteristics and are related closely to varying topography, wave and current characteristics. These facies have been termed in accord with the subenvironments they reflect: (1) seaward slope; (2) bar crest; (3) landward slope; (4) trough; and (5) rip channel. The first four recur where more than one bar is present while the last is confined to the inner system of bars, where distinct rip channels periodically breach the system. Each subfacies is characterized by a distinct assemblage of sedimentary structures which reflects shifts in bedform type with changes in water depth and wave transformation.

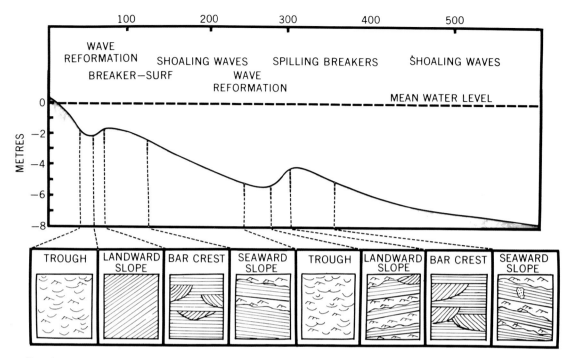

Fig. 4.—Facies model of nearshore barred topography illustrating characteristic sedimentary structures and wave transformation zones.

Bedforms on the seaward slope and crest of the bar are primarily controlled by wave oscillatory and translatory currents and those in the trough and rip channels by unidirectional longshore and rip currents. The landward slope comes under the influence of both types of currents, particularly in the outer system and near the center of crescentic inner bars.

Bedforms within the zones vary with differing wave characteristics. The zones on the bar crest and seaward slope in particular, shift their boundaries with variations in wave height and tidal stage. Most of the preserved sedimentary structures originate under high wave conditions when sediment transport rates are highest and strong currents are generated in the troughs.

The major sequence of structures and associated wave characteristics is illustrated in Figure 4. The following discussion of the subfacies will attempt to define the relationships more closely.

SEAWARD SLOPE FACIES

Bedforms on the seaward slope of the bar are generated by shoaling waves and consist of two principal types—ripples and plane bed. Under low current velocities at the bed, ripples form with crests aligned roughly perpendicular to the direction of predominant wave advance. As current velocities increase, either toward the bar crest or with increasing wave height or period, the ripples are washed out to form a plane bed.

The seaward slope facies of both the inner and the outer system is characterized, therefore, by interbedded sets of small scale ripple cross-lamination which dips predominantly landward, and by seaward dipping, low angle, plane bedding (Fig. 5a, b and f). These may form composite bedsets (Campbell, 1967) of "plane-to-ripple" bedding.

In general, plane bed sets are more common than sets of ripple lamination in the seaward slope facies. This reflects not only the fairly shallow water depths, and thus relatively high current velocities, but also the low rates of sediment transport in ripples formed by oscillatory conditions. As a result only thin units of ripple lamination are preserved. Toward the bar crest the units of plane bed increase in importance and they may occupy almost the whole of the core (Fig. 6c). Where plane beds overly ripples, the contact is usually a sharp seaward dipping erosion surface whereas the transition from plane bed to ripples is usually more irregular. The thickness of both units tends to decrease seaward, again reflecting a decrease in the rate of sediment transport in deeper water.

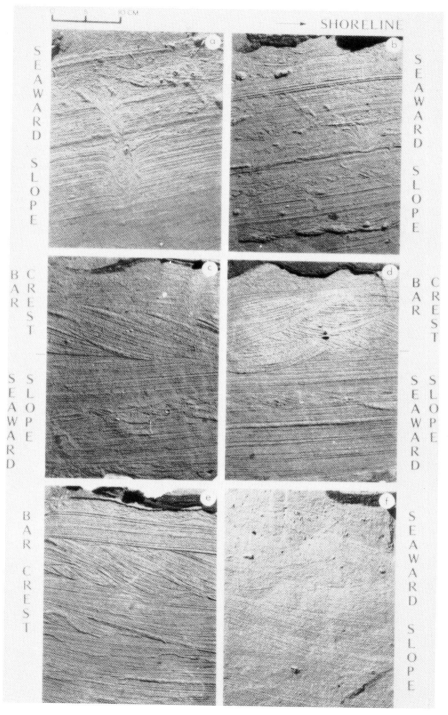

F<small>IG</small>. 5.—Box cores from outer bar illustrating characteristics of sedimentary structures: *a–e*, sequence of cores along one profile across seaward slope (a,b) and bar crest (c,d,e); *f*, seaward slope.

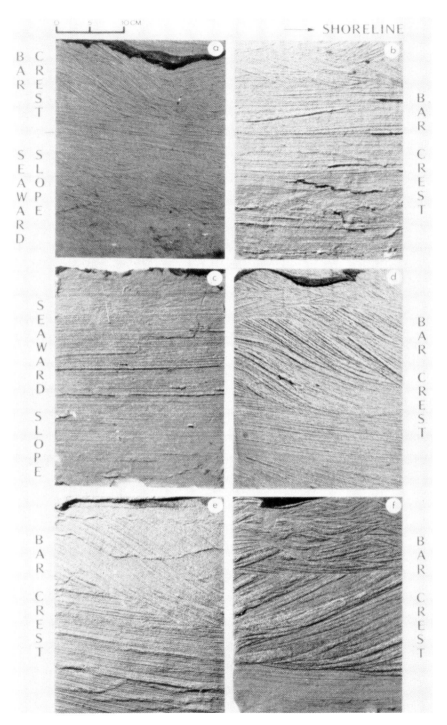

FIG. 6.—Box cores: *a*, seaward slope, inner bar; note that the apparent landward slope of the plane bedding is due to the deviation of the corer from the vertical; *b*, seaward slope, bar crest transition, inner bar; *c*, seaward slope, outer bar; *d*, crest, inner bar; *e*, crest, inner bar; *f*, crest, outer bar.

Sediments on the seaward slope in the outer system are finer than those in the inner system and grain size decreases seaward into deeper water in both systems. Sedimentary structures in the outer system are frequently disturbed by the activities of various marine organisms producing bioturbation structures (Figs. 5a–c, f and 6c) typical of the inner shoreface zone (Howard, 1972). Bioturbation decreases toward the bar crest because of greater and more frequent physical reworking. Bioturbation is rare in the inner system.

BAR CREST FACIES

During high wave conditions the bar crest is an area of shoaling and breaking waves. On the outer bar and most of the inner bars, waves form spilling rather than plunging breakers and the wave form is not completely destroyed across the bar. A true surf zone develops only on the shallowest inner bar and shoal areas. Bedform generation is controlled primarily by waves breaking on the bar, but is also influenced by the interaction of waves with currents flowing seaward across the crest.

The principal bedforms are plane beds, and lunate megaripples similar to those described by Clifton and others (1971). Small-scale oscillation ripples are generated during periods of low wave activity but, because of the low rates of sediment transport, sedimentary structures produced by their migration are usually obliterated during subsequent periods of high wave conditions, particularly in the inner system. The lunate megaripples develop both landward and seaward dipping slip faces on either side of the scour hollow (Fig. 6a). In areas of wave domination the megaripples migrate landward, producing landward dipping cross-stratified units. However, where a seaward flowing unidirectional current is superimposed on the wave orbital currents, the net migration of the lunate megaripples may be seaward. This produces seaward dipping cross-stratification. It occurs primarily in the center of crescentic bars, both in the inner and outer systems, where seaward flowing currents move across the bar crest, but where no topographically defined channel exists.

In the outer system, and on the deeper bars of the inner system, lunate megaripples develop over the entire bar crest. On the shoal areas and broad inner bars, however, a surf zone may develop which causes lunate megaripples to form primarily on the seaward side of the crest and plane bed predominates on the landward side.

The bar crest facies is therefore characterized by interbedded sets of subhorizontal plane beds, developed in somewhat coarser sediments than the seaward slope facies, and by cross-stratified

sets produced by the migration of lunate megaripples. Examples of these structures can be seen in the sequence of cores shown in Figures 5c–e and 6d, e.

Individual sets of plane beds may exceed 20 cm in thickness and have a considerable lateral extent. The dip varies from gently seaward to gently landward, and is controlled by the bar slope at the point of deposition. Landward or seaward migration of the crest may result in both landward and seaward dipping plane bed units being superimposed on one another.

The lunate megaripple cross-stratification can be as much as 15–20 cm in thickness (Fig. 6e) but more frequently is 5–10 cm thick. Each unit extends less than 1 m laterally along the bar and only a few meters normal to the shoreline. Individual laminae within the units frequently have long, curving toesets (Figs. 5e, 6d) but wedge shaped units are also common (Fig. 6e). Most of the megaripple cross-stratification indicates migration nearly perpendicular to the shoreline, but some units indicating oblique movement have been observed.

Seaward dipping units of cross-stratification occur near the center of crescentic bars in both the inner and the outer system (Figs. 6f and 7a, b). Many of the individual foreset laminae are lenticular (Fig. 6f), probably reflecting the pulsations in sediment supply together with lateral transport across the crescentic face under extremely turbulent flow conditions. Fluctuations in the relative strength of waves and seaward flowing currents, and thus in the location of the zone of interaction between them, results in complex interbedding of landward and seaward dipping sets (Fig. 7a).

When the depth of water over the inner bar crest is very shallow, such as during spring low tides, the movement of surf bores across the crest may produce a low accretionary ridge several tens of meters long with a landward slip face 10–20 cm high. It builds landward across the crest and produces a tabular unit of cross-bedding with considerable lateral extent (Davidson-Arnott and Greenwood, 1974).

A few shell fragments may be incorporated in the bar crest sediments but bioturbation structures are almost absent. The bar crest sands have a 'clean' appearance and are generally somewhat coarser and better sorted than those of the seaward slope (Table 3).

LANDWARD SLOPE FACIES

There are numerous differences between the landward slope facies of the inner and outer systems. In the inner system relatively large volumes of sediment are transported over the bar crest during periods of high wave activity and

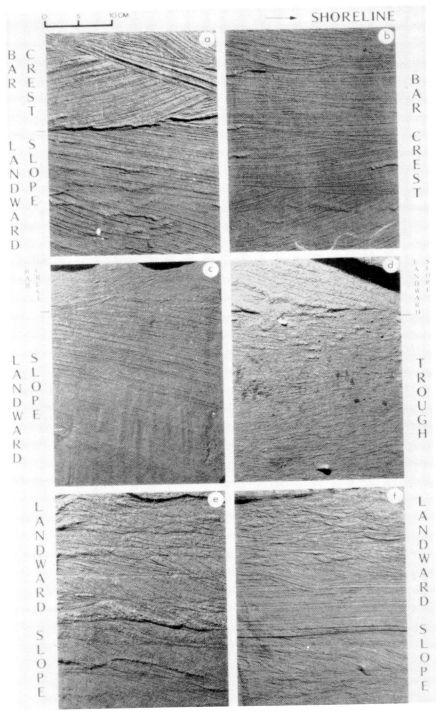

Fig. 7.—Box cores: *a*, crest, outer bar; *b*, crest, inner bar; *c*, landward slope, inner bar; *d*, landward slope—trough junction, inner bar; *e*, *f*, landward slope, outer bar.

TABLE 3.—MEAN AND RANGE OF SIZE-FREQUENCY STATISTICS OF SEDIMENTS FROM THE SEAWARD SLOPE, BAR CREST, LANDWARD SLOPE AND TROUGH FACIES OF THE OUTER SYSTEM. SAMPLES FROM THE LANDWARD SLOPE FACIES HAVE BEEN DIVIDED INTO TWO GROUPS IN ORDER TO SHOW THE CHARACTERISTICS OF SEDIMENTS ACCUMULATING AT THE FOOT OF THE SLOPE.

Facies	$m\phi$			$s\phi$			$sk\phi$		
	min.	av.	max.	min.	av.	max.	min.	av.	max.
Seaward slope	2.19	2.47 (0.18 mm)	2.83	0.36	0.48	0.62	−1.18	−0.59	−0.12
Bar crest	1.84	2.15 (0.23 mm)	2.44	0.39	0.51	0.56	−1.10	−0.15	+0.24
Landward slope	1.30	2.02 (0.25 mm)	2.51	0.39	0.47	0.62	−0.45	−0.09	+0.40
Foot of slope	0.83	1.27 (0.41 mm)	1.75	0.40	0.61	0.86	−0.61	+0.05	+0.42
Trough	1.28	1.92 (0.26 mm)	2.51	0.39	0.64	1.10	−0.87	−0.31	+0.42

are deposited by gravitational avalanching on the landward slope. This is because of the shallower water depths and greater incidence and intensity of wave breaking. The slope is maintained at a steep angle (up to 25°) by the strong longshore currents present in the landward trough which transport much of the sediment delivered over the crest alongshore and eventually offshore. As a result, the landward slope is characterized by plane bedding developed on a steep avalanche slope which produces medium scale planar cross-stratification in cross-section (Fig. 7c). This unit is nearly as thick as the bar is high (up to 1 m) and extends for the full length of the bar (Davidson-Arnott and Greenwood, 1974). The junction with the trough sediments is usually abrupt with little sign of toesets, probably because of transport of sediment by the longshore currents developed in the trough. This can be seen clearly in Figure 7d where the steeply dipping bar sands contrast with the darker trough sands characterized by small scale ripple lamination. The contact is not, however, erosional.

Wave breaking is generally confined to the crest of the bar in the outer system. Strong translatory currents are rarely present and rates of sediment transport are much lower. The landward slope is much more gentle (4.5° average) and there is no evidence of avalanche bedding. In cross-section the bar crest is gently curved and lacks the sharp landward break which is often present in the inner bars. There is a gradual reduction in the effects of oscillatory currents at the bed as water depth increases down the slope. This leads to a reversal of the sequence found on the seaward slope.

The upper part of the landward slope of the outer bar is thus characterized by units of low-angle, landward dipping plane beds and megaripple cross-bedding, the latter often filling the core (Fig. 7e). Toward the bottom of the slope the units of plane bed decrease in thickness, and are interbedded with units of small scale ripple cross-stratification (Fig. 7f).

Sediment size increases down the landward slope, which commonly contains a 10–15 m wide zone of coarse sand and gravel (Table 3) covered with large oscillation ripples. The junction with the trough sediments is usually distinct (Fig. 8a) and is often enhanced by the incorporation of organic material that accumulates at the foot of the bar, and distinctly darkens the trough sediments. In the deeper parts of the outer trough there may be considerable bioturbation.

In the inner system, near the center of crescentic bars, the steep foreset bedding may be interbedded with, or replaced entirely by, seaward dipping cross-stratification resulting from the migration of dunes or megaripples generated by seaward flowing rip currents (Fig. 8b). These units are rare in the outer system, probably because the currents there are much weaker than in the inner system.

TROUGH FACIES

The trough is a zone where longshore currents predominate and wave influence becomes of secondary importance. Under moderate or high wave conditions, waves lose much of their energy on the bar. When they move into the deep water of the trough, the oscillatory currents near the bed are very weak. Once the waves reform in the trough, they begin to shoal again and to control bedform generation.

The characteristic bedforms in the trough are current ripples, primarily oriented normal to the shore under the influence of the longshore currents. The range of orientations does vary somewhat depending on the effectiveness of wave action. The trough facies is thus characterized by small scale ripple lamination similar to that of the seaward slope facies but generally oriented at right angles to the shore (Figs. 7d, 8c, d).

After a storm, organic material such as kelp and eel grass may accumulate to a depth of several cm in the trough. When this is incorporated into the sediments it gives a distinct dark, mottled color which contrasts sharply with the bar sedi-

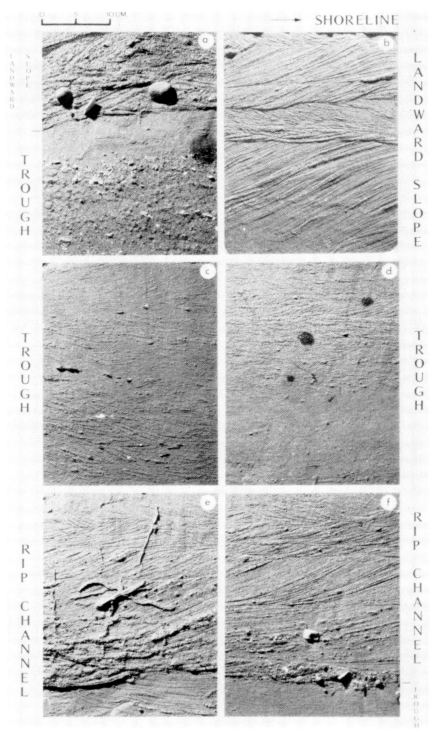

FIG. 8.—Box cores: *a*, landward slope—trough junction, outer bar; *b*, landward slope, inner crescentic bar; *c*, trough, outer bar; *d*, trough, inner bar; *e*, *f*, rip channel, inner system.

ments. Shell fragments which have been swept over the bar are also concentrated in the trough sediments. Although mean sediment size resembles that of the bar, sorting is much poorer and there is a distinct fine component which is not present in the bar sands.

RIP CHANNEL FACIES

The rip channel facies, by definition, is formed in and near the channels that dissect the inner bar system and through which the longshore currents in the trough flow seaward across the breaker line. As in the trough facies, the dominant process controlling bedform generation and movement is the unidirectional current, and wave oscillatory currents are of limited significance. The rip channel facies is distinguished from the trough facies by the presence of seaward dipping cross-bedded units up to 20 cm in thickness. These are produced by migration of megaripples under the influence of unidirectional currents. The crestal form of these bedforms varies between straight and catenary (Allen, 1968) rather than the lunate shape characteristic of the wave-formed megaripples. The distinction between wave-formed and current-formed megaripples in terms of their sedimentary structures is difficult. One common difference, however, is the form of the lower bounding surface to the sets of cross-bedding; the wave-formed lunate megaripples have a curved bounding surface while that of the unidirectional current form is planar. A similar characteristic for ripples has been noted by Boersma (1970).

Because the dominant current is unidirectional, when the longshore current velocities increase near and in the rip channel, the ripples are not washed out to form a plane bed but instead develop into dunes. Highest speeds are usually found in the neck of the rip channel where the volume of flow is greatest and the current is restricted by the sides of the channel. However, if the speeds are high enough, dune formation may extend into part of the trough.

The direction of flow of the rip current can vary considerably, particularly at the seaward side of the rip channel and thus the direction of maximum dip of the cross-bedded units also varies considerably. Examples of the rip channel facies can be seen in Figures 8e and f.

Rip currents transport large volumes of sediment seaward with much of the finer material travelling in suspension. When the rip current flow expands seaward of the breaker zone there is a rapid decrease in speed and much of the sediment is rapidly deposited. In most cases the sediments are probably immediately reworked by wave action. In some areas, however, there is evidence of the effectiveness of this seaward transport preserved in the sedimentary structures.

FIG. 9.—Box core from seaward slope, inner bar, marginal to rip channel illustrating sets of climbing ripple cross-stratification (noted by arrows).

One such example is shown in Figure 9, which shows climbing ripples resulting from the rapid deposition of sediment at the seaward edge of a rip channel by the seaward flowing currents.

Sediments in the rip channel facies are often coarser than those of the trough or bar, particularly near the seaward margin of the facies. Coarse material washed over the bar or moved seaward from the step area during a storm is transported along the bed by the longshore and rip current. It is deposited when the rip current velocity is checked on the seaward side of the rip channel. A fine component derived from sediment settling out of suspension as current speed decreases after a storm may also be present. As in the trough facies, the sediments may have a mottled color due to the presence of organic material.

BEACH FACE

Landward of the inner trough, the waves shoal and break again near the bottom of the swash slope. The general sequence of bedforms found on the seaward slope and bar crest is once more repeated with a complex zone of surf-swash interaction landward of the breaker zone and plane bed on the swash slope itself. Details of the bedforms and structures found in this area have been documented already by Clifton and others (1971) and Davidson-Arnott and Greenwood (1974) and need not be reiterated here.

The effects of the shifting of the bedform zones can be seen in Figure 6a in which the lower half of the core consists of structures of the seaward slope facies and the upper part is lunate megaripple cross-bedding formed at the edge of the bar crest facies. The core was taken across the slip face of an inactive megaripple and both landward and seaward dipping foresets are present. In Figure 6b, plane-to-ripple bed units of the seaward slope facies overlie the coarser plane bedding of a rip channel deposit. The latter has been buried by changes in the inner system topography resulting from the migration of a bar over the old rip channel.

FLOW REGIME CONCEPT AND BEDFORM GENERATION
UNDER WAVE-DOMINATED CONDITIONS

The flow regime concept, developed primarily by Simons and co-workers (Simons and others, 1961; Simons and Richardson, 1961, 1962; Simons and others, 1965) has found a wide application in sedimentology. The basis of the concept is that there exists a definite sequence of bedforms generated as bed current velocities are increased in an alluvial channel with cohesionless bed material. The flow conditions can be divided into a lower flow regime where the bedforms are not in phase with the water surface and an upper flow regime where they are in phase. These are separated by a transition zone where the bed surface is usually flat. The sequence of bedforms in the lower regime is dependent on the size of the material. For fine sand (<0.2 mm) the sequence is: *no movement—ripples—dunes—plane bed*. As grain diameter increases however, the zone of dunes expands and that of ripples decreases until, with coarse sand (1.0 mm or greater), ripples are no longer formed and the sequence becomes: *no movement—plane bed—dunes—plane bed*. Recently, Southard and Boguchwal (1973) have shown that there is a transitional area between the two sequences in which the succession of bedforms is more complex: *no movement—ripples—plane bed—dunes—upper flat bed*.

The usefulness of the flow regime concept in the examination of sedimentary structures lies in the information it can provide on flow and sediment transport conditions. It has been shown by Southard (1971) that if conditions such as sediment density, fluid density and viscosity are held constant, the bed configuration can be described by an unique combination of sediment size, flow velocity and depth of flow. Because, the size and density of sediment composing the structures can be measured, useful information on depth of flow and flow velocity can then be derived by comparison with measured values. The rate of sediment transport increases from the lower towards the upper flow regime and thus identification of the bedform within the flow regime sequence can also provide a rough estimate of sediment transport rates.

The only field application of the flow regime concept to bedforms and structures produced by wave action appears to be that of Clifton and others (1971) and Clifton herein. In the initial study of bedforms and structures in the high energy nearshore along a non-barred coastline, Clifton and others recognized a sequence of five facies in a landward direction from the zone of shoaling waves (Fig. 10). They suggested that the bedforms in these zones could be compared to those in alluvial channels and that the sequence from ripples through lunate megaripples to plane bed, as the wave moved from deep water to the breaker and surf zones, was similar to that from ripples through dunes to plane bed under unidirectional flow. Thus, the zone of asymmetric ripples corresponds to the lower part of the lower flow regime, the lunate megaripples to the upper part of the lower flow regime and the plane bed to the transition zone.

The sequence of structures found on the seaward slope and bar crest facies of both the inner and outer systems in Kouchibouguac Bay does not appear to follow the same sequence as that described by Clifton and others (1971). Instead of the zone of lunate megaripples succeeding the asymmetric ripples, the ripples are succeeded first by plane bed and then by lunate megaripples. This is obviously in conflict with the sequence documented by Clifton and others (1971) and thus deserves further investigation. Landward of the zone of lunate megaripples in Kouchibouguac Bay the sequence is similar to that found in Oregon. In the outer system bar crest, the units of plane beds and cross-bedding are interbedded making identification of the sequence difficult. In the inner system, particularly on the broad shoal areas where a surf zone is developed, the lunate megaripples are succeeded landward by plane bed.

Results of early laboratory studies by Evans and Ingram (1943), Bagnold (1946), Manohar (1955), Kennedy and Falcon (1965), and more recent work using oscillatory flow tunnels by Carstens and others (1969) and Mogridge and Kamphuis (1972) indicate that under symmetric oscillatory flow conditions ripples are washed out to form plane bed as bed velocities and orbital diameters are increased (Figs. 11a, b). A sequence

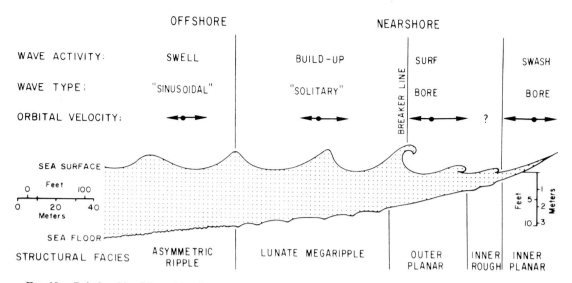

FIG. 10.—Relationship of depositional structures to wave type and activity on a non-barred, high energy coastline, (after Clifton *et al.*, 1971).

similar to that in Kouchibouguac Bay was observed by Inman (1957).

In the oscillatory tunnel experiments, bedform height is compared to the amplitude or diameter of horizontal water motion, which is the most convenient parameter to measure. It seems likely, however, that the most important factor controlling the transition from ripples to plane bed is the maximum orbital velocity at the bed. In Figure 11b the curves for bedform height can be extrapolated to zero bedform height as in Figure 11a. If this is done and all other factors are held constant, it can be seen that for any one orbital diameter, the progression from maximum bedform height to zero bedform height (plane bed) is accompanied by decreasing values for wave period. For a constant orbital diameter this must be accompanied by increasing maximum orbital velocities.

In order to determine whether the results of the laboratory studies in oscillatory flow tunnels were compatible with the observed field data, the results of Carstens and others were used to predict the critical orbital diameter at the bed needed to produce plane bed conditions on the seaward slope of the outer bar. For a wave period of 6.0 seconds and wave heights ranging from 1.0 to 2.0 m (typical of storm waves in the bay) the critical orbital diameter (110 cm) occurs in water depths ranging from 5.2 to 8.7 m assuming a sediment diameter of 0.2 mm. Thus, during a storm, plane bed conditions would be expected to occur for part of the time over the whole of

the seaward slope of the outer bar, with ripples occurring during lower wave heights.

Both the observed sequence in Kouchibouguac Bay and that reported from oscillatory flow tunnel experiments indicate that under symmetric oscillatory flow (Clifton, this volume) the sequence corresponding to the lower flow regime for unidirectional flow is: *no motion—ripples— plane bed.*

The problem then arises of accounting for the zones of lunate megaripples and plane bed found in the breaker and surf zones in Oregon (Clifton and others, 1971) and on the bar crest in Kouchibouguac Bay. Although they occur in shallower water and under higher current velocities than the lower flow regime sequence previously defined, it seems unlikely that the lunate megaripples and plane bed form part of the same sequence. If this were the case they would correspond to the upper flow regime and it is difficult to conceive of conditions under wave action corresponding to the upper flow regime under unidirectional flow. Clifton and others (1971) found that the zone of lunate megaripples coincided with the zone of wave transformation where there was a rapid increase in the landward asymmetry of the orbital velocities at the bed. On this basis they distinguished between the offshore area where orbital velocities are near symmetrical and the nearshore area where they are highly asymmetric landward. It is probable, therefore, that the lunate megaripples result from this change in flow conditions and are not part of the sequence

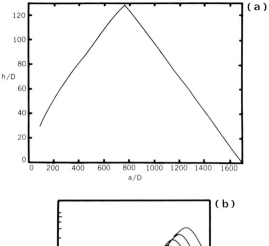

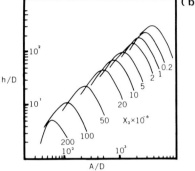

Fig. 11.—*a*, Dimensionless bedform amplitude versus dimensionless orbital amplitude (simplified after Carstens *et al.*, 1971); *b*, dimensionless bedform amplitude versus dimensionless orbital diameter (after Mogridge and Kamphuis, 1972): h = bedform height; D = grain median diameter; a = orbital amplitude; A = orbital diameter (2a); $X_2 = \rho D / \gamma_s T^2$ where ρ = fluid density; γ_s = submerged unit weight; T = period.

generated under nearly equal oscillatory currents. Additional support for this lies in the fact that lunate megaripples are also found occasionally in the lower swash zone (Clifton and others, 1971; Davidson-Arnott and Greenwood, 1974) which is also an area of strong translational currents. As suggested by Clifton and others, the lunate megaripples correspond to dunes, or the upper part of the lower flow regime, and the plane bed in the surf zone corresponds to the transition zone or lower part of the upper flow regime.

It seems, therefore, that there are two distinct flow regime sequences for bedforms in areas of wave domination: (1) a symmetric oscillatory flow regime controlled by near-symmetric oscillatory currents; and (2) a nearshore or asymmetric oscillatory flow regime controlled by highly asymmetric oscillatory and translational currents. In the offshore zone the sequence of bedforms

developed in response to increasing orbital diameter and maximum orbital velocities is: *no movement—ripples—plane bed*. The nearshore sequence, controlled by increasing shoreward asymmetry and bed current velocity is: *no movement—ripples—lunate megaripples—plane bed*.

The actual sequence of bedforms from the offshore zone to the breaker zone will depend on the maximum velocities in the area of change from the symmetric oscillatory flow regime to the asymmetric oscillatory flow regime. The results of Mogridge and Kamphuis (1972) indicate that as wave period increases the initiation of plane bed occurs at greater wave orbital diameters and ripples persist into shallower water (Fig. 11b). With steep, short period waves, bed current velocities high enough to generate plane bed may occur before rapid wave transformation results in the transition to bedforms dominated by highly asymmetric flow. In this case, the sequence of bedforms in a landward direction would probably be: *ripples—plane bed (symmetric flow)—plane bed (asymmetric flow)*. Under long period waves, however, the transition may occur before velocities high enough to generate a plane bed are reached. In this case, the symmetric ripples would be succeeded by asymmetric ripples and by lunate megaripples, producing a sequence: *ripples (symmetric flow)—ripples (asymmetric flow)—lunate megaripples—plane bed (asymmetric flow)*.

The structural sequence observed in Kouchibouguac Bay (ripples—plane bed on seaward slope; lunate megaripples—plane bed on the crest) could, therefore, be achieved either by: (1) the superposition of the two observed sequences, the former produced by very high short period wave conditions during the height of a storm and the latter by lower, longer period waves as the storm abates; or (2) a critical combination of increasing grain size toward the bar crest and wave transformation resulting in a spatially contiguous bedform sequence of: ripples (symmetric)—plane bed (symmetric)—lunate megaripples (asymmetric)—plane bed (asymmetric). This would then provide an explanation for the differences in the sequence observed by Clifton and others and that observed in Kouchibouguac Bay. A more detailed theoretical consideration of the relationships of bedform type to flow conditions and grain size is given by Clifton (this volume).

The application of the flow regime concept in the nearshore area is made even more complex by the presence of a third flow regime sequence, dominated by unidirectional longshore and rip currents, and by the interaction between unidirectional and oscillatory currents. The sequence found under unidirectional currents in the nearshore appears to be similar to that for flow in a stream channel: *no movement—ripples—*

SYMMETRIC OSCILLATORY FLOW
NO MOVEMENT — RIPPLES — PLANE BED

ASYMMETRIC OSCILLATORY FLOW
NO MOVEMENT — RIPPLES — LUNATE MEGARIPPLES — PLANE BED

UNIDIRECTIONAL FLOW
NO MOVEMENT — RIPPLES — MEGARIPPLES — PLANE BED

FIG. 12.—Suggested flow regime sequences in the nearshore area.

megaripples—plane bed.

A further complicating factor is that, although each flow regime sequence is associated with increasing bed velocities, rates of sediment transport vary considerably between similar bedforms in each flow regime. Thus, under symmetric oscillatory flow conditions, there is little or no net sediment transport even with a plane bed, and net rates of transport seaward of the zone of rapid wave transformation are low. Rates of sediment transport are highest in the unidirectional currents where sediment is being transported continuously in one direction, and are intermediate between the two under highly asymmetric or translatory flow because of the occurrence of zero or seaward flow for part of the time.

In conclusion, bedforms in the nearshore area are controlled by three different types of flow conditions, each of which produces a distinct flow regime sequence of bedforms in response to increasing bed velocities (Fig. 12). In the examination of sedimentary structures, care must be taken, therefore, to determine the type of flow under which the structure was formed, particularly in connection with the interpretation of energy levels and rates of sediment transport. Because of the difficulty of distinguishing flow conditions from the individual sedimentary structures, identification of flow conditions probably necessitates identification of the facies type first.

DISCUSSION

The study of bedforms and structures in the barred nearshore environment serves several useful functions. In the first place it provides basic information on the sedimentological characteristics of a depositional environment that has not previously been studied intensely. Also the analysis of bedforms and structures found in each subfacies provides an indication of flow conditions and the direction and rate of sediment transport which control bar dynamics. Further, the subfacies relationships provide a modern analogue for the identification of nearshore barred environments in ancient sedimentary sequences.

In the absence of detailed observations on bedforms under all conditions, the structures provide useful information on bed conditions in the different topographic zones, particularly on

the levels and directions of sediment transport and also differences between inner and outer systems. The structures indicate differences between the two systems in terms of sediment transport over the seaward slope, bar crest and landward slope. Spilling breakers on the outer bar fail to produce large scale surf bores characteristic of the more complete wave collapse in the inner system. The landward slope of the inner bar is therefore characterized by a steep avalanche slip face whereas a lower angle slope in the outer system reflects continual sediment transport by oscillatory wave currents.

The structures also give an indication of the predominant direction of sediment transport. In the trough areas the structures indicate that longshore sediment transport takes place under the influence of longshore currents. In general the seaward slope of the bar (both inner and outer) is an area of landward sediment transport by waves. The existence of seaward dipping crossbedded units in both the inner and outer landward slope and/or bar crest facies of crescentic bars, however, shows that seaward transport of sediment does occur across the bar. This could provide a possible mechanism to explain the maintenance of an equilibrium position and explain why crescentic bars do not migrate continuously shoreward. In contrast, the straight inner bars have structures suggesting continual landward transport over a sharp crest and deposition on an advancing bar front by gravitational slumping. Greenwood and Davidson-Arnott (1975) have shown that straight inner bars do migrate landward but structures in the trough and rip channel facies indicate a seaward flow of sediment which is of significantly higher magnitude than in the outer bar. This acts to reduce the rate of landward migration and trough infilling. Regarding the stability of the crescentic bars, it is interesting to note that the zone of seaward-migrating megaripples is found in the deeper crescent area and not on the shallower shoal or lower areas where landward dipping units occur almost without exception. If this is indeed the mechanism of maintaining equilibrium, then similar facies characteristics should occur in straight bars which also maintain an equilibrium position. Hunter and others (1972), however, note only plane bedding or small scale ripple cross-lamination in the bar crests of straight parallel bars along Padre Island, Texas.

The increasing asymmetry of flow produced by wave shoaling followed by energy loss through spilling breakers suggests that the outer bar is indeed maintained by increasing sediment transport to the point of breaking after which there is a gradual decrease as the wave reforms and water deepens. In contrast the straight inner bar is formed in a distinct surf zone of horizontal translatory currents resulting from greater energy loss on breaking.

The seaward slope facies with composite bedsets of "plane-to-ripple" bedding provides an indicator of storm-induced sedimentation. The sharp erosional contact between successive units is provided by truncation of the ripple cross-bedding. In some seaward slope sequences the total unit is composed of plane bedding suggesting regular removal of the low energy ripple bedding by each storm.

The nearshore bars of Kouchibouguac Bay illustrate certain geometrical and structural characteristics which may provide environmental indices for the interpretation of ancient sandstone bodies. To date no clearly identified wave-formed bars have been documented in the rock record, although "marine bars" have been cited by Masters (1967), Van der Lingen and Andrews (1968), Weidie (1968), Clifton (1972), Hobday and Reading (1972), Brenner and Davies (1973), Exum (1973) and Stricklin and Smith (1973). Although the preservation potential of sediments in the bar form is not very high because the bar itself tends to migrate in response to changing water levels (Saylor and Hands, 1970), preservation is possible under a prograding shoreline situation. The units most likely to be preserved are the lowermost part of the bar slope facies (landward and seaward), together with the trough and rip channel facies. These will be buried under beach face sediment as the progradation proceeds. The bar systems are maintained by sediment transport under storm wave conditions, particularly the outer bar. It is becoming increasingly apparent that the results of higher energy events are the ones most likely to be preserved.

Identification of wave-formed bars in a sedimentary sequence will allow specific environmental interpretations because the bars are only found under restricted, offshore slope, bed material, tidal and wave conditions. It is hoped that the presentation of this detailed facies model for a nearshore barred shoreline will aid in identifying ancient examples.

ACKNOWLEDGEMENTS

This study forms part of a larger project on coastal sedimentation supported by a grant to Greenwood from the National Research Council of Canada (NRCA7956). The basis for the paper forms a part of a doctoral dissertation written by the senior author, which was further supported by a National Research Council of Canada Postgraduate Fellowship. Thanks go to P. Hale, P. Keay and D. McGillivray for their assistance in the field and to P. Hale for photographs of cores from his B.Sc. Research Paper. The staff of the Academic and Electronic workshops helped to design and construct the equipment used in coring and wave and current measurement. We would like to thank the staff of the Graphics and Photography Department at Scarborough College for producing the diagrams and particularly David Harford for the photographs of the peels.

Drs. H. E. Clifton, R. A. Davis Jr. and G. V. Middleton read drafts of the manuscript and we are grateful to them for their constructive criticism. We further benefitted from discussions with Dr. A. V. Jopling. However, the results and interpretations presented are solely the responsibility of the authors.

REFERENCES

ALLEN, J. R. L., 1968. Current ripples: North-Holland Pub. Co., Amsterdam, 433 p.

ANDREWS, P. B., AND VAN DER LINGEN, G. J., 1969, Environmentally significant sedimentological characteristics of beach sands: New Zealand Jour. Geol. and Geophys., v. 12, p. 119–137.

BAGNOLD, R. A., 1946, Motion of waves in shallow water—interaction between waves and sand bottoms: Royal Soc. London Proc., Ser. A, v. 187, p. 1–15.

BOERSMA, J. R., 1970, Distinguishing features of wave-ripple cross-stratification and morphology: Ph.D. Thesis, Univ. Utrecht, 65 p.

BRENNER, R. L., AND DAVIES, D. K., 1973, Storm-generated coquinoid sandstone: Genesis of high-energy marine sediments from the Upper Jurassic of Wyoming and Montana: Geol. Soc. America Bull., v. 84, p. 1685–1698.

BRYANT, E. A., AND MCCANN, S. B., 1973, Long and short term changes in the barrier islands of Kouchibouguac Bay, southern Gulf of St. Lawrence: Canadian Jour. Earth Sci., v. 10, p. 1582–1590.

BURGER, J. A., KLEIN, G. D., AND SANDERS, J. E., 1969, A field technique for making epoxy relief-peels in sandy sediments saturated with salt-water: Jour. Sed. Petrology, v. 39, p. 338–341.

CAMPBELL, C. V., 1967, Lamina, laminaset, bed and bedset: Sedimentology, v. 8, p. 7–26.

CARSTENS, M. R., NEILSON, F. M., AND ALTINBILEK, H. D., 1969, Bed forms generated in the laboratory under an oscillatory flow: Analytical and experimental study: U.S. Army, Corps of Engineers, Coastal Eng. Res. Cent. Tech. Memo. 28, 39 p.

CLIFTON, H. E., 1969, Beach lamination—Nature and origin: Marine Geol., v. 7, p. 553–559.

———, 1972, Miocene marine to nonmarine transition in southern coast ranges of California [abs.]: Am. Assoc. Petroleum Geologists Bull., v. 56, p. 609.

———, HUNTER, R. E., AND PHILLIPS, R. L., 1971, Depositional structures and processes in the non-barred high energy nearshore: Jour. Sed. Petrology, v. 41, p. 651–670.

COOK, D. O., 1969, Sand transport by shoaling waves: Ph.D. Dissertation, Univ. Southern California, 148 p.

DAVIDSON-ARNOTT, R. G. D., 1971, An investigation of patterns of sediment size and sorting in the beach and nearshore area, Kouchibouguac Bay, New Brunswick: M. A. Thesis, Univ. Toronto, 109 p.

——, AND GREENWOOD, B., 1974, Bedforms and structures associated with bar topography in the shallow-water wave environment, Kouchibouguac Bay, New Brunswick, Canada: Jour. Sed. Petrology, v. 44, p. 698–704.

DAVIS, R. A., JR., 1965, Under water study of ripples, southeastern Lake Michigan: Jour. Sed. Petrology, v. 35, p. 857–866.

——, FOX, W. T., HAYES, M. O., AND BOOTHROYD, J. C., 1972, Comparison of ridge and runnel systems in tidal and non-tidal environments: Jour. Sed. Petrology, v. 42, p. 413–421.

EMERY, K. O., AND STEVENSON, R. E., 1950, Laminated beach sand: Jour. Sed. Petrology, v. 20, p. 220–223.

EVANS, O. F., 1941, The classification of wave-formed ripple marks: Jour. Sed. Petrology, v. 11, p. 37–41.

——, AND INGRAM, R. L., 1943, An experimental study of the influence of grain size on oscillation ripple marks: Jour. Sed. Petrology, v. 13, p. 117–120.

EXUM, F. A., 1973, Lithologic gradients in a marine bar, Cadeville Sand, Calhoun Field, Louisiana: Am. Assoc. Petroleum Geologists Bull., v. 57, p. 301–320.

GREENWOOD, B., AND DAVIDSON-ARNOTT, R. G. D., 1975, Marine bars and nearshore sedimentary processes, Kouchibouguac Bay, New Brunswick, Canada: In J. R. Hails and A. Carr (eds.), Nearshore sediment dynamics and sedimentation: John Wiley and Sons, New York, p. 123–150.

HAYES, M. O., (ED.), 1969, Coastal environments, northeastern Massachusetts and New Hampshire: Univ. Massachusetts, Dep. Geol. Coastal Res. Group Contr. 1, 462 p.

HOBDAY, D. K., AND READING, H. G., 1972, Fairweather versus storm processes in shallow marine sand bar sequences in late Precambrian of Finnmark, north Norway: Jour. Sed. Petrology, v. 42, p. 318–324.

HOWARD, J. D., 1972, Trace fossils as criteria for recognizing shorelines in stratigraphic record: In J. K. Rigby and W. K. Hamblin (eds.), Recognition of ancient sedimentary environments: Soc. Econ. Paleontologists and Mineralogists, Spec. Pub. 16, p. 215–225.

HUNTER, R. E., WATSON, R. L., HILL, G. W., AND DICKINSON, K. A., 1972, Modern depositional environments and processes, northern and central Padre Island, Texas: Gulf Coast Assoc. Geol. Socs., Padre Island Natl. Seashore Field Guide, p. 1–27.

INMAN, D. L., 1957, Wave generated ripples in nearshore sands: U.S. Army Corps of Engineers, Beach Erosion Board Tech. Memo. 100, 42 p.

KENNEDY, J. F., AND FALCON, M., 1965, Wave generated sediment ripples: Massachusetts Inst. Technology, Hydrodynamics Lab. Rep. 86, 55 p.

KLOVAN, J. E., 1964, Box-type sediment-coring device: Jour. Sed. Petrology, v. 34, p. 185–189.

KRANCK, K., 1967, Bedrock and sediments of Kouchibouguac Bay, New Brunswick: Fisheries Res. Board of Canada Jour., v. 24, p. 2242–2265.

MANOHAR, M., 1955, Mechanics of bottom sediment movement due to wave action: U.S. Army Corps of Engineers, Beach Erosion Board Tech. Memo. 75, 121 p.

MASTERS, C. D., 1967, Use of sedimentary structures in determination of depositional environments, Mesaverde Formation, Williams Fork Mountains, Colorado: Am. Assoc. Petroleum Geologists Bull., v. 51, p. 2033–2043.

McCANN, S. B., AND BRYANT, E. A., 1972, Beach changes and wave conditions, New Brunswick: Am. Soc. Civil Engineers, Proc. 13th Conf. on Coastal Eng., p. 1293–1304.

McKEE, E. D., 1957, Primary structures in some recent sediments: Am. Assoc. Petroleum Geologists Bull., v. 41, p. 1704–1747.

MOGRIDGE, G. R., AND KAMPHUIS, J. W., 1972, Experiments on bed form generation by wave action: Am. Soc. Civil Engineers, Proc. 13th Conf. on Coastal Eng., p. 1123–1142.

NEWTON, R. S., 1968, Internal structure of wave-formed ripple marks in the nearshore zone: Sedimentology, v. 11, p. 275–292.

REINECK, H. E., 1963, Sedimentgefüge im Bereich der südlichen Nordsee: Senckenb. Naturforsch. Ges. Abh., v. 505, 138 p.

—— AND SINGH, I. B., 1971, Der Golf von Gaeta/Tyrrhenisches Meer: 3. Die Gefüge von Vorstrand- und Schelf-sedimenten. Senckenbergiana Maritima, v. 3, p. 185–201.

—— AND ——, 1973, Depositional sedimentary environments: Springer-Verlag, New York, 439 p.

RISK, M. J., 1967, Shallow water ripple marks in Lake Huron: M.S. Thesis, Univ. Western Ontario.

SAYLOR, J. H., AND HANDS, E. B., 1970, Properties of longshore bars in the Great Lakes: Am. Soc. Civil Engineers, Proc. 12th Conf. on Coastal Eng., p. 839–853.

SIMONS, D. B., AND RICHARDSON, E. V., 1961, Forms of bed roughness in alluvial channels: Am. Soc. Civil Engineers Proc., Jour. Hydraulics Div., HY3, p. 87–105.

—— AND ——, 1962, Resistance to flow in alluvial channels: Am. Soc. Civil Engineers. Trans., v. 127, p. 927–953.

——, ——, AND ALBERTSON, M. L., 1961, Flume studies using medium sand (0.45 mm): U.S. Geol. Survey, Water Supply Paper 1498-A, 76 p.

——, ——, AND NORDIN, C. F., 1965, Sedimentary structures generated by flow in alluvial channels: In G. V. Middleton (ed.), Primary sedimentary structures and their hydrodynamic interpretation: Soc. Econ. Paleontologists and Mineralogists, Spec. Pub. 12, p. 34–52.

SOUTHARD, J. B., 1972, Representation of bed configurations in depth-velocity-size diagram: Jour. Sed. Petrology, v. 41, p. 903–915.

—— AND BOGUCHWAL, L. A., 1973, Flume experiments on the transition from ripples to lower flat bed with increasing sand size: Jour. Sed. Petrology, v. 43, p. 1114–1121.

STRICKLIN, F. L., JR., AND SMITH, C. I., 1973, Environmental reconstruction of a carbonate beach complex: Cow Creek (Lower Cretaceous) Formation of central Texas: Geol. Soc. America Bull., v. 84, p. 1349–1368.

TANNER, W. F., 1959, Shallow water ripple marks varieties: Jour. Sed. Petrology, v. 30, p. 481–485.

——, 1963, Origin and maintenance of ripple marks: Sedimentology, v. 2, p. 307–311.

——, 1971, Numerical estimates of ancient waves, water depth and fetch: Sedimentology, v. 16, p. 71–88.

THOMPSON, W. Q., 1937, Original structures of beaches, bars and dunes: Geol. Soc. America Bull., v. 48, p. 723–751.

VAN DER LINGEN, G. J., AND ANDREWS, P. B., 1968, Grain size parameters and sedimentary structures of a last interglacial marine sand body near Westport, New Zealand: New Zealand Jour. Marine and Freshwater Res., v. 2, p. 447–471.

WEIDIE, A. E., 1968, Bar and barrier island sands: Gulf Coast Assoc. Geol. Socs. Trans., v. 18, p. 405–415.

Sedimentology (1979) **26**, 333–351

Mechanisms of berm development and resulting beach growth along a barrier spit complex

ALBERT C. HINE

University of North Carolina at Chapel Hill, Institute of Marine Sciences,
P.O. Drawer 809, Morehead City, N.C. 28557

ABSTRACT

Weekly topographic profile measurements across a southward migrating recurved-spit complex throughout a summer period have revealed three different mechanisms of berm development, each reflected by a distinctive sedimentary sequence. Each mechanism dominates berm widening along certain sections of the active spit with transition zones separating each one. Along the straight beach sections where a net longshore transport is well developed, sand accumulates at the distal high-tide swash mark during neap tide. These sandy accumulations are neap berms which are later redistributed over the main berm by swash occurring at spring high water. The main berm grows vertically and horizontally as a result. To the south, along the middle portion of the recurved spit, swash bars or ridge-and-runnel systems actively develop, migrate, and weld onto the established berms. This is the second method of berm widening and results from an excess of sand carried into this portion of the spit due to the steadily decreasing transport of the longshore current system. Berm-ridges develop along the southernmost portion of the active recurved spit and represent the third and most rapid form of beach progradation. Wide, broad swash bars build nearly up to the spring high tide level. At neap high tide, the swash cannot extend over this feature. Wave energy is expended on the seaward margin of the swash bar initially developing a low-angle beach face. Rapidly, this beach face steepens and a new berm (beach face and berm top) is developed on top of the swash bar. This berm structure still retains much of its swash bar or ridge appearance, hence the term 'berm-ridge'. Numerous trenches dug into the beach provide data to model the distribution of primary sedimentary structures in recurved spits. Berm-ridges are the most important features along rapidly accreting spits, and structures associated with these features are volumetrically the most significant. Berm-ridges also develop arcuate, vegetated ridges separated by low lying, marsh-infilled swales. These features are commonly seen within barrier islands and designate former inlets.

INTRODUCTION

The berm of a beach has long been understood to be a constructional, morphological feature resulting from the onshore transport of sediments (King, 1972 is a

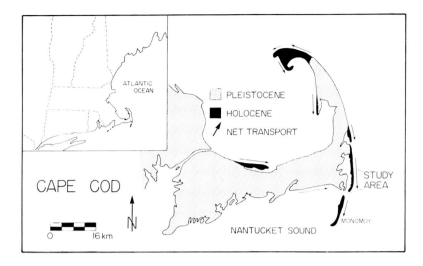

Fig. 1. Location of study area on Cape Cod, Mass. Note Holocene spit development from Pleistocene glacial deposits.

good summary reference). This feature is defined as a 'linear sand body parallel to the shore that occurs on the landward portion of the beach profile. It has a triangular cross-section with a horizontal to slightly landward-dipping top surface (berm top) and a more steeply dipping seaward surface (beach face). This definition incorporates the berm and beach face in Wiegel's (1953) classification' (Coastal Research Group, 1969, p. 455). The berm's topographic profile and general method of emplacement upon a flat, storm beach is also well known (King & Williams, 1949; Hayes, 1969; 1972; 1976; Hayes & Boothroyd, 1969; Davis *et al.*, 1972; Owens, 1977; Owens & Frobel, 1977; and Hine & Boothroyd, 1978). This study, however, demonstrates that berm development and resulting beach growth can occur by at least three different mechanisms, each found along distinct zones of a barrier spit, Nauset Beach, Cape Cod, Massachusetts (Fig. 1).

Each berm type also displays a distinct sequence of primary sedimentary structures revealed by trenches dug into the beach. These structures provide criteria for the recognition of ancient regressive coastal sequences. Berm development analysis also provides insight into the formation of arcuate beach ridges seen so commonly along modern barrier island systems.

GENERAL SETTING AND METHODS

Nauset Beach is a Holocene barrier spit system that has prograded south by recurved spit growth from a Pleistocene glacially-derived headland (Strahler, 1966). Studies of old charts (Goldsmith, 1972; Hine, 1972; 1975) illustrate a near uniform growth of 11 km from north to south during the 1875–1965 period. The southern tip of Nauset Beach is still an actively migrating recurved spit (Fig. 2) which now forms an updrift-offset (Hayes, Goldsmith & Hobbs, 1970) tidal inlet along with Monomoy

Island located on the opposite side. The intertidal portion of the active spit supports flood-oriented sand waves indicating that it lies within the influence of the inlet's northern marginal flood channel (Hayes *et al.*, 1973; Hine, 1975). A few hundred metres to the north of this zone, however, wave activity is the dominant sediment transporting agent.

Two of the beach profiling stations are located close together on the active recurved spit (Fig. 2). The remaining two stations are located further up the barrier spit along straight sections of the beach. Topographic surveying was conducted weekly during the summertime using the Emery (1961) levelling technique. Numerous trenches were dug along the profiles, perpendicular to the beach trend, to study sedimentary structures.

During the survey period (10 June–5 October 1968) no storm waves or large swells occurred so that the beach was in a nearly continuous constructional state. Wave parameters unfortunately were not measured regularly so quantitative relationships between berm type and wave activity could not be established. The field measurements and observations indicate that 40–80 cm high waves were most common with wave periods ranging from 4 to 7 s. Nearby wave gauge data (U.S. Army Corps of Engineers, 1968) and calculated wave energy values show a dominant ENE component which generates the southerly net longshore sand transport (Fig. 3).

Fig. 2. Aerial photo illustrating Nauset Beach, the recurved spit, Chatham Harbour Inlet Monomoy Island, and the upper portions of Cape Cod. Beach profile locations are shown.

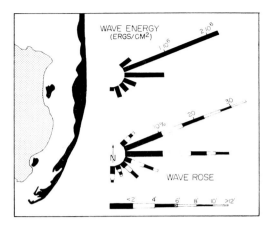

Fig. 3. Wave rose data showing annual wave height, frequency, and direction (U.S. Army Corps of Engineers, 1968). Wave energy values calculated from wave height and frequency data. Dominant wave energy approach is from ENE which sets up the net southerly longshore transport system.

The tides are semidiurnal with little observed diurnal inequality (approximately 15 cm; U.S. Army Corps of Engineers, 1968, P-C-4). The ocean mean tidal range is 210 cm. The maximum difference in tidal range between spring and neap tides is 70 cm (U.S. Dept of Commerce, 1968).

BEACH GROWTH

Neap-berm development

This significant difference in tidal range between spring and neap conditions causes beach growth by the development of small berms on the beach face during spring tide. This occurred most frequently on straight sections of the beach (profile NB-0, Figs 2 and 4).

During the long summer period of fair-weather wave conditions, swash-uprush from waves breaking at neap high tide did not overtop the berm crest. As a result, a small accumulation of sand and gravel developed on the beach face of the berm along the high-tide swash line. This secondary berm with its crest near the neap high-water mark formed within a few tidal cycles and is known as a neap berm (Coastal Research Group, 1969, p. 455). As the tidal range increased with the approach of spring tide, swash-uprush reached higher and higher onto the beach face transporting neap-berm sediments upwards as well. Eventually, swash over-topped the main-berm crest sweeping these sediments onto the main-berm top. As a result, the main berm grew laterally and vertically.

The profile sequence at NB-0 (Fig. 4) shows three periods of neap-berm development (4 July, 18 July, and 15 August) and subsequent main-berm widening (12 July, 28 July, and 29 August). The main berm widened approximately 8 m by the end of summer.

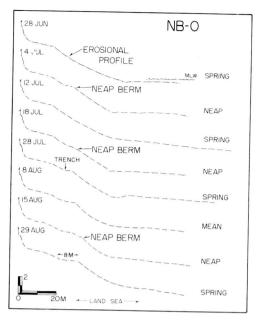

Fig. 4. NB-0 profiles. Profile station is located along straight section of beach (Fig. 2). Berm widening is primarily by alternate development of neap berms (4, 18 July, 15 August) and the subsequent redeposition of this feature by the next spring tides.

Sedimentary structures

The primary structure within a neap berm is essentially conformable, plane, beach-face stratification showing a small bulge or perturbation in the stratification continuity at the point of the neap-berm crest. The neap berms are not preserved regularly as the spring high-tide swash process effectively redistributes the sand along the beach face and up onto the main-berm top. This widened main berm is shown in Fig. 5 where buried, seaward dipping (8–12°), plane beach-face stratification grades upward into near horizontal berm-top plane stratification. The original erosional surface (beach face of 28 June) and truncated berm-top stratification of an earlier berm are clearly evident (Fig. 5).

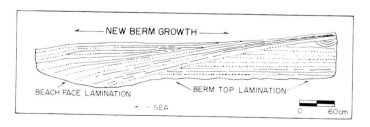

Fig. 5. Line drawing of a trench dug at the NB-0 profile, 28 July (see Fig. 4). Trench clearly showed the buried 28 June beach-face unconformity which truncates older berm-top stratification. Berm widening since 28 June is shown by beach-face stratification grading upward into berm-top stratification. The berm has widened approximately 3 m by this time in the sequence.

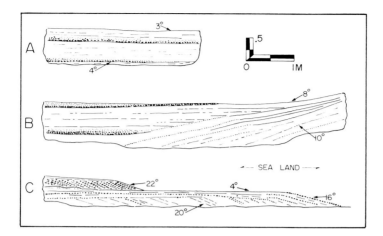

Fig. 6(A). Line drawing from trench cut into berm-top stratification. Two sequences are shown. **(B)** Line drawing from trench cut into berm top and buried beach face stratification illustrates one complete sequence and coarse-grained base of new sequence. **(C)** Line drawing of small berm-ridge. When large amounts of coarse sand or gravel over-top the berm crest, a landward migrating slipface forms which develops steeply dipping planar cross-stratification. This is located high in the berm-top structure.

During neap high tide, gravel from the updrift Pleistocene glacial deposits and marine carbonate debris accumulate along the neap berm and form a line of coarse sediments delineating the distal swash-uprush limit. As the tidal range increases with the approach of spring tide, this coarse sediment is the initial material to be carried over the berm crest and onto the berm top. When maximum spring tide conditions are reached, greater quantities of finer-grained sands are transported over the berm crest burying this initial coarse deposit. Berm-top sedimentation ceases after a certain point when swash-uprush can no longer over-top the berm crest as neap tide approaches. At this time, the cycle recommences as coarse sediment again accumulates on the upper beach face. The resulting structure within the berm is a stacked, rhythmic sequence of thin, coarse-grained, near-horizontal plane stratification covered by and sometimes grading into a thicker zone of fine-grained plane stratification (Fig. 6A,B,C). Trenches cut into other portions of the beach show that up to five distinct sequences are present each with thicknesses of 30–60 cm.

Ridge-and-runnel development

The second process of berm development results from landward-migrating intertidal swash bars welding onto the beach face. This is best illustrated in the profile sequence at NB-1 and NB-2 (Figs 2, 7 and 8). This ridge-and-runnel topography is perhaps the most widely recognized and described constructional beach profile (Cornish, 1898; Gresswell, 1937; 1953; King & Williams, 1949; Hayes & Boothroyd, 1969; Boothroyd, 1969; King, 1972; Sonu, 1968; Hine, 1972; Hayes, 1972; Finley, 1975; Stephen *et al.,* 1975; Owens, 1977; Owens & Frobel, 1977) and commonly occurs during post-storm periods when sand, carried seaward during storm conditions,

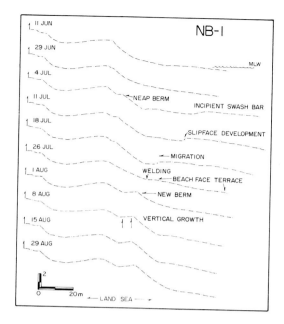

Fig. 7. NB-1 profiles. This station is located near the upper portion of the active recurved spit. This sequence illustrates berm widening by ridge-and-runnel or swash-bar development and subsequent welding of this feature onto the beach face. The low gradient, beach-face terrace feature forms during initial welding (26 July).

rapidly returns to the beach. Intertidal swash-bar development is also common along active recurved spit beaches where the terminus of the longshore transport system is located.

The NB-1 profile is located approximately 3 km north of the active recurved spit in a zone of consistent swash-bar development (Figs 9A,B,C). The profiles from 4 July to 8 August illustrate the following sequence (Fig. 7): (a) initial swash-bar development on the low-tide terrace (4 July); (b) slipface development and migration (11 and 18 July); (c) welding onto beach face creating a flatter profile (26 July); (d) new berm development (1 August); (e) vertical growth of new berm (8 August).

Two significant changes in the beach profile occur during this sequence. First, as the swash-bar slipface begins to weld onto the beach face, its migration rate slows and height decreases. Mid-tide swash transports sand from the swash bar onto the lower beach face. The swash bar loses its distinct form very rapidly (within one or two tidal cycles) as it welds onto the lower beach face. The resulting feature is a beach-face terrace (26 July profile, Fig. 7) which is a broad, gently sloping surface that connects the middle to upper portion of the normal beach face with some point on the low-tide terrace (Coastal Research Group, 1969, p. 456).

Secondly, this new profile being much flatter than the previously established profile is now out of equilibrium with the existing grain size–wave energy relationships which control profile steepness (King, 1972, Chapter 12). Within several tidal cycles, a new steeper beach face is established seaward of the older beach face thus creating the new berm morphology (1 August, Fig. 7).

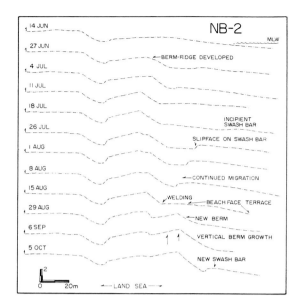

Fig. 8. NB-2 profiles. This station is located along the upper to middle portion of the active spit. Sequence begins with development of a berm-ridge indicative of greater onshore movement of sediment than at NB-1. This sequence also shows more active swash-bar development and subsequent berm widening than NB-1. Berm has widened approximately 68 m by end of field season as a result of these two mechanisms.

The profiles at NB-2, from 18 July to 5 October, also show the same sequence as NB-1. Swash bars are larger, more numerous, and migrate more rapidly at this site than at NB-1. Consequently, newly formed berms are much wider (22 m at NB-2 *v.* 9 m at NB-1).

Sedimentary structures

Sedimentary structures developed by migrating ridge-and-runnel systems and resulting berms have been well described and illustrated in Boothroyd, 1969; Hayes & Boothroyd, 1969; Hayes, Anan & Bozeman, 1969; and Hayes, 1972. Trenches dug into these ridges or swash bars did reveal the typical high angle (21–24°) landward-oriented planar cross-stratification that results from slipface migration. However, thin, planar stratification of lower dip angle (10–14°) consisting of coarser sands occurred at frequent, regular intervals laterally along a trench cross-section (Fig. 10). Observations during a falling tide revealed that the swash-bar slipface is eroded by small waves generated on water temporarily ponded within the runnel. The slipface thus becomes a small, lower-angle beach face with slightly coarser sands accumulating on this surface. During the next rising tide, the slipface reactivates and new, steeper, planar stratification buries this lower angle erosional surface. The lower angle, cross-stratification represents the period of subaerial exposure or low water while the intervening higher angle cross-laminations represent the period of migration during higher water. Each lower angle cross-lamination is a reactivation surface similar to

Fig. 9(A). Aerial photo of beach zone dominated by swash-bar development. Photo taken 3 July. **(B)** Ground photo taken at 18 July (NB-1, Fig. 7) showing active swash bar near lower beach face. **(C)** Aerial photo of NB-1 profile taken 19 July showing same swash bar shown in Fig. 9(B).

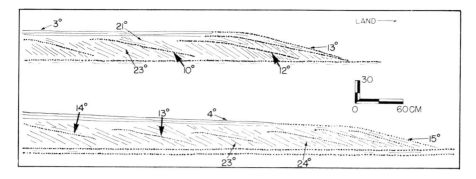

Fig. 10. Line drawings of trenches cut into two different swash bars. Stratification is planar. Two distinct dip angles are shown. The shallower dip (10–14°) consists of coarse sand laminae which develop as small waves erode the slipface during falling water. When the slipface is active, the more dominant, steeper cross-stratification (21–24°) develops.

those described by Collinson (1970) and Klein (1970) and is probably not formed by the constant flow mechanism described by McCabe & Jones (1977).

Situated on top of these slipface-generated structures is near horizontal plane stratification which contributes to the vertical growth of the swash bar. This stratification is generated by upper-regime flow from swash over the bar.

Fig. 11. Ground photo at low water of large (1·7 m high) slipface of a swash bar (pole is 3 m high). Man is standing in a runnel.

Berm-ridge development

The third process of beach growth results from the construction of a berm-ridge. This is defined as a modified ridge or swash bar that develops into a berm on the swash bar's seaward margin (Coastal Research Group, 1969, p. 455). Along areas where swash bars are very well developed, such as an active recurved spit, the bars build vertically so that their top surfaces are near spring high water (Fig. 11). During neap tides, however, the high-tide swash does not extend over the upper reaches of the swash-bar surface. Under these conditions, the gently seaward sloping surface acts as a beach face. As the slope is too flat for an equilibrium beach face, this surface steepens. Consequently, a new beach face is formed on the seaward margin of the swash bar. The resulting feature is called a berm-ridge since it retains the basic geomorphic features of a swash bar (ridge) and a berm. Fraser & Hester (p. 1193, 1977) describe similar features occurring along the Lake Michigan shoreline. They attribute formation to storm waves washing over the foreshore.

A sequence of berm-ridge development is well illustrated by the 14–27 June profiles at NB-2 (Fig. 8) and by the entire summer's profiles at NB-3 (Fig. 12). Since NB-3 is located at the terminus of the longshore transport system, the large net increase in sand has created a wide, flat intertidal/shallow subtidal surface (low-tide terrace) upon which large, broad swash bars have developed (Fig. 13).

During the summer, a number of smaller swash bars migrated up to a large slip-face creating a single, huge swash-bar complex whose active slipface approached 2 m in height by 15 August (Fig. 11). With the addition of another swash bar super-imposed on top (29 August, 6 September) and approaching neap tide, the high-tide swash could not extend over such a broad, high feature. The result was a large berm-ridge developed by 5 October, widening the existing beach by nearly 115 m. The large

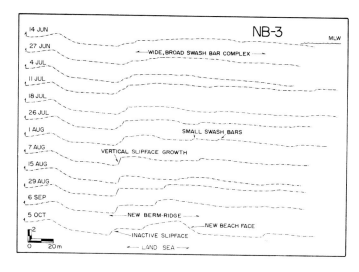

Fig. 12. NB-3 profiles. This station is located on the lower, most active portion of the recurved spit. A broad swash-bar complex has been built up during the summer. Eventually, swash action during neap tide cannot over-top the entire bar. As a result, a new beach face is established seaward of the older beach face creating a berm-ridge structure. This beach zone has widened 115 m.

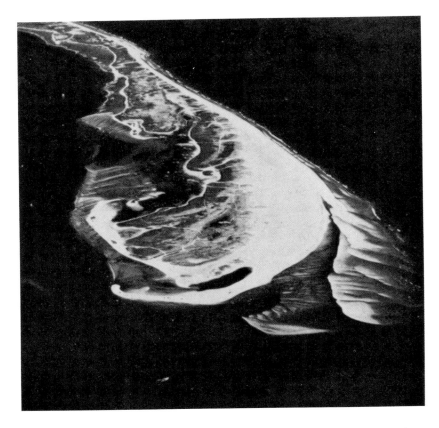

Fig. 13. Aerial photo of lower, active recurved spit illustrating the wide, broad, swash-bar complex at NB-3. Viewer is looking to NNE.

intervening runnel became inactive and filled slowly by the addition of wind trans-ported sands.

Sedimentary structures

Schematic cross-sectional diagrams depicting sedimentary structures within the beach can be drawn based upon trenches dug along these profiles and data from other investigators (Boothroyd, 1969; Hayes & Boothroyd, 1969; Hayes *et al.*, 1969). Figure 14 illustrates a three dimensional view of the beach at NB-2 and NB-3 with a schematic cross-sectional view along the NB-3 profile. A berm-ridge had already been formed at NB-2 (Fig. 4a) and was subsequently widened by swash-bar welding (see Fig. 8). Between these two profile stations on 6 September (Fig. 14A) the berm-ridge structure at NB-2 graded into a wide, broad swash bar at NB-3. By 5 October, the berm-ridge structure had migrated south through the NB-3 profile due to the vertical swash-bar growth and the onset of neap-tidal conditions as explained earlier (Fig. 14B). This migration of the berm-ridge morphology formed a new, straight-berm section in contrast to the older, arcuate-beach section of the recurved spit seen in the background on the figures.

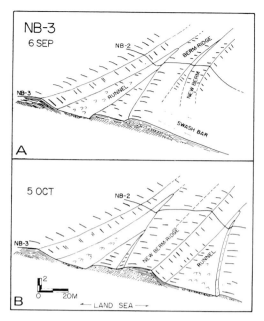

Fig. 14(A). Schematic cross-section and oblique view of lower spit showing profiles NB-2, NB-3 at 6 September. Berm-ridge development is continuing at NB-2, but a wide, broad swash bar remains the dominant feature at NB-3. Swash-bar structure is generally shown to have steep (20–25°) landward dipping, planar cross-stratification formed during slipface migration. These structures are topped by a thin sequence of flat plane stratification formed in the upper-flow regime. **(B)** The berm-ridge morphology has migrated through the NB-3 profile by 5 October. Berm structures consisting of gently, seaward dipping (6–11°) plane stratification (beach face) and near horizontal plane stratification (berm top) plus landward dipping (20–25°) planar stratification rest on top of the earlier swash-bar structures.

Since most of the berm-ridge consisted of several stacked swash-bar sequences, the most common primary sedimentary structure should be landward-oriented, planar cross-stratification of various scales ranging from 30 cm to 2 m in height. Each set of planar cross-stratification should be separated by a thinner set (up to 20 cm) of near horizontal plane stratification representing the swash-bar top. As the beach face was established on the seaward margin of the swash bar, this newly developed profile steepened, and by eroding downward removed a portion of the swash-bar structure. Eventually, a thicker zone (10–30 cm) of seaward dipping (10–14°) plane stratification accumulated representing the build up of the beach face.

The 5 October profile at NB-3 (Fig. 14B) shows a new swash bar approaching the recently developed beach face. This feature welded onto the beach face further widening the beach complex.

The NB-2 profile illustrates both the initial development of a berm-ridge and subsequent berm widening by swash-bar welding (Fig. 15A,B,C). The berm-ridge was developed early in the summer and consisted of berm-top and beach-face plane stratification situated on top of swash-bar structures (Fig. 15A). Figure 15B and C shows schematically the sedimentary structure development of a subsequent berm formed by swash-bar welding. The 5 October profile at NB-2 (Fig. 15C) represents

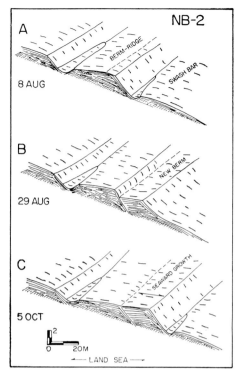

Fig. 15(A). Schematic cross-section and oblique view of the beach at NB-2 during 8 August. A berm-ridge was established earlier in the summer. Diagram depicts a swash bar approaching beach face. **(B)** The swash bar has welded onto the berm-ridge by 29 August. Berm-top and beach-face stratification form on top of welded swash bar. **(C)** By 5 October, the top of the new berm has become even with the berm-ridge producing substantial seaward growth of this feature.

seaward beach growth by the development of three different berms and the imminent development of a fourth as a new swash bar approaches the active beach face.

DISCUSSION AND SUMMARY

Along Nauset Beach three mechanisms of berm development have been observed and measured each occurring along a distinct portion of the barrier spit and each causing the beach to prograde at differing rates. Table 1 summarizes the lateral growth of each berm building mechanism during the 16-week summer period.

Table 1. Growth rates of berm building mechanisms

Berm building mechanism	Seaward growth (16-week period)
Neap-berm development	8 m
Swash-bar welding	22 m
Berm-ridge development	115 m

The increase in beach growth towards the tip of the recurved spit is a function of decreasing longshore transport of sediment due to the changing shoreline orientation. The dominant waves from the NE in this area approach the upper, straight sections of the barrier spit obliquely and set up a southerly longshore transport system. However, near the active spit where the beach is curving away from the ocean into the inlet, the breaker angle increases to the point where longshore transport decreases (U.S. Army Coastal Engineering Research Centre, 1973). Second, the waves are strongly refracted close to the beach face causing wave energy to be diminished due to decreased wave height along a unit width of beach (Zenkovitch, 1967). Sediment is rapidly deposited and forms a broad, shallow subtidal/intertidal terrace upon which develop large swash bars (Fig. 12). These swash bars then migrate towards the beach face in response to locally refracted waves or waves approaching more from the east. The result is widespread swash-bar welding and/or berm-ridge development.

An idealized barrier-spit complex can be postulated based upon the continued beach growth and progradation by these three beach-growth mechanisms (Fig. 16). Since most sediments are deposited nearest the tip of the recurved spit, this area should be dominated by berm-ridge development. These berm-ridges would be separated by wide, deep, relict runnel systems. Ultimately these ridges should establish vegetation, develop dunes, and finally support shrubs and trees. These curved, vegetated beach ridges are very common along barrier-spit systems (Au, 1974; Brauer, 1974; Barwis, 1976; Hayes *et al.*, 1976; Hayes & Hulmes, 1975; Hayes, 1977; Oertel, 1975; Strahler, 1966; Godfrey, 1976; Stapor & Mathews, 1976; Fisher, 1967).

The intervening swales should initially trap wind blown sand. Eventually, marshes should become established, and possibly lens-shaped (cat-eye) fresh-water ponds could be formed (Hayes *et al.*, 1976).

Further up the recurved spit, the swash bars are not as broad or extensive and can migrate up to and weld onto the beach face. There is a transitional zone, such as NB-2, where both berm-ridge development and swash-bar welding can occur. Even

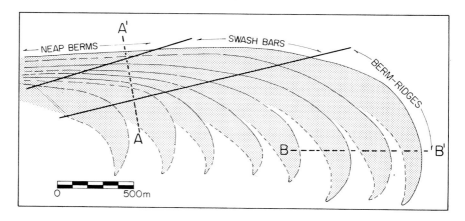

Fig. 16. Idealized barrier-spit complex showing zones where each berm-widening type dominates. Neap-berm growth is the slowest form of beach widening whereas berm-ridge growth is the fastest. Transition zones occur along the boundaries between the berm-growth mechanisms. As the spit migrates, the boundaries migrate as well.

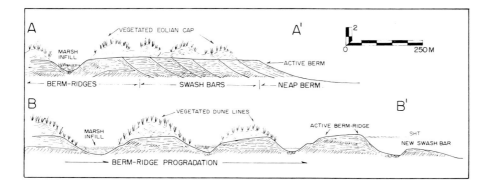

Fig. 17. Schematic sedimentary structure cross-sections across and down the spit complex. Section A–A′ illustrates the gradation from berm-ridge structures in the central portion, through a zone of berms formed by welded swash bars, to the present active berm formed by neap-berm development. Section B–B′ runs parallel to the strandline and crosses a series of berm-ridges which were formed at the active tip of the recurved spit. Muds, marsh, and wind blown sand have partially infilled the swales. The older berm-ridges support vegetated dunes which may eventually become forested.

further up the barrier spit along the straighter portions of the beach, longshore transport is dominant and only neap-berm growth occurs. A transition zone also occurs between the swash-bar welding zone and the neap-berm development zone.

If this barrier spit model is correct (Fig. 16), the largest volume of sand should be incorporated into berm-ridge sedimentary structures and the smallest volume into neap-berm structures. Schematic sedimentary structure cross-sections down the length of the barrier spit and laterally across it are shown in Fig. 17. These highly stylized drawings provide a framework to understand the complex sedimentary sequences that exist within barrier spits or islands formed by migrating recurved spits.

CONCLUSIONS

(1) Three different mechanisms of berm development can occur along an actively migrating spit, each characterizing a distinct zone. These are: (1) neap-berm development; (2) swash-bar welding; and (3) berm-ridge development.

(2) Neap berms are accumulations of sand, gravel, and carbonate debris developed on the beach face when neap high-tide swash is unable to over-top the berm crest. During spring high tide, swash carries sediments composing the neap berm over the crest and deposits them on the berm top. This process occurs primarily along the straight sections of the beach where longshore transport of sand dominates. The development of neap berms and subsequent widening of the main berm is the slowest and least important mechanism of beach progradation.

(3) The welding of intertidal swash bars (ridge-and-runnel system) commonly occurs along the initial curvature of the spit and is the best understood and documented type of berm development. Ridge-and-runnel systems also frequently occur along straight beach sections where onshore sand transport is high. Swash bars migrate across a flat low-tide terrace and weld onto the existing berm creating a

gently seaward dipping beach-face terrace. This new, low-angle beach face rapidly steepens and creates a new berm immediately seaward of the earlier berm. Given a steady sediment supply and no intervening storms, a wide complex can develop consisting of several horizontally stacked berms, each composed of welded swash bars.

(4) Berm-ridges develop along the strongly recurved portion of an active spit and represent the most rapid form of beach progradation. Wide, broad swash bars build nearly up to the spring high tide level. At neap high tide, the swash-uprush cannot extend over this feature. The seaward margin of the swash bar becomes a low angle beach face which steepens causing a normal beach face to develop. This results in a berm structure which still retains much of its swash bar or ridge appearance—hence the term 'berm-ridge'. The wide intervening swales or runnels become partially infilled with mud, wind blown sand, and ultimately marsh growth. The berm-ridges support dune systems which eventually become vegetated with shrubs or trees. These are the arcuate, vegetated beach ridges commonly seen within barrier islands and barrier spits.

(5) An idealized barrier spit would show all three of these mechanisms active along different portions of the spit with the berm-ridges dominant on the active spit tip, swash-bar welding dominant along the middle to upper spit, and neap-berm development dominant along the straight beach. Volumetrically, sedimentary structures associated with berm-ridge development are the most important.

ACKNOWLEDGMENTS

This work was performed while the author was a graduate student at the University of Massachusetts and funded by the Coastal Engineering Research Centre, Contract DACW 72-67-C-004, Miles O. Hayes, principal investigator. David Maleski and James Tolpin assisted in the field. Jon C. Boothroyd assisted greatly by providing valuable discussion and advice. H. E. Reineck, H. T. Mullins, and P. H. Bridges critically reviewed the manuscript.

REFERENCES

AU, SHU-FUN (1974) Vegetation and ecological processes on Shackleford Banks, North Carolina. *National Park Service Scientific Monograph Series,* **6.**

BARWIS, J.H. (1976) Internal geometry of Kiawah Island beach ridges. In: *Terrigenous Clastic Depositional Environments* (Ed. by M. O. Hayes and T. Kana), pp. 11-115–11-125. Tech. Rpt No. 11-CRD, Dept of Geology, University of S. Carolina, Columbia.

BOOTHROYD, J.C. (1969) STOP 19-Crane Beach. In: *Coastal Research Group, Coastal Environments, N.E. Massachusetts and New Hampshire,* pp. 146–173. Cont. No. 1, Dept of Geology, University of Massachusetts, Amherst.

BRAUER, C.D. (1974) *Genetic mapping and erosional history of the surface sediments of Shackleford Banks, North Carolina.* Unpublished M.S. Thesis, Duke University, Durham, N.C.

COASTAL RESEARCH GROUP (1969) *Coastal Environments, N.E. Massachusetts and New Hampshire.* Cont. No. 1, Dept of Geology, University of Massachusetts, Amherst.

COLLINSON, J.D. (1970) Bedforms in the Tana River, Norway. *Geogr. Annlr,* **52,** 31–56.

CORNISH, V. (1898) On sea beaches and sand banks. *Geogr. J.* **11,** 628–651.

DAVIS, R.A., JR, FOX, W.T., HAYES, M.O., & BOOTHROYD, J.C. (1972) Comparison of ridge-and-runnel systems in tidal and non-tidal environments. *J. sedim. Petrol.* **42,** 401–412.

EMERY, K.O. (1961) A simple method of measuring beach profile. *Limnol. Oceanogr.* **6,** 90–93.

FINLEY, R.J. (1975) Hydrodynamics and tidal deltas of North Inlet, South Carolina. In: *Estuarine Research*, Vol. 2, *Geology and Engineering* (Ed. by L. E. Cronin), pp. 277–291. Academic Press, N.Y.

FISHER, J.J. (1967) *Development pattern of relict beach ridges, Outer Banks, barrier chain, North Carolina.* Unpublished Ph.D. Thesis, University of N. Carolina, Chapel Hill.

FRASER, G.S. & HESTER, N.C. (1977) Sediments and sedimentary structures of a beach-ridge complex, southwestern shore of Lake Michigan. *J. sedim. Petrol.* **47**, 1187–1200.

GODFREY, P.K. (1976) Barrier beaches of the east coast. *Oceanus*, **19**, 27–40.

GOLDSMITH, V. (1972) *Coastal processes of a barrier island complex and adjacent ocean floor: Monomoy Island-Nauset Spit, Cape Cod, Massachusetts.* Unpublished Ph.D. Dissertation, University of Massachusetts, Amherst.

GRESSWELL, R.K. (1937) The geomorphology of the south-west Lancashire coastline. *Geogr. J.* **90**, 335–348.

GRESSWELL, R.K. (1953) *Sandy Shores of South Lancashire.* University of Liverpool: Studies in Geography.

HAYES, M.O. (1969) STOP 4—Profile PLB. In: *Coastal Research Group, Coastal Environments, N.E. Massachusetts and New Hampshire*, pp. 50–57. Cont. No. 1, Dept of Geology, University of Massachusetts, Amherst.

HAYES, M.O. (1972) Forms of sediment accumulation in the beach zone. *Waves on Beaches and Resulting Sediment Transport* (Ed. by R. E. Meyer), pp. 297–356. Academic Press, New York.

HAYES, M.O. (1976) Lecture notes. In: *Terrigenous Clastic Depositional Environments* (Ed. by M. O. Hayes and T. W. Kana), pp. 1–130. Tech. Rpt No. 11-CRD, Dept of Geology, University of S. Carolina, Columbia.

HAYES, M.O. (1977) Development of Kiawah Island, South Carolina. *Coastal Sediments '77, Fifth Symposium of the Waterway, Port, Coastal and Ocean Division of A.S.C.E., Charleston, S.C.* 828–847.

HAYES, M.O. & BOOTHROYD, J.C. (1969) Storms as modifying agents in the coastal zone. In: *Coastal Research Group, Coastal Environments, N.E. Massachusetts and New Hampshire*, pp. 245–265. Cont. No. 1, Dept of Geology, University of Massachusetts, Amherst.

HAYES, M.O., ANAN, F.S., & BOZEMAN, R.N. (1969) Sediment dispersal trends in the littoral zone: a problem in paleogeographic reconstruction. In: *Coastal Research Group, Coastal Environments, N.E. Massachusetts and New Hampshire*, pp. 290–315. Cont. No. 1, Dept of Geology, University of Massachusetts, Amherst.

HAYES, M.O., GOLDSMITH, V., & HOBBS, C.H. (1970) Offset coastal inlets: a discussion. In: *Proc. of 12th Coastal Engineering Conf., Washington, D.C.*, pp. 1187–1200.

HAYES, M.O., OWENS, E.H., HUBBARD, D.K., & ABELE, R.W. (1973) The investigation of form and processes in the coastal zone. In: *Coastal Geomorphology* (Ed. by D. R. Coates), pp. 11–41. Publ. in geomorphology, SUNY, Binghamton, N.Y.

HAYES, M.O. & HULMES, L.J. (1975) Relationship of recurved spit growth to barrier island morphology and sedimentation. In: *Program Ann. Meet. Am. Ass. Petrol. Geol. and Soc. econ. Paleont. Miner., Dallas, Texas*, **1**.

HAYES, M.O., FITZGERALD, D.M., HULMES, L.J., & WILSON, S.J. (1976) Geomorphology of Kiawah Island, South Carolina. In: *Terrigenous Clastic Depositional Environments* (Ed. by M. O. Hayes and T. Kana), pp. 11-80–11-100. Dept of Geology, University of S. Carolina, Columbia.

HINE, A.C. (1972) *Sand deposition in the Chatham Harbour Estuary and on the neighbouring beaches, Cape Cod, Massachusetts.* Unpublished M.S. Thesis, University of Massachusetts, Amherst.

HINE, A.C. (1975) Bedform distribution and migration patterns on tidal deltas in the Chatham Harbour Estuary, Cape Cod, Massachusetts. In: *Estuarine Research*, Vol. 2, *Geology and Engineering* (Ed. by L. E. Cronin), pp. 235–252. Academic Press, New York.

HINE, A.C. & BOOTHROYD, J.C. (1978) Morphology, processes, and recent sedimentary history of a glacial-outwash plain shoreline, southern Iceland. *J. sedim. Petrol.* **48**, 901–920.

KING, C.A.M. (1972) *Beaches and Coasts* (2nd edn). St Martin's Press, New York.

KING, C.A.M. & WILLIAMS, W.W. (1949) The formation and movement of sand bars by wave action. *Geogr. J.* **113**, 70–85.

KLEIN, G. DeVRIES (1970) Depositional and dispersal dynamics of intertidal sand bars. *J. sedim. Petrol.* **40**, 1095–1127.

McCABE, P.J. & JONES, C.M. (1977) Formation of reactivation surfaces within superimposed deltas and bedforms. *J. sedim. Petrol,* **47**, 707–715.

OERTEL, G.F. (1975) Post Pleistocene island and inlet adjustment along the Georgia coast. *J. sedim. Petrol.* **45**, 150–159.

OWENS, E.H. (1977) Temporal variations in beach and nearshore dynamics. *J. sedim. Petrol.* **47**, 168–190.

OWENS, E.H. & FROBEL, D.H. (1977) Ridge and runnel systems in the Magdelen Islands, Quebec. *J. sedim. Petrol.* **47**, 191–198.

SONU, C.J. (1968) Collective movement of sediment in the littoral environment. *Proc. of 11th Coastal Engineering Conf., A.S.C.E., London,* Vol. 1, 373–400.

STAPOR, F.W. & MATHEWS, T.D. (1976) Mollusk C-14 ages in the interpretation of South Carolina barrier island deposits and depositional histories. In: *Terrigenous Clastic Depositional Environments* (Ed. by M. O. Hayes and T. Kana), pp. 11-101–11-114. Tech. Rpt No. 11-CRD, Dept of Geology, University of S. Carolina, Columbia.

STEPHEN, M.F., BROWN, P.J., FITZGERALD, D.M., HUBBARD, D.K., & HAYES, M.O. (1975) Beach erosion inventory of Charleston County, South Carolina. *South Carolina Sea Grant Tech. Rpt,* **4**.

STRAHLER, A.N. (1966) *A Geologist's View of Cape Cod.* The Natural History Press, New York.

U.S. ARMY COASTAL ENGINEERING RESEARCH CENTRE (1973) *Shore Protection Manual,* Vol. 1, U.S. Govt Printing Office, Washington D.C.

U.S. ARMY CORPS OF ENGINEERS (1968) Pleasant Bay, Chatham, Orleans, Harwich, Massachusetts. Survey Report. New England Division, Corps of Engineers, Waltham, Mass.

U.S. DEPT OF COMMERCE (1968) *Tide tables, high and low water predictions: east coast of North and South America.* National Ocean Survey, Rockville, Md.

WIEGEL, R.L. (1953) *Waves, tides, currents, and beaches—glossary of terms and list of standard symbols.* Council on Wave Research, The Engineering Foundation, University of California.

ZENKOVITCH, V.P. (1967) *Processes of Coastal Development.* Wiley Interscience, New York.

(*Manuscript received* 27 *April* 1978; *revision received* 8 *November* 1978)

JOURNAL OF SEDIMENTARY PETROLOGY, VOL. 36, NO. 4, PP. 1126–1130
FIGS. 1–2, DECEMBER, 1966

A PROFILE OF THE FOUR MOMENT MEASURES PERPENDICULAR TO A SHORE LINE, SOUTH HAVEN, MICHIGAN[1]

WILLIAM T. FOX, JOHN W. LADD AND MICHAEL K. MARTIN
Williams College, Williamstown, Massachusetts

ABSTRACT

A series of fourteen samples was taken along a profile crossing a beach, berm, foreshore slope, plunge point, nearshore, offshore bar, and offshore area to study the changes in the first four moments. The mean grain size and standard deviation reached a maximum in the plunge zone and were also high on the offshore bar. Skewness and kurtosis values were highest in the nearshore and offshore area. The beach represents a phi normal distribution of fine sand which is mixed with varying amounts of coarser material to form the sediments in the other environments.

INTRODUCTION

A strip of sand beaches encompasses the southern end of Lake Michigan and extends inland for several miles in the area of the Indiana Dunes. The beaches vary from a few feet to several hundred feet wide and are composed of well rounded, fine-grained sand. The sand is distinctively coarser on the gentle foreshore slope which extends from the beach to a pebble zone at the water line. The dominant wind direction is out of the southwest with major storms coming out of the north and northwest. The waves are usually 1 to 3 feet high but may reach heights of 10 to 12 feet in large storms. During and after a storm, the waves first break on the offshore bar, then reform and break again in the plunge zone.

A series of fourteen sand samples was taken along a profile perpendicular to the shore line of Lake Michigan to study changes in the characteristics of the sand in moving from an offshore bar into shallow water and across a plunge zone and onto a beach. The four moment measures—mean, standard deviation, skewness, and kurtosis—were selected for studying changes in the sand-size distribution. By making a traverse across an area which has been under the control of a single set of environmental conditions, including the direction and size of the waves and the velocity of the wind, it should be possible to get a clearer understanding of the sedimentological meaning of the four moments in response to different energy levels across a series of depositional environments.

Several workers in the field of sedimentary petrology have used moment measures as a basis for distinguishing beach, dune, and river sands. Krumbein and Pettijohn (1938) discuss the method of computing the first four phi moments

[1] Manuscript received May 26, 1966.

and their significance. Friedman (1961) has shown that the third moment (skewness) is a sensitive environmental indicator. He plotted skewness against mean grain size for dune and beach sands and ended up with a separation of fields for the two depositional environments. He also plotted skewness against standard deviation, which gave less complete separation of river sands and beach sands. Inman (1952) introduced a graphic method for computing the four moments directly from plots of cumulative frequency distribution. Folk and Ward (1957) used a modified version of the graphic method to determine graphic inclusive measures of the mean, standard deviation, skewness, and kurtosis for the Brazos River bar in Texas. Mason and Folk (1958), using the graphic method, concluded that the differences between beach, dune, and aeolian flats on Mustang Island, Texas, were almost entirely in the tails of the curves which affected skewness and kurtosis. They made an interpretation of the depositional environments by plotting changes in skewness and kurtosis in four traverses across the three environments.

PROCEDURE

Fourteen samples were collected along a 350-foot traverse about 1 mile north of the pier at South Haven, Michigan, which is located on the southeastern shore of Lake Michigan. The profile includes samples from beach, berm, foreshore, plunge point, nearshore, offshore bar, and offshore areas. The sample locations are not evenly spaced but were selected to most effectively demonstrate the differences in the various environments. The fourteen samples were sieved for 15 minutes each on a rotop using a half phi unit sieve interval.

A FORTRAN program to compute the first four moments, including mean, standard devia-

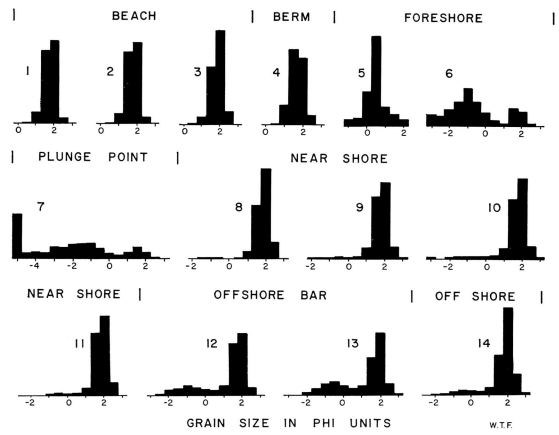

FIG. 1.—Histograms of fourteen samples collected along a profile perpendicular to the shore line at South Haven, Michigan.

tion, skewness, and kurtosis, was written and compiled, using the IBM 7094 computer at the Massachusetts Institute of Technology. The moment measures were computed according to the method outlined in Krumbein and Pettijohn (1938, p. 251).

In the early stages of this project, the four moments were computed using the graphic method outlined by Folk and Ward (1957) modified after the method suggested by Inman (1952). In order to compute the graphic moments, cumulative curves were plotted using the sieve data. From these curves, mean, standard deviation, skewness and kurtosis were computed according to the formulas given in Folk and Ward (1957). The mean and standard deviation values based on the graphic method corresponded quite closely to the first two computed moments. However, the skewness and kurtosis values, especially for the nearshore and offshore areas, differed significantly in the two methods. The large negative skewness values in the near-shore area which were prominent in the com-

puted moments were not observed when the graphic method was used. The tail of coarse material was not detected when the 5th and 95th percentiles were used in the graphic method. The kurtosis values in the nearshore area are also much higher in the computed moments than in the graphic method. For finding mean grain size and standard deviation, the graphic method is perfectly suitable. However, in this study it was not sensitive enough for accurate determination of skewness and kurtosis.

RESULTS

A preliminary interpretation of the energy conditions can be made from a visual inspection of the modal classes and tails on the histograms in figure 1. Samples 1, 2, and 3 which were taken on the beach are unimodal with a modal class of 2 phi units. In moving from the berm across the foreshore to the plunge point in samples 4 through 7, there is a shift in the modal class to the coarser sizes, representing an increase in the energy level and an introduction of a second mode in sample 6 and a third mode in sample 7. Samples 8, 9, 10 and 11, from near shore between the plunge point and the offshore bar, once again display a mode in the 2-phi-unit size like the beach and dune samples, but show distinctive tails in the coarse and of the histogram. Samples 12 and 13 from the offshore bar have the primary mode in the 2-phi-unit class, but show secondary modes in the −1.0 and −0.5 phi classes. These secondary modes are the result of an increase in wave energy on the offshore bar. Sample 14, taken off shore from the sandbar, also shows a primary mode of 2 phi units and a much smaller secondary mode of −0.5 phi units. This sample shows the beginning of the influence of the sand bar on the grain-size distribution in the offshore area.

The distance from the shore line, height above mean lake level, and the four computed moments for each sample are given in table 1. Plots of the topographic profile and the four moments against distance are given in figure 2. The top curve is a 2.5X vertical exaggeration of the topographic profile with a circle for each sample location and a zero line indicating the mean lake level. The sample elevations range from 6.0 feet above, to 5.3 feet below mean lake level.

The second graph in figure 2 is a plot of mean grain size in phi units against distance with zero phi used as a reference line. The mean grain size is plotted with the negative phi units representing the coarser material at the top and the positive phi units or finer material below the zero line. Moving across the beach to the berm (samples 1–4), the mean grain size remains fairly constant, hovering about 1.8 phi units. In moving down the fore shore, the mean grain size increases from 1.68 ϕ at the berm to −0.64 ϕ at lake level. The mean gram size reaches its highest

value of −2.25ϕ at the plunge point which represents the highest energy environment. In the nearshore area between the plunge point and the offshore bar, the mean grain size decreases to about 1.6 ϕ, which is only slightly coarser than the values for the beach. On the offshore bar, where the waves first break, the mean size again increases to about 1.2 ϕ and drops off to about 1.6 ϕ beyond the bar.

The third graph in figure 2 is a plot of standard deviation which is a measure of sorting against distance with a standard deviation of 0.0 used as a reference line. Although mean grain size and standard deviation are theoretically independent, there is a close similarity between the plots of the first two moments. Where there is an increase in mean grain size, there is a corresponding increase in standard deviation. On the beach, the standard deviation values are relatively stable at about 0.36 ϕ, indicating a very well sorted sand. There is a steady increase of the standard deviation across the fore shore to a maximum of 2.26 ϕ at the plunge point. In the near shore area between the plunge point and the bar, the standard deviation values vary around 0.7 ϕ, showing a significant increase over the beach values. On the sand bar, the standard deviation values increase to about 1.25 ϕ and then drop off to about 0.85 ϕ in the offshore area. The three areas of relatively low standard deviation found on the beach near shore and off shore are separated by areas of high standard deviation representing the offshore bar and the plunge point-foreshore areas where energy is concentrated when the waves break. In moving from off shore to near shore and on to the beach, there is a progressive decrease in the standard deviation, indicating an improvement in the sorting.

The fourth graph in figure 2 is a plot of skew-

TABLE 1.—*Location and moment measures for 14 samples taken along a traverse perpendicular to the shore line of Lake Michigan at South Haven, Michigan*

Sample Number	Seaward Distance from Shore Line	Height Above Mean Lake Level	Mean Grain Size	Standard Deviation	Skewness	Kurtosis
	(feet)	(feet)	(phi)	(phi)		
1	−120	6.0	1.723	.359	−.207	3.532
2	−90	3.0	1.738	.359	−.218	3.896
3	−60	3.0	1.818	.361	−.241	3.972
4	−30	3.0	1.680	.401	−.100	3.131
5	−15	1.5	0.469	.596	.060	3.998
6	0	0	−0.640	1.426	.232	2.441
7	3	−1.2	−2.253	2.259	.150	1.948
8	15	−2.0	1.749	.606	−1.419	14.795
9	30	−2.5	1.595	.761	−1.270	10.895
10	100	−3.5	1.593	.857	−1.464	13.594
11	160	−5.2	1.661	.679	−1.232	11.358
12	170	−2.0	1.122	1.247	−.670	3.683
13	200	−2.4	1.063	1.265	−.517	2.979
14	230	−5.3	1.645	.850	−1.011	7.294

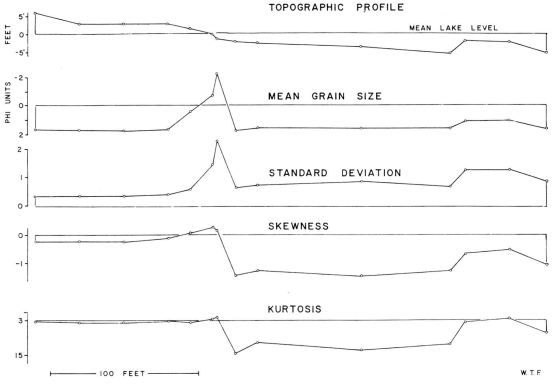

FIG. 2.—Graphs of the topographic profile and the first four moments—mean, standard deviation, skewness, and kurtosis—plotted against distance.

ness against distance with skewness values ranging from 0.232 to −1.464. The beach samples have a slight negative skewness of about −0.2 which can be recognized in the small tail on the coarse side of the histograms in figure 1. Samples 5, 6 and 7 across the fore shore to the plunge point are positively skewed, reaching a maximum at sample 6 with a skewness of 0.232. The positive skewness indicates a tail in the finer material. In sample 6, the coarser mode at −1.0 ϕ has become dominant and the finer mode at 1.5 ϕ to 2.0 ϕ has decreased in amount and is acting like a tail of fine material. In the nearshore samples (8, 9, 10 and 11), the long tail of coarse material gives the sand high negative skewness values close to −1.4. In the offshore bar samples which are bimodal, the finer mode is dominant and the coarser mode is secondary, giving negative skewness values of about −0.6. Off shore, the negative skewness value once more increases to about −1.0. The largest negative skewness values represent long tails of coarse material which usually contain less than 5 percent of the sample. The positively skewed samples are bimodal with the largest mode in the coarser grain sizes.

The lowest plot on figure 2 is a graph of the fourth moment, kurtosis, against distance with kurtosis value of a normal distribution which is 3.0 used as a reference line. The kurtosis values are plotted with zero at the top and 15 at the bottom, so that the general trend of the curve would parallel the trends of the first three moments. Kurtosis values less than 3.0 are considered platykurtic according to Krumbein and Pettijohn (1938, p. 252) and usually result from a bimodal sample. Kurtosis values greater than 3.0 are leptokurtic and indicate a peaked distribution or exceptionally long tails. In contrast with skewness, which indicates on which side of the primary mode the tail is located, kurtosis is a measure of bimodality (platykurtic) or long tails (leptokurtic). The first five samples across the beach and on to the fore shore have kurtosis values slightly greater than 3.0, indicating that they are leptokurtic. Samples 6 and 7 at the bottom of the fore shore and at the plunge point are platykurtic with kurtosis values of less than 3.0. The nearshore samples have kurtosis values greater than 10, resulting from the long tails of coarse material. The long tails make the center of the distribution appear more peaked and therefore give high kurtosis values. The samples on the sand bar have low kurtosis values near that of a normal distribution. The low kurtosis values and negative skewness indicate a bimodal distribution with the dominant mode in the finer grain size. Off shore, the kurtosis value increases again to about 7.3 and resembles the nearshore samples which have high kurtosis values.

CONCLUSIONS

The plots of the four moments against distance are similar in some respects but show their own distinctive characteristics. The mean grain sizes in the beach, nearshore and offshore areas are close to 1.6 ϕ. There are increases in mean grain size where the waves break on the offshore bar and on the beach. The areas of poor sorting, as measured by high standard deviation values, occur on the offshore bar and plunge point-foreshore areas. The standard deviation decreases in steps from the offshore to the near shore areas and on to the beach, indicating progressively better sorting as the material is carried across the sand bar and the plunge zone. The skewness shows slightly negative values on the beach and high negative values in the nearshore and offshore areas. The skewness values are less negative on the bar and positive in the plunge zone. The negative skewness values in the nearshore and offshore areas are probably the result of a tail of coarse material which was swept off the sand bar by the waves, or swept outward from the plunge zone by the backwash of the waves. The positive skewness values at the plunge point are the result of a concentration of coarse granule and pebble-size material in the surf zone, with a secondary mode of fine-sand size. The kurtosis values are slightly leptokurtic across the beach and berm and platykurtic, indicating bimodal distribution in the lower foreshore and plunge zone. The high kurtosis values in the nearshore area are a result of the long tails of coarse ma-

terial which give the curves a peaked appearance. The offshore bar also shows near normal kurtosis values close to 3.0 with a leptokurtic reading in the offshore area. Whereas positive or negative skewness values indicate a tail of fine or coarse material, high kurtosis values are the result of an exceptionally long tail in either the coarse or fine end.

Based on a study of the four moments, it is possible to interpret the changes in energy conditions along a line across a beach through the plunge zone and out to a shallow offshore bar. The four moments reflect the bottom topography and the dissipation of wave energy across the profile. The wave energy is first released on the sand bar where the waves break and move into the near-shore area. The bottom profile in the nearshore area is concave upward, representing equilibrium conditions for the waves encountered. In the nearshore area the waves form again but are smaller because of the energy spent in breaking on the offshore bar. The waves once again break at the plunge point, creating an area of maximum turbulence and release of energy. There is a decrease in energy up the foreshore as indicated by the smaller grain size and better sorting with the maximum of onlap of the waves marked by the berm. On the beach, material from the berm is sorted by the wind, giving a well sorted, fine-grain sand with a small amount of coarse material. In essence, the beach represents a phi-normal distribution of fine sand which is mixed with varying amounts of coarser material to form the sediments in the other environments.

A traverse of closely spaced samples across a shore line is quite effective in interpreting the effects of both wave-energy dissipation and topographic profile on sand-size distribution. Although each moment has its own significance, the four moments must be considered together in making the final interpretation of the energy profile.

REFERENCES

FOLK, R. L., AND WARD, W. C., 1957, Brazos River Bar: a Study in the significance of grain size parameters: Jour. Sedimentary Petrology, v. 27, p. 3–26.

FRIEDMAN, G. M., 1961, Distinction between dune, beach and river sands from their textural characteristics: Jour. Sedimentary Petrology, v. 31, p. 514–529.

INMAN, D. L., 1952, Measures for describing the size distribution of sediments: Jour. Sedimentary Petrology, v. 22, p. 125–145.

KRUMBEIN, W. C., AND PETTIJOHN, F. J., 1938, Manual of sedimentary petrology. Appleton-Century-Crofts, Inc., New York, 265 p.

MASON, C. C., AND FOLK, R. L., 1958, Differentiation of beach, dune, and aeolian flat environments by size analysis, Mustang Island, Texas: Jour. Sedimentary Petrology, v. 28, p. 211–226.

Journal of Sedimentary Petrology, Vol. 28, No. 2, pp. 211–226
Figs. 1–11, June, 1958

DIFFERENTIATION OF BEACH, DUNE, AND AEOLIAN FLAT ENVIRONMENTS BY SIZE ANALYSIS, MUSTANG ISLAND, TEXAS[1]

CURTIS C. MASON AND ROBERT L. FOLK
United States Geological Survey, Brady, Texas and University of Texas, Austin, Texas

ABSTRACT

Mustang Island is a 16-mile-long barrier island on the south Texas Gulf coast. Sediments consist of very well sorted fine sands (mean size 2.82ϕ, average $\sigma_1 = 0.29\phi$), and show exceedingly uniform properties lengthwise of the island. Beach, dune, and aeolian flat environments can be readily distinguished by size analysis. The best means of differentiating them is by plotting skewness versus kurtosis inasmuch as the geologic processes at work have their greatest effect on the tails of the size distribution. Beach sands form normal curves, dune sands are positively skewed but still mesokurtic, and aeolian flat sands are positively skewed and leptokurtic. Sands from the beach are more poorly sorted than those from the other two environments. These differences are extremely significant with P values between .0002 and .0000001. To explain these changes, it is proposed that as sand travels from the beach to the dunes, the coarse end of the parent normal population lags behind, rendering the size curves better sorted and also positively skewed. The aeolian flats are believed to be subject to infiltration of silt from the atmosphere; this imparts a "tail" of fines, registering a marked increase in kurtosis.

INTRODUCTION

Mustang Island, situated on the South Texas coast, separates Corpus Christi Bay from the Gulf of Mexico (fig. 1). It is one of a continuous chain of sand beaches and barrier islands that extend along the western Gulf coast from Louisiana to southern Mexico. Mustang Island trends south-southwest and is approximately 16 miles long and 1 to 3 miles wide; on the northeast it is separated from St. Joseph Island by Aransas Pass, and on the southwest it now merges without break into Padre Island, the pass that formerly existed between them having been closed by storms in 1950.

The nearest weather station is at Corpus Christi where the average annual rainfall is 26.5 inches with a mean annual temperature of 71.0°F. The Köppen classification of the climate is BShn', signifying a hot, semiarid steppe climate with high humidity but no great amount of fog. Normally, the wind blows inland from the southeast at a mean speed of 10 to 12 knots; however, at intervals during the winter strong northerly winds prevail for periods of several days. Waves are usually 1 to 3 ft high, and the slope offshore from the island is very gentle; tides measure only about 2 ft. Hurricanes occasionally form during early fall, and strike any particular point along the Texas coast about once in 25 years.

[1] Manuscript received January 23, 1958.

Except for the small fishing and tourist town of Port Aransas at the north end, the island is sparsely occupied and given over to cattle. A road connecting Port Aransas with the Corpus Christi causeway extends the length of the island, and it is also possible to drive a car along the Gulf beach the full distance; thus surf bathing and fishing is a common activity along the island.

Mustang Island was selected as a testing ground to determine if there exists a statistically significant difference in grain size properties between sands of the various environments on a barrier island. Beach, dune, and aeolian flat environments are well developed here, and it was hoped that a study of the deposits therein might serve as an aid in distinguishing similar environments in ancient sediments. Further, a study of the differences between the sands should aid in understanding the geologic processes at work in the area.

Skewness and kurtosis have been for so many years recorded in a merely perfunctory way (their main purpose seemingly being to beef up tables of data) that there has been considerable question as to whether they had any practical value. Consequently another purpose of this study was to determine if these obscure measures had any utility on Mustang Island. They have met the challenge well; it turns out that these two properties are the very ones that best identify the environments studied!

PHYSIOGRAPHY

All three environments are normally sharply distinguished and extend in narrow strips down the length of the island with little change in width. The Gulf beach averages about 200 ft wide, but may be entirely submerged during very high storm-induced tides. The front part of the beach slopes at an angle of a few degrees and is littered with shell debris; it is separated from the main part of the beach by a sharp break in slope (fig. 2). The main part of the beach is very flat and contains almost no shells (sieving shows less than 0.1 percent of the sample). At the back of the beach is a 150-foot strip of low, overlapping dunes, only about 5 ft high and sparsely vegetated. These grade into a 350-ft wide belt of larger dunes, as much as 20 to 40 ft high and completely stabilized by vegetation, chiefly

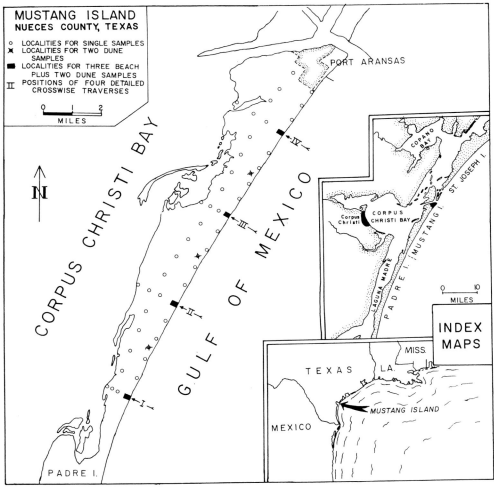

FIG. 1.—Mustang Island, Texas, showing sampling sites. Four traverses were made crosswise of the island (designated I, II, III, and IV). Along each of these crosswise traverses, three beach and two dune samples were taken (position shown by the black block; for details of sample location see fig. 2); and three aeolian flat samples were taken (shown by open circles). Two detailed traverses were made lengthwise of the island, one down the middle of the beach and the other down the aeolian flat (all shown by open circles). Furthermore, midway between each of the four crosswise traverses, a pair of dune samples was taken (shown by the crossed circle symbol).

Fig. 2.—Schematic cross-section of Mustang Island showing detailed location of samples. Distances greatly distorted; the aeolian flat is 1 to 3 miles wide while the beach and dune belt combined average only 500 to 1000 feet wide. The four crosswise traverses consisted of three beach samples (B1, B2, B3); two dune samples, one at each edge of the dune belt (D1, D2); and three samples spaced equally across the aeolian flat (F1, F2, F3). One lengthwise traverse was taken down the mid-beach, at the position of B2; the other lengthwise traverse was down the middle of the aeolian flat, at the position of FM. Additional dune samples were taken at D1 and D2.

sea-purslane and sea-oats. The large dunes form one to three rows parallel with the coast. At several places blowout tongues of bare sand, forming small barchan-type migrating dunes, extend nearly halfway across the island.

The aeolian flat occupies by far the greatest area on the island, beginning abruptly behind the dunes and occupying the remaining 1 to 3 mile width of the island. The term "aeolian flat" is not meant to imply that this large physiographic feature necessarily originated by aeolian action since it may have been formed by washovers or other means. The term merely signifies that the present-day surface skin of sediments over this flat area is now being influenced by wind action. The flat has an elevation of 5 ft or less and is normally smooth and featureless and extensively vegetated with marsh or Bermuda grass. On it there are occasional patches of low vegetated dunes. Low parts of the flat are sometimes flooded at high tide from the lagoon side. Small numbers of cattle graze on this part of the island. The aeolian flat merges with an imperceptibly gentle slope into the lagoon beach, and the water line is extremely irregular with many small peninsulas and islands. The lagoon beach is so poorly differentiated from the aeolian flat that they are considered together in the analytical work. Behind Mustang Island is Corpus Christi Bay, floored with clay or sandy clay and averaging only 12 ft deep.

PROCEDURE

Samples were collected using a grid system. Four crosswise traverses, each consisting of eight samples, were spaced at intervals of 4 miles along the island (fig. 1). On the crosswise traverses, the following samples were taken, designated as shown in figure 2: (1) main beach 3 ft inland from the slope break, B1; (2) middle of the main beach, B2; (3) back of the main beach 5-10 ft in front of the first low dune, B3; (4) halfway up the windward side of the first low dune, D1; (5) halfway down the leeward side of the last large dune, D2; (6) one-third of the way across the aeolian flat, F1; (7) two-thirds of the way across the flat, F2; and (8) at the back of the aeolian flat just above the lagoon shoreline, F3. Two traverses were also taken lengthwise of the island, one down the middle of the main beach and one along the midline of the aeolian flat; these samples were spaced 0.8 miles apart. Two additional dune samples were taken between each of the crosswise traverses. In all, 31 beach samples, 14 dune samples, and 31 aeolian flat samples were analyzed on the grid. To avoid lag sediments, the top inch layer of sand was removed and the sample analyzed was a one inch cube buried an inch below the surface.

The samples were de-salted, disaggregated, and sieved for 15 minutes with a Ro-Tap machine using the following 8-in diameter screens: 2.0ϕ, 2.5ϕ, 2.75ϕ, 3.0ϕ, 3.25ϕ, 3.5ϕ, 4.0ϕ, 4.5ϕ, and pan. Fractions were examined and corrected for aggregates (usually there were none) and weighed to 0.01 gm, but fractions smaller than one gm were weighed to 0.001 gm. Because of the superb sorting of the sand, it was found that if samples weighing 50-60 gm were sieved, the measured phi diameter was consistently 0.05ϕ coarser than when replicate samples of 30-35 gm were used; this is

TABLE 1.—*Distribution of size parameters*

A. DISTRIBUTION OF MEAN SIZE (M_z) VALUES

Environment	Mean of M_z Values	Standard Deviation of M_z Values	Central Two-Thirds	Extreme M_z Values	Character of Distribution
Beach	2.82ϕ (0.142 mm)	0.070ϕ	$2.75\phi–2.89\phi$	$2.65\phi–3.00\phi$	near-normal
Dunes	2.86ϕ (0.138 mm)	0.094ϕ	$2.77\phi–2.95\phi$	$2.69\phi–2.98\phi$	strongly bi-modal, modes 2.80ϕ and 2.96ϕ
Flats	2.83ϕ (0.141 mm)	0.045ϕ	$2.78\phi–2.87\phi$	$2.75\phi–2.89\phi$[1]	near-normal

[1] One aberrant sample from the edge of the lagoon on the south side of the island has $M_z = 2.27\phi$, but this is so far beyond the rest of the samples that it is not considered.

Results of t tests:

Beach versus Dunes, P = .10 (difference dubious).
Beach versus Flats, P = .42 (no difference).
Dunes versus Flats, P = .23 (no difference).

B. DISTRIBUTION OF GRAPHIC STANDARD DEVIATION (σ_I) VALUES

Environment	Mean of σ_I Values	Standard Deviation of σ_I Values	Central Two-Thirds	Extreme σ_I Values	Character of Distribution
Beach	0.309ϕ	0.021ϕ	$0.29\phi–0.33\phi$	$0.26\phi–0.40\phi$	near-normal
Dunes	0.273ϕ	0.026ϕ	$0.25\phi–0.30\phi$	$0.22\phi–0.32\phi$	near-normal
Flats	0.286ϕ	0.023ϕ	$0.26\phi–0.31\phi$	$0.25\phi–0.40\phi$	near-normal

Results of t tests:

Beach versus Dunes, P = .0001 (extremely significant).
Beach versus Flats, P = .0002 (extremely significant).
Dunes versus Flats, P = .07 (difference dubious).

C. DISTRIBUTION OF SKEWNESS (Sk_I) VALUES

Environment	Mean of Sk_I Values	Standard Deviation of Sk_I Values	Central Two-Thirds	Extreme Sk_I Values	Character of Distribution
Beach	$+.03$	.06	$-.03$ to $+.09$	$-.16$ to $+.12$	Slightly bi-modal, modes $-.02$, $+.08$
Dunes	$+.14$	.08	$+.06$ to $+.22$	$+.03$ to $+.26$	Slightly bi-modal, modes $+.06$ and $+.21$
Flats	$+.17$	.07	$+.10$ to $+.24$	$+.04$ to $+.26$	near-normal

Results of t tests:

Beach versus Dunes, P = .00001 (extremely significant).
Beach versus Flats, P = .0000001 (extremely significant).
Dunes versus Flats, P = .22 (no difference).

TABLE 1.—*Continued*

D. DISTRIBUTION OF KURTOSIS (K$_G$') VALUES

Environ-ment	Mean of K$_G$' Values	Standard Deviation of K$_G$' Values	Central Two-Thirds	Extreme K$_G$' Values	Character of Distribution
Beach	.522 (1.09)	.019	.503–.541 (1.01–1.18)	.492–.444 (0.97–1.25)	near-normal
Dunes	.517 (1.07)	.020	.497–.537 (0.99–1.16)	.484–.546 (0.94–1.20)	near-normal
Flats	.546 (1.20)	.024	.522–.570 (1.09–1.33)	.492–.592 (0.97–1.45)	near-normal

Figures in parentheses give equivalent K$_G$ values.

Results of t tests:

Beach versus Dunes, P = .45 (no difference).
Beach versus Flats, P = .0001 (extremely significant).
Dunes versus Flats, P = .0002 (extremely significant).

because of the tendency of the sand to jam up on those screens near the mode. Hence the total sample weight was rigorously maintained at between 30 and 35 gm. Results were plotted as cumulative curves on probability paper using the phi scale (Krumbein, 1934).

Statistical parameters used in describing the grain-size properties of the sand are those proposed by Folk and Ward (1957). These parameters are necessitated because the main differences between Mustang Island samples lie in the far extremes of the distribution, a region not covered by more conventional measures such as Trask's *So* (Trask, 1932), the quartile deviation (Krumbein and Pettijohn, 1938, p. 230) or Inman's (1952) phi deviation measure.

In order to evaluate experimental error—that is, how accurate are the reported values of the various parameters—five samples were selected and each was split into two subsamples. The ten subsamples were given meaningless code numbers by a colleague and returned for sieving and computation. Then the statistical parameters obtained from the two splits of the same sample were compared. For each parameter, the value of the root-mean-square (rms) deviation was computed. The following rms deviations were obtained: Mean (M$_z$), $\pm 0.008\phi$; graphic standard deviation (σ_I), $\pm 0.007\phi$; skewness (Sk$_I$), ± 0.019; transformed kurtosis (K$_G$'), ± 0.0051. This means that if a sample is sieved repeatedly, two-thirds of the analyses will fall within the range of the true value plus or minus one

rms deviation (for example, if a sample with a true M$_z$ of 2.850ϕ and true Sk$_I$ of +.12 is sieved 100 times, then 68 of the sievings will yield M$_z$ values between 2.842 and 2.858, and Sk$_I$ values between +.10 and +.14).

MINERALOGY, GRAIN SHAPE, AND SOURCE OF THE SAND

The sand grains are well sorted but not rounded; consequently the sand is classified as a texturally mature subarkose (Folk, 1954). A count of 540 grains with the petrographic microscope showed 9 percent feldspar (about half orthocase and half microcline), 2 percent chert, 3 percent composite metamorphic quartz and 86 percent common quartz. Inspection of sieved fractions reveals that the samples contain less than 0.1 percent of finely broken shell fragments, nearly all in the coarsest sizes. Bullard (1942) found that the heavy minerals of Mustang Island consist of almost half opaque grains; the chief non-opaque mineral is green hornblende with zircon next and smaller amounts of staurolite, epidote, garnet, and others. Bullard believed that the sand on Mustang Island was drifted southwestward by longshore currents from the Colorado River which reaches the coast about 100 miles to the northeast. This source is indicated by the fact that the Colorado is the only river in Texas that carries large amounts of green hornblende. An unpublished study by Norman Bishop and Charles Mankin, The University of Texas, has revealed that sands in the lower part of the Colorado River carry 5 to 10 percent potash feldspar; thus both light minerals and heavy minerals of Mustang Island indicate derivation from Colorado River detritus.

The grains average subangular (Powers, 1953) but range from very angular to round; it appears that very nearly all the roundness is inherited. Most of the grains are dull-surfaced, and on only a very few is there any sign of incipient edge-rounding of the sharpest corners. Sand from the lower Colorado River shows a very similar assemblage of grain shapes and surface features. Apparently these grains are too fine (2.5ϕ to 3.2ϕ) for beach or dune abrasion to have much effect in modifying the surface features or roundness of individual grains, and these properties are simply inherited from the fluvial assemblage.

FREQUENCY DISTRIBUTION OF VALUES OF MEAN SIZE, STANDARD DEVIATION, SKEWNESS AND KURTOSIS FOR THREE ENVIRONMENTS

For each of the four grain size parameters, smoothed frequency curves have been constructed to show the differences between sands from the beach, dunes, and an aeolian flat. These enable one to compare the range of sorting, skewness, etc. encountered in each environment and also depict the degree of overlap. The raw data from which these frequency distributions are compiled may be inspected in the two scatter plots, figures 8 and 9; data are also shown in table 1.

Mean size (M_z) is determined by the formula

$$M_z = \frac{\phi 16 + \phi 50 + \phi 84}{3}$$

where $\phi 16$ stands for the phi diameter at the 16th percentile of the distribution, etc. Mean grain size of all the environments is very similar (fig. 3) with all of the samples being classified as fine sand, close to the boundary of very fine sand. The beach sands show a nearly normal distribution of mean size, averaging 2.82ϕ (0.142 mm) with a standard deviation of 0.070ϕ. This indicates that the central two-thirds of the samples have mean sizes ranging between 2.75ϕ and 2.89ϕ (0.135 to 0.149 mm). The distribution of mean size for the dune sands

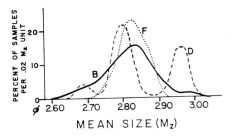

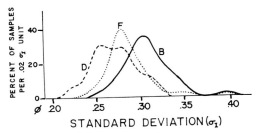

FIG. 3. Frequency distribution of mean size values and graphic standard deviation values for all samples from all environments. Beach, solid line (B); dune, dashed line (D); aeolian flat, dotted line (F). The frequency curves are read as follows: the "beach" curve attains a frequency value of 13 percent at a mean size of 2.80ϕ. This means that 13 percent of the beach samples analyzed had mean sizes between 2.79ϕ and 2.81ϕ (i.e. within the 0.02ϕ interval centered on the specified phi diameter).

In mean size, there is a complete overlap between the environments, with all the samples being classed as fine sand (grand mean 2.83ϕ). The island-wide uniformity in mean size is very striking. Considering the graphic standard deviation, almost all the samples are classed as very well sorted, but among these the beach samples show poorest sorting (average σ_I about $.31\phi$). Frequency distributions of sorting values are nearly normal.

is bimodal with most of the M_z values at about 2.80ϕ and another smaller cluster at about 2.96ϕ. The average dune M_z is 2.86ϕ (0.138 mm) with a standard deviation of 0.094ϕ. The aeolian flat samples have normally distributed M_z values about a mean of 2.83ϕ (0.141 mm) with a standard deviation of 0.045ϕ. The aeolian flat samples are almost unbelievably uniform in mean size; the *extreme* values among the 31 samples sieved are 2.75ϕ and 2.89ϕ, except for one completely aberrant sample at 2.27ϕ, which is omitted from all calculations because it is over 8 standard deviations from the mean.

Are the dune sands really finer than the

beach sands as it appears from the above data? To determine the significance of the difference in mean size between the environments Student's t test (Brownlee, 1948) was applied. This test states the probability (P) that differences in means are due to chance sampling. For example, if P equals .10, it means that there is a 10 percent chance that the apparent differences between two sets of samples are merely accidental. Most workers adopt the convention that P must be less than .05 in order for differences to be considered as significant. For this set of samples P = .10 for beach versus dunes, P = .23 for dunes versus aeolian flat, and P = .42 for beach versus aeolian flat. Thus, our analysis has failed to reveal any significant difference in mean grain size between the environments.

The grand mean (unweighted) for the sediments of the island is 2.832ϕ (0.140 mm) with a standard deviation of 0.070ϕ which means that two-thirds of the samples have mean sizes between 2.76ϕ and 2.90ϕ (0.134 to 0.148 mm). The remarkable similarity between all samples in average grain size indicates a very peculiar set of conditions. Apparently the source supplying sand to Mustang Island contributes only a very limited range of sizes and the environmental processes presently working on the sands are able to effect an extreme degree of homogenization.

Inclusive graphic standard deviation (σ_I) is a measure of sorting, found by the formula

$$\sigma_I = \frac{\phi 84 - \phi 16}{4} + \frac{\phi 95 - \phi 5}{6.6}.$$

If the grain size distribution is Gaussian-normal, 68 percent of the sample will lie within the range of $M_z \pm \sigma_I$. Graphic standard deviation values of all the environments on Mustang Island are close, with almost all the samples being classed as very well sorted (defined as σ_I under 0.35ϕ; Folk and Ward, 1957, p. 13). All of the areas show a nearly normal frequency distribution of graphic standard deviation values (fig. 3). The beach sands are slightly more poorly sorted, having an average σ_I of 0.309ϕ with a standard deviation of 0.021ϕ. This means that the central two-thirds of the beach samples have σ_I between 0.288ϕ and 0.330ϕ. The dune sands have the best

sorting with an average σ_I of 0.273ϕ and a standard deviation of 0.026ϕ. The aeolian flat samples are intermediate in sorting, having an average σ_I of 0.286ϕ with a standard deviation of 0.023ϕ.

By applying Student's t test to this set of samples it was determined that the probability of these differences being due to chance was only .0001 for the beach versus the dunes, .0002 for the beach versus the aeolian flat, and .07 for the dunes versus the aeolian flat. Thus the beach samples are very significantly more poorly sorted than the dune or aeolian flat samples, but the latter two environments have essentially similar sorting.

Skewness (Sk_I) measures the symmetry of the distribution by the formula

$$Sk_I = \frac{\phi 16 + \phi 84 - 2\phi 50}{2(\phi 84 - \phi 16)} + \frac{\phi 5 + \phi 95 - 2\phi 50}{2(\phi 95 - \phi 5)}.$$

Symmetrical curves have $Sk_I = .00$, and as skewness becomes more extreme the value of Sk_I approaches a theoretical maximum of $+1.00$ or -1.00. There is considerable difference in skewness between the beach sediments and the dune and aeolian flat sediments, with most of the beach sediments having nearly symmetrical curves (fig. 4). The dune and aeolian flat samples, on the contrary, are positively skewed (having a tail of fine grains). The beach sediments show bimodality of Sk_I with modes coming at about -0.02 and $+0.08$; the negatively-skewed samples are those nearest the Gulf. The Sk_I distribution of the dunes is weakly bimodal with modes at $+0.06$ and $+0.22$. The aeolian flat samples have a more nearly normal Sk_I distribution, and the primary mode occurs at $+0.16$. Mean and standard deviation of skewness values for the samples from the various areas are as follows: beach $Sk_I = +0.028$ (near-symmetrical), $\sigma 0.060$; dunes $Sk_I = +0.139$ (fine skewed), $\sigma 0.079$; and aeolian flat $Sk_I = +0.169$ (fine skewed), $\sigma 0.068$. Not one of the 45 dune or aeolian flat samples has negative skewness, the smallest value for any sample being $+.03$.

By applying Student's t test, the differences in skewness are extremely significant; the probability of these differences being due to chance is $P = .00001$ for the beach versus dunes, $P = .0000001$ for the beach versus the aeolian flat, and $P = .22$ (non-

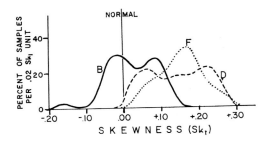

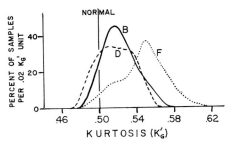

FIG. 4.—Frequency distributions of skewness values and kurtosis values for all environments. Beach, solid line (B); dune, dashed line (D); aeolian flat, dotted line (F). Beaches tend to give nearly symmetrical curves, while dune andaeolian flat samples both show pronounced positive skewness because of a tail of "fines." Considering kurtosis, beaches and dunes yield nearly normal (mesokurtic) curves while the aeolian flat samples are distinctly leptokurtic.

significant) for the dunes versus the aeolian flat. This shows that the dune and aeolian flat sediments are very significantly more fine-skewed than the beach sediments, because of a tail of fines to the right of the mode.

Kurtosis (K_G) measures the normality of a distribution by comparing the sorting in the central part of the curve with the sorting in the tails; if the curve is Gaussian-normal this ratio must be a constant value. The formula used here is

$$K_G = \frac{\phi95 - \phi5}{2.44 \times (\phi75 - \phi25)},$$

and with this formula normal curves (no matter what their overall sorting) have $K_G = 1.00$. A curve with kurtosis of 1.20 is leptokurtic (better sorted in the central part than the tails); the value signifies that, for a given degree of sorting in the central part of the distribution ($\phi25$ to $\phi75$), the spread between the tails ($\phi5$ to

$\phi95$) is 1.20 times as great as it should be if the distribution were normal. For statistical purposes (t tests, computations of standard deviations, means, etc.) it is better if the normalized function

$$K_G' = \frac{K_G}{K_G + 1}$$

is used (Folk and Ward, 1957). In this transformation, normal curves have $K_G' = .50$, leptokurtic distributions have values above this and platykurtic, below this.

The beach and dune sediments are on the mesokurtic-leptokurtic borderline while the aeolian flat sediments are distinctly leptokurtic (fig. 4). The mean and standard deviation of the kurtosis values are as follows: beach $K_G' = .522$ (mesokurtic), $\sigma = 0.019$; dune $K_G' = .517$ (mesokurtic), $\sigma = 0.020$; and aeolian flat $K_G' = .546$ (leptokurtic), $\sigma = 0.024$. All of the kurtosis distribution curves are nearly normal. By applying Student's t test it was determined that the probability of these differences being due to chance was $P = .45$ (insignificant) for the beach versus dunes, $P = .0001$ for the beach versus aeolian flat, and $P = .0002$ for the dunes versus the aeolian flat. This means that the aeolian flat sediments are very significantly more leptokurtic than the dune and beach sediments.

SUMMARY

These results show that it is very easy to distinguish the three environments on Mustang Island by size analysis, despite the phenomenal uniformity of mean grain size. Because differences between samples exist almost entirely in the "tails" of the curves, skewness and kurtosis are the most valuable parameters to use in identifying the environments. Beach samples have normal curves; that is, they are near-symmetrical mesokurtic. Dune samples have curves that are fine-skewed but still mesokurtic. The aeolian flat samples have curves that are both fine-skewed and leptokurtic. The probability that these are chance differences ranges from 1 in 5000 to 1 in 10,000,000!

The following summary key may be used to distinguish the environments on Mustang Island:

Graphic Standard Deviation (σ_I)
   0.21–0.26 probably dune
   0.26–0.28 dune or aeolian flat
   0.28–0.30 indeterminate
   0.30–0.35 probably beach
Skewness (Sk_I)
   $-.20$ to $+.02$ probably beach
   $+.02$ to $+.05$ beach or dune
   $+.05$ to $+.13$ indeterminate
   $+.13$ to $+.30$ dune or aeolian flat
Kurtosis (K_G')
   .47 to .53 beach or dune
   .53 to .55 indeterminate
   .55 to .61 probably aeolian flat

It is evident that the beach sediments are uniquely distinguished by their normality and relatively poor sorting, while the only way to tell dune sands from aeolian flat sands is by kurtosis.

VARIATION IN PARAMETERS LENGTHWISE OF THE ISLAND

In the preceding section we have shown that very significant differences emerge if one compares all the beach sand samples with all the dune or aeolian flat samples. Now it is desirable to investigate if, considering one environment, there is any sys-

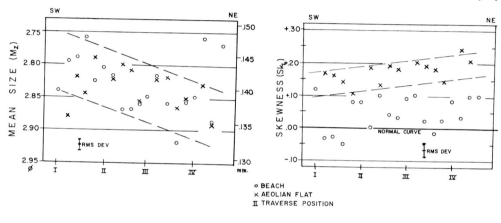

o BEACH
x AEOLIAN FLAT
II TRAVERSE POSITION

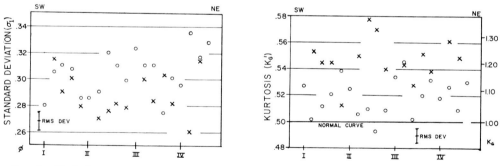

Fig. 5.—Variation in parameters lengthwise of the island. Roman numerals refer to positions of the crosswise traverses, from I at the southwest end to IV near the northeast end of the island. Beach samples shown by open circles, aeolian flat samples by crosses. Mean size shows a dubious tendency to coarsen slightly to the southwest, but there is great sample-to-sample fluctuation. There is no lengthwise change in standard deviation, but the beach samples are rather consistently more poorly sorted. In skewness there is a striking distinction beween beach samples and aeolian flat samples, the latter being in every case more positive-skewed than the beach sample in the corresponding geographic position. The aeolian flat samples appear to be more strongly skewed toward the northeast end of the island. Kurtosis shows no systematic change lengthwise of the island, but the aeolian flat samples are almost always more strongly leptokurtic. Brackets indicate the rms deviation (that is, probable experimental error) for each parameter: it is 68 percent certain that the true value of a parameter for a given sample lies within the bracketed range.

tematic change in parameters lengthwise of the island; that is, do the beach sands become better sorted to the southwest or is there a systematic decrease of kurtosis with distance in the aeolian flat? In studying this aspect, only the beach and aeolian flat samples that occurred along the lengthwise traverse were used—that is, only those taken from the middle of the beach and the middle of the flat (fig. 5). The dune samples were not used because they showed no hint of any lengthwise change. Even on the beach and aeolian flat there was very little systematic lengthwise change in the parameters; values fluctuated slightly from place to place in an apparently random

fashion. Standard deviation and kurtosis showed no trend at all, the aeolian flats remaining consistently better sorted and more leptokurtic all the way down the island. In mean size (M_z), however, both beach and aeolian flat samples apparently coarsen from about 2.85ϕ at the northeast end to 2.80ϕ at the southwest end of the island. But there is so much scatter about this trend that the t test shows that the difference is probably not significant (comparing the M_z values of the northeast half of the island with those from the southwest gives $P=.10$; that is, there is one chance in ten that the apparent change is accidental). Skewness shows no systematic change down

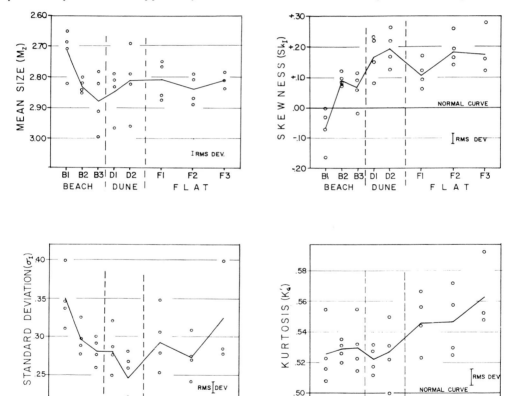

FIG. 6.—Detailed variation in parameters crosswise of the island. Sample location designations (B1, D2, etc. are as shown in fig. 2. Each small circle represents an analyzed sample from one of the four crosswise traverses; the solid line shows the mean value obtained by averaging the results from the four traverses. Mean size is coarsest near the Gulf but otherwise shows little change. Sorting is best at the rear of the dunes. Skewness and kurtosis both increase in passing from the Gulf toward the lagoon side of the island. Rms deviation brackets have the same significance as before.

the beach, but in the aeolian flat skewness apparently decreases from about $+.20$ at the northeast end to $+.14$ at the southwest end (figs, 5, 7). Comparing the northeast half of the aeolian flat with the southwest half, the t test gives $P=.04$, so that this may be a real change.

SIGNIFICANCE OF SAMPLE-TO-SAMPLE FLUCTUATION

Because values of the parameters fluctuate along the island (fig. 5) the question arises as to whether this variation is a gradual change between the sampling points or if the scale of fluctuation is much smaller than the sampling interval. For example, if the mean size at a hypothetical station A is 2.80ϕ and the mean size at station B is 2.90ϕ, then if one took four samples spaced at equal distances along a line between A and B, would the resulting values show a gradual transition (for example, 2.82ϕ, 2.84ϕ, 2.86ϕ, and 2.88ϕ) or a random fluctuation (for example, 2.88ϕ, 2.76ϕ, 2.89ϕ, and 2.82ϕ)? To check this, four additional equispaced samples were taken between one pair of regular grid sampling points on the beach and four more in a similar pattern on the aeolian flat. It was found that the parameters varied rapidly between grid sampling points, and, as a matter of fact, all size parameters fluctuated just as much between two successive sampling points on the original grid (0.8 mile apart) as they fluctuated the entire distance down the island (16 miles)! As a consequence the scale of fluctuation in parameters is less (perhaps much less) than 1000 feet.

VARIATIONS OF PARAMETERS ACROSS THE ENVIRONMENTS

Four crosswise traverses, spaced at intervals down the island, were taken. In these, as has been mentioned, three samples were taken from the beach (one nearest the water just above the break in slope, one in the middle, and one at the back of the beach near the dunes), two from the dunes (one next to the beach, the other next to the flat) and three spaced across the flats (figs. 1, 2). Heretofore all the samples from a particular major environment have been considered together; but it is found that even within one environment there is a gradual transverse change in that samples

nearer the Gulf have different properties from those farther away. The parameters varied as shown in figure 6.

Mean Size.—The coarsest sediments analyzed were on the beach nearest the Gulf, for here $M_z=2.71\phi$. The sediments became finer as the beach was crossed until $M_z=2.88\phi$ on the backshore near the dunes. Mean size increased again in the dunes and then stayed nearly constant across the aeolian flat with $M_z=2.82\phi$.

Standard Deviation.—Sorting on the beach near the Gulf was poorest with a standard deviation of 0.35ϕ. Sorting was much better on the back of the beach and in the first dunes with $\sigma_I=0.28\phi$ and continued to improve to 0.25ϕ on the lee side of the large dunes. Sorting became progressively poorer on the aeolian flat, reaching a value of 0.32ϕ near the lagoon.

Skewness.—On the beach nearest the Gulf the sediments were negatively skewed (-0.07), while at the back of the beach skewness changed markedly to $+.08$. The dune and aeolian flat samples were even more positively (fine) skewed, with skewness averaging $+.15$ to $+.20$. Figure 7 is a fence diagram which shows the variation in skewness both lengthwise and across the island.

Kurtosis.—Values of kurtosis were nearly constant at $K_G'=.525-.530$ for both the beach and dune sediments. Sands became abruptly more leptokurtic on the aeolian flat $(K_G'=.54)$ and climbed to $.56$ for the sediments near the lagoon.

INTERRELATIONSHIP OF SIZE PARAMETERS

In order to see if the four size parameters on Mustang Island were interrelated, six scatter plots were made by coplotting each of the pairs of parameters (Folk and Ward, 1957). However, because of the extremely small range of mean size values (2.65ϕ to 3.00ϕ) and similarly small range of standard deviation values (0.22ϕ to 0.40ϕ), no plots using either of these two parameters resulted in any significant trends or correlations. An example of one of these is the plot of mean size versus standard deviation (fig. 8) which shows that for Mustang Island sorting is practically independent of mean size. The relatively poor sorting of the beach samples is evident on this diagram.

The only plot that shows any correlation

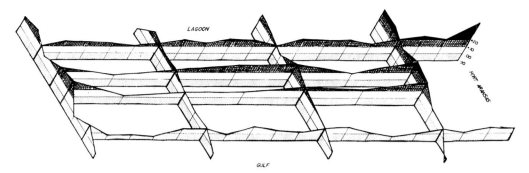

FIG. 7.—Fence diagram, showing variation of skewness over Mustang Island. "Fences" trending to the upper left connect the four crosswise traverses, from Gulf at bottom to lagoon at top; the crosswise distances are greatly exaggerated. The long "fences" represent the lengthwise traverses, in order from the bottom; (1) mid-beach traverse, (2) and (3) dune traverses, and (4) aeolian flat traverse. Note increase in skewness away from the Gulf (readily visible by following each crosswise traverse, skewness values over +.10 shown in heavy shading) and increasing skewness to the northeast (upper right) in the aeolian flat.

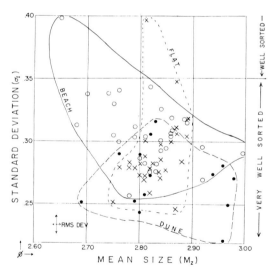

FIG. 8.—Scatterplot of mean size versus graphic standard deviation for all Mustang Island samples. Open circles, beach; filled circles, dune; crosses, aeolian flat. Except for the fact that the beaches are more poorly sorted, there is considerable overlapping of environments; that is this diagram is not very useful in distinguishing these sediments on Mustang Island. Furthermore there is very little overall trend between grain size and sorting except that within the beaches the coarser samples have poorest sorting. Reliability of each data point is indicated by the rms deviation brackets.

between parameters is the plot of skewness versus kurtosis (fig. 9), which shows that high positive skewness is in general associated with leptokurtosis. On this diagram, too, the best differentiation of the samples from the three environments is accomplished: the beach sands yield nearly normal curves, dune sands have nearly normal kurtosis but are positively skewed, while the aeolian flat samples are positively skewed and have high kurtosis.

Why should the plot of skewness versus kurtosis be the most valuable one to use in identifying the environments on Mustang Island? Apparently it is because the source area supplied sand of very uniform mean grain size and superb sorting, and these more basic properties of the sediment are thereby fixed and can only be slightly modified by the dune or beach environments. However, slight differences in mode of transport apparently affect the tails of the distribution considerably, and the character of the tails is precisely what kurtosis and skewness are designed to measure. Only a small amount of sand need be added to or subtracted from the tails to change these parameters greatly, while a large amount of material must be added (or subtracted) to change the mean size or standard deviation substantially. An analogy may be drawn here between sphericity and roundness of pebbles. With a given distance of transport, roundness changes more significantly than sphericity because roundness measures easily-changed small-scale features (sharpness of corners) while sphericity depends upon the major dimensional ratio which requires much more energy to change, hence is more a function of source.

HYPOTHESIS TO EXPLAIN THE SEDIMENT CHANGES

Heretofore no attempt has been made to explain why the dune sands are better sorted than the beach sands or why the beach sands give normal curves and the aeolian flat samples are positively skewed and leptokurtic. In searching for the geologic reason behind these changes there seems to be no way to prove or disprove the correctness of our hypothesis. The mechanism we propose fits the known facts; whether it is truly the correct mechanism is unknown.

We have seen that skewness and kurtosis

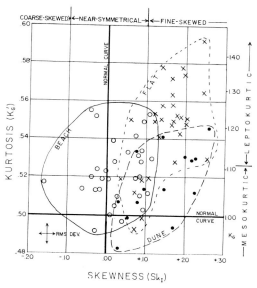

SKEWNESS (Sk$_I$)

FIG. 9.—Scatterplot of skewness versus kurtosis. Open circles, beach; filled circles, dune; crosses, aeolian flat. This plot is the best means of distinguishing environments on Mustang Island, because the differences between environments are reflected only in the tails of the grain size curves; and skewness and kurtosis are purposely designed to measure the properties of the tails. Beach samples give near-symmetrical, mesokurtic to slightly leptokurtic curves; dune samples are fine-skewed and mesokurtic; and aeolian flat samples are both fine-skewed and leptokurtic.

offer the best means of identifying the environments, that standard deviation also helps, but mean size is worthless. Consequently, differences between samples must be due to additions to, or subtractions from, the "tails" of the grain size curves while the bulk material remains essentially constant. Folk and Ward (1957) proposed that unimodal sediments gave normal curves, and that the cause of skewness and kurtosis was the addition of minor amounts of other normal populations to the sediment—often in amounts not even sufficient to form a secondary mode. Adding 5–10 percent of finer material to a normal population, for example, imparts positive skewness and leptokurtosis. The hypothesis developed below depends on this assumption of modal mixing.

First, one must assume that the direction of sand transport is from the beach to the dunes to the aeolian flat (a direction favored by the prevailing wind). All the sand samples from all environments have as their nucleus a normally-distributed population of grains. This population stays pretty constant in mean (2.80–2.85ϕ) and standard deviation (.28–.30ϕ) although slight fluctuations do occur. This nucleus forms the great bulk of all samples; it is impossible to calculate its exact proportion, but a careful guess would indicate that it forms from 80 to 95 percent of every sample. The differences in environments (which show up as differences in standard deviation, skewness and kurtosis), then are achieved by adding (or subtracting) small amounts of sand to the tails of this nucleus population. At the beach nearest the Gulf, to the nucleus population is added a very small amount of a coarser mode at about 2.0ϕ (?), averaging perhaps 2–5 percent of the sample. These rough figures are obtained by determining where the cumulative curve departs from a straight line on probability paper; beach analyses follow a straight line until they reach about 2.25ϕ (fig. 10) where they begin to curve off slightly. Addition of this slight coarse tail to the parent population (fig. 11) accounts for (1) a somewhat higher standard deviation, (2) slight negative skewness, and (3) slight leptokurtosis. This coarse mode is not shell fragments (which at the most comprise 2 to 5 percent of the fraction coarser

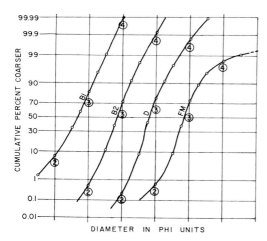

FIG. 10.—Representative cumulative curves from Mustang Island, plotted with probability ordinate. Circled numbers refer to phi diameters of the curves to which they are appended; that is all curves shown have medians between 2.7ϕ and 2.9ϕ. B1 is a typical curve for a beach sample nearest the Gulf; it is the only one that shows negative skewness. B2 is a typical sample from mid-beach, and shows the nearest approach to a normal curve, even when the distribution is carried past the 99.9 percentile. Curve D is a typical dune sample, showing positive skewness (the curve starts to "tail off" to the right after it passes the 90 percentile). Curve FM is a typical aeolian flat sample; note sharp "tailing off" past the 90 percentile, due to addition of a small amount of very fine sand and silt grains. This infiltered fine tail is responsible for the strong positive skewness and leptokurtosis; the central part of the distribution (ϕ25 to ϕ75) is still well sorted, but the tails are now relatively poorly sorted and this imparts a high kurtosis.

than 2ϕ, which itself makes up no more than 2 percent of the sample) but seems actually to be distinct population of coarser quartz grains. This mode is so small in quantity that its very presence is debatable, however.

In the rest of the beach, samples vary from normal curves to those having slight positive skewness (figs 10, 11). Apparently now the coarser mode has dropped out, and these samples represent in essence the unmodified nucleus population because they give curves that are most nearly normal and also have a sorting value coinciding with the average for all samples.

The change from beach to dunes is accompanied not only by improvement in sorting but, strangely enough, also by

abrupt development of strong positive skewness. Usually the change in sediments from a normal curve to a positively-skewed one is accompanied by poorer sorting because of the addition of a finer mode to the main population (Folk and Ward, 1957). However, it is possible to obtain a positively-skewed distribution from a normal one by two processes: (1) addition of fine material, the more common process, or (2) subtraction of the coarse end of a normal distribution. On Mustang Island the second process has seemingly operated as the sand travels from the beach to the dunes; elimination or lagging behind of the coarse end of the normally distributed nucleus population results in both improvement in sorting and development of positive skewness, because the curve is now rendered asymetrical with a "pseudo-tail" in the fines (fig. 11).

In the aeolian flat, the curves remain postively skewed and become markedly leptokurtic as the sorting worsens. This can be interpreted as the result of adding a fairly large amount of material (probably windborne infiltration) to the fine end of the distribution (fig. 11). It is estimated that this fine material has a mode at about 4ϕ (silt to very fine sand) and averages about 5–10 percent of the total sample (fig. 10).

One of the notable characteristics of Mustang Island samples is their tendency to be leptokurtic (table 2; fig. 9). Only six of the 76 samples had kurtosis values under 1.00 (K_G' under .50). This prevalence of kurtosis values slightly over $K_G = 1.00$ seems to be a common feature in samples that are essentially pure sands. One does not have to search far for a reason, however; leptokurtosis is caused by additions of a small amount of a secondary mode (say 3–20 percent) to a primary mode (Folk and Ward, 1957, fig. 19). Addition of this secondary mode serves to worsen sorting in the tails of the distribution while the sorting in the central part of the distribution remains good, hence the curves become leptokurtic. Apparently, then, few sands consist entirely of one mode, and most have small amounts of some secondary mode either coarser or finer than the main mode; this is seemingly the case on Mustang Island.

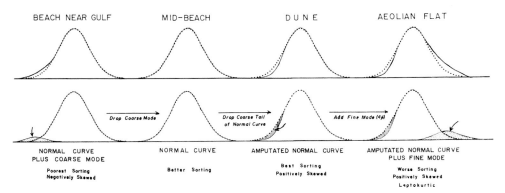

Fig. 11.—Hypothesis to explain the development of different types of grain-size curves on Mustang Island. The direction of transport is assumed to be from the Gulf Beach (left) towards the aeolian flat (right). In each diagrammatic figure, the dotted curve represents a standard Gaussian-normal distribution, of constant shape and placed at constant position to serve as a reference mark. The solid-line curves in the upper row of figures represent the type of frequency curve obtained upon analysis of the actual samples; usually, it departs somewhat from the standard Gaussian-normal curve. The lower set of figures is an attempt to explain *why* the actual sample curve departs from the reference Gaussian curve. It is proposed that a normally-distributed nucleus population forms the great bulk of all samples, and that differences between samples (expressed as departures from normality) are caused by addition or subtraction of grains near the tails of this nucleus population.

The beach near the Gulf is negatively skewed; this is believed to be because of the addition of a very small amount of coarse mode to the nucleus normal population of grains. The mid-beach curve seems to consist very nearly of the pure nucleus normal population of grains; apparently the coarse mode has lagged behind and disappeared, thus the sorting is slightly improved. In passing from the beach to the dunes, the grains in the coarse end of the normal population apparently lag behind; thus the coarse tail is "amputated" (shaded area), causing positive skewness and further improvement in sorting. In the aeolian flat, a fine tail is added by infiltration of 4ϕ material settling out from the atmosphere; this produces marked positive skewness, strong leptokurtosis, and poorer sorting. These causative mechanisms are all hypothetical but appear to fit the observed facts.

TABLE 2.—*Classification of samples as to normality of the distribution*

(Limits after Folk and Ward, 1957)

SKEWNESS

	Coarse-skewed $(Sk_I < -.10)$	Near-symmetrical $(Sk_I -.10$ to $+.10)$	Fine-skewed $(Sk_I > +.10)$
Beach	1	27	3
Dune	0	6	8
Flat	0	6	25
Total	1	39	36

KURTOSIS

	Platykurtic $(K_G'$ under .475)	Mesokurtic $(K_G' .475–.525)$	Leptokurtic $(K_G'$ over .525)
Beach	0	20	11
Dune	0	8	6
Flat	0	6	25
Total	0	34	42

CONCLUSIONS

Some source (probably the Colorado River) contributes normally-distributed, well-sorted and exceedingly uniform fine sand to Mustang Island, accounting for the remarkable constancy in size and lack of change lengthwise of the island. A coarse quartz mode is retained or added to the normally-distributed sediment only on that part of the main beach nearest the water, possibly because of the higher energy levels existing there. As the sand is blown from the beach and heaped into dunes, the coarse end of the normal size distribution lags selectively behind because the wind cannot carry the coarser grains as easily; thus the dunes become positively skewed and better sorted (fig. 11).

The aeolian flats are very level, grass-covered, and lie at a low elevation. Hence small quantities of coarse silt or very fine sand settle out from the atmosphere and accumulate in the flat, probably filtering down between the coarser grains. The coarse silt cannot be removed from the flat because of its relative inaccessibility to wind erosion. This infiltered silt tail (fig. 11) imparts positive skewness and leptokurtosis. Source of the silt is not known; it appears to be most abundant at the north end of the island (because skewness is most extreme there (figs. 5, 7), and could conceivably be blown from the mainland during "northers."

This study has shown that grain size analysis is quite successful in distinguishing three environments on Mustang Island and in showing what geologic processes operate to differentiate them. The best way to identify the environments is by plotting skewness against kurtosis, because these properties reflect the changes in the tails of the distribution and the tails are most sensitive to transportive mechanisms. Further studies are being undertaken to see if the same principles apply elsewhere along the Texas coast.

ACKNOWLEDGEMENTS

This paper is the result of a Master's thesis submitted by Mason (1957) to the Geology Department, The University of Texas; the thesis was supervised by Folk. Edward C. Jonas and Raymond C. Staley also served on the thesis committee and offered helpful comments. Dr. Howard Odum assisted in sample collecting and made available the facilities of the University of Texas Marine Station at Port Aransas, and Dr. H. Gordon Damon made many suggestions. Maxine Welch Mason assisted greatly in preparation of the drawings.

REFERENCES

BROWNLEE, K. A., 1948, Industrial experimentation. Chemical Publishing Co., Brooklyn, 168 p.
BULLARD, F. M., 1942, Source of beach and river sands on the Gulf coast of Texas: Geol. Soc. America Bull., v. 53, p. 1021–1044.
FOLK, R. L., 1954, The distinction between grain size and mineral composition in sedimentary-rock nomenclature: Jour. Geology, v. 62, p. 344–359.
FOLK, R. L., AND WARD, W. C., 1957, Brazos River bar: a study in the significance of grain size parameters: Jour. Sedimentary Petrology, v. 27, p. 3–26.
INMAN, D., L., 1952. Measures for describing the size distribution of sediments: Jour. Sedimentary Petrology, v. 22, p. 125–145.
KRUMBEIN, W. C., 1934, Size frequency distribution of sediments: Jour. Sedimentary Petrology, v. 4, p. 65–77.
KRUMBEIN, W. C., AND PETTIJOHN, F. J., 1938, Manual of sedimentary petrography. D. Appleton-Century, New York, 549 p.
MASON, C. C., 1957, Sediments of Mustang Island, Texas: unpubl. Master's thesis, The University of Texas.
POWERS, M. C., 1953, A new roundness scale for sedimentary particles: Jour. Sedimentary Petrology, v. 23, p. 117–119.
TRASK, P. D., 1932, Origin and environment of source sediments of petroleum: Gulf Publ. Co., Houston, 323 p.

JOURNAL OF SEDIMENTARY PETROLOGY, VOL. 37, No. 1, PP. 128–156
FIGS. 1–31, MARCH, 1967

SEDIMENTATION OF BEACH GRAVELS: EXAMPLES FROM SOUTH WALES[1]

BRIAN J. BLUCK
Department of Geology, University of Glasgow, Glasgow

ABSTRACT

On the basis of particle shape the surface layers of some South Wales beaches are subdivided into four zones:— a large disc zone landward, typified by cobble sized discs, having on its seaward side the imbricate zone composed mainly of imbricate disc-shaped pebbles. Seaward of the imbricate zone lies the infill zone where spherical and rod shaped pebbles (drawn from a reservoir, underlying the large disc zone, and in which there are particles with a shape and size making them potentially capable of rapid seaward transport) infill a framework of spherical cobbles fringing the seaward margin. The spherical cobble framework is called the outer frame.

Particle shapes are not so much made as used on these beaches; and particle shape differentiation is related to settling velocity, pivotability, and ability to filter through the porous gravels. Discs are not produced by a special feature of marine abrasion: the most oblate discs are found in areas least worked on by the sea.

Composition is a function of particle size and shape; particle size and shape vary systematically across the beach; so composition and maturity indices are also seen to vary in a similar way. In the reworking of the boulder clays, which forms a source for much of these marine gravels, two processes are recognised: the post glacial weathering of the boulder clays and abrasion on the beach. Both are selective in that they affect the labile (in this case a subgreywacke) more than the stable (in this case, quartzites). Weathering and abrasion work to split greywackes into discs. At the same time destruction of this kind in always reducing the number of large and increasing the number of small particles, produces a size maturity correlation where the coarser grains are more mature than equivalent sizes in the original boulder clay, but possibly the finer are less mature than equivalent sizes in the original boulder clay. As abrasion further continues, (exemplified here on one beach) the composition shape function begins to disappear, and maturity greatly increases with size.

Particle size parameters vary across the beach. Changes in standard deviation and skewness are, to a considerable extent, effected by either the removal from, or addition of small coarse modes to large fine. Size frequency and shape frequency are combined in an attempt to understand more fully the type and extent of sediment movement taking place in these gravels.

The beaches are divided into two types: the one on breakdown building up to the seaward a succession of coarse spherical cobbles infilled with spherical and rod shaped pebbles; the other an alternation of beds containing spherical and rod-shaped grains with beds of disc-shaped grains.

INTRODUCTION

Numerous well developed gravel beaches of believed storm origin are found on the South Wales (U.K.) coastline which faces the dominant westerly winds. This study is concerned with the particle shape, size, and lithological composition of six of these beaches positioned between Sker Point and Nash Point (fig. 1). The coastline is at present one of submergence (Strahan, 1896; Strahan and Cantrill, 1904, p. 104), but oscillations of the post glacial shoreline have been a marked feature. The gravels of the present day beaches are backed by Recent gravel whose level is several feet higher. This older gravel is overlain by sand dunes.

The Ogmore gravel beaches are backed by low cliffs of Triassic breccias and Carboniferous Limestone or low sand dunes, and they face open sandy beaches. The Newton beaches, on the other hand are backed by fairly high dunes, face wide stretches of sandy beach, and lie adjacent to the Ogmore River. Much of the gravel on the

Newton beaches is mixed with sand, some of which is known to have come from the dunes. Sker beaches are situated on a rocky coastline, and are usually found in small coves backed by low dunes, Sker Point beach is situated on a headland, is backed by low lying dunes, faces a rock platform of Triassic conglomerate, and is one of the highest beach bars studied. Cwm Nash beach is situated in a small cove in a coastline which has high cliffs of Liassic limestone. The beach is backed by a small valley and has a rock platform in front of it. Like Sker Point, Cwm Nash receives relatively intensive wave attack, and the beach bar is correspondingly high.

In all, six beaches were sampled, and many more studied; but the beaches at Sker Point and Newton were sampled more intensively than the others.

PARTICLE SHAPE

The gravel beaches at the outset were sampled for particle shape using the method suggested by Krumbein (1953) and Krumbein and Miller

[1] Manuscript received June 30, 1966.

(1953), but once it became apparent that a zonal arrangement of particle shape existed on the beach, further sampling was not based on a statistical plan, but rather directed towards those parts of the investigation which would throw more light on the means of particle movement.

The shape of the particle was classified according to the Zingg (1935) classification, while sphericity, calculated according to Krumbein (1941b), is determined in only a few samples, since this measure is inherently ambiguous (van Andel, Wiggers, and Maarleveld 1954, p. 105; Sneed and Folk, 1958, p. 122; Bluck, 1965, p. 241). Approximately 50 particles were measured from each of the size grades and each of the localities shown in figures 1 and 4. The samples included particles of various lithology: in these gravels the type of source rock exerts very little control over the essential particle shape make-up of the beach.

The data are presented in two ways: the proportion of particle shapes are recorded for each size grade (fig. 2), and the size frequency mea-

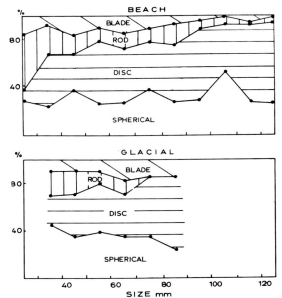

FIG. 2.—Shape composition of beaches and glacial boulder clay. Beach sample, 5,300; boulder clay, 600 particles.

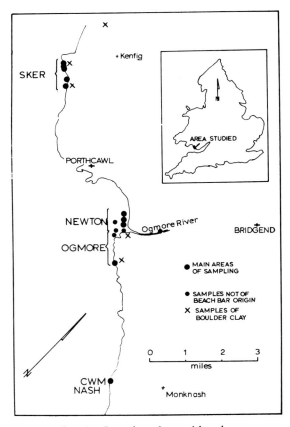

FIG. 1.—Location of gravel beaches.

surements are combined with the particle size shape data to give an estimate of the actual numbers of variously shaped particles there are in a sample (fig. 3). In figure 2 the proportion of differently shaped particles for each size is given for all beaches, but is obtained from only those samples collected by means of a grid; other samples were biased towards certain zones. Whilst significance has not been calculated on any of these data, there is clearly an abundance of spherical and disc shaped grains in all sizes (cf. Bluck, 1965, p. 241, fig. 14), with the exception of the 20–30 mm. grade where there is an abundance of rod shaped fragments. Although the proportion of differently shaped particles varies from size to size, there is a general trend to these variations with an increase in the proportion of discs with increasing size, and a corresponding decrease in rods and blades. In comparison with the particle shape composition of the boulder clays, beaches have smaller proportions of spherical shaped fragments in many of those size grades common to both deposits. A marked decline in the proportion of rod shaped particles takes place in the 70–80 mm. sizes of the boulder clays which also have a slightly higher proportion of blades in the larger sizes; this latter characteristic would follow from the observations of Holmes (1960, p. 1653), if blades are assumed to be an "immature" shape. A combination of shape size frequency is given for all

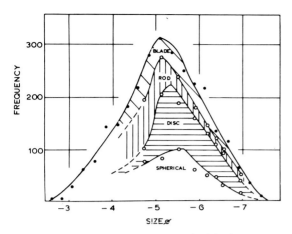

FIG. 3.—Size frequency combined with the proportions of various shapes in given size grades so as to give an estimate of the actual numbers of differently shaped particles on the beach.

beaches studied (fig. 3), including only those samples collected with the aid of the grid. Disc shaped fragments are by far the most abundant, and the highest percentage of discs is found in the size class which is also the modal size class of the gravel. This is not the case with any other shape; spherical grains, for example, are present in greater proportion in a size class which is larger than the modal size class of the sediment and rods in a smaller size class. The reasons for these features are not yet understood.

Measurements of particle shape-size of gravels from two selected beaches are shown in figure 4, where a general increase in the percentage of spherical and rod shaped particles takes place towards the seaward margin. Only in one of the six beaches studied is there an increase in the proportions of spherical and rod shaped fragments in a perpendicular direction, for instance, along the beach. The most landward margins of all the beach bars are composed of gravels which have a high proportion of disc shaped grains in the larger size classes, spherical and rod shaped fragments being almost confined to the lower size ranges. Since the modal grain size of the sediment is lower than sizes in which there is a high proportion of discs, disc shaped fragments are not the most abundant variety in these gravels (fig. 7). Deposits with the characteristics listed above make up the *large disc zone*. Immediately seaward of the large disc zone are deposits characterized by a high proportion of disc shaped grains in all sizes studied. And, in addition, the modal grain size of the deposit falls in the same size range which contains the highest proportion of discs. Moreover, the deposits flanking the seaward margin of the large disc

zone are the only ones where grain imbrication is particularly well displayed, and these gravels consequently constitute the *imbricate zone*, although imbrication may be seen in deposits occurring elsewhere on the beach. Outside the imbricate zone, is an area composed of gravels which have a large proportion of spherical and rod shaped fragments in all the sizes studied. This area normally has a sheet of sand bordering the imbricate zone (that is on the landward fringe), over which particles move very rapidly, and in view of this the sheet of sand is referred to as the "sand run." The particles moving across the sand run accumulate on the seaward side to form a narrow band composed of spherical and rod shaped pebbles, where the modal grain size of the deposit is also the size having the highest proportion of either rod or spherical grains. Seaward of this again is an area where the spherical and rod shaped pebbles are infilling a framework of larger cobbles. Trenching has shown that all three deposits described represent the stages of infilling a cobble frame, and for this reason the three deposits comprise the *infill zone;* but all three are not always present in the infill zone. All zones in figure 4 refer only to the surface layers of the deposit.

The cobble sized deposits, composed primarily of spherical grains, which fringe the very seaward gravel bar margin is called the *outer frame.* Here, the size grade with the highest proportion of spherical particles is coincident with the modal grain size of the sediment.

Landward Particle Movement; Build up of the Bar

The gravel bars were built up during storm conditions (Lewis, 1931). In nearly all the beaches studied, the presence of gravel (which often contains disc shaped boulders, up to a metre across) above or on the high water mark confirms this view. Net landward movement during normal sea conditions is small (cf. Kidson and Carr, 1959, p. 386) and mainly confined to disc shaped pebbles. Fleming (1964, p. 115), in tank experiments, demonstrated a migration of "non spherical" grains up the beach.

It is suggested that during storm conditions fragments of all shapes were thrown forward by the waves, but discoidal particles being easily plucked from the sea floor; being lighter than, for example, a sphere of similar median diameter; and when in suspension having a lower settling velocity than any other shaped particle (Wadell, 1934; Krumbein, 1942; McNown and Malaika, 1950; Albertson, 1953; Briggs and others, 1962) were larger than, or, if of the same size, thrown further than any other particle being moved by the wave.

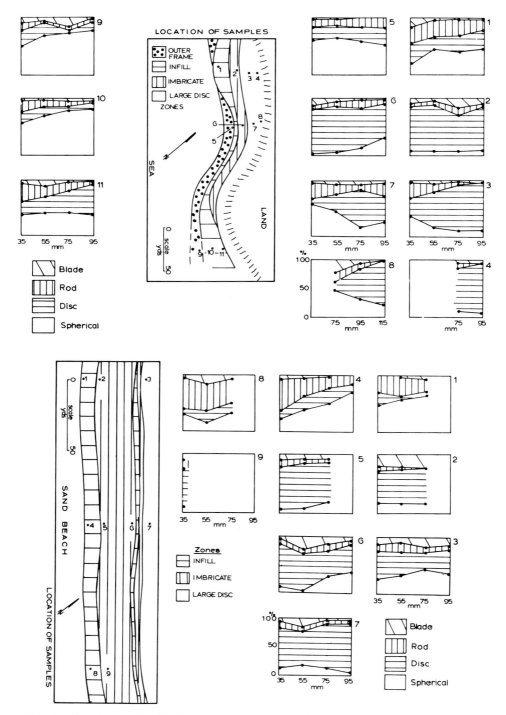

FIG. 4.—Showing the distribution of particle shapes and zones on two of the beaches studied.
Top diagram, Sker; bottom, Newton.

Conversely, the presence of large spherical shaped fragments at the foot of the bar may be partly due to their high settling velocity. During storm conditions, when moved, they were either smaller than or, if of the same size, thrown a shorter distance than other shaped grains. Spherical and disc shaped grains are end members of series of shapes all having different settling velocities; rods and blades falling somewhere between the two extremes (Krumbein, 1942; McNown and Malaika, 1950; Albertson, 1953; Briggs and others, 1962).

On one occasion, after moderately rough seas, spherical particles were found blanketing the various zones already established on the beach. The paucity of disc shaped fragments in this blanketing deposit is believed to be due to the lack of discs on the seaward bar margin, from where the deposit had been derived, that is from the infill and outer frame zones.

Seaward Particle Movement; Breakdown of Storm Beach

Particle movement during the erosive period of the gravel beach development takes place within the beach on the landward side, and also on the beach surface, normally seen on the seaward areas.

Movement within the beach.—Movement within the beach has been demonstrated by a study of the distribution of painted particles from known positions. And such movement is most common in the gravels underlying the large disc zone. The backwash of waves breaking on the porous frame travels through the gravel, rather than on the gravel surface and in its passage combs finer material seaward the size and shape of which depend upon the size and geometry of the gravel pore space: the gravel in this upper part of the beach therefore acts as a sieve on the infiltering particles (fig. 26). Insufficient data are as yet available to describe fully the shape sorting mechanism taking place in this sieving process, but it is known that spherical particles, on some beaches at least, move more quickly through the pores than do other shapes. The large disc zones of these beaches have aprons of spherical pebbles a few feet seaward of bands of seaweed, which mark the turning points of the flood tides; and these spherical pebbles are interpreted as having moved through the cobble frame of the large disc zone. The pore geometry not only varies with position on the beach (since shape and size of beach gravels vary in an areal fashion), but also varies in the same spot with changing sea conditions. Thus on some gravel beaches there is a tendency for rod shaped grains to orientate themselves in a direction perpendicular to beach strike; in others the gravel is seen to slump sea-

ward, and in these a random particle orientation is likely. It might well be that the condition of rod particles, with their long axea dipping towards the sea precedes the slumping in that it provides a fabric facilitating mass movement.

Movement on the surface.—In traction spherical and rod shaped particles tend to move faster than the discoidal (Krumbein, 1942, p. 625); discs have a lower pivotability than rods and spherical (Shepard and Young, 1961, p. 198; Kuenen, 1964a, p. 207). These facts were demonstrated on the beach by painting particles of various shapes and size, placing them in a line parallel to the shore, and noting their distribution after a tide. Thus, on all the beaches studied spherical and rod shaped particles are transported seaward by the backwash and accumulate on the seaward fringe of the gravel bar (fig. 4, 5).

Generally speaking spherical and rod shaped fragments respond in a similar way to the forces applied to them by the water; this is demonstrated by the close positive correlation between the number of rod and spherical grains present in the samples (fig. 6). Moreover, most samples have more spherical than rod shaped fragments. But in parts of the imbricate zone at Sker Point, the lower sizes particularly have more rod than spherical particles (fig. 4). This fact is in evidence elsewhere, although is not true at Cwm Nash (fig. 5). The reason for the higher percentage of rods in the imbricate zone of the many beaches is clearly displayed in the field, where rod shaped pebbles are caught up in the irregular surface offered by the imbricate fabric. Here they lie with their long axes parallel to the beach strike lodged in hollows which face the land (since imbricate pebbles normally dip towards the sea.) Observations made on the beach during sediment movement showed that spherical grains, on the other hand, move with greater ease through this picket of imbricate particles. When the direction of imbrication is reversed, the hollows between the discs face the sea and the rods are released.

This lateral filtering of particles according to their shape also takes place in the outer frame, and can be demonstrated at Sker Point. At localities 9, 10, 11, (fig. 4, Sker), situated in the infill zone and outer frame, there is a seaward decline in the proportion of rods, but an increase in the proportion of spherical particles. This, again, can be related to the nature of the floor over which the grains are transported: the spherical grains are better suited to travel through cobble frame, since the rods, being moved with greater speed when they are orientated with their long axis parallel to the beach, are least capable of moving through the pores of the cobbles when in this alinement.

There is a seaward decline in the size grade which has the highest proportion of disc shaped pebbles. The modal grain size of the gravel is smaller than that size with the highest proportion of discs on the landward bar margin, and greater than the modal size with the highest proportion of discs on the seaward bar fringes. Both modal grain size of the gravel and the size grade with the highest proportion of discs are coincident in the sediments of the imbricate zone, which is situated somewhere between the two other locations (fig. 7). These features concerning the disc shaped particles are common to all the beaches. In addition, there is an overall change in the shape of the discs from land to sea; the discs on the landward side are more oblate than those on the seaward, thus giving the impression of a very gradual change in the shapes of fragments across the beach.

The positive correlation between the number of discs and the number of blades in each of the samples indicates that both shapes respond in a similar way to the forces applied to them by the water (fig. 6). Discs are known to possess a low pivotability and therefore tend to move more slowly in traction. But pivotability is also a function of size as well as shape, and in these beaches the landward increase in the size grade with the highest proportion of discs is believed to be an expression of the two factors, shape and size, controlling pivotability.

The reason for the greater abundance of disc shaped particles in the imbricate zone is related to the amount of sediment reworking taking place there. Of the lag gravels, this is the one nearest to the sea, and is therefore subjected to more intensive current action: and since spherical and rod shaped particles are continually moving seaward and disc tending to lag, the more reworking by the sea the fewer spherical and rod shaped particles will remain on the imbricate zone. There are always the by-passing grains extracted from gravels to the landward, but these are few in number (fig. 7). A state of equilibrium is therefore approached when, in these lag gravels, the grain size of the sediment is coincident with that size class having the highest proportion of discs. It follows, therefore, that the deposits to the landward (the large disc zone) have not reached a condition of equilibrium, in the sense that given the same conditions of reworking and a long period in which seaward particle movement takes place, the spherical and rod shaped grains will continue to be removed from the zone. The large disc zones, and the deposits underlying them, are reservoirs of spherical and rod shaped grains which are potentially capable of rapid seaward transport.

Whilst the discs lag, they are by no means stationary—although the mechanism of seaward movement is not easily detected. Discs are seen to move like wheels (Owens, 1908, p. 418;

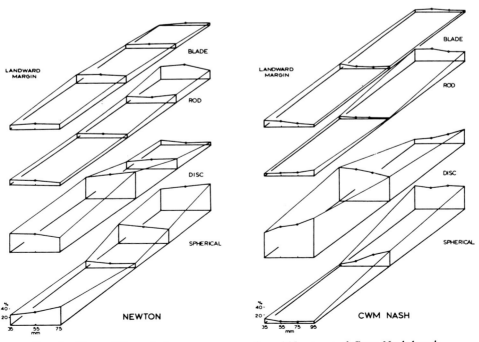

FIG. 5.—Shape differentiation across one section of Newton and Cwm Nash beach.

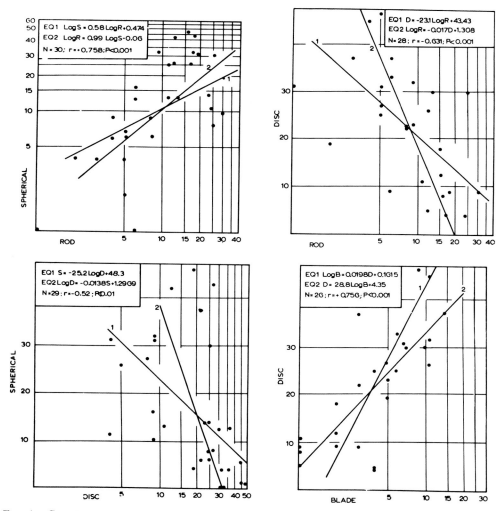

FIG. 6.—Correlation between the numbers of variously shaped particles found in each sample of size range 16–48 mm.

Bagnold, 1940; Kuenen, 1964a, p. 37), but this is not considered to be the important method of disc transportation here, and is commonly seen taking place on sandier beaches. The discs in the imbricate zone move in a number of ways, the most important of which are not yet determined. Imbricate discs nearest the sea often dip at a lower angle than those immediately landward (see also Krumbein, 1939, p. 702); and, as diagrammatically shown in figure 8, this, by means of a caterpillar-like action, allows the imbricate zone to move slowly seaward. The movement is irregular, with the result that disc pebbles in this zone have highly irregular dip values, from 0°–85° (see also Krumbein, 1939, fig. 18). The backwash is observed to play a major role in the

formation of imbrication (but see Frazer, 1935, p. 980). The percolation of the backwash downward through the underlying porous gravel produces imbrication dipping seaward; but where there is a strong backwash or an impermeable bed below the discs, imbricate pebbles may sometimes dip landward, or in some cases imbrication is completely destroyed. On the other hand, where the discs are particularly large, and the gravel very porous, there is insufficient strength in the backwash to effect the imbrication of the discs (fig. 30 B, C.).

The change in the dip of imbrication at the seaward end of the imbricate zone, is related to the change in the permeability of the underlying beds where they are more permeable towards the

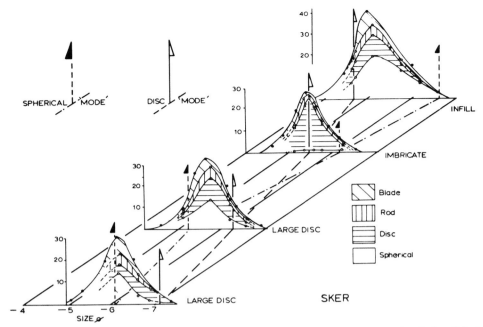

Fig. 7.—An example of the combination of shape/size/frequency across a beach at Sker Point. 'Mode' refers to the size range containing the highest proportion of the stipulated shape, and is determined by the use of a moving average. The scale on the left of the frequency curves indicates the numbers of all the particles.

landward regions, being underlain by gravel, and relatively impermeable on the seaward side being underlain by sand (fig. 26). Thus the concentration of water along the sand surface in the backwash, displaces the foot of the pebbles which are in contact with the sand surface.

The "broken-up" imbrication (fig. 8) is also considered to be a form of disc movement. It may be due to a strong backwash flipping over the discs (Twenhofel, 1950, fig. 24), or the rotation of the underlying spherical pebbles (fig. 8B). But it is also conceivable that the orbital movement of passing waves may induce this reversal in disc dip.

SPHERICITY

The changes in the sphericity/size relationship across the beach is given in figure 9, where a general increase in sphericity is indicated in a seaward direction (Krumbein and Griffith, 1938, fig. 6) for particles of the same size; and an increase in sphericity with size. The standard deviation of sphericity (fig. 9) shows a general increase with increasing size, and in a seaward direction for all sizes studied. The facts presented in figure 9 may well indicate that selective shape sorting is indeed less selective when large grains are being moved, and when turbulent conditions are presumably present; and that shape sorting is more selective in what it leaves behind than in

what it removes: or that particles which roll have a wider range of sphericity than those which lag.

In respect to the gravels found on these beaches where the initial deposit was laid down by storm waves of high energy, and with a large suspended load, the following points may be made:—

(1) Where the highest proportion of discs falls in a size grade larger than the modal

MIGRATION OF DISCS

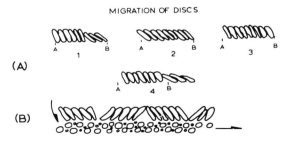

Fig. 8.—Mechanism of disc migration. (A) successive stages in the movement are represented by 1, 2, 3, 4. By displacing a few of the discs at the seaward end of the column (1), and with the others conforming to this new dip (2), the particles are able to move past stationary points, A and B as in 3. The process begins again as in 4. The arrows in (B) represent the direction of backwash movement.

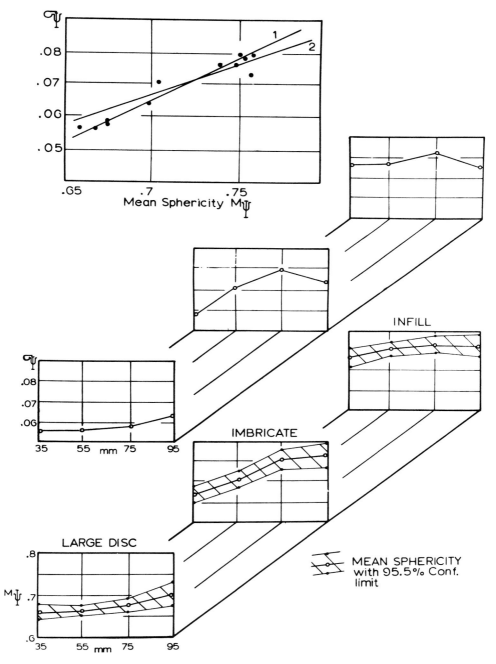

Fig. 9.—Variation of mean sphericity ($M\psi$) with size and position across the beach. Standard deviation of sphericity ($\sigma\psi$) is plotted against mean sphericity, where Eq. 1 is $\sigma\psi = 1.8M\psi - 0.063$; Eq. 2 is $M\psi = 0.64\sigma\psi + 0.438$; and $r = +0.85$; $n = 12$; $p = <0.001$. The example is taken from Cwm Nash at stage 2 (of the Sker type beach).

size of the sediment, reworking is not complete, and in that sense the sediment in question is not in equilibrium with its new conditions.

(2) Where the highest proportion of discs falls in a size grade which is the same as the modal size grade of the sediment, reworking is complete, and in that sense the sediment is in equilibrium with its new conditions.

(3) Where the highest proportion of either spherical or rod shaped grains is found in the same size grade as the modal size of the sediment, then uniform deposition by a similar means of transport is indicated.

(4) Where the disc mode falls in a size grade lower than the modal size grade of the sediment, either the deposit is made up of a coarse tractive load sediment (spherical and rod) and a fine suspended load sediment (which includes many discs); or two modes of tractive transport

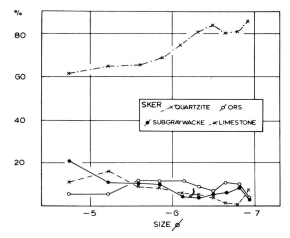

Fig. 11.—Lithological composition plotted against size. O.R.S. = Old Red Sandstone.

has taken place—rapid movement of spherical and rod shaped grains to the site of sediment accumulation, and a slower movement of discs (e.g. by shuffling) to the same site. In both instances the discs are found above the spherical and rod shaped fragments in the succession.

LITHOLOGICAL COMPOSITION

The beach pebbles lithologically resemble the rock types which compose the adjacent cliffs. Thus the beach at Cwm Nash is composed almost exclusively of Liassic limestones (with the anticipated marked absence of shales); the beach at Sker Point of particles found in the surrounding boulder clay and Triassic conglomerate; and the beaches near Ogmore of fragments similar to those found in the nearby boulder clay, Triassic breccias, and also fragments of adjacent Carboniferous Limestone. With the possible exceptions to be noted later, in each beach there is no reason to suspect the presence of an additional source whose general composition is dissimilar to those now found fringing the beaches. Nevertheless, shoreward migration of exotic pebbles (?ships ballast) on a nearby beach at Newton is evident. Lithological composition is given in figures 10, 11, 12.

The quartzite particles vary in their composition and texture, and are, for the most part, probably derived from the Namurian, Lower and Middle Coal Measures of the South Wales Coalfield. These highly quartzose rocks have grain sizes ranging from fine sand to fine pebble, and in nearly all examples seen in thin section the grains are pressure welded. The subgreywacke is a fairly friable, poorly sorted quartz rich rock with

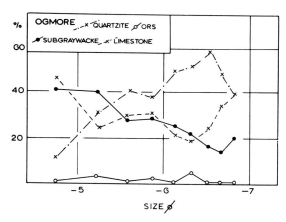

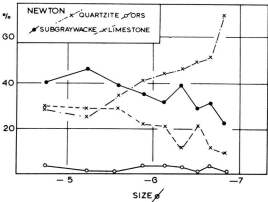

Fig. 10.—Lithological composition plotted against size. O.R.S. = Old Red Sandstone.

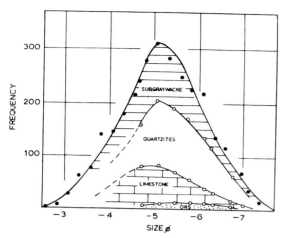

FIG. 12.—Size frequency combined with lithological composition to give an estimate of the actual numbers of different lithological types occurring on the beach. O.R.S.=Old Red Sandstone.

tough, and quartzitic with some pressure welding, although some have a calcite cement.

A trial test was conducted on the quartzites in order to determine whether they behaved more or less as a single unit. That they did behave in a similar way was confirmed by subdividing them into dark (with fine grain size) and light (with coarse grain size) and comparing their variability when plotted against size, although the finer grained group seemed to be the more labile. However, with the distribution of both types of quartz being fairly uniform, grouping them together is not considered to be a serious error.

Composition is a function of size (Davis 1958), and in Newton, Ogmore and Sker (figs. 10, 11), quartzite increases with increasing size, whilst limestone and subgreywacke percentage decrease with increasing size. The percentage of large limestone fragments is high in Ogmore, which is backed by limestone cliffs. Quartzites are the most abundant lithology (fig. 12). Figure 13 shows that in the gravels of Newton beach there is a strong positive correlation between the number of disc shaped particles and the number of subgreywacke particles per sample, and in the same way for spherical and quartzite. There is no significant correlation between the blade and limestone particles, but further sampling may prove the low value of r ($r=.23$; $n=.30$; $p=>.0.1$) to be significant. Whilst correlations of the same type and magnitude were obtained from Ogmore, the gravels at Sker Point yielded a diminished, and not always significant correlation between similarly paired observations. In the samples of boulder clay so far studied, there is no significant correlation between the number

some evidence of pressure welding. The intergranular pore space is filled with clay minerals, but the most important attribute of the subgreywacke is the ease with which it splits along the bedding planes. The rock, quite singular in character, is derived from the Upper Coal Measures of South Wales, where it is known as the Pennant Sandstone. The limestones vary considerably in texture; the Liassic ones are aphanitic, and the Carboniferous ones are mostly bioclastic with grain size varying mainly from fine to coarse sand. Triassic particles are calcareous silts ones, and the Old Red Sandstones are

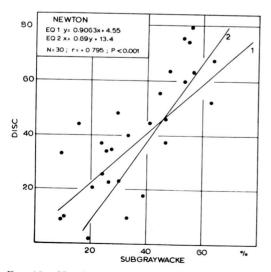

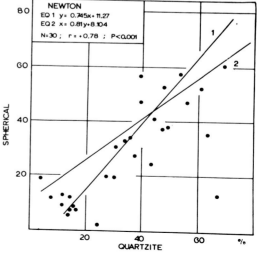

FIG. 13.—Number of discs per sample plotted against the number of subgreywacke fragments from the same samples; the same thing is plotted with spherical and quartzite. Particle sizes range from 16–128 mm.

of spherical and quartzite particles, nor between the number of discs and subgreywacke per sample. It seems reasonable to assume that even after more boulder clay samples have been taken, these correlations will, at the very most, be small—although perhaps significant.

The reasons why the subgreywacke makes disc shaped particles are to be found in the ease with which it splits along the bedding planes, rather than any mineralogical attribute. Weathering taking place during the interval between glacial deposition and marine erosion is an important factor in controlling size (Davis, 1951, p. 187) and shape of particles being made available to the beach. Observations have shown that sometime during the post-Glacial interval flat disc or blade shaped particles are produced from spherical and rod shaped subgreywacke grains; weathering opens the planes of weakness in these particles so that on slightest impact they break into a number of platy fragments. The quartzites on the other hand show little or no effect of weathering in the boulder clay, and although no significant correlation is found in the boulder clay between spherical and quartzite grains, it is the fact that weathering has so depleted the number of spherical subgreywacke particles and in so doing, so multiplied the number of discs and blades of this lithology that a strong correlation exists between subgreywacke and disc, and quartzite and spherical. That is to say, if there is later to be found a correlation between quartzite and spherical particles in a more extensive study of the boulder clay the accentuation of this correlation, as seen in the beach, is due to the incidental association of quartzite with subgreywacke, rather than some other factor inherent in the quartzite so as to make it spherical.

The relationship between shape and lithology, as outlined above, does not imply, at least on the beaches studied here, that the lithological composition of the source rock exerts any commanding influence over the shape composition of the beaches. Whether the beaches are backed by limestone (Cwm Nash) or boulder clay (Ogmore, Newton and Sker) the same shape differentiation obtains. Surf action, with perhaps the exception of the friable subgreywacke, does not so much make a shape (Landon, 1930, p. 445; Marshall, 1929, p. 344; Cailleux and Tricart, 1963, p. 269; Emery, 1960, p. 185; Kuenen, 1964b, p. 37) as use a shape already in existence, and in respect to the beaches studied here, the contributing areas have been sufficiently well endowed with all shapes so as to permit a uniform type of shape differentiation on all of them.

Within each beach composed of polygenetic gravels, there is a lithological compositional zoning with the zones running parallel to the shoreline and where quartzite and O.R.S. particles tend to concentrate on the seaward, and subgreywacke on the landward parts of the beach. This variation in lithological composition is more marked in those beaches which have a strong correlation between shape and lithology (fig. 14, 15). It is evident that shape sorting has incidentally produced a sorting out of particles in terms of their lithological composition.

Where the migration seaward of beach gravels brings about a succession comprising deposits of different zones there is also a succession of gravels with quite different composition (fig. 28). It is clear therefore that any vertical change in the particle composition of a gravel or conglomerate, even when particles of the same size are being compared, cannot without due caution be ascribed to changes in provenance: and if shape sorting is or has been effective in the deposit examined, then a rapid lateral change in lithological composition is also to be anticipated in any sampling programme.

Maturity of the Gravels: the Reworking Process

Maturity is calculated on the basis of including limestone and subgreywacke as being labile, and quartzite and Old Red Sandstone as being stable. The maturity index is therefore:

$$\frac{\text{Quartzite} + \text{O.R.S.}}{\text{Limestone} + \text{Subgreywacke}}$$

As to be expected from compositional variations, maturity increases with increasing grain size, and changes with position on the beach (fig. 16, 17, 18). The imbricate zone has the lowest maturity, and the infill zone and outer frame the highest. Included in the figures 16 and 17 is the maturity of the boulder clay also plotted against grain size, where there is little or no definite maturity changes over the size ranges studied. Limestones are not present in the boulder clay, so that given no additional source of gravel, the difference between the maturity (excluding limestone) of the boulder clay and the marine gravels, for each grain size, will give some indication of the combined effects of weathering processes which have affected the particles in the boulder clay since its laying down, and the processes of marine abrasion on particles released to the beach.

The respective effects of weathering and marine abrasion on the maturity are difficult to isolate. Both weathering and abrasion, in preferentially breaking down the subgreywacke particles to a greater number of smaller sizes, is continually increasing the maturity of the higher size grades, but reducing the maturity of the

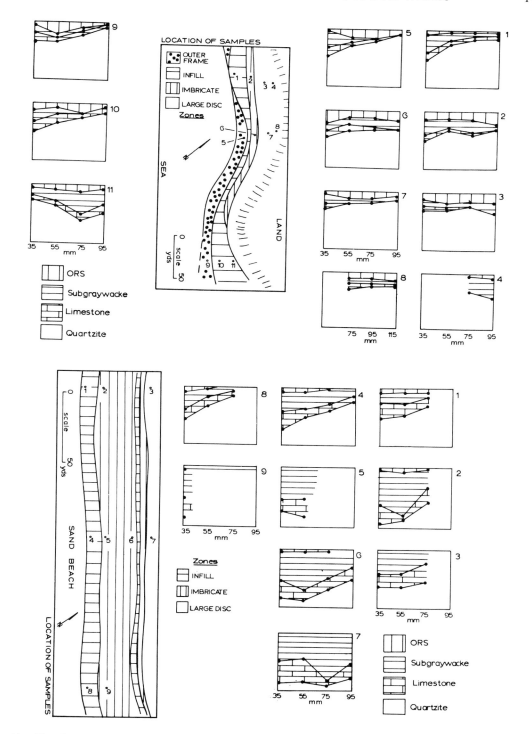

FIG. 14.—Showing the distribution of lithological types, and how this distribution changes between zones. O.R.S. = Old Red Sandstone. Top diagram, Sker; bottom, Newton.

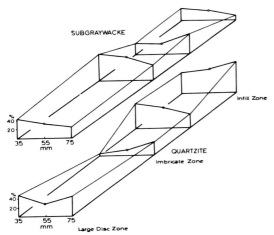

FIG. 15.—Diagram to illustrate the differences in lithological types between zones on a sector of the Newton beach.

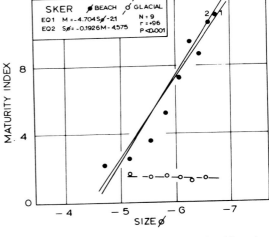

FIG. 16.—Maturity of the beach and boulder clay gravels plotted against size: data for Sker Point.

lower. The rate of supply of labile constituents to the lower size grades is probably logarithmic and, when all things are taken into account, might well produce a maturity curve similar to figures 16 and 17. Also abrasion generally increases with increasing size (Daubree' 1879; Marshall, 1927; Krumbein, 1941a, Kuenen, 1956), so the increase in maturity with size in figures 16 and 17 may also reflect this factor (although Kuenen, 1964b, p. 34, found no increase with size, in the erosion of particles subjected to surf-like action). Con-

sidering now the differences in maturity (excluding limestone) of different shaped particles, it is known from observation that in the weathering process subgreywacke particles become more oblate: gravel lying at the foot of one boulder clay exposure contained many large subgreywacke discs. Since the number of discs so produced is a multiple of the number of other shapes from which they are derived, such as spherical and rods, one would therefore expect the disc fraction of the marine gravels to be

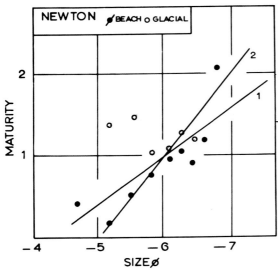

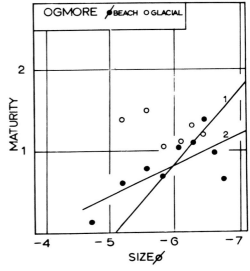

FIG. 17.—Maturity of the beach and boulder clay gravels plotted against size: data for Newton and Ogmore. In Newton EQ.1 is $M = -0.624\ S - 2.761$; and EQ. 2 is $S = -0.9954\ M - 4.989$; where $r = +0.79$; $n = 9$; $p = <0.02$. In Ogmore EQ. 1 is $M = -0.357\ S - 1.13$; and EQ. 2 is $S = -1.279\ M + 4.889$; where $r = 0.677$; $n = 9$; $p = <0.02$.

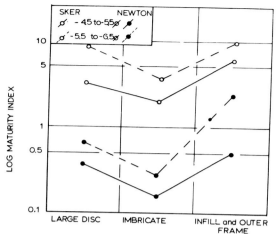

FIG. 18.—Maturity changes across the beach

spherical. That this is so is demonstrated in figure 19. But the maturity of the beach disc particles is much higher than one would have expected from weathering alone: small samples of disc fragments, rather angular in outline and in a part of the large disc zone immediately backed by boulder clay, gave maturity values of 2 for -5.5ϕ and 2.9 for -63ϕ (fig. 19). This deposit, little worked on by the sea, is believed to be fairly representative of the material supplied to the beach after the weathering of the boulder clay, and the differences between the maturity values of this deposit and the maturity values for the beach is a result of beach abrasion. Meager though this information is, it assumes a greater importance when it is considered in the light of foregoing conclusions. Large discs move only during storm conditions when they are ultimately thrown forward in the advancing storm waves. And in order to account for the increase in disc maturity with increasing size, it is suggested that abrasion takes place mostly during storm conditions. Under these conditions impact breakage would be high, and even higher

either less mature than that of the boulder clay, or if more mature, the difference between the maturity index of the two deposits to be far smaller in the case of discs than in the case of

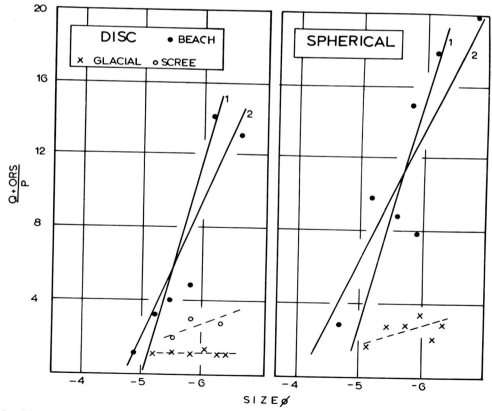

FIG. 19.—Maturity of disc and spherical particles plotted against size, the data is taken from Sker Point. In discs EQ. 1 is $M = -7.1\ S - 3.33$; EQ. 2 is $S = -0.0991\ M - 4.952$; where $r = +0.84$; $n = 6$; $p = <0.05$.

for larger discs where a greater weight is involved.

Since it is an observable fact that under normal sea conditions, spherical and rod shaped particles of the diameter about -5ϕ move more rapidly than any other sizes, all spherical and rod shaped fragments which were collected for mechanical analysis were plotted on probability paper on the chance that a size deficiency would appear; a size deficiency rather higher than the expected one is seen (fig. 20), but the reason for this is not certainly known.

The beach at Sker Point is markedly more mature than those at Ogmore and Newton; and if the supply of limestone to all beaches is assumed to be fairly constant (by leaving out limestone, all three beaches give essentially the same maturity curves as before) there are a number of other possible explanations for this relationship which readily present themselves. Undoubtedly, the Ogmore River has brought in some subgreywacke particles; samples of the gravels of this river obtained less than a mile from the river mouth contained well over 80 percent subgreywacke in all size grades from 35-95 mm. Also, Newton and to a lesser extent Ogmore have a high sand content which could well serve to hinder erosion (Kuenen, 1964b, p. 35, showed this effect of high sand concentration in experiments). The Sker Point beach, on the other hand, being situated on an exposed headland, is more vulnerable to wave attack (the storm beach is far higher here than anywhere else) and also has less sand mixed in with the gravel than seen elsewhere. There is not obvious contamination by a gravel source other than the boulder clay. But, in the lower size grades, the maturity of the Newton and Ogmore beaches is lower than the maturity of the adjacent boulder clays. This may be due either to contamination or to the increase in smaller labile particles consequent on the breakdown of large.

The observed maturity differences across the beaches follows from selective shape sorting already referred to in the discussion of lithological composition.

From the foregoing data and discussion, the following points may be made in respect to these gravels. Where there has been little abrasion or no prolonged weathering of this mixed rock suite there is only a minor correlation between lithology and shape, and maturity and size. But in the early stages of weathering and/or erosion there is a marked correlation between lithology and shape and a somewhat less marked correlation between maturity and size; the shape-lithology correlation is partly the expression of how this maturity/size correlation is being achieved, by the splitting of subgreywacke par-

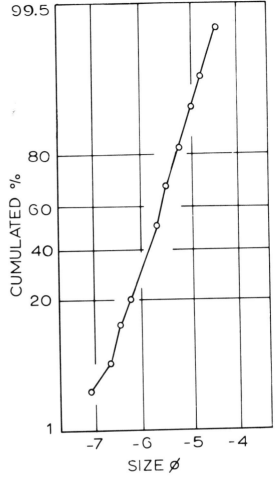

Fig. 20.—Cumulative frequency percentage curve for all spherical particles included in samples collected for size sorting.

ticles along bedding planes to form discs. At this stage there may even be a decrease in the maturity of the smaller grains: Ogmore and Newton might (with the reservations already referred to) be examples of this stage. With more intensive weathering or, as in the case studied here, erosion, the shape/lithology correlation becomes smaller, and confined to the smaller sizes (since the number of labiles are reduced by becoming smaller in size) and the shape lithology correlation of the stable lithological types, if such a correlation exists, will remain. Sker Point beach is an example of this phase. Maturity-size correlation will produce a steep curve which will, as erosion proceeds, continue to steepen to approach parallelism to the size axis as a power function. (see table 1).

TABLE 1.—*The maturing process of the marine gravels intensity and/or period of weathering and/or abrasion*

A	B	C
(i) No variation of maturity with size (ii) No correlation between shape and lithology	(i) Maturity varies with size (ii) Smaller sizes are less mature than equivalent size grade in source rock (iii) Good correlation between lithology and shape.	(i) Maturity greatly increases with increasing size (ii) All size grades larger than granule are more mature than same size grades in source rock (iii) Correlation between lithology and shape best developed in the smaller size grades.
e.g BOULDER CLAY	e.g. NEWTON and OGMORE	e.g. SKER POINT

PARTICLE SIZE PARAMETERS

Beaches were sampled for size parameter data in a similar way as outlined for the study of particle shape. The intermediate axis of the particle was used to describe the size attributes. The relevant statistics of the total random beach sample is given in figure 21, where the standard deviation compares well with the recorded values of Krumbein and Griffith (1938, p. 636), Emery (1955, p. 47), where his Trask sorting values have been transformed to standard deviation using the graphs of Friedman (1962, fig. 9) and Steinmetz, (1962, p. 65), who utilized the long axis of the particle. However, the values of standard deviation are not uniformly distributed over the beaches; this measure changes markedly in a direction perpendicular to beach strike (Krumbein and Griffith, 1938, fig. 4).

Skewness is derived from the third moment, and is calculated in the way outlined by Krumbein and Pettijohn (1938) and (Griffith, 1960, p. 574), and also shows a marked change in value across beach strike. Kurtosis, derived from the fourth moment, varies in a similar direction.

An estimate of the particle size parameters of the gravels as originally laid down by the advancing storm waves, was obtained for four samples (table 2). This original or parent deposit, undoubtedly modified by the backwash of the depositing storm waves, has its coarser frame infilled with granules and sand (fig. 31), and is found near the high tide mark. Seaward of this parent deposit there were no extensive spreads of gravel, as is common when reworking of the storm beach has taken place. These four samples are amongst the worst sorted seen on the beach.

The particle size parameters will be discussed within the framework of the zones already established on these beaches.

Large Disc Zone

The average grain size of gravels in the large disc zone ranges from -6.6ϕ on the landward to 5.7ϕ on the seaward side. The gravels are comparatively well sorted, display symmetrical frequency curves, and generally a high positive kurtosis (fig. 22). The sediment has an open framework, with a poorly developed preferred orientation; discs often lie flat on the surface, and occasionally rod shaped grains have long axes dipping seaward.

The large disc zone is least worked on by the sea; it straddles the high tide mark. But this zone, although retaining some of the characteristics of the parent deposit, is distinctive by virtue of the small amount of reworking which has taken place here. Figure 7, which shows two typical size-frequency-shape curves for this deposit, illustrates the presence of two important components: a coarse grained disc fraction, and a frequency mode predominantly composed of spherical and rod shaped particles; the finer

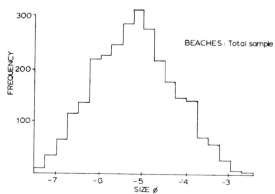

FIG. 21.—Frequency size curve for all the randomly collected beach samples.

TABLE 2.—*Particle size parameters of parent gravel*

Mdϕ	σ	Skϕ	Kϕ
−4.436	0.5701	−0.599	−1.05
−3.991	0.7121	−1.062	+0.54
−4.357	0.6312	+0.285	−2.83
−5.125	0.5189	−0.279	+0.18

grades comprise a similar mixture of shapes as does the mode.

The low standard deviation and the high positive kurtosis are the result of the reworking of a parent deposit with particle size parameters somewhat similar to that as shown in table 2 and figure 23. Particles which were mostly of a size smaller than -5ϕ, and probably also less pivotable particles of a larger size than this, were at an early stage lost during the period when the open framework was formed; the lag concentrate of large discs (fig. 4) left particularly on the top layer of the sediment is thought to indicate the removal of spherical grains from the coarse end of the frequency distribution. With the development of an open frame, the backwash in percolating through the gravel pores, could no longer concentrate sufficient energy to move the gravel with any speed even though the gravel contained particles normally capable of rapid movement in traction, that is spherical and rods. The formation of a porous frame prohibited the development of a negatively skewed distribution typical of lagged gravel.

The Imbricate Zone is typified by gravels which have an average grain size of -5.2ϕ, are comparatively well sorted and have variable skewness and kurtosis values which by and large average out 'normal' (fig. 22). The modal size grade of the gravel contains the highest proportion of discs. These pebbles normally form an open framework, but there is very little downward and lateral filtering due to the proximity of the sand floor (fig. 26).

In comparison with those of the large disc zone the gravels of the imbricate zone are far more worked on by the sea, and for that reason reflect less the nature of the parent deposit; but many of the discs were probably derived from the areas now occupied by the large disc zone, and therefore transported seawards (see fig. 23). The disc part of the frequency distribution represents a lag deposit (in the sense that it moves seaward a lot slower than any other group of particle shapes), whilst spherical and rod shaped grains are only in transit from the landward beach bar to the seaward margin. The frequency distribution may therefore be looked upon as a large and basic or stable population of discs, upon which is superimposed a minor and transient population of spherical and rods; the size parameters of the discs change when traced

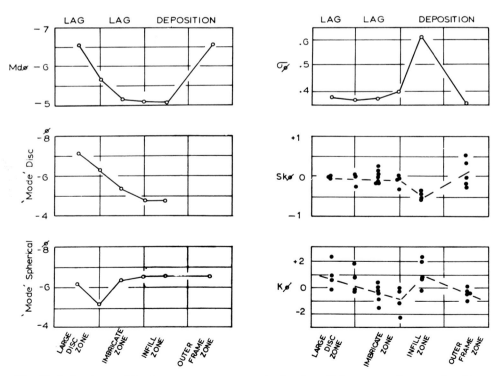

Fig. 22.—Variation in particle size parameters across the beaches. Mdϕ=mean diameter in phi; $\sigma\phi$=phi standard deviation; Skϕ=phi skewness; Kϕ=phi kurtosis. The disc 'mode' and the spherical 'mode' represent an average of the size classes which have the highest proportion of these respective shapes for several samples taken from the zones indicated.

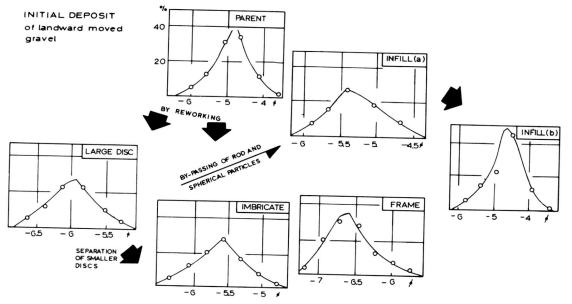

FIG. 23.—Diagram illustrating the shapes of selected size frequency curves for various zones, and their suggested origin.

seaward, and those of the spherical and rod pebbles vary with the availability and selection of these grains from the reservoir situated landward.

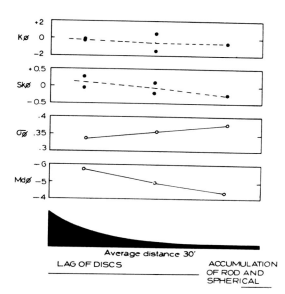

FIG. 24.—Variation in size frequency parameters across the imbricate zone. Mdϕ = mean diameter; 6ϕ = phi standard deviation; Skϕ = phi skewness; Kϕ = phi kurtosis. The silhouette is a diagrammatic representation of the profile of this zone and is based on actual observations.

The particle size parameters across the imbricate zone are given in figure 24. The samples were obtained from a beach which had just been worked on by a receding tide. Grain size diminishes seaward, this being due to a decline in the size of the discs more than compensating for a slight increase in the number of spherical and, to a lesser extent, rod shaped grains which slightly increase in size in that direction. The seaward increase in the standard deviation is mainly due to the spread produced by a disc population decreasing in size, mixing with a population of mainly spherical and some rods, increasing in size. The spherical and rod shaped particles being larger in size and smaller in number than the discs at the seaward end, tend to impart a negative skew to the frequency distribution. But on the landward side the gravels have a positive skew due to the presence of a minor amount of particles, particularly rods (of slightly smaller size than the imbricate discs) being wedged in the disc picket. Kurtosis is difficult to interpret in figure 24 but seems to become negative when traced towards the sea, probably due to the spherical and rod shaped grains, accumulating on the seaward end producing a second, albeit smaller, size mode.

Outer Frame Zone

Gravels of the outer frame have a mean size -6.6ϕ, and are the best sorted gravels on the beach; their frequency distributions have skewness values which vary considerably, but as a generalisation may be said to be positive skew and negative kurtosis. The modal size grade has the highest proportion of spherical and rod shaped fragments. The particles form a framework which is up to 2 feet thick and which is underlain by sand or rock. Little is known about the formation of this deposit other than it was derived from the landward, and in that event it may be that the larger fragments were moved off the storm beach in preference to small (see King, 1959, Joilieff, 1964, p. 80, although this latter writer records 4″–5″ particles travelling slower than 2″–3″). But there is always the possibility that both large and small fragments were taken off the gravel bar, and the smaller have since been removed. The positive skew present in some of these gravels would perhaps indicate this former mechanism. Observations made on the beach indicate that pebble or granule material with a low standard deviation tends to move en mass, and creep along towards the sea: but any material larger than this creeping gravel moves rapidly in traction, overtaking the finer grained constituents. It is conceivable that this difference in type and form of movement of different sized gravel happened during the early stages of beach bar breakdown, and so led to the accumulation of the outer frame. Such forms of movement would be particularly helped where the beach slope is high: the larger grains having a greater momentum than the small: or may be partly due to the fact that the larger grains are not hindered by being caught in the pores between smaller. This latter origin implies a bimodal grain distribution in the lower part of the beach bar to where these cobbles were moving; and it is significant that gravel of the size range about -5.5 to -6.5ϕ is retained in the large disc zone as an open framework in the way already outlined, thus leading to a deficiency of this size, and a relative pebble and cobble abundance on the seaward fringe (fig. 20).

Infill Zone

This zone contains gravels which fall into two groups: those which form a thin band of spherical and rod shaped pebbles on the seaward side of the imbricate zone, and those to seaward again, where spherical and rod shaped pebbles, infill the outer frame (fig. 26).

The spherical and rods accumulating to the immediate seaward of the imbricate zone have an average grain size of -5.1ϕ. Their size frequency curves have comparatively high standard deviation of 0.4ϕ, negative skew, and a negative kurtosis. These pebbles are drawn from the landward situated reservoir (which underlies the large disc zone (fig. 26), and across the im-

bricate zone, which acts as a picket. The sizes of particles in this zone depend upon what is made available for transportation from the reservoir, the sea conditions, and the nature of the openings between the imbricate discs in the imbricate zone. Where the migrating particles have the same size as the openings offered by the discs then movement is hindered (this being strong in the case of rods). Particles larger or, perhaps to a lesser degree, smaller than this size tend to make a more important contribution to the deposits accumulating on the seaward fringe of the imbricate zone. It follows then that these particular deposits of the infill zone have a fairly high standard deviation, and a negative kurtosis with a tendency towards bimodality (fig. 22, 23). The negative skew of the distribution is acquired in two possible ways: finer constituents tend more to remain trapped in the imbricate picket or the finer particles are more rapidly moved than coarse on the flat surface (around 3–5°) and transported out of the gravel and seawards.

Seaward, spherical and rod shaped pebbles and granules infill the outer frame to give rise to a deposit with an average grain size of -5.1ϕ with (excepting the 'parent' gravel) the poorest sorting in the beach, and having a strong negative skew, and a positive kurtosis.

Since at least two distinctive sediments of widely different average grain size are mixed to form the gravels of the infill zone, the high value of standard deviation is to be expected. Moreover the negative skewness is the result of an excessive amount of fine gravel infilling the pore space within a coarse sediment; and the positive kurtosis is possibly the result of lateral filtering through the pores. However when this pore infilling takes place, grain to grain contacts of the outer frame are sometimes lost: cobbles are found dispersed throughout the gravel and entirely surrounded by the finer, seaward moving gravels. But the absence of a frame does not imply the simultaneous deposition of the cobbles and the pebble-granule sized material (Plumbley, 1948, p. 542–545, Potter, 1955, p. 17); the cobbles of the outer frame were present on this seaward fringe long before the finer grained material arrived. Whilst there may be more than one way in which this framework of cobbles is broken down, the mechanism of its disintegration has been observed operating in one instance. The infilling of the outer frame zone is sometimes accomplished by the seaward movement of a wedge of fine gravel which may be preceded by a thin veneer of spherical and rod shaped, medium sized pebbles. Backwash, concentrated on the surface of this fine gravel mass grows turbulent around the projecting cobbles of

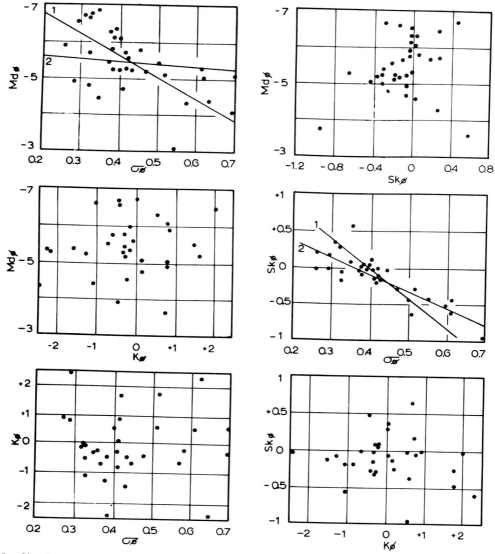

FIG. 25.—Size frequency parameters plotted against each other. In the plot $\sigma\phi/\mathrm{Md}\phi$, $r = -0.3435$; $n = 34$; $p = <0.05$: In the plot $\mathrm{Sk}\phi/\sigma\phi$, $r = -0.753$; $n = 35$; $p = <0.001$.

the frame, effects the removal of some of them, leaving others dispersed in the matrix of finer material. Dispersive stress, increasing with increasing grain size (Bagnold, 1954, p. 62), could also be a factor in frame disintegration (see fig. 30D, E)

Plots of various parameters of the size frequency distribution are given in figure 25. Standard deviation decreases with increasing size and this is to be expected since the lag gravels (with the exception of the outer frame, which may not be a lag deposit) are normally coarse and have lost size grades during reworking. In comparison,

the curves of a similar plot made by Folk and Ward (1957, p. 17, fig. 10) show gravel of about -3ϕ to be fairly well sorted for a fluvial gravel. Skewness versus size shows no well developed correlation (cf. Folk and Ward, 1957, p. 19, fig. 12; Friedman, 1961, p. 518, fig. 2, for sand sized material, Friedman, ibid, p. 517, coarse sand and gravel), and neither does kurtosis versus size. Standard deviation increases with the approach of high negative skewness values. This follows from the fact that the increase in the standard deviation is accomplished by adding a small amount of coarse material to a greater population with a finer mode such as imbricate zone. There are variants of this: the removal of the coarser part of a distribution lowers standard deviation, and produces positive skew such as large disc zone. And the addition of a large amount of fine to a small amount of coarse material produces the same effect of increasing standard deviation and giving a negative skew such as infill zone. For a similar plot Folk and Ward, (1957, fig. 14) found a circular distribution over a much wider range of standard deviation values. But even taking same ranges (converting Folk and Ward's data by means of the graphs produced by Friedman, 1962), the nature of the correlation is evidently different.

In comparing standard deviation of sphericity (fig. 9) with standard deviation of size frequency both appear to increase seaward (excluding the outer frame); and this might well indicate that where there is strong size sorting, there is also strong shape sorting.

Whatever the ultimate cause may be of these changes in the statistical parameters associated with size sorting, it is evident that they are less useful in subdividing the beach bar than the shape-size procedure adopted here and elsewhere (Bluck, 1965); and since it is from an analysis of the beach bar zonal development that the mechanics of sediment movement is deduced, mechanical analysis can only be regarded as an inferior tool to the point of being supplementary. These shortcomings of the particle size parameters may be due either to their relative insensibility or acute sensibility to the recording of such a variety of hydrologic and other factors which are known to exist on the beach. The imbricate zone, for example, has a

wide range of standard deviation, skewness and kurtosis (figs. 22, 24), which fall well within the ranges of such values obtained from other zones; yet the essential nature of this zone is easily ascertained from the size-shape data, and size-shape-frequency data. The relative ease with which the size frequency responds to conditions of the environment is therefore demonstrated by this example. But mechanical analysis does not itself possess the means by which these changes in standard deviation, skewness and kurtosis may be elucidated: within the size frequency distribution are lumped together different shaped particles each of which respond differently to different conditions, or respond differently to the same condition. This defect is overcome by the use of the shape-size-frequency technique, the great advantage of which is that it dissects the frequency curve in such a way as to permit a more direct analysis of where, to what extent, and how gravel movement is, or has taken place in the area represented by the sample.

DEVELOPMENT OF THE GRAVEL BEACHES

The gravel beaches studied in detail can be conveniently subdivided into two groups: the Sker type and the Newton type, each of which behaves in a slightly different way during break down, but they were both built up in essentially the same way.

Sker Type

This type of gravel beach is found at several localities in the Sker district, Ogmore and Cwm Nash, and includes five of the six beaches studied. They all have a large disc zone, an im-

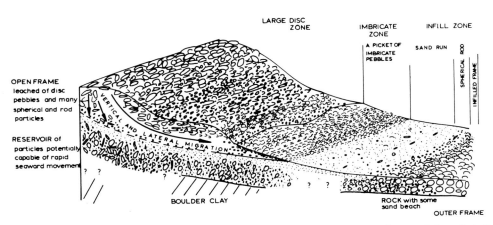

FIG. 26.—A composite diagram showing a part of the Sker Point storm beach. The diagram is based partly on a number of trench sections.

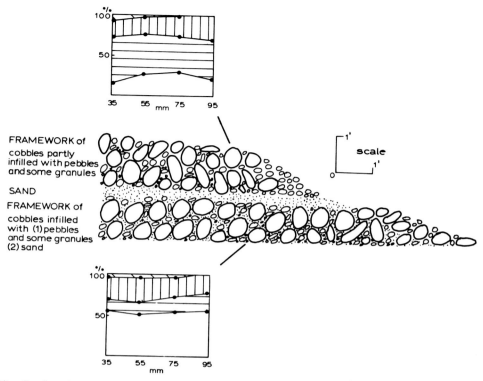

FRAMEWORK of
cobbles partly
infilled with pebbles
and some granules

SAND

FRAMEWORK of
cobbles infilled
with (1)pebbles
and some granules
(2) sand

scale

FIG. 27.—Section of a trench cut into the seaward end of the Cwm Nash storm beach. The figure also shows the percentages of various fragments shapes in the stipulated size ranges; the ornament is as for figure 4.

bricate zone, an infill zone and an outer frame. Observations made over a period of 3 years have shown that the development of the Sker type beach bar is as follows:—

(a) The 'initial' form comprises a ridge of gravel positioned on or about the high tide mark, and a thin fringe of gravel on the seaward side. The whole bar is composed of variously shaped fragments the inter-pore space of which is infilled with sand and granules. The large discs are only beginning to be further concentrated. On the seaward side the imbricate zone is only impersistently developed, and well mixed with spherical and rod shaped fragments. Imbrication is only weakly developed. The outer frame is normally fairly well established at this time.

(b) After a while four zones become fairly well established; the large disc, imbricate, infill and outer frame. The large disc zone has a considerable residuum of large discs and an open framework, which slows down the abstraction of spherical and rod shaped particles. Underneath this zone is a reservoir of sand and gravel (fig. 26)

which is subjected to movement through the developing frame; the frame acts as a sieve on this moving material. The im-bricate zone is now fairly well established and has a fairly short, steep asymptotic profile, and a seaward decline in disc size. On the seaward side of this imbricate zone the infill zone comprises the sand run, the thin strip of spherical and rod pebbles, and an area where infilling is taking place. At this stage in the bar development the outer frame is filled, and the sequence resulting is as shown as one in figure 27 and is found on several beaches. The beach bars shown in figures 3, 4 and 5 were sampled at this stage.

(c) Following the creation of the zones, further modification is apparent by the growth of the large disc zone. This growth entails further removal of spherical and rod shaped grains on the landward, with the accumulation of a residuum of discs. But seaward extension is affected by the migration of discs as shown in figure 29 out over the infilled frame, or even as a component of frame infill. The extension of the imbricate zone introduces a further hindrance to the rapid seaward transport of spherical and rod shaped grains.

Smaller and/or less spherical cobbles and large pebbles, released from the reservoir underlying the disc zone, move seaward and extend the outer frame ahead of the migrating pebble and granule sized material, or adds another outer frame above the already existing infill zone.

A model for the succession built up during the breakdown of a storm beach of this type is given in figure 29. Although part of this modal succession has been proved to exist on one beach (for 1 and 2 of figure 29, see figure 28), that part designated 3 has not been seen on the present day beaches, but has been seen in some marine gravels related to an earlier sea level. These older gravels were excavated to a maximum depth of 15 feet by a mechanical shovel. In the exposed sections there were some beds of cross bedded gravel, with the cross bedding dipping towards the land. However, the landward movement of a flat topped gravel bar, whose particle shape composition compared well with the particle shape composition of the older cross bedded gravel, was seen seaward of the infill zone at Newton: it was not seen to migrate over the infill zone, but it does seem likely that bar migration of this type would give rise to the landward dipping cross bedded gravels.

In the excavated sections of the older beach deposits, thick beds of gravel were seen to dip seaward at slight angles: this seaward dip of gravels also obtains on the present day beach during the bar breakdown, and with a higher content of sand in the bar, this angle of deposition is possibly higher. Dune sands, following on top of these inclined gravels produce a succession which appears to be unconformable, but which is in fact the normal succession of regression with offlap.

Newton Type

The beach at Newton, similar to the Sker type in many ways, has the same stages in breakdown; but differs in having a higher proportion of sand and no outer frame on the immediate seaward side of the infill zone (fig. 31 A). There is a rather poorly developed frame some 60 yards seaward of the gravel beach, but it is not certain if this is genetically related to the beach bar itself; it might be related to gravel movement at the mouth of the Ogmore River. Instead of there being one imbricate zone and one area of spherical and rod pebble accumulation, there are up to three of each in the stage corresponding to (c) of the Sker type. And with the seaward migration of these three or less zones a succession, as shown in figure 28 is produced (see also figure 29). Once again the succession in figure 29 is hypothetical in that it assumes no

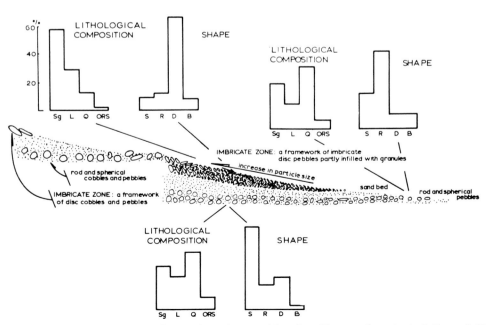

FIG. 28.—Section obtained from trenches cut into the gravel beach at Newton. S=spherical; R=rod; D=disc; B=blade. Sg=subgreywacke; L=limestone; Q=quartzite; ORS=Old Red Sandstone.

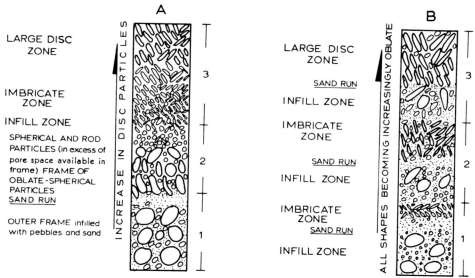

FIG. 29.—Model successions built up by the complete breakdown of the storm beaches. A is the Sker type and succession designated 1 overlain by 2 have been recorded in a few instances; the complete sequence has not been observed. B is the Newton type and once again the succession 1 overlain by 2 has been seen but the complete sequence has not.

landward migration of gravel during a period of complete breakdown of the bar. In marked contrast to the succession produced by the breakdown of the Sker type bar, this Newton type shows an increase in the size of the spherical and rod shaped fragments upward in the succession (fig. 28).

CONCLUSIONS

Differently shaped particles react differently to water flow, and this is an important characteristic of these marine gravels which permits a subdivision of the beach into zones. Disc shaped fragments behave quite differently from either spherical or rod, but behave in a similar way to blade. These features may be related to settling velocity or 'flume behaviour,' where on a smooth, unobstructed floor, spherical and rod shaped grains move faster than discs or blades. But the beach surface is seldom smooth and unobstructed, and in the reaction between particle and floor, another shape sorting factor is seen to operate—shape filtering. In this process, particles, because of their shape, cannot easily move through the obstructions, and therefore constitute a lag deposit.

Size frequency analysis, itself of secondary importance in the study of marine gravels, can be used with advantage when combined with shape. In combining shape-size-frequency it is possible to assess the degree to which the deposit in question has come to terms with those factors of the environment which are acting on the sediment at the time of sampling. Where the modal size of the sediment is coincident with the size having the highest proportion of discs, then a state of equilibrium is achieved in a gravel undergoing lag; where the modal size of the sediment is coincident with the size having the highest proportion of spherical or rod shaped particles, then fairly uniform conditions of deposition from the tractive load are taking place.

Tractive transport on the beach is seen to take three forms: the most common is rolling, where the particle caught in the force of the backwash moves along the surface with which it is predominantly in contact. Disc shaped grains shuffle along, and some grains move collectively in a form called surface creep. Surface creep is found in gravels with a low standard deviation, and occurs when the backwash water, percolating through the sediment, mobilises the layer and effects its slow movement seawards. This form of movement is achieved in two ways:— (a) No effective turbulence is caused by large grains being surrounded by finer: there is an even distribution of the energy expended on the sediment surface by the water movement. (b) The sizes of the pores within the sediment mass and on the surface of the sediment are such that few grains are either large enough to roll on the surface and bridge the gaps between grains, or small enough to migrate through the pores.

The anomalous situation is seen where coarse

FIG. 30.—A. Gravel beach and bar, Sker Point. Stage 2 of breakdown. B. Large disc zone Sker Point. C. Imbricate zone, Sker Point: pebbles do not show imbrication. D. Outer frame, Sker Point. E. Infill zone, Sker Point, spherical and rod shaped particles are infilling a frame of cobbles, which is partly broken up.

FIG. 31.—A. Gravel beach, Newton, at stage 2 of breakdown. B. Imbricate zone, Sker Point, showing the large spherical particles concentrating on the seaward side, and the finer grains trapped within the picket of imbricate pebbles on the landward side. The photograph was taken after particles of the outer frame had been thrown up over the imbricate zone. C. Section cut into the parent gravel, showing lag of discs at the top (large disc zone) underlain by beds rich in spherical and rod shaped pebbles and granules, and finally a sand filled gravel at the bottom. Newton. D. Gravel beach at Newton in stage 1 of its development. Beach cusps of the type shown are common in this phase of bar development.

grains outstrip fine. On the beaches this phenomenon is believed to be due to: (a) If it is considered that the weight, and the discoidal shape of a particle are factors hindering its movement in traction, then it follows that large spherical grains will move when smaller discs will remain. (b) Large grains will move on the surfaces of small by bridging the gap between these smaller grains. This factor is extremely important where the small sized sediment moves either by shuffling (imbricate discs) or by creep.

Both composition and maturity are a function of size and shape on these beaches, and for that reason vary markedly and systematically within the beach environment. There is no correlation between maturity and size in the source rocks of these gravels, and the value of maturity is low. Weathering of this source gravel (boulder clay) produces an increase in maturity with increasing size, and abrasion on the beaches accentuates this trend by further reducing the numbers of large labile fragments. It seems likely that erosion would continue to produce a maturity-size power function. Shape-lithology correlation is believed to be a characteristic of a phase in the maturing process of these gravels. The sequence of gravels in order of increasing maturity is— boulder clay—the Newton and Ogmore beaches—the Sker beaches. This sequence correlates with an increase in energy supplied to effect the erosion of the gravels: this being based on inference in the case of the glacial environment, but based on evidence in the case of the beaches. The main landward part of the storm

beach may be looked upon as being a reservoir of sand and gravel slowly being released to the sea. This reservoir is capped by a zone of large discs representing the lag product of gravel leaching. In time a shape differentiation takes place throughout the bar with discs travelling seaward far slower than spherical and rod: the stage of bar breakdown can be ascertained from the length of the imbricate zone, which increases with the continued reworking of the gravel. The history of bar breakdown is written, in converse, in the deposits accumulating at its foot, and these sequences have been observed in older post-glacial deposits.

The possibility of disc shaped fragments being made by special features of marine abrasion is not supported by the data obtained here. The largest discs are the most angular and the most oblate; and the most oblate discs are found in areas which are least worked on by the sea, such as in the large disc zone, near the high tide mark. The most oblate discs have the least independent evidence of the type abrasion envisaged by some as effecting a flattening of particles. Selective sorting controls the shape distribution of a population of grains, and impact breakage during storm conditions is the favoured means of beach particle abrasion for discs at least.

ACKNOWLEDGEMENTS

It is a pleasure to thank Professor T. N. George for his critical reading of the manuscript.

REFERENCES

ALBERTSON, M. L., 1953, Effect of shape on the fall velocity of gravel particles: Fifth Hydraulics Conf. Proc. Univ. Iowa, Iowa City. p. 243–261.
BAGNOLD, R. A., 1940, Beach formation by waves; some model experiments in a wave tank: Jour. Inst. Civil Engineers, v. 15, p. 27–52.
———, 1954, Experiments on the gravity free dispersion of large solid spheres in a Newtonian fluid under shear: Roy. Soc. Lond. Proc. A. v. 225, p. 49–63.
BLUCK, B. J., 1965, The sedimentary history of some Triassic conglomerates in the Vale of Glamorgan, South Wales: Sedimentology, v. 4, p. 225–245.
BRIGGS, L. I., McCULLOCH, D. S., AND MOSER, F., 1962, The hydraulic shape of sand particles: Jour. Sedimentary Petrology, v. 32, p. 645–656.
CAILLEUX, A., AND TRICART, J., 1963, Initiation a l'etude des sables et des galets: Centre de documentation universitaire, Paris. Tome 1.
DAVIS, S. N., 1951, Studies of Pleistocene gravel lithologies in Northeastern Kansas: State Geol. Survey Kansas Bull. 90, p. 173–192.
———, 1958, Size distribution of rock types in stream gravel and glacial till: Jour. Sedimentary Petrology, v. 28, p. 89–94.
EMERY, K. O., 1955, Grain size of marine gravels: Jour. Geology, v. 63, p. 39–49.
———, 1960, The sea off Southern California: A modern habitat of petroleum. John Wiley and Sons, Inc., New York, 366 p.
FRAZER, J. H., 1935, Experimental study of the porosity and permeability of clastic sediments: Jour. Geology, v. 43, p. 910–1010.
FLEMING, N. C., 1964, Tank experiments on the sorting of beach material during cusp formation: Jour. Sedimentary Petrology, v. 34, p. 112–122.
FOLK, R. L., AND WARD, W. C., 1957, Brazos River bar: a study in the significance of grain size parameters: Jour. Sedimentary Petrology, v. 27, p. 3–26.
FRIEDMAN, G. M., 1961, Distinction between dune, beach and river sands from their textural characteristics: Jour. Sedimentary Petrology, v. 31, p. 514–529.
———, 1962, On sorting, sorting coefficients and the lognormality of the grain size distribution of sandstones: Jour. Geology, v. 70, p. 737–753.

GRIFFITHS, J. C., 1962, Statistical methods in sedimentary petrography: *in* MILNER, H. B., Sedimentary Petrography: Allen and Unwin, London, p. 565–617.

HOLMES, C. D., 1960, Evolution of till-stone shapes, Central New York: Geol. Soc. America Bull., v. 71, p. 1645–1660.

JOLLIFFE, I. P., 1964, An experiment designed to compare the relative rates of movement of different sizes of beach pebbles: Proc. Geol. Assoc. London, v. 75, p. 67–86.

KIDSON, CLARENCE., AND CARR, A. P., 1959, The movement of shingle over the sea bed close inshore: Geog. Jour., v. 125, p. 380–389.

KING, C. A. M., 1959, Beaches and Coasts. Edward Arnold and Company, London.

KRUMBEIN, W. C., 1939, Preferred orientation of pebbles in sedimentary deposits: Jour. Geology, v. 47, p. 673–706.

———, 1941a, The effect of abrasion on the size, shape and roundness of rock fragments: Jour. Geology, v. 49, p. 482–520.

———, 1941b, Measurement and geological significance of shape and roundness of sedimentary particles: Jour. Sedimentary Petrology, v. 11, p. 64–72.

———, 1942, Settling-velocity and flume-behaviour of non-spherical particles: Trans. Am. Geophys. Union, v. 23, p. 621–633.

——— 1953, Statistical designs for sampling beach sand: Trans. Am. Geophys. Union, v. 34, p. 857–866.

KRUMBEIN, W. C., AND GRIFFITH, J. S., 1938, Beach environment in Little Sister Bay, Wisconsin: Bull. Geol. Soc. America, v. 59, p. 629–652.

KRUMBEIN, W. C. AND MILLER, R. L., 1953, Design of experiments for statistical analysis of geological data: Jour. Geology, v. 61, p. 510–522.

KRUMBEIN, W. C., AND PETTIJOHN, F. J., 1938, Manual of sedimentary petrography. D. Appleton-Century-Crofs, Inc., New York.

KUENEN, P. H., 1956, Experimental abrasion of pebbles 2 rolling by current: Jour. Geology, v. 64, p. 336–368.

———, 1964a, Pivotability studies of sand by a shape sorter: *in* Developments in sedimentology, v. 1, Deltaic and shallow water marine deposits. Elsevier Publ. Co. Amsterdam.

———, 1964b, Experimental abrasion: 6. Surf action: Sedimentology, v. 3, p. 29–34.

LANDON, R. E., 1930, An analysis of beach pebble abrasion and transportation: Jour. Geology, v. 38, p. 437–446.

LEWIS, M. V., 1931, The effect of wave incidence on the configuration of a shingle beach: Geog. Jour., v. 78, p. 129–148

MARSHALL, P., 1927, The wearing of beach gravels: New Zealand Inst. Trans., v. 58, p. 507–532.

———, 1929, Beach gravels and sand: New Zealand Inst. Trans., v. 60, p. 324–365.

McNOWN AND MALAIKA, J., 1950, The effect of particle shape on the settling velocity at low Reynolds numbers: Trans. Am. Geophys. Union, v. 31, p. 74–82.

OWENS, J. S., 1908, Experiments on the transporting power of sea currents: Geog. Jour. v. 13, p. 415–425.

PLUMBLEY, W. J., 1948, Black Hill terrace gravels a study in sediment transport: Jour. Geology, v. 56, p. 526–577.

POTTER, P. E., 1955, The petrology and origin of the Lafayette gravel. Part I. Mineralogy and petrology: Jour. Geology, v. 63, p. 1–38.

SHEPARD, F. P., AND YOUNG, R., 1961, Distinguishing between beach and dune sands: Jour. Sedimentary Petrology, v. 31, p. 196–214.

SNEED, E. D., AND FOLK, R. L., 1958, Pebbles in the Lower Colorado River, Texas. A study in particle morphogenesis: Jour. Geology, v. 66, p. 114–150.

STEINMETZ, RICHARD, 1962, Sampling and size distribution of quartzose pebbles from three New Jersey gravels: Jour. Geology, v. 70, p. 56–73.

STRAHAN, AUBERY., 1896, On submerged land surfaces at Barry, Glamorganshire: Quart. Jour. Geol. Soc. London, v. 52, p. 474–489.

STRAHAN AUBERY, AND CANTRILL, T. C., 1904, The geology of the South Wales Coalfield. Part VI. The country around Bridgend: Mem. Geol. Survey Great Britain.

TWENHOFEL, W. H., 1950, Principles of sedimentation. McGraw-Hill Book Co. Inc., 673 p.

VAN ANDEL, T. H., WIGGERS, A. J., AND MAARLEVELD, G., 1954, Roundness and shape of marine gravels from Urk (Netherlands): a comparison of several methods of investigation: Jour. Sedimentary Petrology. v. 24, p. 100–116.

WADELL, HANKON., 1934, The coefficient of resistance as a function of Reynolds number for solids of various shapes: Jour. Franklin Inst., v. 217, p. 459–490.

ZINGG, TH., 1935, Beitrag zur schotteranalysis: Schweiz. Min. u. Pet. Mit., v. 15, p. 39–140.

PHYSICAL PROCESSES AND FINE-GRAINED SEDIMENT DYNAMICS, COAST OF SURINAM, SOUTH AMERICA[1]

JOHN T. WELLS AND JAMES M. COLEMAN
Coastal Studies Institute, Louisiana State University
Baton Rouge, Louisiana 70803

ABSTRACT: The prograding Holocene mud wedge between the Amazon and Orinoco Rivers in the trade wind belt of northeastern South America provides a modern-day example of muds accumulating under moderate wave-energy conditions. Gigantic shore-attached mudbanks (10 km × 20 km), composed partly of thixotropic fluid-mud gel, front this coast every 30–60 km to form a buffer to wave attack and a temporary storage for fine-grained sediments. This mesotidal coast (tide range ~2.0 m) with gentle offshore slope (0.0006) allows the exposure twice a day of extensive tidal flat deposits, which are backed by mangrove swamps on a well-developed chenier-plain complex. Field experiments were conducted in Surinam during 1975 and 1977 to provide new information on process-form relationships in this interesting but unusual muddy environment.

Simultaneous measurements of waves, currents, tide elevation, suspended-sediment concentration, and variations in mud density show that soft intertidal and subtidal muds are suspended at both tide and wave frequency. Suspended-sediment concentrations typically exceed 1,000 mg/l at the surface as incoming solitary-like waves partially disperse fluid mud into overlying water on a falling or rising tide. Redeposition of mud may occur near time of high tide. The strong attenuation of shallow-water waves by these muds provides conditions that are favorable for further sedimentation.

High concentrations of suspended fluid mud, together with solitary-like waves from the northeast throughout the year, can lead to extraordinarily high net sediment transport rates in the nearshore zone. Calculations based on solitary-wave theory and on data obtained from this study indicate that $15\text{-}65 \times 10^6$ m^3 of mud can move along shore each year without involving breaking waves, the concept of radiation stress and a nearshore circulation cell, or bedload transport. Farther offshore, outside the zone of wave dominance, wind-driven currents and the Guiana Current combine to transport muds to the northwest, consistent with the observed direction of mudflat migration.

INTRODUCTION

The open, unprotected coast of northeastern South America, subject to moderate levels of wave energy from the outer continental shelf, is for several reasons an unusual environment with respect to process-response relationships. First, the nearly 1,600 km of shoreline between the Amazon and Orinoco Rivers is an accreting muddy coast, and thus provides a contradiction to long-held beliefs that muds accumulate only in quiet, wave-free environments by slow processes of deposition. Second, this coast is one of only a few in the world where present-day processes have formed muds into linear, shore-attached, migrating shoals that are similar in morphology to the sandy shoals reported by Swift et al. (1972a, b) off the east coast of the United States. Finally, accumulations of tenacious fluid-mud gel, referred to locally as "slingmud," front the coast periodically to form an inaccessible shoreline at low tide that serves as a buffer to wave attack and a storage facility for fine-grained sediments. The major purpose of this paper is to present results of field studies that provide information on the behavior of fine-grained sediments, particularly fluid mud, and the effects of these muds on coastal processes.

The mud-bound coast of the Guianas (French Guiana, Surinam, Guyana) and other muddy coasts worldwide can be characterized by extremely high suspended-sediment concentrations in coastal waters, often exceeding 1,000 mg/l at the surface (Wells and Coleman, 1977), and by beaches composed of silts, clays, and shell debris, backed by salt marshes or mangrove swamps. The presence of heavily sediment-laden water affects water column dynamics, such as rate of wave attenuation. Muddy shorelines often respond differently to coastal processes than shorelines formed from sand-sized particles.

[1]Manuscript received November 24, 1980; revised June 9, 1981.

JOURNAL OF SEDIMENTARY PETROLOGY, VOL. 51, NO. 4, DECEMBER, 1981, p. 1053–1068
Copyright © 1981, The Society of Economic Paleontologists and Mineralogists 0022-4472/81/0051-1053/$03.00

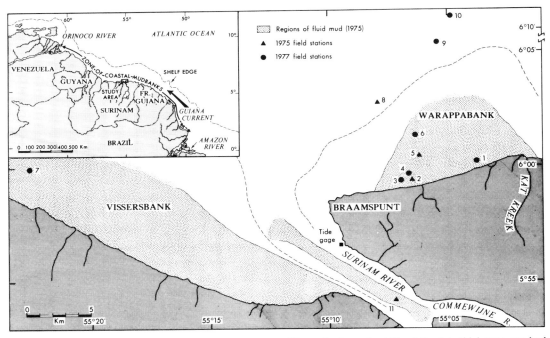

FIG. 1.—Index map showing locations of field stations. Water depths and width of the intertidal zone are both highly variable as a result of mudbank migration, fluid-mud suspension and deposition, and phase of the tide (3-m contour referenced to mean low water). Inset map shows the Guiana Current and zone of coastal mudbanks. Twenty-seven to thirty mudbanks are present on the inner continental shelf between the Amazon and Orinoco Rivers (for greater morphological detail see Rine, 1980).

In the coastal system under consideration (Fig. 1) fine-grained sediments enter the Atlantic Ocean from the Amazon River and are trapped on the inner shelf by an estuarine-type circulation as they settle from suspension; currents near the bottom have a net movement in an onshore direction, whereas those on the surface have a net movement offshore (Eisma, 1967; Gibbs, 1976). Transport by the Guiana Current and by littoral currents then spreads these fine-grained sediments to the northwest to form the coastline of the Guianas. Clay-rich sediments have been prograding offshore since the beginning of the Holocene, and today form a wedge of mud that reaches 25 m in thickness along the coast of Surinam (Rine and Ginsburg, 1978).

Subaqueous mud shoals appear near the Brazil-French Guiana border and recur every 30–60 km to the northwest. At the mouths of the Orinoco River in Venezuela mudbanks merge with recent deltaic deposits (van Andel, 1967). Although the processes responsible for formation of these mudbanks are unknown, the presence and movement of mudbanks have

been documented from nautical charts since the 1600s. Early hydrologic surveys revealed average migration rates of 1.5 km/yr (Allersma, 1971) and affirmed the fact that these mudbanks, although exposed to wave forces from the Atlantic Ocean, were able to maintain their identity for decades. Mudbanks are typically 10–20 km in the alongshore dimension and extend up to 20 km offshore. Maximum relief is less than 5 m, and mudbanks thin both seaward and landward, with gentle topographic undulations (<0.5 m) sometimes extending to a water depth of 20 m. Delft Hydraulics Laboratory (1962) observed 21 mudbanks between Waini River, Guyana, and Cayenne, French Guiana, during coastal reconnaissance in 1961, and reported that most opened to the east with angles of 20–30° to the shoreline.

Fluid mud is associated with—and found in the vicinity of—mudbanks and is partially exposed at low tide as extensive subaerial tidal flats (Fig. 2). Consistency varies considerably, from dense yogurt-like material to soft coffee-colored mud with density only slightly greater

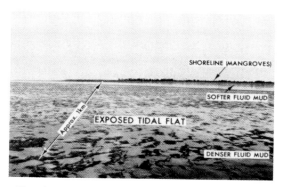

FIG. 2.—Mudflat exposed at low tide on western flank of Warappabank. Softer (less dense) fluid muds near the shoreline can be identified in this photograph by the thin layer of clear water that overlies them.

the Guiana coast, three have dealt primarily with morphology and sedimentology (Vann, 1959; Augustinas, 1978; Rine, 1980) and three with coastal dynamics and physical processes (Delft Hydraulics Laboratory, 1962; NE-DECO, 1968; Wells, 1977). Several shorter papers have been published on coastal processes, hydrographic observations, and shoreline evolution (Diephuis, 1966; Eisma, 1967; Allersma, 1971; Gibbs, 1976; Wells and Coleman, 1977; Wells et al., 1979). Despite these and other efforts, however, our understanding of certain aspects of physical processes on muddy coasts is in an early stage of development. Additional research is required in areas such as transport of mud by waves and processes of suspension and deposition.

DATA ACQUISITION

The country of Surinam, located midway between the Amazon and Orinoco Rivers, has coastal conditions that are representative of the 1,600 km of muddy coast in northeast South America and for this reason was selected as the field area. The months of data acquisition, August through October (1975, 1977), are typically dry and winds are moderate (<3 m/ sec). Data were collected at ten field sites along the coast of Surinam and one site in the Surinam River entrance (Fig. 1).

Simultaneous measurements of wave height and period, near-bottom variations in fluid-mud density, suspended-sediment concentration, and tide elevation were made at stations over Warappabank and Vissersbank, regions where fluid mud up to 1.5 m thick was found to blanket the bottom (sites 1–7, Fig. 1). Wave data were also taken farther offshore where substantial quantities of fluid mud are lacking (sites 8–10, Fig. 1). Each field station was occupied for several hours to several days.

Water depths at low tide ranged from 0 m (intertidal mudflat) to 10 m (site 10). When fluid mud was present, the bottom was defined as the surface of the fluid-mud layer, even though survey instruments could penetrate through it to more consolidated sediments below (Odd and Owen, 1972). In all cases, fluid mud is a distinguishable horizon that can be detected by depth sounders, bottom probes, and occasionally by lead line soundings.

Wave data were taken with a pressure-type

than that of water. Following Krone's (1962) definition, dense "suspensions" are referred to as fluid mud (also slingmud, liquid mud, fluff mud, soft silt, slib, and creme de vase) when the concentration of sediment in water exceeds 10,000 mg/1, which corresponds to a sediment-water density of 1.03 g/cm^3 at 35‰ salinity. Softer muds that dewater rapidly after subaerial exposure are covered by several centimeters of clear water (Fig. 2). As first observed by Zonneveld (1954) and later reported by NEDECO (1968), fluid mud occurs most commonly on the lee side or western flank of mud shoals, after being eroded from the eastern edges. Details of the mechanism whereby fluid mud is transported from east to west, presumably in suspension, are unknown and pose one of the major unanswered questions concerning mudbank propagation.

A distinct erosion-accretion cycle of approximately 30 years duration is associated with the migration of mudbanks past a given point (Delft Hydraulics Laboratory, 1962). In interbank areas, plunging breakers may impinge directly upon stands of mangroves at high tide, whereas in shoal, fluid-mud regions waves are severely attenuated and virtually absent at the shoreline. Periodically mudflats become welded to the shoreline, *Avicennia* mangroves colonize, and soils begin to ripen. Previous shorelines are marked by the small quantities of sand introduced from local rivers and wave-reworked shell debris supplied from the shelf, which have formed linear detrital bodies on the broad chenier-plain complex.

Of the major field studies conducted along

wave gage fabricated at Coastal Studies Institute (sites 1–9) and a Datawell Wave Rider Buoy (site 10). A tide record was obtained using a similar system, a battery-powered pressure-transducer water-level gage, that was fastened to a platform in the Surinam River entrance. Two minutes of tide data were recorded continuously on a Rustrak recorder every 30 min. A 60-sec time-constant filter in the tide gage removed high-frequency surface waves. Variations in mud and near-bottom water density, obtained simultaneously with

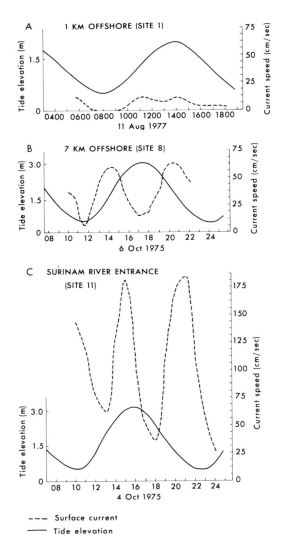

FIG. 3.—Relationship between tidal current and water-surface elevation on intertidal bank (A), interbank area (B), and Surinam River entrace (C). Current falls to zero in intertidal area when mud is exposed at low tide (A).

wave data, were determined from time series measurements of pressure variations in or just above the fluid-mud layer. Two Statham pressure transducers formed the sensing unit of this prototype instrument, which was capable of providing both mean and fluctuating components of density to an accuracy of at least 0.004 g/cm^3 (details in Wells, 1977; Wells et al., 1979; Fredericks and Wells, 1980). All wave and fluid-mud density data were recorded as analog signals on a two-channel Gould Brush Strip Chart Recorder. Before reaching the recorder, signals were processed electronically to remove high-frequency noise (>10 Hz) and to enhance resolution.

Current speed and direction profiles were made at some locations (sites 1, 3, 7, 8, 11, Fig. 1) from an anchored boat. These data were obtained with a Marine Advisors Q-15 ducted current meter. In water depths greater than 2 m profiles were taken at 0.5-m intervals. When water depths were less than 2 m currents were measured at a single mid-depth position.

Water samples for suspended-sediment determinations were taken with a Van Dorn sampler and analyzed using a Millipore pressure filtration system, following standard techniques (Wells and Coleman, 1977). Shallow cores and bottom grab samples were taken for routine sedimentological and soils analysis. In soft muds the Van Dorn sampler and plastic water bottles were used to obtain bottom samples. Bottom depths were determined with a Raytheon Model 731 electronic depth recorder and occasionally by lead line soundings. Positioning was by horizontal sextant angles.

RESULTS

Tide Elevation and Current Strength

Mean tide range decreases from more than 8 m at the Amazon River entrance to less than 1 m off the Orinoco River delta (NOAA Tide Tables, 1980). Tides along the coast of Surinam have a mean range of 1.8 m with spring and neap ranges of 2.8 m and 1.0 m, respectively, and display a well-behaved, semi-diurnal periodicity; during the period of field studies in 1975 and 1977 mean tide range was 1.85 m and 1.70 m, respectively. Phase of tide in the fortnightly spring-neap cycle controls the width of the intertidal zone, which, depending on bottom gradient, varies in Surinam from less than 2 km to over 4.5 km (see Fig. 2B in the paper by Wells and Coleman which immediately follows this one in this issue).

Observed tide height/current velocity relationships are given in Figure 3 for intertidal, subtidal, and river entrance environments. Current speeds in the intertidal zone over Warappabank (Fig. 3A) are on the order of 10–20 cm/sec; maximum measured current in this environment was over 30 cm/sec at 1 m above the bottom (site 3). Current speeds fall to zero for 1–3 hr each tidal cycle when muds are exposed intertidally. Farther seaward, in the subtidal environment, current speeds are 30–50 cm/sec and the tide height/current velocity relationship is often one of a standing wave (Fig. 3B). Maximum measured surface and bottom currents in subtidal portions of Warappabank were 66 and 47 cm/sec, respectively (site 8). All speed and direction measurements taken for at least a full tidal cycle indicate the presence of a residual current, setting to the northwest, which attains maximum surface speeds of 10–20 cm/sec.

Tidal currents in local estuaries, such as the Surinam River entrance, are extremely strong (Fig. 3C); sustained speeds of over 2 m/sec were recorded during a spring tide in 1975. Net nontidal flow in the Surinam River entrance was observed to be deflected west, and currents move across Vissersbank (Fig. 1) rather than out onto the shelf through the river channel.

Examination of data in NEDECO (1968) shows that outside the coastal boundary layer, a region perhaps 20–40 km wide, current strength increases as a strong oceanic current, the Guiana Current, sweeps the coast from southeast to northwest, moving as an extension of the North Equatorial Current off Brazil (Metcalf, 1968). Current speeds are reported to be, on the average, 0.5–0.9 m/sec (NEDECO, 1968). Although current measurements were not taken in the Guiana Current on the outer continental shelf for the present study, it is assumed that the effect of this current is reflected in the residual currents reported above for the inner continental shelf.

Wave Characteristics

Examination of deepwater wave statistics indicates that moderate to high wave energy levels are expected seaward of the outer continental shelf (8°N, 54–57°W) (U.S. Naval Oceanographic Office, 1963). Waves on the shelf, averaged through the year, are typically 1–2 m high and exceed 4 m less than 1 percent of the year (NEDECO, 1968). Moreover, highest waves coincide with periods of strongest winds (February–May), whereas lowest waves coincide with periods of weakest winds (June–November); average period is 6–8 sec, with swell from North Atlantic storms occasionally exceeding 15 sec. Data tables in NEDECO (1968) show that sea and swell arrive from the northeast quadrant during all months of the year, with 50 percent arriving from N50°E to N70°E. Waves gradually refract in propagating across the shelf and, as observed in this study, impinge upon the shoreline at angles of N3–8°E. A typical section of wave record and the associated spectrum from the

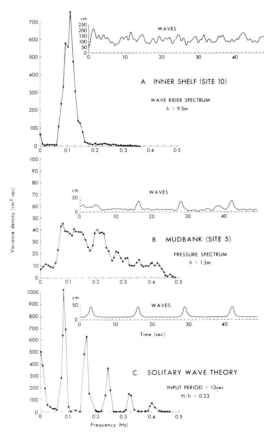

FIG. 4.—Typical wave records and wave spectra from inner continental shelf (A), mudbank area (B), and from solitary-wave theory (C). Data taken during low to moderate winds (<3 m/sec).

TABLE 1.—*Rate of wave energy loss, coast of Surinam, computed from wave spectra taken at 22, 11, and 4 km offshore*

Experiment	H_1 (cm)	T_1 (sec)	h_1 (m)	H_2 (cm)	T_2 (sec)	h_2 (m)	Energy Loss (%)	H_3 (cm)	T_3 (sec)	h_3 (m)	Energy Loss (%)
1	89	7.0	8.7	32	7.0	5.8	87	24	11.1	2.4	93
2	86	8.8	8.3	26	9.2	5.5	91	20	10.8	2.0	95
3	88	8.7	7.9	28	8.8	5.0	90	19	13.6	1.6	95
4	93	9.3	7.1	32	9.2	4.7	88	19	9.9	1.3	96
5	92	8.8	7.5	27	9.1	4.6	91	22	13.7	1.2	94

Note: H = wave height, T = wave period, h = water depth, and subscripts 1, 2, and 3 denote outer, intermediate, and inner wave stations, respectively.

inner continental shelf (field site 10) show 0.5–1.0-m-high waves with a well-defined spectral peak at a period of 8 sec (Fig. 4A). Wave data taken seaward of subtidal fluid muds always display narrow spectral peaks as a result of relatively uniform trade winds from the northeast.

Measurements from our studies show that, as waves propagate into shallow water over a fluid-mud bottom, pronounced changes in profile and amplitude occur (Fig. 4B). Examination of 20-min time series records taken at stations 1–10 during all stages of the tide indicate that, when incoming waves first propagate as shallow-water waves (water depth/wave length < 0.05), they are deformed and solitary-like wave profiles result (Fig. 4B). Solitary waves are characterized descriptively as isolated crests separated by flat troughs lying at still-water level (Fig. 4C). Wave crests are steep yet symmetrical, and their lateral continuity, as determined from aerial observations, may be several kilometers. Wave spectra over a fluid-mud bottom become broad, with many spectral peaks, and resemble the perfect solitary-wave spectrum shown in Figure 4C in that spectral peaks often occur at harmonic frequencies.

In regions between mudbanks where the bottom is consolidated clay and fluid mud is lacking, waves are more sinusoidal and break as plunging breakers at the shoreline. Breaking waves in interbank areas produce an abrasion platform of firm clay, backed by thin detrital accumulations of sand and shell.

The conventional shoaling transformation whereby wave height initially decreases and then increases rapidly prior to breaking does not exist when the bottom is composed of fluid mud. Instead, wave height is continuously and strongly attenuated as waves travel toward shore with a solitary-like profile; most waves do not reach the shoreline, nor do they break.

Those waves that do break are typically spilling breakers.

Rate of loss of wave energy has been quantified from time series data taken simultaneously at three field sites (10, 9, 6, Fig. 1) along a line oriented parallel to the direction of incoming waves. Wave energy is proportional to the square of wave height (using linear wave theory) and can be computed as the variance, σ^2, of the wave spectrum (see CERC, 1973)

$$\sigma^2 = \int_0^\infty E(\omega) \, d\omega \qquad (1)$$

where $E(\omega)$ is the energy spectrum function. Table 1 gives results of these calculations for five experiments conducted on August 20, 1977. The bottom along the line of wave travel was composed of fluid mud 10–50 cm thick. From the outer station, 22 km offshore, to the intermediate station, 11 km offshore, rates of energy loss were 87 to 91 percent; total wave energy loss from the outer station to the inner station, 4 km offshore, ranged from 93 to 96 percent. Visual observations affirmed the belief that between the inner station and the shoreline waves were completely attenuated without breaking. Average wave period does not vary significnatly from the outer to intermediate stations but appears to increase from

TABLE 2.—*Properties of coastal fluid muds, Surinam, South America*

Bulk density	1.03–1.25 g/cm³ (1030–1250 kg/m³)
Water content	64–96%
Voids ratio	4–62
Median particle size	0.5–1.0 micron (disaggregated)
Viscosity	0.02–210 poises
Organic content	1.5–2.2%
Mineralogy	10–30% kaolinite
	10–30% illite
	5–20% smectite
	15–40% quartz

TABLE 3.—*Maximum and minimum surface suspended-sediment concentration, coast of Surinam*

Field Site		Range in Water Depth	Concentration (10^2 mg/l)	
			Maximum	Minimum
1		0.0–2.0	3.33	0.21
2		0.0–2.0	2222.85*	26.57
3	Intertidal	0.0–2.0	52.34	1.09
4	and	0.5–2.5	17.75	0.67
5	Nearshore	1.0–3.0	37.49	0.34
6		1.5–4.0	11.19	0.82
7		0.5–2.5	24.51	2.75
8		4.0–7.0	0.81	0.16
9	Offshore	4.5–8.0	0.34	0.14
10		9.0–11.5	No data taken	
11	River entrance	5.0–8.0	11.98	0.49

*Samples from surface of fluid mud exposed at low tide.

the intermediate to inner stations as a result of selective attenuation of higher frequency waves (Table 1).

Fluid-Mud Dynamics

Mass physical properties of coastal fluid muds in Surinam, determined by standard (ASTM) laboratory procedures, are given in Table 2. Whereas the exact combination of properties that govern the behavior of clays is complex and controversial (Partheniades, 1971), those listed in Table 2 are perhaps the most important. Characterized descriptively, Surinam muds are extremely fine, have high organic content, and exhibit very low strength.

In general, waves and currents maintain large volumes of fine-grained sediment in suspension, making the nearshore waters of Surinam among the muddiest in the world. Samples taken in this study indicate that suspensate concentrations in regions of fluid-mud bottom are orders of magnitude higher than those reported for interbank areas (NEDECO, 1968) and may attain surface-water values of several thousand milligrams per liter (Table 3). Intertidal and nearshore waters are more turbid than offshore (Table 3), and near-bottom are more turbid than surface waters, even in interbank areas (Fig. 5).

Aerial reconnaissance shows that inshore of approximately 15–20 km, shoreward of the high-current-velocity region of the Guiana Current, waters are especially muddy at low tide. Samples from field sites 1–7 reveal that suspended-sediment concentrations begin to increase at or near mid tide, reach a maximum about low tide, then decrease up to the following high tide. Sediment concentrations farther offshore or between mudbanks, sites 8–10,

show no systematic variation with stage of tide (Fig. 5).

Much of our information concerning suspension processes has been obtained by monitoring pressure variations in the upper 0.5 m of fluid mud, then converting these to units of density using a hydrostatic pressure concept

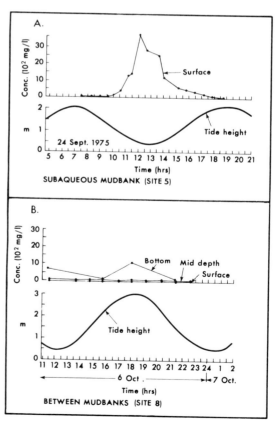

FIG. 5.—Variations in suspended-sediment concentration over mudbank (A) and between mudbanks (B).

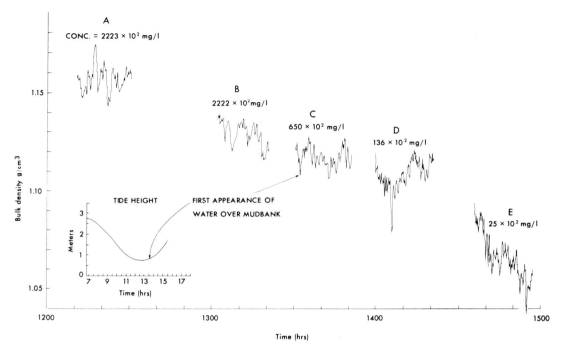

FIG. 6.—Time series of bulk density variations in upper 0.5 m of fluid mud, beginning at low tide, field site 2. Values above time series sections A-B are sediment concentrations in exposed fluid-mud layer; values above time series sections C-E are average suspended-sediment concentrations in water after tide has begun rising over mudflat.

(Wells, 1977; Wells et al., 1979; Fredericks and Wells, 1980). In general, apparent variations in mud density can result from suspension or deposition, gain or loss of pore waters, and advection of sediment past instrument sensors. By obtaining measurements over a range of fluid-mud densities (1.03–1.24 g/cm³) with sensors at several depths relative to the surface of the fluid-mud layer, we have been able to examine details of near-bottom processes in a variety of situations, from which generalizations have been made concerning sediment suspension and movement.

Variations in differential pressure occur at three predominant frequencies: tide (~12.4 hr), wave (5–10 sec), and intermediate (30 sec–5 min). Figure 6 shows results of a 3-hr experiment beginning at low tide that documents variations in pressure (density) during a rising tide on an intertidal mudflat. Five time series sections, each approximately 20 min, show a gradual decrease in bulk density from 1.16 to 1.05 g/cm³ between low tide and mid tide. Of particular interest are the facts that density began to decrease before rising waters reached the field site and that after approxi-

mately 1430 hr the rate of decrease in mud density accelerated concurrently with mixing of mud in overlying water. Higher frequency density perturbations that occur on a time scale of minutes are common in this and other time series records and often become more intense as wave height increases.

Substantial variations in mud density occur at wave frequency, and muds with density less than 1.20 g/cm³ respond rapidly to the passage of waves (Fig. 7). As each wave approaches instrument sensors, density gradually increases, then at the instant of wave crest passing, falls rapidly before once again beginning a gradual climb. Careful examination of density variations in both sections of time series in Figure 7 reveals that the magnitude of these variations is less at LW (1255 hr) than at ~1.5 hr before LW (1115 hr). Further, a slight shift downward in absolute position of the density line indicates that mud was less dense at LW than previously and, therefore, that some suspension had taken place.

Intermediate frequency pressure variations have been noted in all time series records, even in muds as dense as 1.24 g/cm³ (Fig. 8).

The characteristic features are that pressure disturbances generally last from 30 sec to 5 min and that pressure nearly always returns to nominal values. The differential pressure event recorded in Figure 8 was in the upper 30 cm of mud, which had a density of 1.20 g/cm^3. Units of pressure (dynes/cm^2) were retained in this time series record because the disturbance in subbottom pressure field, to be discussed later, was not attributed to a variation in mud density.

DISCUSSION

Fluid-Mud Formation, Suspension, and Redeposition

The traditional concept that muds accumulate only in quiet, wave-free environments is clearly not applicable when the supply of fine-grained sediments is extremely large. Indeed,

the only prerequisites for fluid-mud formation appear to be high suspended-sediment concentrations and rapid sedimentation. The fact that soft, muddy bottoms can attenuate wave energy rapidly after initial deposition helps promote sedimentation even further and leads to fluid-mud deposits on mudbanks in Surinam. A review of the literature indicates that fluid muds are deposited along other coastlines subject to at least moderate wave energy levels from offshore: Louisiana coast (Morgan et al., 1953; Wells and Roberts, in press); southwest coast of India (Moni, 1971; Nair, 1976); west coast of Korea (Wells and Huh, 1979); and east coast of China bordering the Gulf of Po Hai (Zenkovitch, 1967).

Details of the processes by which fluid muds form are known only from static laboratory conditions and are summarized by Krone (1962, 1963), Pierce and Williams (1966),

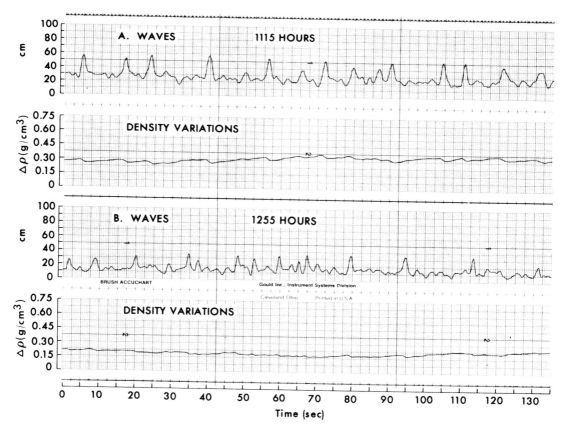

FIG. 7.—Wave-by-wave variations in near-bottom fluid-mud density recorded during the passage of waves at 1.5 hr before LW (A) and at LW (B). Slight decrease in magnitude of density variations in (B) is a result of removal of 10–20 cm of fluid mud between instrument sensors.

INTERMEDIATE FREQUENCY PRESSURE VARIATION

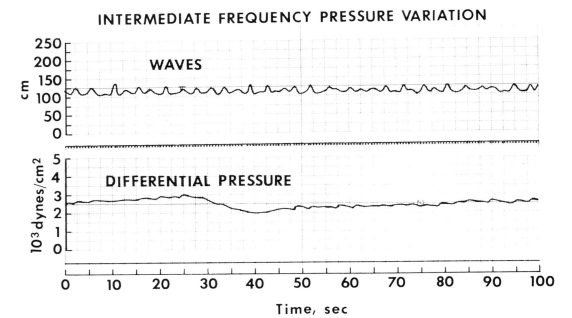

FIG. 8.—Variation in differential pressure in the upper 0.5 m of fluid mud as a result of mass movement, field site 3. The rapid decrease, followed by gradual increase, in differential pressure between instrument sensors suggests the initiation of flowsliding.

Migniot (1968), and Owen (1970a, 1970b). Observations from field investigations suggest, however, that fluid-mud formation in nature is a rapid and dynamic process. Kirby and Parker (1977) have found that estuarine fluid muds are suspended and redeposited at tidal frequency and form progressively thicker accumulations on the spring tide to neap tide cycles as current velocities decrease. During the formation process an interface settles from the surface while a second interface moves upward from the bottom; eventually they meet to form a density gradient that is sharp enough to return sufficient energy for detection by echo sounder. Once formed, fluid mud consolidates slowly as pore waters are expelled through drainage wells. Stirring by waves slows down the consolidation process, and, unless muds are exposed subaerially for several days, consolidation is usually interrupted as newly formed fluid muds are suspended and redeposited many times (Wells, 1977).

Variations in density of fluid muds examined in the present study (Figs. 6 and 7) result from suspension of sediment at tide and wave frequencies. As tide rises over mudflats, incoming waves gradually suspend the fluid muds, thereby causing a decrease in mean density between instrument sensors (Fig. 9). In the case of the 3-hr experiment shown in Figure 6, the drop in average density from 1.16 to 1.05 g/cm^3 resulted from the suspension of at least 40 cm of fluid mud. Although the experiment was terminated at mid-tide and further details of the suspension process could not be monitored, fathometer profiles, near-bottom samples, and bottom probes indicated that this mud was redeposited near time of high water. The fact that fluid muds reappear at the

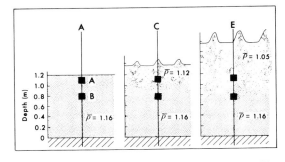

FIG. 9.—Suspension of fluid mud by solitary-like waves. (A, C, and E refer to sections of time series in Fig. 6.) Within the mud layer A and B show positions of pressure transducers.

same location on successive days provides further evidence that massive suspension is followed by rapid redeposition later in the tidal cycle.

The considerable variation in bulk density of fluid mud prior to the first impingement of waves (Fig. 6, sections A and B) was the result of interstitial pressure waves from offshore, which, in low-density muds, generally precede the arrival of surface waves. The first 1.5 hr of data (Fig. 6) support observations that low-density intertidal muds ($\rho < 1.20$ g/cm^3) become measurably diluted by water associated with rising tide even before waves are large enough to be recorded. The rapid decrease in density, beginning in time series E, indicates that rate of suspension is increasing, perhaps as a result of total bed failure from stress levels higher than bulk shear strength, as observed in the laboratory by Ariathurai and Krone (1975). Even so, average suspended-sediment concentrations decrease in water over the fluid-mud layer (Figs. 5A and 6), since

tide elevation rises faster than the fluid-mud layer is suspended from the bottom.

Wave-by-wave suspension, superimposed on the longer trends described above, can be used to explain the variations in mud density shown in two sections of time series data in Figure 7. As each wave passes instrument sensors, a cloud of sediment is instantly suspended, then advected in the direction of wave travel as it begins to settle. This wave-by-wave process is shown diagrammatically in Figure 10. At time t_1, prior to the arrival of a wave crest, 8 cm of fluid mud covers the lower pressure transducer. At time t_2 the bed is instantly suspended and a dense cloud of muddy water extends to the surface. Some of the sediment may be advected by shoreward-directed currents under the wave crest, thus causing a decrease in the average density between the two pressure sensors. The trend toward increasing density, beginning after t_3, results from particle settling and initial reformation of the fluid-mud layer after the wave crest has passed. Par-

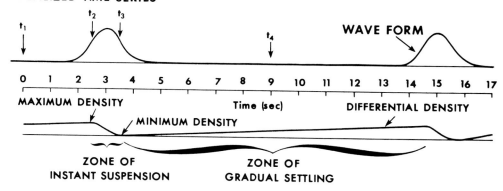

a. **IDEALIZED TIME SERIES**

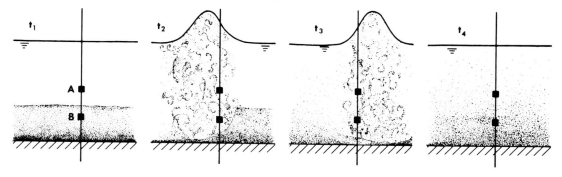

b. **SEQUENCE OF SUSPENSION-DEPOSITION**

Fig. 10.—Wave-by-wave near-bottom density variations as explained by sediment suspension and deposition (see text).

ticles may settle as a unit from a mass that fails under the shear of a passing wave but rapidly regains its structure as a fluid mud during the settling process, then forms an interface that quickly collapses to give an overall high settling rate. Time t_4 represents the return to initial bed state; near-bottom density increases during the settling process between passage of wave crests. As more and more mud is removed from the bottom, the mean density and the magnitude of fluctuating density components decrease. Estimates based on position of pressure sensors relative to the fluid-mud surface and the mean density of fluid mud between the sensors indicate that 10–30 cm of bottom mud can be suspended each hour, provided the density is less than 1.20–1.22 g/cm^3.

Examination of numerous time series records indicates that the intensity of this suspension process depends upon mud density and, to a lesser extent, wave height. If bulk density exceeds 1.25 g/cm^3, muds appear to be virtually resistant to suspension at wave and tide frequencies, even though tidal currents exceed 50 cm/sec (Fig. 3B) and wave-induced current surges exceed 65–80 cm/sec for durations of a few seconds (10-sec solitary waves with average heights of 30–50 cm). However, higher waves during the months of February–May could result in a seasonal cycle of erosion in the more consolidated muds.

Transportation of Mud

The fact that suspensate concentrations in coastal waters range anywhere from 100 to 10,000 mg/l (Table 3), depending on water depth, stage of the tide, wave height, and bottom consistency, suggests that sediment transport rates may be enormous, even under relatively weak currents. Recent estimates indicate that approximately 20–40 percent of the total sediment load from the Amazon River makes its way northwestward along the coastlines of French Guiana, Surinam, and Guyana (Eisma and van der Marcel, 1971) and results in one of the highest annual littoral transport rates in the world. Approximately 150 × 10^6 m^3/yr of "through transport" takes place in the form of suspended sediment, and another 100 × 10^6 m^3/yr moves as a result of the propagation of coastal mudbanks to the northwest (summarized as order of magnitude estimates from

Delft Hydraulics Laboratory, 1962; Gibbs, 1967; NEDECO, 1968; Allersma, 1971; and Eisma and van der Marcel, 1971).

Previous investigators have generally attributed these exceedingly high longshore transport rates to suspension of mud by wave orbital scour, followed by transport to the northwest within the Amazon Mud Stream by the Guiana Current. The main strength of the Guiana Current, however, is 100–200 km offshore, in a region where suspended-sediment concentrations are reported to be less than 10 mg/l (Gibbs, 1976). Closer inshore, within the Amazon Mud Stream (20–40 km offshore), residual currents are only 10–20 cm/sec, but suspensate concentrations are 1–3 orders of magnitude greater than in the Guiana Current (Table 3). We suggest, therefore, that most transport takes place in the dynamic nearshore and inner shelf region, which extends perhaps as far offshore as the fluid muds that are associated with mudbanks, and that waves are responsible for much of the transportation as well as suspension of sediment.

The finding in this study that suspensate concentrations are highest in fluid-mud regions where solitary-like waves occur, combined with the fact that 93 percent of sea and swell arrive at the coastline between N30°E and east (NEDECO, 1968), suggests that a tremendous potential exists for sediment transport by waves acting alone. In theory, a solitary wave is a wave of translation whereby water particles move only in the direction of wave travel. When waves approach the shoreline from an angle, a longshore transport component is produced. Laboratory studies on solitary waves have shown that if wave profile is similar to that given by theory, then particle trajectories are unidirectional and each wave clearly produces a mass transport (Daily and Stephen, 1953). Numerous observations in this and other field studies (for instance, Inman et al., 1963) have provided qualitative verification that particle velocity is greater in the onshore direction under crests than in the offshore direction under troughs of shallow-water solitary-like waves.

Wells et al. (1979) have found, by taking mass transport of suspended sediment, as applied to surf-zone problems, that longshore sediment transport rates of 15–65 × 10^6 m^3/yr are possible from waves acting alone. The computations were made using data from Table 3 under the assumption of true solitary-wave particle velocities and the simplification of a uniform return flow between mudbanks. Figure 11 shows sediment transport rates as a function of wave period for the inner 5 km of shelf. These values give order of magnitude agreement with previously cited transport rates of 250×10^6 m³/yr, since these previous estimates were made for a 30-km-wide cross section. That is, if one-sixth of 250×10^6 m³/yr moves alongshore in a band that is only 5 km wide, the width of the hypothetical mudbank used in our calculations, then the transport rates become 42×10^6 m³/yr.

Although transport velocities in the above calculations are taken to be those of true solitary waves, no data are available to substantiate this quantitatively. Values derived are thus considered to give an upper bound for longshore transport by the solitary-wave mechanism. A potentially high transport rate by solitary waves is of particular significance in light of the fact that waves are severely attenuated

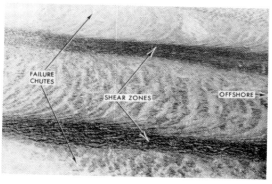

FIG. 12.—Flowslide chutes bounded by composite shear zones, Warappabank. Photo taken east of field site 1 at low tide. Scale: area covered is 1.5 m × 2.2 m.

and seldom expend their energy by breaking. The implication is that breaking waves and the conventional momentum flux approach to sediment transport problems may not be applicable along extremely muddy shorelines, yet transport rates may still be substantial.

Further evidence for transport of mud by waves was noted in the nearshore region and on the beach face by Augustinas (1978). Fluid muds were found to be pushed against steep slopes, covering the foreshore and sometimes even the backshore. Numerous coastal indentations were filled with fluid mud, similar to pocket sand beaches along a rocky shoreline. The onshore component of transport by solitary waves would tend to trap muds in the nearshore region, particularly if muds are moved en masse by waves, as suggested by Delft Hydraulics Laboratory (1962).

Intermediate frequency pressure variations such as those shown in Figure 8 may be the result of onshore transport en masse by waves or offshore mass movement by flowsliding. Systems of linear failure chutes bounded by well-formed shear zones have been noted by Wells et al. (1980) to carry muds seaward at rates of 1–10 cm/min during low tide (Fig. 12). Gradients in pore water pressure or variations in thickness of mud over instrument sensors are recorded as pressure variations and are indications of mass movement (flowsliding) offshore. Flowslide movement may be significant as a transport mechanism for returning tidal flat muds to the wave-dominated environment from which they were derived. The lack of hurricanes and severe storms appears to preclude offshore movement of mud

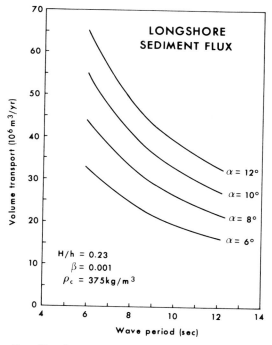

FIG. 11.—Longshore sediment transport as a function of wave period. α = wave angle to shoreline, β = offshore slope, ρ_c = sediment concentration of transported sediment mass, and H/h = wave height/water depth ratio used in calculations. High-frequency waves that approach shore from steep angles are able to transport the largest volumes of suspended muds.

by winter- and spring-season storm waves.

In addition to wave-induced currents, sediment is also transported to the northwest by the residual Guiana Current and by wind-driven currents. Seaward of perhaps 5 km, where muds are subtidal and solitary-like waves are not as common, the Guiana Current becomes more important and assumes a larger role in the transport of sediment. For example, along the neighboring shoreline of Guyana (Fig. 1), Delft Hydraulics Laboratory (1962) has reported residual currents of 15–40 cm/sec seaward of the nearshore and inner shelf, regions where waves are less important.

Wind-driven currents are estimated to be moderate as a result of winds from the east to northeast at an average speed of ~3 m/sec. Because of the nearly coast-parallel orientation, winds do not pile up water but instead induce gentle longshore currents. Utilizing wind data given in NEDECO (1968) and a theoretical model given by Murray (1975), we calculate speeds of wind-driven currents on the inner shelf to be 12–18 cm/sec 90 percent of the year.

Interruptions in the longshore transport of mud may occur temporarily each time a mudbank migrates past a river mouth. Tidal currents exceeding 2 m/sec (Fig. 5C) sweep coastal muds into and out of local rivers with the flood-ebb cycle. However, severe siltation problems and high turbidities (Table 3) in the Surinam River entrance (Harbormaster, Paramaribo, pers. comm.) suggest that some muds derived from offshore remain in the rivers, especially during periods of mudbank passage. Despite the intensity of tidal currents in the Surinam River entrance, the immense transport of muds alongshore causes a deflection of this and other river mouths to the west (Fig. 1).

Regardless of the exact combination of forces that operate from the shoreline to the shelf edge, all available data show a movement of water to the northwest, consistent with observed direction of sediment transport and mudbank migration. Further research along the world's muddy coastlines should be directed toward partitioning total sediment transport into that which results from wave-induced, wind-induced, or ocean currents, and toward an understanding of current speeds and associated shear stresses required to initiate suspension in muds of various consistencies.

CONCLUSIONS

1) The prograding muddy coast of northeastern South America indicates that muds can accumulate in moderate-wave-energy environments. Linear mud shoals, composed partly of fluid muds, change rapidly in time and space, primarily as a result of suspension and transport by waves. Wave-induced currents on the inner shelf and the residual Guiana Current on the outer shelf are responsible for much of the sediment that is transported to the west.

2) As waves propagate over banks of fluid mud they lose nearly all of their energy through attenuation, without breaking, and are deformed into solitary-like wave profiles. As a result, when fronted by fluid mud, muddy coasts are able to protect their shorelines.

3) In mud where density is less than $1.20–1.22$ g/cm^3, suspension takes place at wave and tidal frequencies and a periodic exchange between suspended sediment and fluid mud results. Suspended-sediment concentrations over subtidal and intertidal muds may reach several thousand milligrams per liter as fluid mud is dispersed into overlying waters.

4) Seabed variations in density of coastal fluid muds at wave frequency indicate that clouds of sediment are suspended and may be advected toward shore. Onshore transport may be partially balanced by offshore gravity transport from flowslides.

5) Currents induced by solitary waves can explain longshore volume transport rates of $15–65 \times 10^6$ m^3/yr without involving breaking waves or the concept of radiation stress and a nearshore circulation cell, as normally applied to sandy coasts.

ACKNOWLEDGMENTS

This research was performed under a contract between the Coastal Sciences Programs, Office of Naval Research, Arlington, Virginia 22217, and the Coastal Studies Institute, Louisiana State University, Baton Rouge. Cooperation and field support were provided by Drs. R. A. Cambridge, E. H. Dahlberg, and Th. E. Wong, Government Service for Mining and Geology, Ministry of Development, and Mr. A. M. Sutmuller and his staff, Hydraulic Research Division, Ministry of Public Works and Traffic, Paramaribo, Surinam. Technical assistance in the field was provided by R. G. Fredericks and E. A. Bishop. Mrs. Gerry

Dunn prepared the illustrations. We thank P. A. Byrne and Wm. J. Wiseman, Jr., for reviewing an early draft of the manuscript and D. Nummedal and D. W. McGrail for critical review of the final draft.

REFERENCES

ALLERSMA, E., 1971, Mud on the oceanic shelf off Guyana: Symposium on Invest. and Resources of Caribbean Sea and Adjacent Regions, UNESCO, Paris, p. 193–203.

VAN ANDEL, T. H., 1967, The Orinoco Delta: Jour. Sed. Petrology, v. 37, p. 297–310.

ARIATHURAI, R., AND KRONE, R. B., 1975, Mathematical modeling of sediment transport processes in estuaries, in Wiley, M., ed., Estuarine Processes, Vol. II, Circulation, Sediments, and Transfer of Material in the Estuary: Academic Press, p. 98–106.

AUGUSTINAS, P. G. E. F., 1978, The changing shoreline of Surinam (South America): [unpub. Ph.D. dissertation]: The Netherlands, Univ. Utrecht, 232 p.

Coastal Engineering Research Center, 1973, Shore protection manual: Washington, D.C., U.S. Army Corps of Engineers, 3 v.

DAILY, J. W., AND STEPHAN, S. C., 1953, The solitary wave—its celerity, profile, and internal velocities and amplitude attenuation in a horizontal smooth channel: Proc. Third Conf. Coastal Engr., Cambridge, MA, p. 13–30.

Delft Hydraulics Laboratory, 1962, Demerara Coastal Investigation: The Netherlands, Delft, 240 p.

DIEPHUIS, J.G.H.R., 1966, The Guiana coast: Tijdschr. Kon. Ned. Aardr. Gen., v. 83, p. 145–152.

EISMA, D., 1967, Oceanographic observations on the Surinam shelf: Hydrographic Newsletter, Spec. Pub. 5, p. 21–53.

EISMA, D., AND VAN DER MARCEL, H. W., 1971, Marine muds along the Guyana coast and their origin from the Amazon Basin: Contrib. Mineral. Petrology, v. 31, p. 321–324.

FREDERICKS, R. G., AND WELLS, J. T., 1980, High precision instrumentation system for sea bed pressure measurements in muddy sediments: Proc. Oceans 1980 Conf., p. 226–230.

GIBBS, R. J., 1967, Geochemistry of the Amazon River system, part I, the factors that control the salinity and the composition and concentration of the suspended solids: Geol. Soc. America Bull., v. 78, p. 1203–1232.

———, 1976, Amazon River sediment transport in the Atlantic Ocean: Geology, v. 4, p. 45–48.

INMAN, D. L., GAYMAN, W. R., AND COX, D. C., 1963, Littoral sedimentary processes on Kauai, a subtropical high island: Pacific Science, XVII, p. 106–129.

KIRBY, R. R., AND PARKER, W. R., 1977, The physical characteristics and environmental significance of fine-sediment suspensions in estuaries: Estuaries, Geophysics, and the Environment, National Academy of Sciences, Washington, D.C., p. 110–120.

KRONE, R. B., 1962, Flume studies of the transport of sediment in estuarial shoaling processes: final rept.: Berkeley, Univ. California Hydraulic Engr. Lab. and Sanitary Engr. Research Lab., 110 p.

———, 1963, A study of rheologic properties of estuarial sediments: Berkeley, Tech. Bull. 7, Univ. California Hydraulic Engr. Lab. and Sanitary Engr. Research Lab., 91 p.

METCALF, W. G., 1968, Shallow currents along the northeastern coast of South America: Jour. Marine Res., v. 26, p. 232–243.

MIGNIOT, C., 1968, A study of the physical properties of various forms of very fine sediment and their behavior under hydrodynamic action: La Houille Blanche, no. 7, p. 591–620.

MONI, N. S., 1971, Study of mudbanks along the southwest coast of India: Proc. Twelfth Conf. Coastal Engr., Washington, D.C., p. 739–750.

MORGAN, J. P., VAN LOPIK, J. R., AND NICHOLS, L. G., 1953, Occurrence and development of mudflats along the western Louisiana coast: Tech. Rept. 2, Coastal Studies Inst., Louisiana State Univ., 34 p.

MURRAY, S. P., 1975, Trajectories and speeds of wind-driven currents near the coast: Jour. Physical Oceanography, v. 5, p. 347–360.

NAIR, R. R., 1976, Unique mud banks, Kerala, Southwest India: Am. Assoc. Petroleum Geologists Bull., v. 60, p. 616–621.

NEDECO, 1968, Surinam transportation study: The Hague, Netherlands Engr. Consultants, 293 p.

NOAA Tide Tables, 1980, East coast of North and South America: U.S. Dept. Commerce, 293 p.

ODD, N. V. M., AND OWEN, M. N., 1972, A two-layer model of mud transport in the Thames estuary: Proc. Inst. Civ. Engr., Supplement Paper 7517S, p. 175–205.

OWEN, M. N., 1970a, Properties of a consolidating mud: Wallingford, England, Rept. No. INT 83, Hydraulics Research Station, 90 p.

———, 1970b, A detailed study of the settling velocities of an estuary mud: Wallingford, England, Rept. No. INT 78, Hydraulics Research Station, 40 p.

PARTHENIADES, E., 1971, Erosion and deposition of cohesive materials, in Shen, H. W., ed., River Mechanics: Boulder, Colorado State Univ. Press, p. 25-1–25-91.

PIERCE, T. J., AND WILLIAMS, D. J., 1966, Experiments on certain aspects of sedimentation of estuarine muds: Proc. Inst. Civ. Engr., v. 34, p. 391–402.

RINE, J. M., 1980, Depositional environments and Holocene reconstruction of an argillaceous mud belt—Suriname, South America [unpub. Ph.D. dissertation]: Univ. Miami, 222 p.

RINE, J. M., AND GINSBURG, R. N., 1978, A cyclic sedimentary sequence created by migrating mud banks on an open Holocene shelf, Suriname, S. A.: Geol. Soc. America Abstracts, v. 10, p. 478.

SWIFT, D. J. P., HOLLIDAY, B., AVIGNONE, N., AND SHIDELER, G., 1972a, Anatomy of a shore face ridge system, False Cape, Virginia: Marine Geology, v. 12, p. 59–84.

SWIFT, D. J. P., KOFOED, J. W., SAULSBURY, F. P., AND SEARS, P., 1972b, Holocene evolution of the shelf surface, south and central Atlantic shelf of North America, in Swift, D.J.P., Duane, D. B., and Pilkey, O. H., eds., Shelf Sediment Transport: Processes and Pattern: Stroudsburg, PA, Dowden, Hutchinson, and Ross, p. 499–574.

U.S. Naval Oceanographic Office, 1963, Oceanographic atlas of the North Atlantic Ocean: Dept. Navy Pub. No. 700, Sea and Swell, 227 p.

VANN, J. H., 1959, The physical geography of the lower coastal plain of the Guiana coast: Tech. Rept. 1, Dept.

Geography and Anthropology, Louisiana State Univ., 91 p.

WELLS, J. T., 1977, Shallow-water waves and fluid-mud dynamics, coast of Surinam, South America [unpub. Ph.D. dissertation]: Coastal Studies Inst., Louisiana State Univ., 99 p.

WELLS, J. T., AND COLEMAN, J. M., 1977, Nearshore suspended sediment variations, central Surinam coast: Marine Geology, v. 24, M47–M54.

WELLS, J. T., AND HUH, O. K., 1979, Tidal flat muds in the Republic of Korea: Chinhae to Inchon: Office Naval Res. Sci. Bull, v. 4, p. 21–30.

WELLS, J. T., COLEMAN, J. M., AND WISEMAN, W. J., Jr., 1979, Suspension and transportation of fluid mud by solitary-like waves: Proc. Sixteenth Conf. Coastal Engr., Hamburg, Germany, p. 1932–1952.

WELLS, J. T., AND ROBERTS, H. H., in press, Fluid mud dynamics and shoreline stabilization: Louisiana Chenier Plain: Proc. Seventeenth Conf. Coastal Engr., Sydney, Australia.

WELLS, J. T., PRIOR, D. B., AND COLEMAN, J. M., 1980, Flowslides in muds on extremely low angle tidal flats, northeastern South America: Geology, v. 8, p. 272–275.

ZENKOVITCH, V. P., 1967, Processes of coastal development: New York, Wiley Interscience, 738 p.

ZONNEVELD, J. I. S., 1954, Observations along the coast of Surinam: Tijdschr. Kon. Ned. Aardr. Gen., v. 71, p. 18–51.

PERIODIC MUDFLAT PROGRADATION, NORTHEASTERN COAST OF SOUTH AMERICA: A HYPOTHESIS[1]

JOHN T. WELLS AND JAMES M. COLEMAN
Coastal Studies Institute, Louisiana State University
Baton Rouge, Louisiana 70803

ABSTRACT: The Guiana Coast of northeastern South America, backed by mangrove swamps and fronted by migrating mudflats and associated subtidal mudbanks, has developed during the Holocene as a prograding mud wedge from Amazon-derived sediment. A hypothesis is offered for the periodic stabilization of shifting mudflats, a process that has been recognized previously as the mechanism for initiation of new land growth. The hypothesis assumes that solar semiannual and 18.6-yr tidal components allow abnormal exposures of coastal mudflats and conditions that are favorable for establishment of *Avicennia* mangroves. Once colonized, mangrove roots displace muds upward, thus decreasing the frequency of tidal inundation and increasing the ability of vegetation to trap and hold muds. Based on estimated rates of root growth and forecasted tide records for the coast of Surinam, land elevation will increase by 25 cm in 10 yr and frequency of tidal inundation above 2.45 m (8.0 ft) will decrease from 106 to 2 per year during the same period.

INTRODUCTION

The Guiana coast of northeastern South America between the Amazon and Orinoco rivers is one of only a few true chenier plain coasts in the world (Augustinus, 1978; Otvos and Price, 1979). It bears remarkable similarity to the Louisiana chenier plain in that 1) fine-grained sediments supplied by a major river, the Amazon, have caused progradation during the Holocene, thus forming a Holocene mud wedge up to 25 m thick (8 m thick in Louisiana), and 2) mudflats are separated by sand/shell chenier ridges in alternating patterns of coarse versus fine sedimentation (Fig. 1). In addition to being approximately five times as long and twice as wide (Rine, 1980), the Guiana coast differs from the Louisiana chenier plain in that mangrove swamp rather than brackish marsh forms a substantial part of the vegetation between chenier ridges.

Evolution of the Guiana coast over the past 6,000 yr has been that of an accretionary coast built up by deposition of mudflats that subsequently become colonized by vegetation and remain as permanent features. Because mudflats and associated subtidal mudbanks migrate alongshore from southeast to northwest at average rates of 1.5 km/yr (NEDECO, 1968), permanent progradation occurs only when

[1]Manuscript received November 24, 1980; revised June 9, 1981.

shifting muds are stabilized. Overall deposition of mud is interrupted at times by erosional periods during which sand/shell beaches are formed by wave action (Vann, 1969). These beaches become isolated as chenier ridges by subsequent periods of mud accretion. Perhaps the two major unanswered questions concerning the evolution of this immense system are 1) what is the detailed mechanism of mudflat-mudbank movement and 2) what leads to periodic stabilization whereby westward-moving mudflats settle in front of the coast and thus initiate a new phase of land growth? New data that pertain to the question of transport of muds have been given by Wells and Coleman (see paper preceding this one in this issue); the purpose of this paper is to address the second question by proposing a hypothesis for the establishment of subaerial mudflats.

Tidal Mudflats

Intertidal mudflats, the subaerial extensions of subtidal mudbanks or mud shoals, front the coast of northeastern South America every 30–60 km (Delft Hydraulics Laboratory, 1962). A typical mudflat-mudbank system is 10–20 km wide, extends 20 km offshore, and may contain on the order of 10^9 m^3 of mud, nearly all of which has been derived from the Amazon River (NEDECO, 1968). Intertidal exposures normal to the shoreline range from approximately 2–5 km; slopes are less than 0.05

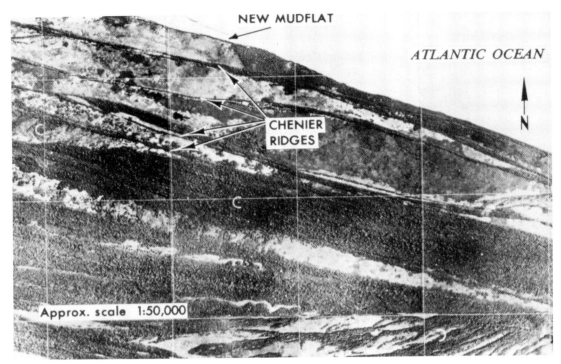

Fig. 1.—Subparallel chenier ridges separated by swamp and marshland vegetation, eastern Surinam coast. For location map, see Wells and Coleman in paper preceding this one in this issue.

degree. Similar features occur along the Louisiana coast (Morgan et al., 1953; Wells and Roberts, in press), southwest coast of India (Moni, 1971; Nair, 1976), and the China coast in the vicinity of the Yangtse River (J. D. Milliman, pers. comm.).

A well-defined 30-yr cycle of erosion/accretion (at a given location) is associated with mudflats and mudbanks because of their migratory nature. Thixotropic fluid muds that accumulate on the western flanks of mudflats and mudbanks (Zonneveld, 1954) provide shelter from wave attack and allow a temporary period of coastal accretion. In interbank areas between mudbanks waves impinge directly on the shoreline and produce an abrasion platform of clay as the shoreline is rapidly eroded. As the mudflat-mudbank system moves from southeast to northwest, so do locations of erosion and accretion. Major mechanisms for movement of the fluid muds that control accretion/erosion cycles are waves, wind-driven and tidal currents, and the Guiana Current (Wells and Coleman, in paper preceding this one in this issue).

Occasionally a wedge of mud becomes permanently attached to the shoreline and is rapidly colonized by mangroves. Such an event is usually attributed to sea level variation and, in fact, NEDECO (1968) implied that virtually the entire evolution of the Guiana coast can be explained in terms of variations in eustatic sea level, which some 50 years ago settled into an accelerated rate of rise of 1.1 mm/yr. An alternate explanation for mud stabilization is that periodic failure of the trade wind system to develop results in calmer sea conditions and enhanced sedimentation (Vann, 1969). Although gradual adjustments in sea level and variations in climatic conditions certainly have been important to coastal evolution during the Holocene, we are of the opinion that low-frequency tidal components, in combination with rapid mangrove growth, are immediately, and in some cases fully, responsible for subaerial mudbank establishment.

Hypothesis

Through the examination of long-term forecasted tides and estimated rates of root growth in *Avicennia* mangroves, we propose the hypothesis that 1) low-frequency tidal constituents (6-mo and 18.6-yr period) allow abnormal exposures of fluid muds which 2) begin to consolidate and gain strength rapidly as mangroves become established, and 3) during mangrove establishment are elevated substantially by subsurface root growth, which leads to a greatly reduced frequency of tidal inundation.

DISCUSSION

Figure 2A illustrates the effect of the 6-mo solar semiannual (S_{SA}) and 18.6-yr tidal components on the average high-water elevation for the period 1958–1978 at the Surinam River entrance (for location see Fig. 1, Wells and Coleman, in paper preceding this one in this

issue). Vertical excursion in monthly averages in less than a 10-yr period extends from a high of 2.28 m in October 1959 to a low of 2.14 m in June 1967 (14 cm), an amount greater than the rise (5.5 cm), by NEDECO's (1968) estimate, in eustatic sea level since the early 1900s. Although these are averages, each based on approximately 60 high water (HW) estimates, the fact remains that the solar semiannual and 18.6-yr tidal constituents are present in the astronomical tides and can become important because of low meteorological tides and gentle offshore gradients. Whereas absolute maximum and minimum inundation cannot be obtained from monthly averages alone, information on frequency and relative magnitude of HW events can be obtained and is useful.

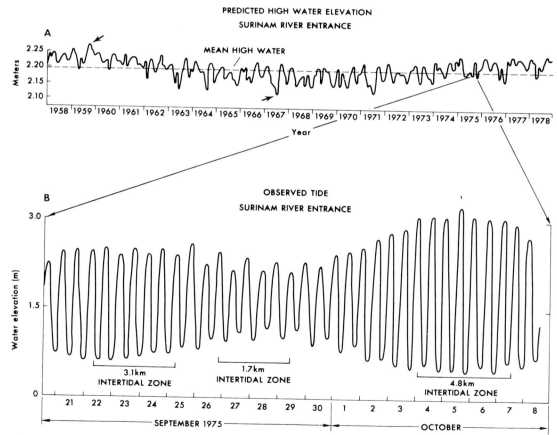

FIG. 2.—Average predicted HW elevations, Surinam River entrance, for the period 1958–1978(A) and observed tide, Surinam River entrance, showing width of intertidal zone at various tidal ranges (B). Arrows in (A) designate times of maximum (1959) and minimum (1967) elevation in combined S_{SA} (solar semiannual) and 18.6 yr cycle. Record from gage shown in (B) not tied into geodetic or leveling net.

If one assumes an average slope of 0.0005 (0°01′30″) then some 320 m of land would be exposed by a 14-cm decrease in water level. Because the variation in spring to neap high water greatly exceeds 14 cm (Fig. 2B), the numbers of importance are those that indicate how many consecutive days a given area remains dry. During the single spring-neap cycle in Figure 2B, 1.5 km of mud was exposed at HW neap tide that was not exposed at HW spring tide. However, duration of subaerial exposure was for only a few days (Fig. 2B). The potential effect of the additional 14 cm is shown in Figure 3 by a histogram of frequency exceedence versus time for 1967 and 1977, the years coinciding with the trough and crest of the 18.6-yr cycle, respectively. If one assumes forecasted tides are accurate, then in January and June 1967 no tide exceeded 2.45 m (8.0 ft) above mean low water (MLW), and the number of times that the other months ex-

ceeded this level ranged from one-half to three-quarters that in 1977. Furthermore, during certain years (1968) average monthly tide never exceeded mean high water (MHW), whereas during other years (1958 and 1977) average monthly tide never fell below MHW (Fig. 2A). Forecasted tides have been used in these calculations because 20-yr records of observed tides were not available to us; they nevertheless indicate that in a statistical sense the S_{SA} and 18.6-yr tidal constituents provide long periods of mud exposure.

Numerous investigators have cited the role of dense *Avicennia* (black mangrove) and *Rhizophora* (red mangrove) forests in reducing current velocities and damping waves, thus promoting sedimentation (e.g., Chapman, 1976). The basic requirement for initial mangrove establishment during the first two weeks after propagules fall from parent trees is that only a few millimeters of water be present. Mangroves are reported to be established between MHW neap (Diemont and van Wijngaarden, 1975) and MHW spring tide (Baltzer, 1969; Steinke, 1975). Prior to initial development of the root system, survival appears to depend overwhelmingly on the number of consecutive days without flooding (Chapman, 1976). After establishment of the root system, regular inundations have little effect on growth (Steinke, 1975) and, at this point, mangroves begin to influence coastal progradation by the volume of sediment displaced by roots and perhaps also by sediment trapped in the dense root network.

In theory, if the rate of increase in root volume with time and rate of decrease in sediment volume due to compaction are known, then the variation in land elevation can be determined. Unfortunately, even though visual observations indicate dense mangrove growth below MHW (Fig. 4), measurements of root volumes have never been made and estimates must suffice. Mature mangroves in eastern Surinam are 10–20 m high (Pons and Pons, 1975) with roots accounting for one-half of the total biomass. In other areas roots up to 20 m long with average diameters of 15 cm have been measured (S. A. Snedaker, pers. comm.). A density of 25 trees per 300 m^2 area, each tree with a root volume of 3.5 m^3 in the upper 30 cm of sediment, would displace 87.5 m^3 of sediment, leading to an overall vertical displacement of 29 cm (volume displaced divided by

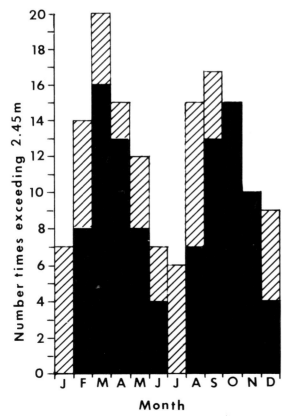

FIG. 3.—Frequency versus time for the 1967 trough(solid) and 1977 crest (ruled) of the 18.6 yr cycle showing number of times tide exceeds 2.45 m (8.0 ft).

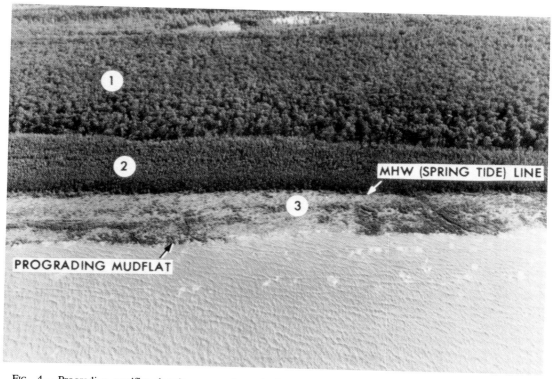

FIG. 4.—Prograding mudflat showing successive colonization by *Avicennia* (black mangrove), eastern Surinam coast (1 is oldest, 3 is youngest).

area). If simultaneously with root growth soil compacts from a density of 1.25 to 1.45 g/cm^3, then the ground level decreases by 4 cm to give a net rise in elevation of 25 cm (Fig. 5). The result would be a substantial decrease in the number of inundations at any given stage of the tide. Inundation frequently decreases from a high of 106 two years after initial colonization to a low of 2 inundations per year after ten years of growth (Fig. 5).

The effect of low-frequency tidal components is also important because, once muds have been exposed to drying, bulk density increases during the same time period in which vegetation is becoming established. Figure 6 shows that, as bulk density increases linearly, apparent viscosity increases exponentially in fine-grained sediments. Laboratory studies have shown that viscosity correlates well with shear strength (Owen, 1970). Thus a small increase in density may lead to a large increase in strength, and, once density exceeds 1.20–1.22 g/cm^3 (Wells and Coleman, in paper preceding this one in this issue), sediment becomes

very difficult to resuspend by small waves in the nearshore.

In summary, long periods of lower than normal tide (months to years) create conditions favorable for mangrove establishment, which in turn lead to large displacements of sediment. During initial months of mangrove colonization, muds consolidate and gain sufficient strength to withstand subsequent erosion. Once vegetation is established, the growth rate of mangrove roots offsets the effect of further consolidation and soil elevation begins to rise. Because erosion and accretion occur simultaneously in the Guianas, migrating mudflats would most likely stabilize at locations where they happen to front the coast during the combined lows in 18.6-yr and S_{SA} cycles. That is, permanent accretion could be expected once every 18.6 yr, but only at locations fronted by mudflats. By comparing aerial photographs of the Surinam coast, Augustinas (1978) concluded that overall accretion took place from 1966–1970, a period of time that coincided with minimum HW elevations as-

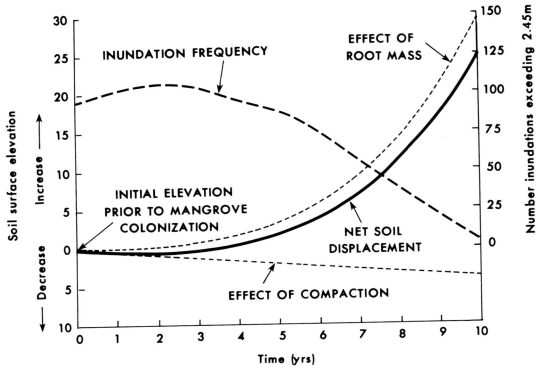

FIG. 5—Net soil displacement (solid line) and frequency of inundation (heavy dashed line) versus time. Soil surface elevation increases from root growth and decreases from dewatering and compaction (thin dashed lines).

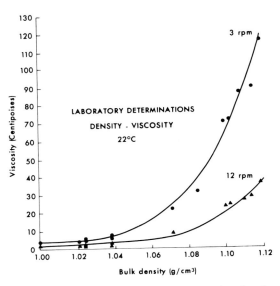

FIG. 6.—Bulk density versus apparent viscosity for Surinam muds at shear rates of 3 and 12 rpm.

sociated with the 18.6-yr cycle (Fig. 2A). To our knowledge the mechanism discussed in the above paragraphs has never been addressed in the literature, and, as a hypothesis, should be field tested to determine its importance in coastal progradation and evolution.

ACKNOWLEDGMENTS

We thank H. E. Clifton and R. L. Phillips for critical reviews of the manuscript. This research was supported by the Coastal Sciences Program, Office of Naval Research, under a contract with Coastal Studies Institute, Louisiana State University.

REFERENCES

AUGUSTINAS, P. G. E. F., 1978, The changing shoreline of Surinam (South America) [unpub. Ph.D. dissertation]: The Netherlands, Univ. Utrecht, 232 p.
BALTZER, F., 1969, Les formations végétales associées au delta de la Dumbéa (Nouvelle-Calédonie): Cahiers

Outre-mer, Sér. Géol. 1, p. 59–84.

CHAPMAN, V. J., 1976, Coastal Vegetation: New York, Pergamon Press, 292 p.

DELFT HYDRAULICS LABORATORY, 1962, Demerara Coastal Investigation: The Netherlands, Delft, 240 p.

DIEMONT, W. H. AND VANWIJNGAARDEN, W. 1975, Sedimentation patterns, soils, mangrove vegetation, and land use in the tidal areas of West-Malaysia: Proc. Inter. Symposium on Biology and Management of Mangroves, Honolulu, Hawaii, v. II, p. 513–528.

MONI, N. S., 1971, Study of mudbanks along the southwest coast of India: Proc. Twelfth Conf. Coatal Engr., Washington, D.C., p. 739–750.

MORGAN, J. P., VAN LOPIK, J. R., AND NICHOLS, L. G., 1953, Occurrence and development of mudflats along the western Louisiana coast: Tech. Rept. 2, Coastal Studies Inst., Louisiana State Univ., 34 p.

NAIR, R. R., 1976, Unique mud banks, Kerala, Southwest India: Am. Assoc. Petroleum. Geologists Bull., v. 60, p. 616–621.

NEDECO, 1968, Surinam transportation study: The Hague, Netherlands Engr. Consultants, 293 p.

OTVOS, E. G., AND PRICE, W. A., 1979, Problems of chenier genesis and terminology—an overview: Marine Geology, v. 31, p. 251–263.

OWEN, M. N., 1970, Properties of a consolidating mud: Wallingford England, Rept. No. INT 83, Hydraulics Research Station, 90 p.

PONS, T. L., AND PONS, L. J., 1975, Mangrove vegetation and soils along a more or less stationary part of the coast of Surinam, South America: Proc. Inter. Symposium on Biology and Management of Mangroves, Honolulu, Hawaii, p. 548–560.

RINE, J. M., 1980, Depositional environments and Holocene reconstruction of an argillaceous mud belt—Suriname, South America [unpub. Ph.D. dissertation]: Univ. Miami, 222 p.

STEINKE, T. D., 1975, Some factors affecting dispersal and establishment of propagules of *Avicennia marina* (Forsk.) Vierh: Proc. Inter. Symposium on Biology and Management of Mangroves, Honolulu, Hawaii, p. 402–414.

VANN, J. H., 1969, Landforms, vegetation and sea level change along the Guiana coast of South America: Buffalo, Tech. Rept. 3, State Univ. College, 128 p.

WELLS, J. T., AND ROBERTS, H. H., in press, Fluid mud dynamics and shoreline stabilization: Louisiana chenier plain: Proc. Seventeenth Conf. Coastal Engr., Sydney, Australia.

ZONNEVELD, J. I. S., 1954, Observations along the coast of Surinam: Tijdschr. Kon. Ned. Aardr. Gen., v. 71, p. 18–51.

Reprinted from BEACH AND NEARSHORE SEDIMENTATION, SEPM Special Publication No. 24,
PP. 169–187, FIGS. 1–23, October 1976

INTERACTION OF BIOLOGICAL AND GEOLOGICAL PROCESSES IN THE BEACH AND NEARSHORE ENVIRONMENTS, NORTHERN PADRE ISLAND, TEXAS

GARY W. HILL AND RALPH E. HUNTER [1]
U.S. Geological Survey, Corpus Christi, Texas 78411

ABSTRACT

Padre Island, a barrier island off the southern Texas coast, experiences a low tidal range, is affected by waves of moderate height, and the northern part of the island is composed largely of fine sand. The seaward part of the island and the adjacent nearshore can be differentiated geomorphically into a beach (backshore and foreshore) and a bar-trough system.

Macrobenthos zonation is related to geomorphic features and can be defined in terms of species distribution and density, diversity-equitability, and niche classification. Dominant species characterize each landform: *Ocypode quadrata* (ghost crab) is concentrated in the beach, and *Callianassa islagrande* (ghost shrimp) and *Mellita quinquiesperforata* (sand dollar) are mainly in the nearshore bar-trough system. Diversity is lowest in the backshore and highest in the foreshore and the bar-trough system. The backshore has a homogeneous trophic nucleus (scavengers) and the foreshore and bar-trough system have a mixed trophic nucleus of suspension and deposit feeders.

Characteristic depositional structures are common to each landform: (1) beach, gently seaward-dipping planar laminations produced by wave swash; (2) bar-trough system, small-scale lenticular crossbedding usually without any well-defined preferred orientation of dip direction and produced by deposition on sand ripples, planar lamination produced when bar crests are planar because of high waves, and medium-scale cross-bedding produced by migrating megaripples and dipping in the direction of the longshore current. The depositional structures commonly are destroyed by organisms. Characteristic biogenic sedimentary structures are found in each geomorphic element. Variation in the areal density, size, morphology, and orientation of *O. quadrata* burrows can be used to define subenvironments of the beach. Deep oblique to vertical burrows of *C. islagrande* and shallow horizontal intrastratal trails of *M. quinquiesperforata* characterize the bar-trough system.

INTRODUCTION

Studies of modern marine environments have long been used to provide an insight into the processes that created the sedimentary rocks found in ancient basins. In particular, elements of the modern beach and littoral environments are detailed to serve as models in documenting the facies changes from marine to nonmarine. This paper describes the results of a detailed study of biological and geological features in the Texas Gulf Coast beach and nearshore environments and discusses the nature of, and balance between, biological and physical processes.

Although much has been written about the geology (King, 1972) and biology (Pearse, Humm, and Wharton, 1942) of beaches and their adjacent environments, relatively little work has been directed toward the interaction of physical and biological factors in controlling the sedimentary features of beach and nearshore environments. Studies in the United States on animal-sediment relationships have largely been restricted to the Atlantic coast, especially Georgia (Howard and Frey, 1973). In Texas, animal-sediment relationships in the neritic environment have received meager study. Biogenic structures common to

modern depositional environments of northern Padre Island were briefly described by Hunter and others (1972), and the relationship of variations in morphology, distribution, and density of ghost crab *Ocypode quadrata* (Fabricius) burrows to the physical zonations of the beach environment was described by Hill and Hunter (1973).

ENVIRONMENTAL SETTING

Geographic setting.—Padre Island is the southernmost part of a gently curving chain of barrier islands and spits that stretches some 322 km along the Texas coast from the Brazos River delta on the northeast to the Rio Grande delta in the southeast. Padre Island itself extends a distance of 177 km without a permanently open natural pass and is divided only by Mansfield Pass, an artificial cut which is maintained by dredging. The beach and nearshore section of the South Bird Island 7.5-minute quadrangle, which is typical of northern Padre island, served as the principal study area (Fig. 1).

Climate.—Padre Island has a subhumid to semiarid warm-temperature climate. The mean annual rainfall at Corpus Christi is 66.9 cm; the mean monthly temperature varies from 14.1° C in January to 29.0° C in August, and the mean annual temperature is 22.1° C (NOAA, 1974). The mean annual wind speed is 5.3 m/sec, and the resultant wind direction is 121°. The climate becomes more

[1] Present address: U.S. Geological Survey, Menlo Park, Calif.

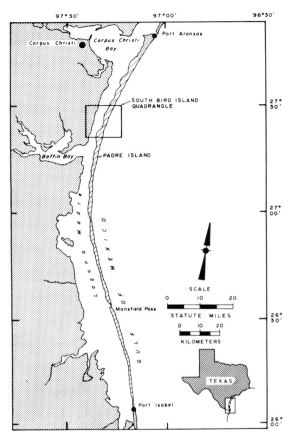

FIG. 1.—Index map of study area. Padre Island is obliquely hachured.

humid and less windy along the coast to the northeast; for those reasons, the role of wind in shaping landforms and transporting sand is and has been greater on Padre Island than on the northeastern part of the Texas barrier chain.

Tides, water properties, and wave climate.—The Padre Island shore is microtidal, having a mean diurnal range of 51.8 cm at Port Aransas (NOAA, 1975). The mean monthly water temperature at Port Aransas varies from 13.6° C in January to 30.0° C in August, and the mean annual water temperature is 22.7° C (NOAA, 1973). The mean monthly salinity, calculated from the water density at Port Aransas, varies from 29.5‰ in May to 36.6‰ in August, and the mean annual salinity is 32.0‰ (NOAA, 1973).

Few data exist regarding wave climate. The heights of breaking waves are normally 0.3 to 1.0 m by visual observation. Breakers higher than 2 m occur several days per year, largely during storms in the fall, winter, and spring. Waves

approach the coast from the southeast during the summer and dominantly from the northeast during the winter.

Sediment.—The mean grain size of shell-free beach sand along northern Padre Island is in the range 2.5 to 3.0 ϕ and is well sorted (Hayes, 1964; Dickinson, 1971). Shells and shell fragments other than *Donax* are not abundant on the beach and nearshore. However, shells of many different molluscs have formed surficial layers in the outer trough at times when it was cut to an unusually great depth, and pipe cores show that shell layers occur at depths greater than 0.7 m beneath the beach surface. These shells are derived from shelly sands that underlie the more recent, nearly shell-free sands.

Geomorphology.—Northern Padre Island and the adjacent inner shelf are marked by a set of elongate, shore-parallel geomorphic units (Fig. 2). The geomorphic units with which this paper is concerned are the beach and inner part of the shoreface.

The beach along most of northern Padre Island is bounded landward by a vegetated foredune ridge. Where vehicular traffic is permitted on the beach, the beach-foredune boundary is sharply defined. Where vehicular traffic has been banned on a section of beach within Padre Island National Seashore, patches of vegetation have become established on the backshore, and since 1971 have caused the growth of small dune mounds that tend to obscure the beach-foreshore boundary. The permanence of this dune growth remains to be tested by a major hurricane. Beach studies for this report were carried out largely within this untrafficked zone, where the influence of man is minimal. Here the beach normally consists of a gently sloping (<2°-5°) foreshore, 25-45 m wide, and a nearly horizontal backshore, 65-115 m wide, at an elevation of 1.5-2.0 m above low water (Fig. 2).

The beach along northern Padre Island has not migrated measurably in any systematic way from the position surveyed in 1877 and shown on the first reliable map published in 1882 (Hunter and Dickinson, 1970). Hurricanes, however, cause striking temporary erosion, producing a gently sloping, nearly planar hurricane beach (Hayes, 1964). Sand eroded from the beach during hurricanes is gradually carried back by normal wave activity and results in the rebuilding of the normal backshore and foreshore (Fig. 2). The backshore may persist for several years between hurricanes because it is outside the influence of normal wave action after its full development.

A low-tide terrace often makes up the seaward part of the intertidal zone. Nearly as often, however, this terrace is replaced by an ephemeral swash bar (ridge) and runnel. A topographic step

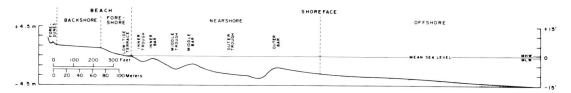

Fig. 2.—Profile of northern Padre Island beach and shoreface. The morphology is typical of northern Padre Island during summer conditions. An ephemeral bar and runnel commonly replace the low-tide terrace.

usually occurs at the seaward edge of the low-tide terrace.

The shoreface, which is the relatively narrow, steep, inner part of the continental shelf, can be divided into nearshore and offshore parts. Only the former is part of this study. The nearshore part of the shoreface consists of a series of bars, typically three along this section of coast, having intervening troughs (Fig. 2). The bars on this part of the Texas coast are generally straight, continuous, and aligned parallel to shore. The bars are remarkably stable in a dynamic sense. They shift back and forth and change shape as wave conditions change, but seldom are destroyed, migrate onto the beach, or grow from a previously planar bottom. In unusually calm weather, however, the inner bar migrates shoreward and becomes irregular in plan view as tongues of sand are built from the bar into the inner trough. In the late summer of 1974, this migration proceeded to the extent that the inner trough was filled and the inner bar was planed off. In contrast, during the passage of Hurricane Fern in September 1971, the outer bar was planed off and the outer trough was filled.

Hydrodynamic processes.—The swash zone, the dynamic zone dominated by wave runup and backswash, coincides with the foreshore during normal wave and tide conditions. The backshore, in contrast, is inactive during fair weather except for the generally landward transport of sand by wind. Because of the dampness of the sand due to its low elevation, wind erosion seldom lowers the level of the backshore by more than a few centimeters. Wave swash reaches the backshore several times a year, mostly during winter storms, but only hurricanes cause severe erosion.

The nearshore is the dynamic zone dominated by breaking waves and by wave-induced currents. Breaking waves and surf are confined mainly to the bars and to the edge of the beach with the waves tending to reform in the troughs. The waves are seldom so small that they do not break on the inner bar, but breaking is commonly absent on the outer bars.

The prevailing longshore currents vary seasonally, being mostly to the south in winter and to the north in summer. The strongest currents, more than 1 m/sec, are mainly to the south and occur several times a year, mostly during winter storms. Rip currents commonly flow seaward across the bar crests when waves are breaking on the bars. Aerial photographs taken about a half-hour apart show that the rip currents migrate with the longshore current. The absence of rip-current channels across the bars is probably related to the migration of the rip currents.

The strongest onshore- and offshore-directed water motions in the nearshore are the oscillatory motions due to waves. The oscillations are markedly asymmetric: the onshore pulses reach higher maximum velocities but are of shorter duration than the offshore pulses (Clifton, this volume). This asymmetric oscillatory water motion can transport sand landward even in the absence of superimposed net currents.

Observations of slightly negatively buoyant drifters and of plumes from anchored dye packets show that net onshore near-bottom currents are common on the seaward sides of the bars and on the bar crests. Similar observations show that net offshore, near-bottom currents occur on the landward sides of the bars and in the troughs when waves are breaking on the bars. Although the sand-transporting power of these offshore bottom currents has not been documented, they may be the main factor in promoting bar stability by counteracting the tendency of the asymmetric oscillatory water motion to transport sand landward.

METHODS

Biota.—From January 1971 to February 1975, numerous transects were made perpendicular to the shoreline across northern Padre Island from the foredune ridge to the outer bar in the bar-trough system. Bulk sediment samples for biota were taken along each transect, and a constant volume of sediment, to a depth of 15 cm and having a surface area of 0.01 m^2, was recovered by pipe coring. The bulk samples were washed through a 0.5 mm mesh sieve. Organisms recovered were fixed in 10 percent formalin, preserved in 45 percent isopropyl alcohol, and later identified and counted in the laboratory.

Biota of the beach and nearshore was quantitatively sampled in the summer of 1972 and in the winter and spring of 1973 and 1975. Burrows of the larger crustaceans, particularly *Ocypode quadrata*, were examined during all seasons from 1971 to 1975.

The spacing of sample stations along each transect varied according to the subenvironment being sampled. Sample stations on the backshore and foreshore were spaced 8 m and 3 m apart, respectively. In the nearshore, divers using SCUBA took samples in the deepest part of each trough and on each bar crest.

To ensure representative sampling of large deep-burrowing organisms, different sampling techniques were used. The local distribution and density of the ghost crab *Ocypode quadrata* were determined by marking out 3 m wide strips perpendicular to the shoreline and divided into sections 3 m square from the waterline to the foredune ridge. Within each section, the number of ghost crab burrows was counted and their diameter, length, morphology, and orientation were measured. To determine more accurately the distribution-density of *Callianassa islagrande* Schmitt, two methods of counting burrow openings were used. During spring low tides, a tape measure was placed across the foreshore perpendicular to the shoreline, and *C. islagrande* burrow openings were counted in each square meter along the tape. In the surf zone, a diver dropped a metal loop, 30 cm in diameter, onto the bottom in each trough and on each bar crest and counted the burrow openings inside the loop. A benthic suction sampler modified from Brett (1964) was also used to collect organisms quantitatively from sediment depths as great as 1 m.

Sediments.—Relatively undisturbed box cores (10 × 14 × 20 cm) and pipe cores as much as 1.3 m long were collected from the beach and bar-trough system. In the laboratory, the cores were opened and X-ray radiographs and epoxy casts were made for the analysis of physical and biogenic sedimentary structures.

A modification of burrow-casting techniques (Mayou, Howard, and Smith, 1969), and trenching were used to determine burrow morphologies. Burrow casts were made using epoxy and fiberglass resins.

Laboratory techniques.—X-ray radiographic examinations of biogenic sedimentary structures were made using a 3 cm wide plexiglas aquarium having a continuous water-circulation system (Fig. 3). Sediment erosion or deposition in the aquarium was maintained at various rates. Radiographs were made using a portable industrial X-ray unit equipped with a beryllium window hotshot head and type-M industrial X-ray film.

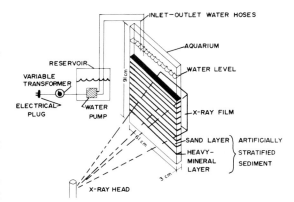

Fig. 3.—Schematic diagram of aquarium, X-ray, and continuous water-circulating system used to study species-specific biogenic sedimentary structures under laboratory conditions.

BIOTA

Community structure.—The 660 short pipe cores taken at 110 sample stations along four transects on the northern Padre Island beach and bar-trough system yielded 4,546 individuals belonging to 27 macrobenthic species representing several taxonomic groups (Table 1). The distribution and density of *Ocypode quadrata*, as indicated by their burrows, were determined at 597 sample stations (3 m² each) along 27 transects which contained 2,800 burrows. An additional 387 *O. quadrata* burrows were examined to determine burrow orientation. Burrows of *Callianassa islagrande* were studied at 76 stations along four transects.

Most of the species are represented by few individuals. Seventy-seven percent (3,443 individuals) belong to the single most frequently occurring taxon (haustoriid amphipods), and 99 percent (4,450 individuals) belong to the five most frequent species. In contrast, 1 percent (96 individuals) of the biota comprises 81.5 percent of the species (Tables 1 and 2).

TABLE 1.—NUMBER OF SPECIES AND SPECIMENS COLLECTED FOR ALL SAMPLES FROM ALL STATIONS

Taxa	No. of species	No. of specimens
Crustacea	9 (33.5%)	3,550 (78%)
Polychaeta	9 (33.5%)	691 (15%)
Mollusca	4 (15%)	194 (4%)
Echinodermata	3 (11%)	99 (2%)
Others	2 (7%)	12 (1%)
	27 (100%)	4,546 (100%)

TABLE 2.—COMPARISON OF NUMBER OF SPECIES AND SPECIMENS COLLECTED IN THE BEACH AND BAR-TROUGH SYSTEM OF NORTHERN PADRE ISLAND

| | Beach | | | Bar-trough system | |
	Backshore		Foreshore		
No. of stations	40		46	24	
Total no. of species	6		21	19	
Total no. of specimens	335		2,337	1,874	
No. of species:					
Crustacea	2 (33.3%)		9 (43%)	5 (26%)	
Polychaeta	2 (33.3%)		9 (43%)	7 (37%)	
Mollusca	0		2 (10%)	4 (21%)	
Echinodermata	0		1 (10%)	3 (16%)	
Others	2 (33.3%)		0	0	
Most abundant:					
2 species	322 (96%)		2,076 (89%)	1,656 (88%)	
5 species	334 (99.7%)		2,272 (97%)	1,844 (98%)	
No. of specimens:					
Crustacea	272 (81%)		1,712 (73%)	1,551 (83%)	
Polychaeta	51 (15%)		579 (25%)	76 (4%)	
Mollusca	0		45 (2%)	149 (8%)	
Echinodermata	0		1 (1%)	98 (5%)	
Others	12 (4%)		0	0	
Most common species:	Haustoriidae	272	Haustoriidae 1,656	Haustoriidae	1,514
	Scolelepis squamata	50	*Scolelepis squamata* 420	*Donax variabilis*	142
	Staphylinidae	9	*Lumbrineris* sp. 133	*Mellita*	
			Donax variabilis 39	*quinquiesperforata*	93
			Lepidopa websteri 24	*Lumbrineris* sp.	65
				Pinnixa chacei	30

The taxonomic group comprising the greatest number of individuals collected was Crustacea (78%) followed by Polychaeta (15%), Mollusca (4%), and Echinodermata (2%). Other taxonomic groups accounted for less than one percent of the total specimens collected (Table 1).

Two macrozoobenthic communities and an intervening ecotone, each related to a specific geomorphic feature (Table 3), are defined by the zonation in distribution and density of the most common and/or conspicuous species (characteristic species, Table 4; Fig. 4).

The backshore contains the fewest zoobenthic species and individuals compared with the other landforms in this study (Table 2). Some of these species, among which the haustoriid amphipods and the polychaete worm *Scolelepis squamata* (Müller) are most common, are restricted to the

TABLE 3.—COMMUNITIES AND RELATED GEOMORPHIC FEATURES OF THE NORTHERN PADRE ISLAND BEACH AND BAR-TROUGH SYSTEM

Community	Geomorphic feature
Ocypode	Backshore
Ecotone	Foreshore
Callianassa-Donax-Haustoriidae	Bar-trough system

seaward edge of the backshore (Fig. 4). Because these species represent landward extensions of populations more abundant in other subenvironments and occupy a restricted zone, they are not characteristic of the backshore in general. The ghost crab *Ocypode quadrata* is a large conspicu-

TABLE 4.—CHARACTERISTIC MACROZOOBENTHIC SPECIES OF COMMUNITIES FOUND IN THE BEACH AND BAR-TROUGH ENVIRONMENTS OF NORTHERN PADRE ISLAND

	Sand beach community	Bar-trough community
1st order	*Ocypode quadrata*	*Callianassa islagrande*
		Donax variabilis
2nd order	*Scolelepis squamata*	*Mellita quinquiesperforata*
3rd order	—	Haustoriidae
Influents	Staphylinidae	*Lumbrineris* sp.

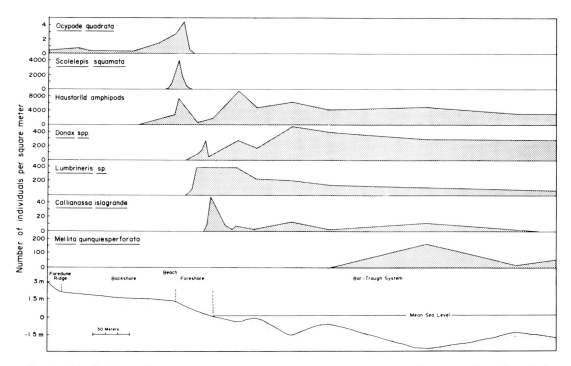

FIG. 4.—Distribution and zonation of macrobenthos on the beach and bar-trough system of northern Padre Island.

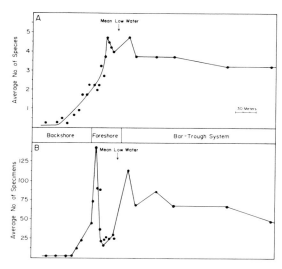

FIG. 5.—Cross section of the northern Padre Island beach and bar-trough system. *A*. Distribution of species. *B*. Distribution of individuals.

ous organism that is found everywhere in the backshore in relatively small numbers (Fig. 4) and is considered a first-order characteristic species of the backshore (Table 4). The backshore community was named after this species— *Ocypode* community. Rove beetles (Staphylinidae) are abundant in the backshore, but the 0.5 mm mesh size of the sieves used in collecting samples was not small enough to collect them quantitatively.

The second largest number of zoobenthic species and individuals is found in the bar-trough system (Table 2). Characteristic species that are distributed throughout the bar-trough system (Table 4) include haustoriid amphipods, the bivalve *Donax variabilis* Say, the polychaete worm

TABLE 5.—DIVERSITY AND EQUITABILITY VALUES OF MACROZOOBENTHIC ASSEMBLAGES RELATED TO SPECIFIC GEOMORPHIC FEATURES COMMON TO NORTHERN PADRE ISLAND

Landform	Diversity	Equitability
Backshore	0.6280	0.2950
Foreshore	.9327	.1070
Bar-trough System	.8054	.1047

TABLE 6.—PERCENTAGES OF BIOMASS FOR EACH TROPHIC TYPE FOUND IN DIFFERENT NERITIC MACROZOOBENTHIC COMMUNITIES ON NORTHERN PADRE ISLAND

Trophic type	*Ocypode* community	*Collianassa-Donax*-Haustoriidae community
Suspension feeders	< 10%	28%
Detritus feeders	> 90%	70%
Carnivores	< 1%	2%
Trophic nucleus	Homogeneous	Mixed

Lumbrineris sp., and the ghost sprimp *Callianassa islagrande* (Fig. 4). The sand dollar *Mellita quinquiesperforata* (Leske) is not found landward of the crest of the middle bar. Because of the large numbers of haustoriid amphipods and *Donax*, and the restricted distribution of the large conspicuous *Callianassa islagrande*, the macrozoobenthic community of the bar-trough system was named the *Callianassa-Donax*-Haustoriidae community.

Samples from the foreshore yielded the greatest number of species and individuals (Table 2). The foreshore represents an ecotone—a boundary between two adjacent communities. Species common to the backshore and foreshore include *Ocypode quadrata* and staphylinid beetles. Species common to the bar-trough system and foreshore include haustoriid amphipods, *Scolelepis squamata*, *Callianassa islagrande*, *Donax variabilis*, and *Lumbrineris sp.* (Fig. 4, Table 2). To further distinguish the ecotone from either adjacent community, the densities of some characteristic species found in the two communities are greatest in the foreshore. Both *Ocypode quadrata* and *Callianassa islagrande* reach their greatest density in the foreshore, but their distribution patterns generally do not overlap (Fig. 4). The polychaete *Scolelepis squamata* is almost totally limited in its distribution to the upper foreshore, where it attains very high densities (Fig. 4).

Diversity-equitability.—As a measure of processes operating in an ecologic system, diversity reflects external environmental stresses as well as internal stability and productivity (Beerbower and Jordan, 1969). Diversity was determined by simply counting the number of species and individuals in each sample and also by calculating the Shannon diversity index.

Both the number of species (Fig. 5a) and the number of individuals (Fig. 5b) increases seaward across the backshore, rises sharply in the foreshore, and then gradually declines across the bar-trough system. A slight reduction in the number of species and a large drop in the number of total individuals seems to occur just landward of the mean low water line. Howard and Dörjes (1972) noticed a similar reduction of species and individuals landward of the low water line on

Sapelo Island, Georgia. On Padre Island, this zone of reduced density generally corresponds to the plunge point of waves on the lower foreshore, suggesting that extreme turbulence near the bed may play a role in causing this reduction.

The Shannon diversity index, H (Shannon and Weaver, 1963), is an approximation of the Brillouin index.

$$H = - \sum_{i=1}^{N} P_i \ln P_i \qquad (1)$$

0 1 2 3 4 cm

FIG. 6.—X-radiograph of box-core peel from crest of inner bar. Planar lamination probably formed by deposition on planar bed.

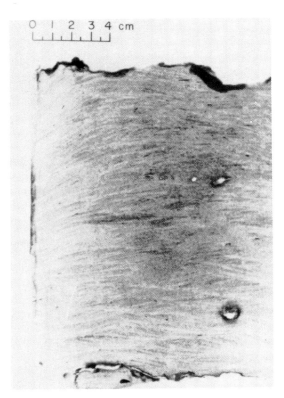

FIG. 7.—X-radiograph of box-core peel from inner trough. Small-scale cross-bedding formed by ripple migration; contortion of bedding at edges of peel is artificial.

where P_i = the number of individuals of the ith species divided by the number of individuals of all species in a sample, and n = the number of species in the sample. It is influenced by two components: the total number of species present (species-richness component) and the evenness of distribution of the individuals among the different species (equitability component). Whereas the number of species depends primarily on the structural diversity of a habitat, equitability is more sensitive to the stability of physical conditions. To separate the two components of the Shannon diversity index, Lloyd and Ghelardi's (1964) equitability index, E, was used:

$$E = si/s \qquad (2)$$

where s = observed number of taxa, and si = calculated number of taxa whose random properties yield the diversity H.

Equitability decreased seaward from the backshore to the bar-trough system (Table 5). The bar-trough system has a higher diversity index

(Table 5) than the backshore (Table 2, Fig. 5a), but the greatest diversity index is found in the foreshore or intertidal zone. Such an abundance of species is explained in the biological concept of the ecotone or "edge effect"; when two habitats come together, the edge between the two will be more favorable as a habitat then either type considered alone.

Niche classification.—According to Scott (1972), the two most important parameters of the niche hypervolume are the feeding habit and the position of each species relative to the sediment-water interface (its substrate niche).

Trophic groupings are formed by listing species (trophic types) in order of decreasing biomass. The dominant species, whose combined biomass is greater than 80 percent of the total sample, form the trophic nucleus, which may be classified as either homogeneous (consisting of species of a similar feeding type) or mixed (consisting of species of different feeding types) (Rhoads, Speden and Waage, 1972).

FIG. 8.—X-radiograph of box-core peel from inner trough. Medium-scale cross-bedding formed by migration of megaripples; the cross-bedding dips in the direction of the longshore current.

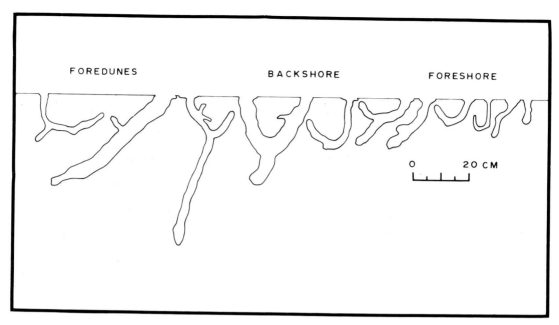

Fig. 9.—Representative *Ocypode quadrata* burrows of a beach cross section, northern Padre Island (from Hill and Hunter, 1973).

Samples within each community were grouped together, and species were listed by trophic types to determine the composition of the trophic nucleus. On the basis of percentages of biomass, the trophic nucleus of the *Ocypode* community is homogeneous, and the *Callianassa-Donax-*Haustoriidae community is mixed (Table 6). Detritus feeders dominate both communities. Scavengers, however, are prevalent on the backshore, whereas deposit feeders abound in the bar-trough system.

Closely associated with the substrate and its condition is the mode of movement or attachment of benthic animals. Thorson's (1957, p. 461) classification of three "ecologically different groups of benthic marine animals" was used: (1) epifauna, animals occupying area upon the substrate; (2) infauna, animals occupying sediment volume; and (3) vagrant invertebrates.

The majority of benthic organisms found in the beach and surf environments are infaunal forms. The environments are too harsh for epifauna to exist. Animals such as *Donax* and haustoriid amphipods, living near the sediment-water interface without the protection of an open burrow for downward escape, are streamlined and possess the ability to burrow rapidly when dislodged from the sediment.

SEDIMENTARY STRUCTURES

Physical sedimentary structures.—The domi-

nant internal structure produced by wave swash on the beach is gently seaward-dipping planar lamination (McKee, 1957; Milling and Behrens, 1966; Moiola and Spencer, 1973). Some irregular stratification is produced on the backshore by scour and deposition around stranded debris and by the growth of incipient dunes. Cores suggest that such irregularities are less common at depths below 0.5 m. Most of the beach sand body was probably deposited on foreshores, and most of

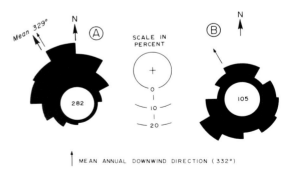

Fig. 10.—Orientation of *O. quadrata* burrows, defined as the direction of burrow descent. Number in the center of each circle indicates the number of burrows measured. Data plotted in 30° classes. *A.* Orientation of backshore burrows. *B.* Orientation of burrows in the interdune flats.

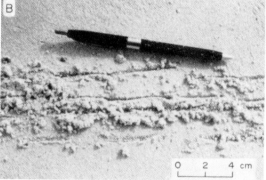

FIG. 11.—Lebensupurren produced by *O. quadrata.*
A. Mound of sand around burrow opening resulting
from digging activities. *B.* Trackway.

the sand was probably deposited rapidly during
post-hurricane recovery periods.

Three kinds of bed configurations and corresponding internal structures produced by wave
and current action on fine-grained sand have been
found in the bar-trough system of northern Padre
Island. These are plane beds with planar lamination, ripples with small-scale cross-stratification,
and megaripples with medium-scale cross-stratification.

Plane beds occur on the bar crests whenever
the waves are large enough to break and extend
down the sides of the bars. Deposition sometimes
occurs on such surfaces, producing planar lamination (Fig. 6). The laminae tend to be similar
in thickness to adjacent laminae, suggesting that
each lamina is the product of a single wave in
a series of similar waves.

Ripples occur at depths greater than those in
which plane beds are generated under equivalent
conditions and as a result tend to be restricted
to the troughs between bars. In the transition
from rippled to plane beds, the ripples are destroyed during the peak of each passing wave

surge and form again during the deceleration of
the surge. In somewhat deeper water, the ripples
become permanent, but their asymmetry reverses
as wave surge oscillates. These very active ripples,
of the type called "nonorbital" by H. E. Clifton
(this volume), range from 5 to 10 cm in spacing,
are less than 1 cm high, and have flat, wide troughs
and long straight crests. They are aligned parallel
to the waves or, if a longshore current is present,
at some angle between the waves and the direction
normal to the current. The internal structure
produced by the migration of these ripples is
poorly known; if the ripples climb at a very low
angle, the resulting structure may closely resemble
planar lamination.

In the deeper parts of the troughs, during low
and moderate wave activity, the ripples are less
active. These less active ripples tend to be larger
and steeper than the "nonorbital" ripples, have
spacings as much as 15 cm, have rounded troughs
and no distinct asymmetry, are short-crested, and
form an irregular branching pattern. The complexity of the plan-view pattern is probably due
to the interference of wave surge, the net offshore
flow, and the longshore current. The internal

FIG. 12.—X-radiograph of box-core peel from the
backshore. Sand intensely bioturbated by rove beetles
(Staphylinidae). Because of the small size of the beetles,
the sand was not displaced very far, and stratification
is still visible. Gas-bubble cavities are still preserved
near the base.

structure produced by deposition on rippled surfaces in the interbar troughs is small-scale lenticular cross-bedding without any well-defined preferred onshore or offshore component of foreset dip direction but at times having preferred longshore components, which, however, are subject to reversals (Fig. 7).

Longshore currents exceeding about 0.5 m/sec produce megaripples ranging from 10 to 60 cm in height. Megaripples produced by both north-flowing and south-flowing currents have been observed. The internal structure produced by migration of the megaripples is medium-scale (defined here as units 4 to 100 cm thick) cross-bedding that dips in the direction of the current (Fig. 8). This cross-bedding commonly dips at angles less than the angle of repose and in places at angles as low as 10°. Currents that flow along the leeward slopes of megaripples, rather than currents that flow down these slopes, as suggested by Imbrie and Buchanan (1965), are probably the most common cause of the low dip angles that are typical in shallow marine cross-bedding.

Ripples having spacings of 0.3 m or more can exist in shelly sand adjacent to small ripples in fine-grained sand. Sand that is sufficiently shelly for the existence of large ripples is rarely found off northern Padre Island but is common off central Padre Island. The orientation and symmetry of these ripples varies. Onshore-facing lunate megaripples have been seen on the landward side of the inner trough, and offshore-facing megaripples were observed at the same time on the seaward side of the inner trough. Symmetric, shore-parallel, large wave ripples and longshore-facing, current-generated megaripples have been observed in shelly sand in the middle and outer troughs.

Biogenic sedimentary structures.—Distinctive biogenic sedimentary structures are produced by many of the macrozoobenthic organisms found in the beach and bar-trough system of northern Padre Island. These biogenic sedimentary structures help to define the macrobenthos zonation and may be related to specific geomorphic features.

Variation in areal density, size, morphology, and orientation of *Ocypode quadrata* burrows can be used to define subenvironments of the beach (Hill and Hunter, 1973). An increase in burrow diameter, length, and complexity of shape (Fig. 9) coupled with a decrease in burrow density (Fig. 4) from the upper foreshore to the back edge of the beach, differentiates beach subzones. Burrows in the backshore show a preferred orientation, descending in a northwest direction (Fig. 10a). Laboratory experiments and field observations under varying wind conditions show that this orientation is controlled by the direction of

Fig. 13.—Filled rove-beetle burrows penetrating a heavy mineral layer exposed by wind scour on the backshore.

onshore winds. In contrast, burrow orientation is random in the interdune flats of the foredune ridge, where wind shadows occur (Fig. 10b).

Other lebenspurren produced by *O. quadrata*, such as mounds of excavated sand around burrow openings, trackways, and feeding pellets (Fig. 11), are normally destroyed by wind and wave activity. The ghost crabs will inhabit any large burrow found on the backshore, such as those made by the south Texas pocket gopher *Geomys personatus* (True).

Intense burrowing by rove beetles (Staphylinidae) on the backshore produces bioturbated sediments (Fig. 12). The presence of rove beetles on the backshore is marked by small burrow openings (1 mm) and stringers of loose sand pushed from the burrows. Filled rove beetle burrows can be observed on the beach when a heavy-mineral layer is exposed by wind scour (Fig. 13).

The south Texas pocket gopher, *G. personatus*, which is found in great numbers on the eolian flats of Padre Island, produces a large distinct burrow found occasionally on the beach. The

FIG. 14.—Burrow of the south Texas pocket gopher on the backshore of northern Padre Island. *A.* Mounds of sand excavated from the burrow. *B.* Excavated burrow revealing a somewhat sinuous morphology.

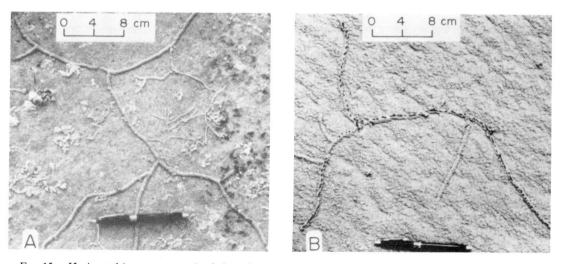

FIG. 15.—Horizontal burrow network of *Omophron* beetle larvae on the backshore of northern Padre Island. *A.* Undisturbed burrow. *B.* Burrow showing peck marks of birds searching for food.

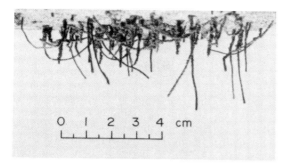

FIG. 16.—Epoxy burrow casts of the polychaete worm *Scolelepis squamata.*

are capsule shaped and about 19 mm in length and 7 mm in diameter (Davis, 1966). A typical mound of sand measured 10 to 15 cm in height, 48 to 60 cm in diameter, and consisted of 4.5 to 6.5 kg of sand.

A horizontal burrow network produced by the larvae of the beetle *Omophron sp.* (Fig. 15a) is occasionally found along the landward edges of the backshore. This distinctive burrow system is a feeding target for birds which methodically peck the burrow when searching for the larvae (Fig. 15b).

The upper foreshore is characterized by the dense vertical burrows of the polychaete worm *Scolelepis squamata* (Fig. 16). The burrows have a thin mucoid lining. Lebensspuren, such as footprints, produced by shorebirds feeding along the upper foreshore are superficial and easily destroyed by wave swash. Pecking marks made by shorebirds when searching for polychaetes, mole crabs, or *Donax* reach depths of as much as 30 mm and could be preserved.

Lebensspuren found in both the foreshore and the bar-trough system include the small body-sized burrows of the coquina clam *Donax variabilis* just below the substrate surface and a bioturbated sediment produced by numerous haustoriid

burrows are horizontal, slightly sinuous, average 10 cm in horizontal diameter, 13 cm in vertical diameter, and lie about 25 cm below the sand surface (Fig. 14). Most of the burrows terminate near the seaward edge of the backshore, where the water level is very close to the sediment surface. One burrow system excavated on the backshore was more than 35 m long and had short side branches. These side branches normally contain a food cache or fecal pellets. The fecal pellets

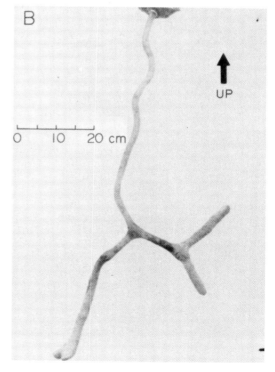

FIG. 17.—*Callianassa islagrande* burrow. *A.* Narrow upper section of burrow. *B.* Fiberglass cast of main burrow.

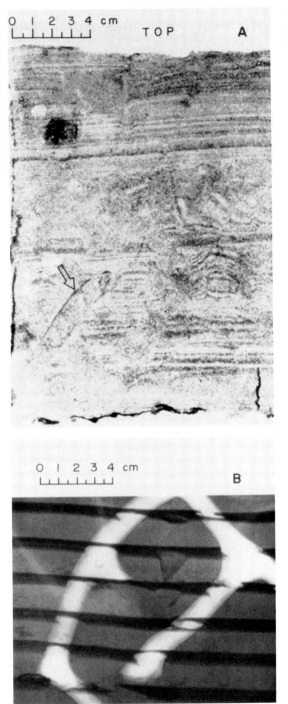

amphipods. The subvertical burrows of the polychaete *Lumbrineris* sp. are common in the lower
foreshore and inner trough.

In the bar-trough system, the large conspicuous
burrowing animals can be divided into two broad
groups based on gross burrow orientation. Species
that produce deep vertical burrows are dominant
in the inner surf zone, whereas species that burrow
horizontally are more common in the outer nearshore. The ghost shrimp *Callianassa islagrande*
constructs deep, nearly vertical burrows (Fig. 17)
to depths of a meter or more and is the dominant
burrowing species throughout the nearshore. The
length of the narrow (6–7 mm) upper section of
the *C. islagrande* burrow depends on the rate
of sediment deposition. The narrow section of
the burrow is almost never present on bar crests.
Burrows of *C. islagrande* are well defined in cores
by their morphology, size, and cemented walls
(Fig. 18). Surface expressions of ghost shrimp
burrows include chimney structures, mounds of
sediment, conical depressions, and simple burrow
openings (Fig. 19).

C. islagrande produce large numbers of fecal
pellets that measure approximately 0.75 to 1.0
mm in diameter and 2 to 3 mm in length. These
fecal pellets consist largely of clay-size material
(97%) and are found locally in rings around the
burrow openings of the ghost shrimp burrows at
low tide (Fig. 20a). Dense accumulations of *C.
islagrande* fecal pellets are commonly found along
strand lines on the beach (Fig. 20b). These fecal
pellets are also concentrated in troughs between
ripples where they become covered by sediment
(Fig. 20c). Although the fecal production rate was
not determined for *C. islagrande* on Padre Island,
C. major Say was found to produce about 456
pellets per burrow per day in the sand-beach
community at Sapelo Island, Georgia (Frankenberg, Coles, and Johannes, 1967).

Sediment excavated by *C. islagrande* during
its deposit-feeding process may be redeposited
at a level higher or lower than the level from
which it was removed. Under laboratory conditions, *C. islagrande* was found to dispose of
excavated sand by redepositing it in abandoned
feeding burrows at all levels in the sediment
column and by venting it out the burrow opening
at the sediment surface (Fig. 21).

Although the burrows of *C. islagrande* are lined
to increase the wall strength, the burrows occasionally collapse, thereby producing a variety of

FIG. 18.—X-radiographs of *C. islagrande* burrows. *A.*
Box-core peel from the lower foreshore showing a well
defined *C. islagrande* burrow and other irregularly
shaped burrows, and an intensely bioturbated interval
between intervals having partially preserved bedding;
the planar bedding was formed by wave swash. *B.*
Burrow made in a narrow aquarium under laboratory
conditions.

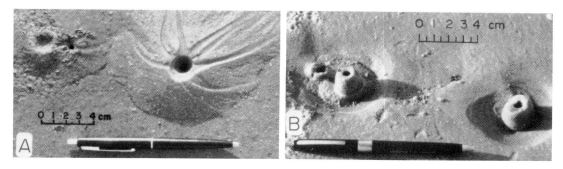

FIG. 19.—Surface openings to *C. islagrande* burrows. *A.* Mound produced by excavated sand vented by the organism from burrow opening. *B.* Chimney structure produced when sand is eroded away from burrow near surface opening.

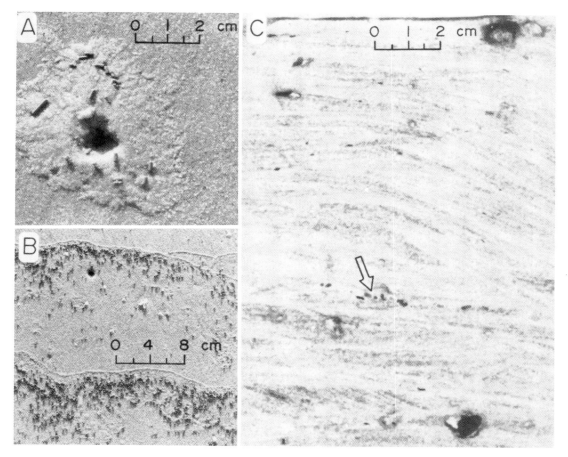

FIG. 20.—Fecal pellets of *C. islagrande*. *A.* Around burrow opening during low tide. *B.* Along strand lines on the upper foreshore. *C.* X-radiograph of box-core peel showing fecal pellets buried along a depositional surface in the inner trough.

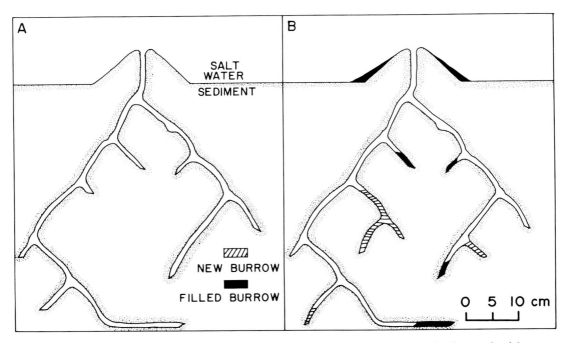

FIG. 21.—Redeposition of excavated sediments by *C. islagrande* while deposit feeding under laboratory conditions, as determined by time-lapse X-ray radiography. *A.* Morphology of the burrow at the start of the experiment. *B.* Morphology of the burrow 24 hours into the experiment.

sedimentary structures (Fig. 22). Nodular wall structure is common to callianassids found on the East Coast of the United States (Weimer and Hoyt, 1964). A general lack of obviously nodular structure in the burrow wall of recently constructed ghost-shrimp burrows has been observed in this study, both in the field and in the laboratory.

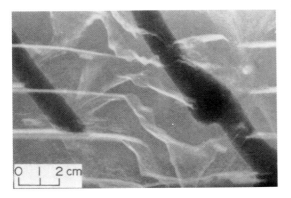

FIG. 22.—Sedimentary structures produced by the collapse of *C. islagrande* burrows under laboratory conditions. Heavy-mineral layers (light areas) bounded on each side by fine sand layers (dark areas).

Rarely, the thicker, stronger, somewhat nodular walls of older(?) *C. islagrande* burrows have been seen on the middle and outer bar crests.

Intrastratal trails probably produced by the horizontal burrowing of sand dollars *Mellita quinquiesperforata* (Fig. 23) are common seaward of the middle bar in the surf zone. Less common but conspicuous horizontal burrowers and surface crawlers include the olive shell *Oliva sayana* Ravenel, moon shell *Polinices duplicatus* (Say), and the auger snail *Terebra salleana* Deshayes.

Although distinct biogenic structures are common in the beach and nearshore sands of northern Padre Island, the burrowing activities of the organisms are even more strikingly manifest in the essentially complete homogenization of the nearshore sands below a thin surficial layer. Pipe cores as long as 1.5 m show that lamination is almost completely absent at depths greater than 0.3 m below the sediment-fluid interface in the nearshore. In fact, seaward of the middle bar, lamination seldom extends more than 2 cm below the sediment surface.

On the beach, lamination is found down to a sharp contact at a level near mean low water. Below this contact, the sand is completely homogenized and contains shells and shell fragments of Gulf origin. This shelly sand is apparently a nearshore deposit that predates the beach. The lower foreshore deposits above this older deposit are alternating beds of highly bioturbated sand and relatively undisturbed laminated sand. Farther landward on the beach, the sands above the older deposit are well laminated, having thin shelly layers in the lower part. The shelly layers were probably derived from the older deposit. Some *Callianassa* burrows occur in the lower part, at levels corresponding to the lower foreshore. Burrows typical of the upper foreshore and backshore occur near the top.

Although Moore and Scruton (1957) suggested that the absence of visible physical sedimentary structures in shoreface sands of the Texas coast might be the result of rapid deposition of well-sorted sand, this hypothesis must be ruled out. Downward increases in the degree of bioturbation, remnant wispy inhomogeneities of irregular shape, and the random orientation of shell fragments are definitive evidence that the absence of lamination is due to bioturbation. The degree of bioturbation is related to changes in the balance between biogenic and physical sedimentary structures.

The balance between biogenic and physical sedimentary structures at depth changes significantly over relatively short periods of time. As the beach and nearshore are rebuilt following erosion caused by severe storms such as hurricanes, the newly deposited sediment is well laminated down to depths as great as one meter, and little biogenic activity is evident. As biological populations destroyed by a major storm become reestablished, distinct biogenic sedimentary structures and bioturbated sediments become more common. Within a few years, the sediment at depths greater than a few centimeters has been worked and reworked by organisms, resulting in a high degree of homogenization.

Given the fact that the uppermost part of the inner nearshore sand is often well laminated, the general absence of lamination at greater depths must be largely the result of the activities of deep-dwelling burrowers. *Callianassa islagrande* is the only organism that seems capable of performing this work. Laboratory experiments to determine burrowing rates and patterns under varying environmental conditions showed that *C. islagrande* is capable of reworking 17 percent of the upper one meter of sediment in the inner nearshore each year.

SUMMARY

Macrobenthos zonation and characteristic sedimentary structures relate to geomorphic features and dynamic zones along the coast. Perhaps the most striking aspect of the interaction of biologic and geologic processes in this area is the destruc-

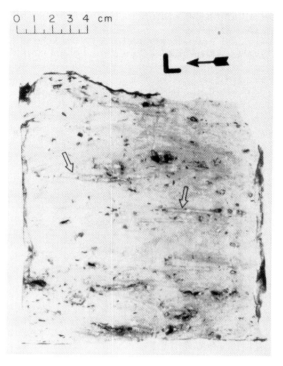

FIG. 23.—X-radiograph of box-core peel from the outer bar in the surf zone showing abundant horizontal burrows in shelly sand, probably produced by sand dollars *Mellita quinquiesperforata*. Orientation of peel is perpendicular to shoreline (L).

tion of such a large fraction of the depositional structures by burrowing organisms. Macrobenthos zonation can be defined in terms of species distribution and density, diversity-equitability, and niche classification. Characteristic sedimentary structures common to each landform include depositional structures and biogenic structures. However, biogenic sedimentary structures are most effective in defining beach subzones, whereas physical sedimentary structures are most useful in defining subzones of the inner nearshore.

The *Ocypode* community is found primarily on the backshore and upper foreshore and is characterized by low species diversity, low density of individuals, and infaunal forms which are primarily detritus feeders, mainly scavengers. The dominant internal depositional structure of the backshore is gently seaward-dipping planar lamination produced by wave swash. The burrows of the ghost crab *Ocypode quadrata* are the dominant biogenic sedimentary structures on the backshore. *O. quadrata* burrows are larger in diameter, extend deeper into the sediment, and have a more complex morphology than those in the upper foreshore. In the backshore, a substantial amount of the depositional structures are preserved because the only deep-burrowing form, *Ocypode quadrata*, does not occur in great numbers, is not active during winter months, and does not construct extensive burrows.

Specific to the bar-trough system, the *Callianassa-Donax*-Haustoriidae community is characterized by comparatively high diversity of infaunal species, most of the many individuals belonging to a few species. The trophic nucleus of this community is mixed, although detritus feeders, mainly deposit feeders, are dominant. Three kinds of sedimentary structures produced by waves and currents are common in the bar-trough system: (1) small-scale lenticular cross-bedding, usually without any well-defined preferred orientation of dip direction produced by deposition on sand ripples; (2) planar lamination produced when bar crests are planar because of surge caused by large waves; and (3) medium-scale cross-bedding dipping in the direction of the longshore current produced by migrating megaripples. *Callianassa islagrande* burrows are the dominant biogenic sedimentary structure throughout the bar-trough system. Horizontal intrastratal trails of *Mellita quinquiesperforata* are abundant seaward of the middle bar. Depositional structures in this zone are preserved in only the upper 30 cm because the deeper sediment is reworked continually by the deep-burrowing species, *Callianassa islagrande*, which occurs in relatively dense population, is active during all seasons, and continually reworks its extensive burrow system.

The ecotone or boundary between the communities of the backshore and the bar-trough system is in the foreshore. The greatest diversity and density of macrozoobenthic organisms, all of which are infaunal forms, are found in the ecotone. Species common to both adjacent communities are abundant but locally restricted in the foreshore. The trophic nucleus of the ecotone is mixed. As in the backshore, the dominant internal depositional structure in the foreshore is gently seaward-dipping planar lamination produced by wave swash. Highest densities of the large conspicuous burrows of *O. quadrata* and *C. islagrande* occur in the upper and lower foreshore, respectively. In the sediment column of the foreshore, alternating zones of bioturbated sediment and well preserved depositional structures are common. Considering the high densities of organisms in this landform, it is surprising that any depositional structure is preserved.

ACKNOWLEDGEMENTS

We are indebted to Drs. J. W. Tunnell, Texas A&I University at Corpus Christi, Texas; H. E. Clifton, U.S. Geological Survey, Menlo Park, California; and L. E. Garrison, U.S. Geological Survey, Corpus Christi, Texas, for their critical reading of the manuscript. Ronald J. Miller, Michael E. Dorsey, Kenneth A. Roberts, and Jack L. Kindinger of the U.S. Geological Survey, Corpus Christi, Texas, are thanked for their invaluable assistance in field sampling and laboratory work.

REFERENCES

BEERBOWER, J. R., AND JORDAN, D., 1969, Application of information theory to paleontologic problems: Taxonomic diversity: Jour. Paleontology, v. 43, p. 1184–1198.
BRETT, C. W., 1964, A portable hydraulic diver operated dredge-sieve for sampling subtidal macrofauna: Jour. Marine Res., v. 22, p. 205–209.
DAVIS, W. B., 1966, The mammals of Texas: Texas Parks and Wildlife Dept. Bull., v. 41, 267 p.
DICKINSON, K. A., 1971, Grain-size distribution and the depositional history of northern Padre Island, Texas: U.S. Geol. Survey Prof. Paper 750-C, 6 p.
FRANKENBERG, D., COLES, S. L., AND JOHANNES, R. E., 1967, The potential trophic significance of *Callianassa major* fecal pellets: Limnology and Oceanography, v. 12, p. 113–120.
HAYES, M. O., 1964, Grain size modes in Padre Island sands: Gulf Coast Assoc. Geol. Socs., Field Trip Guidebook 1965 Ann. Meeting, p. 121–216.
HILL, G. W., AND HUNTER, R. E., 1973, Burrows of the ghost crab *Ocypode quadrata* (Fabricius) on the barrier islands, south-central Texas: Jour. Sed. Petrology, v. 43, p. 24–30.
HOWARD, J. D., AND DÖRJES, JURGEN, 1972, Animal-sediment relationships in two beach-related tidal flats: Sapelo Island, Georgia: Jour. Sed. Petrology, v. 42, p. 608–623.
——, AND FREY, R. W., 1973, Characteristic physical and biogenic sedimentary structures in Georgia estuaries: Am. Assoc. Petroleum Geologists Bull., v. 57, p. 1169–1185.
HUNTER, R. E., AND DICKINSON, K. A., 1970, Map showing landforms and sedimentary deposits of the Padre Island portion of the South Bird Island 7.5 minute quadrangle, Texas: U.S. Geol. Survey, Misc. Geol. Inv. Map I-659.
——, WATSON, R. L., HILL, G. W., AND DICKINSON, K. A., 1972, Modern depositional environments and processes, northern and central Padre Island, Texas: Gulf Coast Assoc. Geol. Socs., Field Trip Guidebook 1972 Ann. Meeting, p. 1–27.
IMBRIE, JOHN, AND BUCHANAN, HUGH, 1965, Sedimentary structures in modern carbonate sands of the Bahamas:

In G. V. Middleton (ed.), Primary sedimentary structures and their hydrodynamic interpretation: Soc. Econ. Paleontologists and Mineralogists, Spec. Pub. 12, p. 149–172.

KING, C. A. M., 1972, Beaches and coasts: St. Martin's Press, New York, 570 p.

LLOYD, M., AND GHELARDI, R. J., 1964, A table for calculating "equitability" components of species diversity: Jour. Animal Ecol., v. 33, p. 217–225.

MAYOU, T. V., HOWARD, J. D., AND SMITH, K. L., 1969, Techniques for sampling tracks, trails, burrows, and bioturbate textures in unconsolidated sediments: Geol. Soc. America Spec. Paper 121, p. 665–666.

MCKEE, E. D., 1957, Primary structures in some recent sediments: Am. Assoc. Petroleum Geologists Bull., v. 41, p. 1704–1747.

MILLING, M. E., AND BEHRENS, E. W., 1966, Sedimentary structures of beach and dune deposits—Mustang Island, Texas: Univ. Texas, Inst. Marine Sci. Pub., v. 11, p. 135–148.

MOIOLA, R. J., AND SPENCER, A. B., 1973, Sedimentary structures and grain-size distribution, Mustang Island, Texas: Gulf Coast Assoc. Geol. Socs. Trans., v. 23, p. 324–332.

MOORE, D. G., AND SCRUTON, P. C., 1957, Minor internal structures of some recent unconsolidated sediments: Am. Assoc. Petroleum Geologists Bull., v. 41, p. 2723–2751.

PEARSE, A. S., HUMM, H. J., AND WHARTON, G. W., 1942, Ecology of sand beaches at Beaufort, N.C.: Ecol. Mon., v. 12, p. 136–180.

RHOADS, D. C., SPEDEN, I. G., AND WAAGE, K. M., 1972, Trophic group analysis of Upper Cretaceous (Maestrichtian) bivalve assemblages from South Dakota: Am. Assoc. Petroleum Geologists Bull., v. 56, p. 1100–1114.

SCOTT, R. W., 1972, Preliminary ecological classification of ancient benthic communities: 24th Internat. Geol. Congr. Proc., Sec. 7, p. 103–110.

SHANNON, C. E., AND WEAVER, W., 1963, The mathematical theory of communication: Univ. Illinois Press, Urbana, 117 p.

THORSON, G., 1957, Bottom communities (sublittoral or shallow shelf): *In* J. W. Hedgpeth (ed.), Treatise on marine ecology and paleoecology: Geol. Soc. America Mem. 67, v. 1, p. 461–534.

U.S. NATIONAL OCEANIC AND ATMOSPHERIC ADMINISTRATION, 1973, Surface water temperature and density, Atlantic coast, North and South America: Natl. Ocean Survey Pub. 31-1.

——, 1974, Local climatological data, annual summary with comparative data, 1974, Corpus Christi, Texas: Natl. Environmental Data Service.

——, 1975, Tide tables, 1975, east coast of North and South America: Natl. Ocean Survey.

WEIMER, R. J., AND HOYT, J. H., 1964, Burrows of *Callianassa major* Say, geologic indicators of littoral and shallow neritic environments: Jour. Paleontology, v. 38, p. 761–767.

JOURNAL OF SEDIMENTARY PETROLOGY, VOL. 42, No. 3, p. 608-623
FIGS. 1-14, SEPTEMBER, 1972

ANIMAL-SEDIMENT RELATIONSHIPS IN TWO BEACH-RELATED TIDAL FLATS; SAPELO ISLAND, GEORGIA

JAMES D. HOWARD

Skidaway Institute of Oceanography, Savannah, Georgia 31406

AND

JURGEN DÖRJES

Institut for Meeresgeologie und Meeresbiologie—"Senckenberg," Wilhelmshaven, Germany

ABSTRACT

Two tidal flats associated with barrier island beaches have been examined in a cooperative study between a geologist and a biologist. The results of this work point out the interaction of physical and biological factors in controlling the sedimentary record of two similar subfacies.

In the two flats described, sand size is similar and both flats occur as parts of barrier island beaches. The resulting depositional record is different, however, because of slight differences in the geographic settings and the responses of physical and biological processes to these differences. Similarities do exist in terms of the high degree of biogenic reworking which characterizes both tidal flats.

Fifty species of macrobenthic organisms were found to inhabit each of the two tidal flats examined. Twenty-seven of these occupied both flats. At Nannygoat flat where mud is an important sediment constituent (5 to 16 percent), polychaetes made up 38 per cent of the fauna and crustaceans 36 percent. At Cabretta flat where mud comprises a much smaller fraction (0.5-1.5 percent), polychaetes accounted for 28 percent of the species and crustaceans represented 40 percent of the species.

If these two flats were preserved in a depositional sequence, they would both be lens or wedge-shaped sand bodies composed of bioturbated sand and both would be incorporated into a normal beach sequence. They would differ, however, in the percentage of mud fraction and in the type of specific trace fossils found.

INTRODUCTION

This paper reports a detailed study of the animal-sediment relationships of two specific local clastic sedimentary environments and is a cooperative effort between biology and geology. Possibly it will seem to represent too much zoology for geologists and vice versa. However, most of those working in present-day sedimentary environments are struck by the profound effect which organisms have in effecting sedimentation and modifying the resultant sediments. In this study we have examined two tidal flats on Sapelo Island, Georgia.

The two flats studied are shown in Figure 1. Nannygoat Tidal Flat (fig. 2a and b) is located on the south end of the main Sapelo Island beach (Nannygoat Beach) just inside Doboy Sound. This flat has been in existence for many years as indicated by aerial photographs from the middle 1930's. Cabretta Tidal Flat (figs. 2c and d), in contrast, is a very recently formed flat developed behind a shoaling spit which has built southward from a tidal inlet. This is apparently an environment in transition and it is anticipated that this flat will, in a few years, be filled-in and overlain by a backshore and dune field.

METHODS

Animal Collection

During spring low tides, when the vertical tide range was approximately 2.4 m, transects were made across the 350 m wide Cabretta Flat and the 75 m wide Nannygoat flat, from the lower part of the beach slope to the low tide level occurring on the day of sampling. On each transect bulk sediment samples for animals, spaced 20 m or 50 m apart, were taken and a constant volume of sediment, to a depth of 50 cm and a surface area of 0.2 m², was recovered. The number of stations occupied along each transect thus depended on the width of the tidal flats; at Cabretta flat, eight samples were taken and at Nannygoat flat six samples were taken. The bulk sediment samples were washed through a sieve with 0.8 mm² mesh. The animals recovered were preserved in formalin and later identified and counted in the laboratory.

Sediments

Oriented, undisturbed rectangular gallon-can cores and vibrocores up to 1.5 m in length were collected from each of the tidal flats during the summers of 1969 and 1970. The cores were opened in the laboratory and x-ray radiographs and epoxy casts were made for analysis of physical and biogenic sedimentary structures. The cores were subsampled for textural analysis. The sediments were wet sieved to determine the percentage of fine fraction (<0.060 mm), sand fraction (0.060 to 2.0 mm) and coarse fraction (>2.0 mm). The sand fraction was run through a Woods Hole-type sediment analyzer for grain size characteristics.

NANNYGOAT TIDAL FLAT SEDIMENTS

Geologic Setting

The Nannygoat tidal flat lies in a protected bight where the Nannygoat beach recurves into Doboy Sound (figs 1 and 2a). The two subtle bulges of the beach (x and y of fig. 2a) serve to protect the flat from wave energy. During periods of onshore winds from the southeast this flat is protected from strong wave action by the extensive shoal system developed at the mouth of Doboy Sound. Due to the water circulation pattern in Dobby Sound, a lens of organic-rich sediment-laden waters stalls in this area of the beach during high tide and permits abundant organic material to accumulate on the

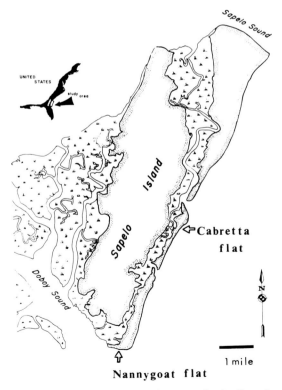

Fig. 1.—Sketch map of Sapelo Island, Georgia showing location of Cabretta tidal flat and Nannygoat tidal flat.

flat and provides an abundant food resource for deposit and suspension feeding organisms of the flat.

Although the present position of the tidal flat is the result of accretion to this portion of the beach during a storm in 1964, aerial photographs from 1940's and 1950's indicate that a muddy tidal flat has existed here for at least 30 years.

Sediments

Sediments of the tidal flat represent a mixture of sand and mud. The mud throughout most of the flat ranges from 5 to 10 percent although locally mud accumulations may be as much as 16 percent and near the margins of the flat where the beach sand encroaches on the flat, it accounts for less than one percent of the sediment. Mean grain size of the sand fraction is 2.4ϕ to 2.7ϕ with 2.6ϕ most common.

The sand fraction is derived from sediments brought to the tidal flat from the main part of the beach as is shown by similar grain size, sorting, and composition. The fine fraction, on the other hand, which is absent in the adjacent beach, is derived from a primary and a secondary source. A primary source is the mud deposited directly from the suspended load of the highly turbid waters of Doboy Sound. This material, which settles out of suspension during slack tides, is high in organic matter and is the primary food for the numerous suspension and deposit feeding organisms of the tidal flat. The fecal material of these organisms is the secondary source of the tidal flats muds. Fecal material actually represents the major sedimentary constituent of fines in the tidal flat. During low tides, the surface of the flat is covered by low-amplitude ripple marks and each ripple trough acts as a collecting point for fecal material. In some instances the fecal material may be so dense that large areas of the flat are completely covered by a fecal pellet layer. Many of the recognizable mud layers in cores from the tidal flat are made of fecal mud, although in the deeper parts of the meter-long cores, it is not always possible to recognize discrete fecal pellet morphology in the mud layers due to compaction. A detailed examination of fecal pellet muds was not made but it is obvious from the presence of fecal concentrations around burrow openings that a significant amount of the material is contributed by the burrowing shrimp *Callianassa* sp. and the polychaete worms *Onuphis microcephala* and *Diopatra cuprea* (fig. 3).

Other materials which contribute to the composition of the tidal flat sediments include plant debris and shell fragments. The plant material

FIG. 2.—Nannygoat and Cabretta tidal flats. a) Aerial view of the south end of Sapelo Island and Nanny-goat tidal flat. Black line marks the location of transect. b) Surface view of Nannygoat tidal flat, illustrating ripple-marks and tubes of *Onuphis microcephla* during low tide. c) Aerial view of Cabretta Island and Cabretta tidal flat. Black line marks the location of transect. d) Surface view of Cabretta flat, showing ripple-marks during low tide.

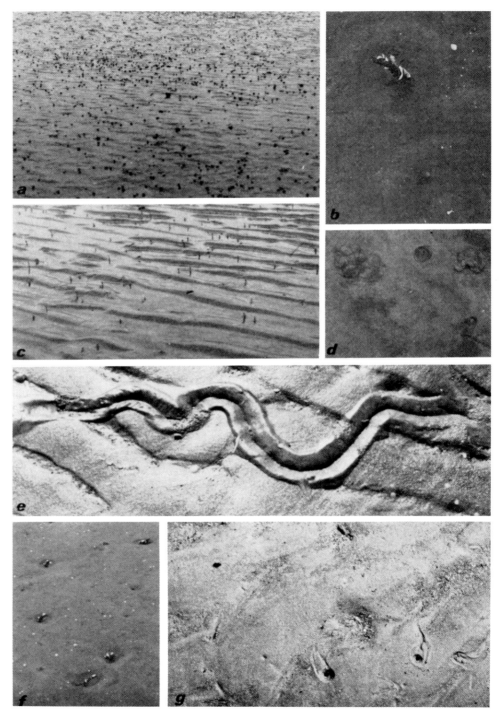

Fig. 3.—Characteristic physical and biologic features on the Nannygoat flat surface. a) *Nassarius vibex* feeding on the flat surface. b) Upper part of the burrows of *Diopatra cuprea*. c) *Onuphis microcephala* tubes. d) Feeding hole and fecal mound of *Balanoglossus sp.* e) Trace of *Polynices duplicatus*. f) *Diopatra cuprea* tubes. g) Entrance holes of *Callianassa* burrows.

is present as finely divided fragments of the marsh grass *Spartina* which settle with the mud fraction. Recognizable shell fragments are relatively scarce and normally account for less than one percent of the tidal flat sediments. For the most part this represents single valves of the small clams *Mulinia* and *Donax*. The only dense accumulations of shells occur where the tidal flat merges with the normal beach.

Geometry and Sediment Distribution

Based on analysis of cores, photographs from the past 30 years, and bathymetry of the adjacent Doboy Sound, it appears that Nannygoat tidal flat is a wedge shaped deposit. Over the past 30 years, the south end of Sapelo Island has been migrating to the south based on the evidence from aerial photographs. The presense of beach ridges curving into Doboy Sound suggest that this process has been in effect for a much longer time but it is not known how long a tidal flat has been present in this area. Within the period of time of aerial photo coverage, however, it appears that the tidal flat has prograded southward into Doboy Sound in response to the southward building of the whole Sapelo Island beach (Hoyt and Henry, 1965). Following the prograding of the flat into Doboy Sound, the beach on the north side of the flat has likewise prograded southward over the flat. This has resulted in a higher sand-mud ratio on the north side of the flat. Likewise the east and west margins of the flat show a high sand-mud ratio due to the presence of sand introduced from the protecting forelands (x and y of fig. 2a). Thus, the cores with the greatest percentage of mud layers are found in the central portion of the flat. This is based on percent of mud layers in meter-long cores which show a greater increase in the presence of mud layers in the southern and western parts of the flat.

It is assumed that if the south end of the island continues to migrate one would find preserved there a lens of tidal flat sediments between an underlying estuarine record and an overlying beach sequence. It is more likely, however, that, in the case of the Georgia coast, the inlet to Doboy Sound will shift again to the north and erase at least a portion of the tidal flat record.

Lateral continuity of units in this small subfacies is possible to a limited extent. Beds can be traced in the muddier portion of the flat based on a similar type of bioturbation and by similar zones of mud layer concentration. These beds can be traced parallel to shoreline over a distance of 300 meters. Most likely these are lenses of rather small lateral extent.

Sedimentary Structures

Biogenic sedimentary structures dominate over physical structures in the Nannygoat tidal flat. These result to some extent from constructed burrows of the infauna, but a general bioturbation and reworking are by far the most abundant feature.

Surface Features

During low tide the surface of the southend flat is covered by low amplitude ripple marks which commonly have a height of 1.5 to 3.0 cm and an average wave length of 4 to 6 cm (figs. 2b and 3). These ripples commonly strike N60E to N70E and reflect the dominant wave energy from the southeast. Examination of the internal structures shows both onshore and offshore dip of ripple laminations, but onshore directions are much more abundant. The troughs of nearly all surface ripplemarks are filled with fecal material and organic detritus as discussed previously; these fine grained accumulations are readily identified in cores by the presence of mud flasers. Numerous interruptions in the ripple-marked surface are created by biogenic activity on the flat surface (fig. 3). These include surface trails made by crabs and snails, burrow openings and fecal castings by animals living in the flat, and by feeding excavations made by sting-rays. The latter made depressions as deep as 30 cm with a surface diameter of up to 1 m. Such depressions are important to the local conditions of sedimentation on the tidal flat. When the rays abandon these feeding holes the depressions serve as traps for sediment and commonly act as catchments for the fine and lightweight fraction and especially for fecal material. This activity can result in lenses of nearly pure fecal mud which are commonly encountered in the tidal flat cores.

Internal Structures

In all cores taken on the tidal flat, some indication of preserved ripple laminations was found but, for the most part, the sediments show considerable reworking by burrowing organisms. Examples of this are shown in Figure 4 which are x-ray radiograph prints of surface can cores taken across the Nannygoat tidal flat. Figure 4a is from the beach-tidal flat margin, Figure 4b from the center of the flat and 4c from the low tide line. Ripple laminations are obvious at the tops of all cores. Based on observations made on the flat at various levels, it is apparent that the rising tide and onshore currents act to form ripple laminations and the falling tides truncate or modify them. Figure

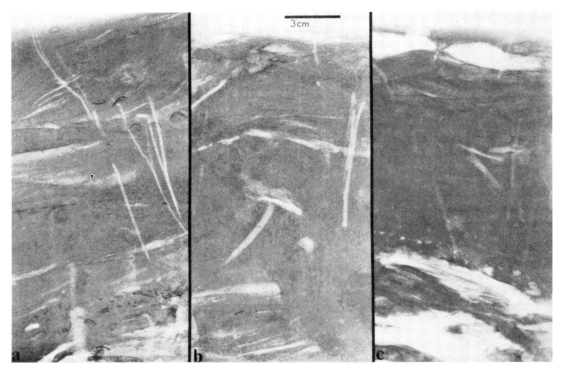

Fig. 4.—Prints of x-ray radiographs made from cores taken on Nannygoat tidal flat surface, Sapelo Island, Georgia. a) Core taken at tidal flat beach contact. This core showed the best preservation of physical sedimentary structures seen anywhere on the tidal flat. In the upper part of the core are landward dipping ripple laminations with fecal mud flasers (white on radiograph print). In the middle section of the print there is evidence of bioturbation by amphipods which has produced the disrupted laminations. In the bottom one-fourth of the core is a shell concentration made up of single valves and fragments of *Mulinia*. At the base of this core are biogenically reworked mud layers. Several inclined worm tubes cut across the upper two-thirds of the core. b) Core from the center of the Nannygoat flat. Ripple laminations are preserved at the top of the core. Remnant stratification can be recognized in the upper and lower thirds of the core due to the presence of fecal mud flasers (white on the radiograph print). Isolated lenses of mud truncated by areas of highly bioturbated sand indicate that the mud layers were once more laterally continuous. This core is about 50 percent reworked by organisms. c) Core from the low tide line of the Nannygoat tidal flat. Lenses of mud (white on the radiograph print) and ripple laminations are present in the upper one-fourth of the core. The middle portion of the core is made up of biogenically reworked sand with some worm tubes cutting through. The lower one-fourth of the core is composed mostly of thick mud layers.

4a, from the tidal flat-beach transition, shows the best preserved ripple laminations and represents the highest energy in the environment. This is also the only core with any significant amount of shells and shell fragments. In all of the radiographs, presence of mud flasers (white on x-ray print) are obvious. As mentioned previously, these result from ripple trough-filling by fecal material and organic detritus.

In all of the cores taken on Nannygoat tidal flat the most abundant sedimentary structures result from bioturbation by burrowing organisms. In Figure 4b and c, primary stratification is nearly absent due to the high degree of biogenic reworking. The plot of animal density (fig. 5) indicates that these are areas of greatest density of individuals and greatest variety of species. The only distinct structures are the occasional polychaete worm tubes. The generally blurred or "fuzzy" character of the sediment texture in 4b and c results from bioturbation produced by amphipods (Howard an Elders, 1970) and isopods which are present in great numbers in this area. In spite of the well preserved physical structures in Figure 4a, amphipod and isopod bioturbation is obvious as are the tubes of *Onuphis*.

ANIMALS

The six samples taken on Nannygoat flat yielded 3,462 individuals belonging to 50 macrobenthic species representing the following taxonomic groups.

Taxa	Number of Species	% Species
Polychaeta	19	38
Crustacea	18	36
Mollusca	9	18
Echinodermata	1	2
Nemertini	1	2
Enterpnuesta	1	2
Chelicerata	1	2

Most individuals of these species are sparse. Seventy-one percent (2468 individuals) belong to the five most frequently occurring species and eighty-five percent (2952 of the total individuals) belong to the ten most frequent species. In contrast, only 15 percent of the individuals belong to 83 percent of the species (Table 1).

The taxonomic group represented by the greatest density and abundance at Nannygoat flat is the Crustacea, which constitutes 2544 (73.5 percent) of the total individuals (Table 1). Only 629 individuals (18 percent) belong to the Polychaeta and 272 (8 percent) to the Mollusca. All other groups recorded include less than 0.5 percent of the total individuals.

The distribution and zonation of animals relative to sediments and geomorphology of the flat are shown in Figure 5. A restricted group of animal species occurs in the lower part of the beach slope on the landward margin of the flat which is marked by a relatively clean sand. These species, some having high densities of individuals, are the bivalve *Donax variabilis*, the polychaete worm *Nerenides agilis*, and the enteropneust *Balanoglossus sp.* Nevertheless, most of the species recorded inhabit the wet, muddy sand flat. In addition to the amphipods *Bathyporeia sp.* and *Acanthohaustorius sp.*, the most abundant individuals are species of the polychaete worms *Onuphis microcephala, Nephythys picta, Glycera dibranchiata, Heteromastus filiformis, Diopatra cuprea, Nereis succinea,* and *Spiophanes bombyx,* and the crustaceans *Chiridotea caeca, Pinnixa chaetopterana, Callianassa sp.,* and the bivalve *Mulinia lateralis*.

Both the number of species (fig. 6a) and the number of individuals (fig. 6b) increase more or less consistently from the lower part of the beach slope to low water level. The sligh reduction in total individuals at station 5, 20 m landward of the low water line, seems to be real although no apparent changes occur in the physical setting.

The only obvious differences in the sedimentological and geomorphological conditions at Nannygoat flat are the contrasts between the steeper beach slope, having relatively dry, clean sand and the continually wet area of the muddy flat. Both are inhabited by characteristic species

Fig. 5.—Numerical distribution and zonation of macrobenthos on Nannygoat flat (LWL—low water line).

TABLE 1—*Comparison between numbers of species and specimens living on Cabretta and Nannygoat tidal flat*

	Cabretta flat	Nannygoat flat
Type of sediment	medium fine sand/fine sand	medium fine sand/muddy sand
Number of stations	8	6
Number of species	50 (100%)	50 (100%)
Number of specimens	20606 (100%)	3462 (100%)
Number of species:		
Crustacea	20 (40%)	18 (36%)
Polychaeta	14 (28%)	19 (38%)
Mollusca	6 (12%)	9 (18%)
Echinodermata	2 (4%)	1 (2%)
Others	8 (16%)	3 (6%)
Most abundant		
5 species	19479 (95%)	2468 (71%)
10 species	20273 (98%)	2952 (85%)
Number of specimens:		
Crustacea	19482 (94%)	2544 (73.5%)
Polychaeta	671 (3%)	629 (18%)
Mollusca	406 (2%)	272 (8%)
Others	64 (1%)	17 (0.5%)

Most common species:	Cabretta		Nannygoat	
	Acanthohaustorius sp.	15363	*Bathyporeia sp.*	1320
	Bathyporeia sp.	3680	*Acanthohaustorius sp.*	511
	Nerenides agilis	391	*Onuphis microcephala*	284
	Donax variabilis	307	*Haustorius sp.*	182
	Onuphis microcephala	138	*Heteromastus filiformis*	171
	Haustorius sp.	130	*Donax variabilis*	132
	Neohaustorius schmitzi	128	*Mulinia lateralis*	106
	Nephtys picta	57	*Neohaustorius schmitzi*	102
	Parahaustorius longimerus	45	*Chiridotea caeca*	78
	Tellina texana	34	*Nephtys picta*	66
	Spiophanes bombyx	28	*Pinnixa chaetopterana*	65
	Limulus polyphemus (juv.)	27	*Monoculodes sp.*	47
	Olivia sayana	26	*Callianassa sp.*	43
	Solen viridis	25	*Gammarus sp.*	36
	Callinassa major	25	*Glycera dibranchiata*	33
	Magelone sp. I	18	*Nerenides agilis*	25
	Chiridotea caeca	18	*Corophium simile*	16
	Balanoglossus sp.	17	*Gammaridea sp.*	14
	Ogyrides alphaerostris	17	*Parahaustorius longimerus*	13
	Gammarus sp.	10	*Spiophanes bombyx*	12

that are capable of making distinctive burrows or burrow structures (fig. 7 and 8). The lower part of the steeper beach slope is characterized by the dense vertical burrows of the spionid annelid *Nerenides agilis,* the small body-size burrows of the bivalve *Donax variabilis* just below the substrate surface, and sediment bioturbation by numerous amphipods. In addition, the enteropneust *Balanoglossus sp.* (fig. 3d), constructing typically u-shaped burrows, occupies the area between the beach slope and the tidal flat. In contrast, the muddy flat is characterized by the long tubes of the polychaete *Onuphis microcephala* (mucoid tubes covered with sand grains) (fig. 3c), and *Diopatra cuprea* (chitinous tubes incorporating shells, shell fragments,

and plant detritus) (Myers, 1970) (figs. 3b and f). Other importatnt species include the polychaete *Heteromastus filiformis* and the ghost shrimp *Callianassa sp.* living in branch-shaped burrows having one or more passages to the substrate surface. Less abundant on the muddy flat are the bivalve *Mulinia lateralis* and the mole-crab *Lepidopa websteri* (Howard, 1968). Both burrow into the sediment; the first sits relatively deep in the sediment, reaching the surface with its long siphons, while the second digs small holes into the surface, probing for enemies or food by means of its long antennae. The snails *Nassarius vibex* (fig. 3a) and *Polynices duplicatus* (fig. 3e) feed on the sediment surface, making meandering trails.

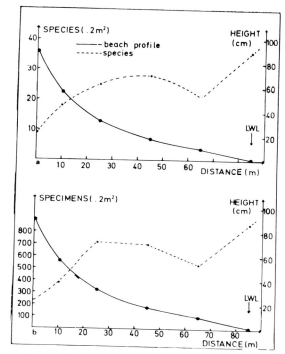

FIG. 6.—Nannygoat tidal flat. a) Distribution of species. b) Distribution of individuals.

CABRETTA TIDAL FLAT
Geologic Setting

The Cabretta flat stands in strong contrast to Nannygoat flat because of its local geographic setting (fig. 1 and 2c). At Cabretta the flat merges landward with a beach as does Nannygoat flat. Seaward, however, it is protected by an intertidal shoal which shields the flat from the open sea. Also, the Cabretta flat is open on the north and south ends so that during beginning ebb and late flood tides a tidal creek just to the north crosses its surface. The reason for this is that the flat has formed behind a spit which over the past 15 years has built southward from the tidal creek entrance. This situation results in a facies of relatively clean sand because the fines that settle out during slack flood are later transported out of the environment. It is likely that with time the spit will close off, and this flat will become a sediment trap and then eventually build up to form a beach.

Sediments

Sediments of the Cabretta flat are consistently low in fine fraction with no sample containing more than 1.5 percent finer than sand; the samples with the least fine fraction contained 0.5

percent. Mean grain size is 2.2ϕ to 2.4ϕ which is in the same size range as the adjacent beach. Very few shells were found in the flat, and material coarser than sand was less than one percent in all cores. Most of this material is derived from the laterally adjacent beaches and to some extent from erosion of Pleistocene outcrops in the nearby tidal creek. The Cabretta flat sediments differ from those of the Nannygoat flat in that they possess a higher percentage of heavy mineral fraction and essentially no fine fraction.

Geometry and Sediment Distribution

The Cabretta tidal flat is an elongate wedge-shaped deposit. On the landward side, it wedges out against a normal beach foreshore and seaward against a beach on the spit (fig. 2c). To the north the flat passes into the shoal which has formed at the mouth of the tidal creek where the shoal joins the island. To the south, the flat is transitional with normal shoreface sediments where the shoal ends.

Sedimentary Structures

Here, as in the Nannygoat tidal flat, the biogenic sedimentary structures are dominant over physical sedimentary structures. In this case, however, the bioturbation is much more subtle and less diverse in origin.

Surface Features

Across the entire Cabretta flat the surface is characterized by ripple marks (fig. 2d). Here, however, one finds no fecal muds or organic detritus trapped in the ripple troughs. The ripples are formed by wave action during high tide and current action when the trough drains during ebb tide. Thus, in the higher parts of the flat, the ripple crests normally parallel the shoreline and in the lower part of the flat, cusp ripples are

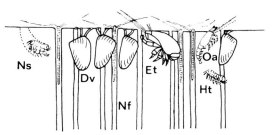

FIG. 7.—Location of most important animals and burrows in the clean sand of the beach slopes of both tidal flats. (Dv = *Donax variabilis*, Et = *Emerita talpoidea*, Ht = *Haustorius sp.*, Nf = *Nerenides agilis*, Ns = *Neohaustorius schmitzi*, Oa = *Ogyrides alphaerostris*.)

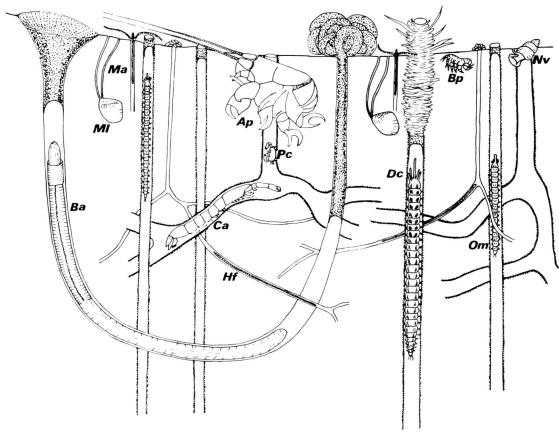

Fig. 8.—Burrowing characteristics of the most important animals, burrows, and tubes in the muddy sediments of Nannygoat tidal flat. (Ap = *Albunea paretii,* Ba = *Balanoglossus sp.,* Bp = *Bathyporeia sp.,* Ca = *Callianassa sp.,* Hf = *Heteromastus filiformis,* Om = *Onuphis microcephala,* Dc = *Diopatra cuprea,* Ma = *Magelone sp.,* Ml = *Mulinia lateralis,* Nv = *Nassarius vibex,* Pc = *Pinnixa chaetopterana.*)

found which show a southward current direction where the flat drains to the south parallel to the shoreline.

Surface features other than ripple marks, however, are relatively few. The only major exception are the sand castings of the Balanoglossoid worms (fig. 3d) and the occasional markings made by molluscs and sand dollars (fig. 9). Feeding holes formed by rays which were abundant on Nannygoat flat are generally absent on the flat at Cabretta.

Internal Structures

By far the most abundant internal sedimentary structures are the ubiquitous though subtle bioturbate textures created by amphipods. Generally in any shallow core taken on the Cabretta tidal flat, one will find some evidence of primary physical sedimentary structures in the form of ripple laminations. These are especially common

at the top of the cores. At a depth of 2 or 3 cm, however, these rapidly decrease in abundance and instead one finds only complete bioturbation by amphipods. The only major exception to this is found on the landward margin at the flat where typical beach stratification becomes obvious.

Figure 10 shows x-ray radiograph prints of cores taken from the Cabretta tidal flat. Figure 10a represents the maximum of biogenic reworking in the cores. Current ripples are present at the top of the core and there is a subtle hint of stratification throughout the core. It is considered unlikely that the ripple lamination is of much significance in that the entire core has been bioturbated by amphipods. This imparts to the radiograph print a delicate mottled appearance and indicates that the amphipods have reworked essentially every sand grain. The only major recognizable biogenic structures are the

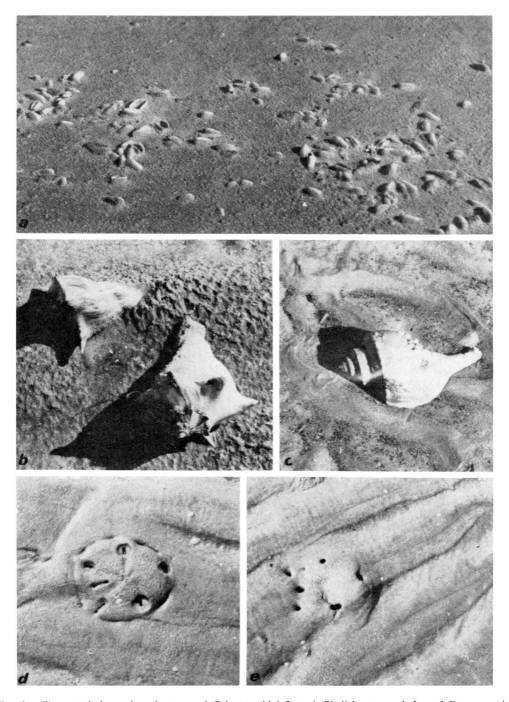

FIG. 9.—Characteristic surface features of Cabretta tidal flat. a) Shell layer consisting of *Donax variabilis* valves, b and c) *Busycon carica* and *B. canaliculatum* washed up on Cabretta tidal flat by surf. d and e) *Mellita quinquiesperforata* just below the sediment surface.

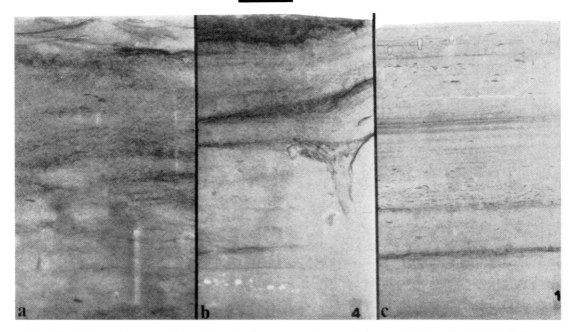

3 cm

FIG. 10.—Prints of x-ray radiographs made from cores taken on Cabretta tidal flat, Sapelo Island, Georgia. a) Core showing high degree of biogenic reworking. Surface shows ripple laminations enhanced by heavy mineral layers. Elsewhere in this core there is only a subtle hint of primary physical stratification. The "fuzzy" texture throughout most of this radiograph print is typical of the bioturbation produced by amphipods. In the lower one-third of this core there are some larger biogenic structures perhaps produced by snails or mole crabs. b) Core showing remnant stratification which has been reworked by amphipod burrowing. The conical structure on the right is the upper portion of a *Balanoglossus* burrow. c) Core from the marin of the Cabretta tidal flat. In this print typical foreshore beach stratification is obvious. However, careful examination shows that even here there has been considerable disturbance of the stratification by amphipods (especially in the lower one-third) and by the small surf clams *Donax* which are visible in life position near the surface of the core.

coarse mottles which have resulted from bioturbation by large organisms. The particular organism which authored this structure is unknown but perhaps it marks the passage of the snail *Olivia* or the mole crab *Albunea* (Os and Ap in fig. 14).

Figure 10b shows slightly more evidence of primary physical sedimentary structures. This is somewhat misleading because this core contains more heavy minerals (dark areas in the radiograph print) than in Figure 10a. Thus, even though the amphipods have extensively rearranged the sands, the location of the heavy mineral zones help to define the original structures. Of particular interest here, however, is the feeding cone and biogenic reworking by the sand worm (enteropneust) *Balanoglossus*. The organism which makes the sand castings shown in Figures 3 and 14 also makes these cone shaped depressions when it draws down sand to

be injested.

Figure 10c is of interest in comparison to the preceding illustration as it represents an x-ray radiograph print of a core taken on the margin of the flat where it merges with the normal foreshore Cabretta Island beach. The sand is of the same size and composition as in the flat but here continual tidal reworking and breaking wave-energy results in the dominance of physical over biogenic sedimentary structures. Even there, however, one can see that amphipods and the surf clam *Donax* have influenced the postdepositional modification of primary physical sedimentary structures.

Animals

The eight samples taken on Cabretta flat produced 20,606 individuals (Table 1) belonging to 50 macrobenthic species. These were distributed among eight systematic groups, as follows:

Taxa	Number of Species	% Species
Crustacea	20	40
Polychaeta	14	28
Mollusca	6	12
Echinodermata	2	4
Coelenterata	3	6
Nemertini	2	4
Enteropneusta	2	4
Chelicerata	1	2

Very few species are truly abundant on the flat. The five species occurring most fequently include 19,482 individuals or 95 percent of the total fauna. The ten most fequently occurring species include 20,273 individuals or 98 percent of the total fauna. Thus 10 percent of the recorded species comprise more than 95 percent of the total individuals (Table 1).

The most abundant individuals belong to species of the Crustacea. This taxonomic group includes 94 pericent of the individuals. Only 6 percent of the individuals belong to the Polychaeta (3 percent), Mollusca (2 percent), and other groups (1 percent) (Table 1).

The distribution and zonation of animals in relation to topography of the beach-flat is shown in Figures 11 and 12. The numerous individuals of the amphipod species *Haustorius sp.* and *Neohaustorius schmitzi* occur only in a narrow zone of the beach slope; during low tide this sand is relatively dry. Species such as the bivalve *Donax variabilis* and the polychaete *Nerenides agilis,* and the crustacean *Chiridotea caeca* are usually found in narrow zones within the middle and lower parts of the beach slope. The main habitat for most of the species found on Cabretta flat is the continually wet, fine sand of the actual sand flat. Here the most abundant species are the amphipods *Acanthohaustorius sp.* and *Bathyporeia sp.* Also very common are the polychaetes *Onuphis microcephala, Nephtys picta,* the crustacean *Callianassa major,* and the molluscs *Olivia sayana, Solen viridus,* and the enteropneust *Balanoglossus sp.* Some species, such as the coelenterates *Renilla reniformis, Haliactis sp.,* and the cumacean *Oxyurostylis smithi,* are able to live only a very short time above the low water line. These species ordinarily inhabit the bottom sediments of the runnel, which is commonly covered by water during ebb tide. Other species, including the polychaete *Spiophanes bombyx* and the bivalve *Tellina texana,* have their main distribution in the runnel but are also able to settle in the lower, continually moist parts of the sand flats. The distribution and horizontal zonation of some of the most important and abundant species are shown in Figure 12c.

The number of species in Cabretta flat is relatively constant from station to station; important minima are located at the lower part of the steeper beach slope and at the steeper ridge slope (fig. 12b), but neither of these belongs to the true flat environment. Nevertheless, both minima are located in similar topographic areas, subject to similar hydrographical conditions. Wave action along the lower parts of the steeper slopes, about 50 cm above low water level, is higher than on the planar flat. Very few species, some represented by high numbers of individuals, are able to exploit these extreme hydrographical conditions.

The number of individuals present increase constantly from the lower part of the beach slope to the upper part of the sand flat (fig.

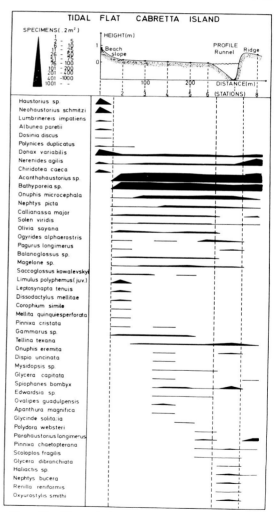

Fig. 11.—Numerical distribution and zonation of macrobenthos on Cabretta tidal flat (STLWL = spring tide low water line).

12a), where the first maximum occurs. From here to the bottom of the runnel, the number of species decreases rapidly. A second maximum occurs near the top of the ridge and then abundance decreases again seaward. The first maximum is formed by numerous individuals of the two amphipod species *Acanthohaustorius sp.* and *Bathyporeia sp.* The second maximum consists mostly of the polychaete *Nerenides agilis,*

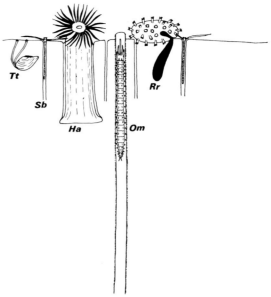

FIG. 13.—Location of most important animals, burrows, and tubes in the runnel of Cabretta tidal flat. (Ha = *Haliactus sp.,* Om = *Onuphis microcephala,* Rr = *Renilla reniformis,* Sb = *Spiophanes bombyx,* Tt = *Tellina texana.*)

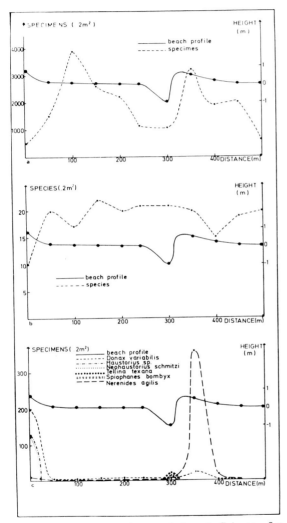

FIG. 12.—Specific characteristics of Cabretta flat animal distribution. a) Distribution of individuals showing maxima in the upper part of the flat and in the ridge slope, and minima in the runnel and near the low water line. b) Distribution of species showing minima in the lower beach slope and the ridge slope. c) Zonation of some of the most important species on Cabretta tidal flat. In relation to recurring geomorphological and physical conditions (beach slope and ridge slope) some of the species (*Donax variabilis, Nerenides agilis*) occur in two separate zones.

which also lives in the beach slope (fig. 12c).

The different topographic features in the area of Cabretta flat are: the beach slope, the planar flat, the runnel, and the ridge. Most of these are characterized by specific animals (figs. 7, 13 and 14) that build tubes or burrows in the sediment. The lower part of the beach (Fig. 7) and the upper part of the ridge, situated at the same height above mean low water level, are characterized by the dense, vertical burrows of the spionid worm *Nerenides agilis,* the small domiciles of the bivalve *Donax variabilis* (Frey and Howard, 1969), and the burrowing activity of numerous amphipods (Howard and Elders, 1970), just below the substrate surface (fig. 7). In contrast, the main flat (fig. 14) is characterized by the long, vertical muddy-walled tubes of the ghost shrimp *Callianassa major,* (Weimer and Hoyt, 1964), the branched u-shaped burrows of the enteropneust *Balanoglossus sp.,* and the arenaceous mucous tubes of the polychaete *Onuphis microcephala* which was illustrated by Frey and Howard (1969). In the runnel itself (fig. 13), only a few burrowing animals live; in addition to the polychaete *Onuphis microcephala,* these include the sand-burrowing anthozoans *Haliactis sp.* and *Renilla reniformis,* the latter supported by its soft stalk in the sediment. Species such as *Busycon carica* (fig. 9b), *B. canaliculatum* (fig. 9c) and *Mellita quinquiesperforata* (fig. 9d, 9e), as well as the

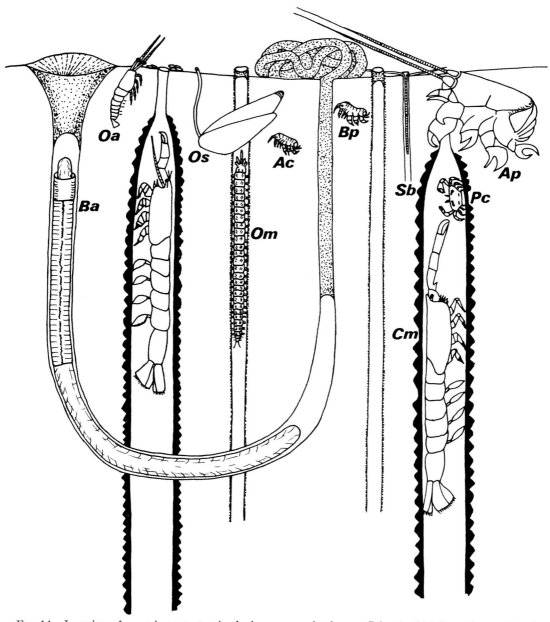

Fig. 14.—Location of most important animals, burrows, and tubes on Cabretta tidal flat. (Ac = *Acantho-haustorius sp.,* Ap = *Albunea paretii,* Ba = *Balanoglossus sp.,* Cm = *Callianassa major,* Os = *Olivia sayana,* Pc = *Pinnixa chaetopterana,* Sb = *Spiophanes bombyx,* Om = *Onuphis microcephala,* Bp = *Bathyporeia sp.* Oa = *Oryrides alphaerostric.*)

shells of several pelecypod species (fig. 9a), are frequently washed up on the Cabreeta flat.

COMPARISONS AND CONCLUSIONS

The number of macrobenthic species found at Cabretta flat and at Nannygoat flat (Table 1) is the same and the number of mutually character-

istic species is high. Slightly more than one third (27) of the total species were found in both areas. One third (20) were observed only on Cabretta beach, and one third (23) only at Nannygoat beach. The major differences in number of individuals (Table 1) can be attributed only to the abundance of the amphipods

Acanthohaustorius sp. and *Bathyporeia sp.* on Cabretta flat. No important differences exist after subtraction of these amphipods from the total number of individuals. More important are the differences in percentage composition of the different taxonomic groups (Table 1). At Cabretta flat 40 percent of the total species are crustaceans and only 28 percent are polychaetes, whereas at Nannygoat flat 38 percent of the total species are polychaetes and 36 percent are crustaceans. The same tendency has been recorded in the number of individuals. This trend apparently shows that the number of species and individuals of crustaceans decrease with increasing content of mud in the sediment, the opposite being true of polychaetes.

One other important difference is the contrasting composition of these basic communities. The snail *Olivia sayana,* the ghost shrimp, *Callianassa major,* and the shrimp *Ogyrides alphaerostris* are very characteristic of clean sandy areas, whereas the polychaetes *Heteromastus filiformis* and *Diopatra cuprea,* the bivalve *Mulinia lateralis,* and the ghost shrimp, *Callianassa sp.* prefer a higher content of mud in the sediments.

Both of the small tidal flats discussed in this paper would, if preserved in a depositional sequence, appear as lens or wedge shaped bodies of highly bioturbated sand. They are both composed of sand with the same grain size as the adjacent beach. Nannygoat flat is considerably higher in fine fraction and the alternating layers of sand and mud would give distinct clues to the energy fluctuations which operate here. This would not be at all obvious in the case of Cabretta flat because of the tidal creek influence which effectively removes the fine fraction that normally would accumulate. However, the presence of a highly bioturbated lens of sediment incorporated into an otherwise normal beach sequence should alert the investigator that something unusual has occured.

In so far as potential trace fossils are concerned, the two different species of *Callianassa* would be very obvious in that *C. major* makes a considerably larger, through structurally similar, burrow than *C. sp.* In addition, in this instance, at least, *C. major* builds a nearly vertical burrow which penetrates to a meter or more in depth whereas *C. sp.* builds a burrow which seldom exceeds 15 cm in depth.

ACKNOWLEDGEMENTS

We acknowledge the assistance of our colleagues Robert W. Frey of the University of Georgia and Gunther Hertweck or Senckenberg Institute who assisted in sampling and gave constructive remarks in the manuscript preparation. George Remmer of S.U.N.Y. Stoneybrook and Jim Kirchhoffer of Antioch College are thanked for their assistance in field sampling. This study was conducted as part of research supported by the Oceanographic Section of the National Science Foundation under Grants GA-719 and GA-10888.

REFERENCES

FREY, R. W. AND J. D. HOWARD, 1969, A profile of biogenic sedimentary structures in a Holocene barrier island-salt marsh complex, Georgia. Trans. Gulf Coast Assoc. Geol. Soc., V. 19, pp. 427–444.

HOWARD, J. D., 1968, X-ray radiography for examination of burrowing in sediments by marine invertebrate organisms. Sedimentology, V. 11, pp. 249–258.

HOWARD, J. D. AND C. A. ELDERS, 1970, Burrowing patterns of haustoriid amphipods from Sapelo Island, Georgia. In: Crimes, J. P. and J. C. Harper, Editors, *Trace Fossils,* Geol. Jour., Spec. Issue 3, pp. 243–262 (Liverpoool).

HOYT, J. H. AND V. J. HENRY, JR., 1965, Significance of inlet sedimentation in the recognition of ancient barrier islands. Guidebook Wyo. Geol. Assoc., p. 190–194.

MEYERS, A. C., 1970, Some paleoichnological observations on the tubes of *Diopatra cuprea* (Bosc) : Polychaeta, Onuphidae. In: Crimes, J. P. and J. C. Harper, Editors, *Trace Fossils,* Geol. Jour. Spec. Issue, 3 pp. 331–334 (Liverpool).

WEIMER, R. J. AND J. H. HOYT, 1964, Burrows of *Callianassa major* Say, geologic indicators of littoral and shallow neritic environments. Jour. Paleo., V. 38, pp. 761–767.